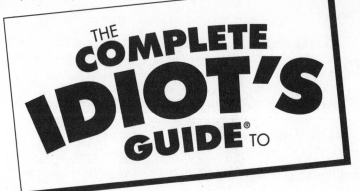

The Mafia

Second Edition

by Jerry Capeci

ALPHA

A member of Penguin Group (USA) Inc.

For my wife, Barbara, who still makes it all worthwhile

ALPHA BOOKS

Published by the Penguin Group

Penguin Group (USA) Inc., 375 Hudson Street, New York, New York 10014, U.S.A.

Penguin Group (Canada), 10 Alcorn Avenue, Toronto, Ontario, Canada M4V 3B2 (a division of Pearson Penguin Canada Inc.)

Penguin Books Ltd, 80 Strand, London WC2R 0RL, England

Penguin Ireland, 25 St Stephen's Green, Dublin 2, Ireland (a division of Penguin Books Ltd)

Penguin Group (Australia), 250 Camberwell Road, Camberwell, Victoria 3124, Australia (a division of Pearson Australia Group Pty Ltd)

Penguin Books India Pvt Ltd, 11 Community Centre, Panchsheel Park, New Delh—110 017, India

Penguin Group (NZ), cnr Airborne and Rosedale Roads, Albany, Auckland 1310, New Zealand (a division of Pearson New Zealand Ltd)

Penguin Books (South Africa) (Pty) Ltd, 24 Sturdee Avenue, Rosebank, Johannesburg 2196, South Africa

Penguin Books Ltd, Registered Offices: 80 Strand, London WC2R 0RL, England

International Standard Book Number: 1-59257-305-3
Library of Congress Catalog Card Number: 2004113218

09 08 07   8   7   6   5   4

Interpretation of the printing code: The rightmost number of the first series of numbers is the year of the book's printing; the rightmost number of the second series of numbers is the number of the book's printing. For example, a printing code of 04-1 shows that the first printing occurred in 2004.

Printed in the United States of America

Note: This publication contains the opinions and ideas of its author. It is intended to provide helpful and informative material on the subject matter covered. It is sold with the understanding that the author and publisher are not engaged in rendering professional services in the book. If the reader requires personal assistance or advice, a competent professional should be consulted.

The author and publisher specifically disclaim any responsibility for any liability, loss, or risk, personal or otherwise, which is incurred as a consequence, directly or indirectly, of the use and application of any of the contents of this book.

Most Alpha books are available at special quantity discounts for bulk purchases for sales promotions, premiums, fundraising, or educational use. Special books, or book excerpts, can also be created to fit specific needs.

For details, write: Special Markets, Alpha Books, 375 Hudson Street, New York, NY 10014.

Publisher: *Marie Butler-Knight*
Product Manager: *Phil Kitchel*
Senior Managing Editor: *Jennifer Chisholm*
Senior Acquisitions Editor: *Paul Dinas*
Development Editor: *Jennifer Moore*
Production Editor: *Janette Lynn*

Copy Editor: *Molly Schaller*
Cartoonist: *Shannon Wheeler*
Cover/Book Designer: *Trina Wurst*
Indexer: *Angie Bess*
Layout: *Becky Harmon*
Proofreading: *Donna Martin*

Contents at a Glance

Appendixes

Contents

Foreword

A few months ago I was asked to fill in for Jerry Capeci in a weekly online discussion at *Slate Magazine* about *The Sopranos*—that wonderful HBO series that has captured the soap opera–like yin and yang of La Cosa Nostra at the turn of the century.

I was happy to do it, but said I felt like a bishop who had been asked to substitute for the pope. I knew the liturgy but couldn't bring the same authority to the pulpit.

Jerry Capeci is the *capo di tutti capi* of mob writers. Has been for years. And this funny, entertaining, and chock-a-block full-of-information book is the essence of who he is and what he has done during more than three decades of tracking organized crime. Nobody does it better.

The mob, of course, has fallen on hard times. Its glory days are long past. But its glory was more myth than reality anyway. It was Mario Puzo and Francis Ford Coppolla who gave us the noble crime boss. Don Corleone never really existed. Instead, we've had crazy psychopaths like Albert Anastasia (no relation) and Nicky Scarfo, celebrity dons like Al Capone and John Gotti, and treacherously ruthless mob bosses like Vito Genovese and Vincent Gigante.

These are the guys, along with their associates, *comares* (pronounced goom-*odds*), and sycophants, that Capeci gives us in *The Complete Idiot's Guide to the Mafia*.

In easy, understandable terms, he has captured the essence of La Cosa Nostra.

Now he's revised the package, adding even more insights and providing just the right blend of pathos and humor.

For the old-time wiseguys the idea was to make money, not headlines. For those true believers, the Mafia really was a way of life. There's a lot of that in this book.

But there are also plenty of the "holy-shit-can-you-believe-it" escapades that put the lie to the image of the clever, taciturn don and his loyal band of followers.

In general, the mobsters who dominated La Cosa Nostra at the turn of the century were not true believers. The Mafia wasn't a way of life, but a way to make money—strictly a business proposition.

And when these guys found themselves jammed up, looking at a 40-year prison stint in some RICO murder and conspiracy case, they made a business decision. How do I cut my losses?

You can almost hear the infamous Salvatore "Sammy the Bull" Gravano asking that question as he decides to give up John Gotti. (Here, of course, you could substitute the names of dozens of other mob turncoats who have followed that same path. All have gotten headlines. But few have gotten the book contract and movie deal that added to Gravano's riches.)

What was La Cosa Nostra?

Honor and loyalty? Fuhgeddaboudit.

"The daily routine involves grit, grime, self-interest, lying, cheating, backstabbing, pettiness, spontaneous violence, stupidity, betrayal, and many other acts that conjure up the idea of killers without honor who will do almost anything to make a buck."

That's Capeci on La Cosa Nostra.

Nobody knows it better.

—George Anastasia

George Anastasia covers organized crime for the *Philadelphia Inquirer.* He is the author of four books about the mob. His latest, *The Last Gangster* (ReganBooks, 2004), made the *New York Times* bestseller list.

Introduction

The Mafia fascinates people everywhere. Two books that Gene Mustain and I wrote about John Gotti, *Mob Star* in 1988 and *Gotti: Rise and Fall* in 1996, were very well received. So was our updated edition of *Mob Star* in 2002, as well as the first edition of *The Complete Idiot's Guide to the Mafia* in 2002. *The Godfather* movie packed theaters, as did its two sequels. As the twenty-first century unfolds, the highly acclaimed HBO series *The Sopranos* is flying high. Viewers are already salivating over the sixth and final season that is not due until 2006! My GangLandNews.com website (www. ganglandnews.com) averages more than 250,000 unique visitors a month. There is no doubt—America loves the Mafia.

But what is it that fascinates us? I am not a shrink, but I think people from all walks of life, from every corner of the globe, love to be scared. We pay money to go on rides and to see movies that scare us. Others spend a lifetime putting their lives in danger as they scale mountains or jump out of planes with no more than a bit of cloth to save them. Perhaps reading about the Mafia and watching mob characters on the screen provides enough of a hint of danger to be attractive.

My neighbor, who wishes to remain anonymous, told me he had it all figured out. He said we are all frustrated by irritating things in our lives that we are helpless to do anything about. Maybe a motorist who gave you the finger and his horn as he cut you off, or the counterman in the deli who ignored you and served customers who came in after you. Secretly, my neighbor thinks, we would like to be feared a little by such people so they would be nicer to us. He thinks following the Mafia lets us fantasize a little about having this kind of power. I shut him up by saying, "How would you like to worry every day that your best friend was going to put a bullet in the back of your head?"

In this book, I describe the real Mafia. The focus is on the unique American version of the Sicilian Mafia that developed in the twentieth century. Unlike the Sicilian version, La Cosa Nostra wasn't restricted to males of Sicilian heritage, but men whose roots went back to all parts of Italy. Additionally, although the core of La Cosa Nostra is its Italian-American members, the organization couldn't function without thousands of associates who are of just about every nationality that can be found in North America.

This book makes no apologies for writing about the Mafia. At the height of its power, La Cosa Nostra only had about 3,500 members nationwide. Collectively, the various families exerted incredible power that influenced politics, the price of numerous commodities, the cost of various services, the affairs of major unions, the results of many court cases, and many other facets of North American life. Its power was so great that it took a major, sustained effort by the federal government to bring it under a semblance of control. This book is not about Italian-Americans. It's about gangsters who happen to be, for the most part, of Italian-American lineage.

This updated edition of *The Complete Idiot's Guide to the Mafia* contains seven new chapters (Part 6, "The New Millennium") that detail new developments and emerging trends in the twenty-first century, as well as new insights into prior events that have come to light from new turncoats and investigative efforts by the law enforcement community.

Of course, saying that La Cosa Nostra has this incredible power begs the question of how it acquired and maintained it. I'll take you through the early days as the families began to form, to the golden years of Prohibition, and to the era of gambling, drugs, and labor racketeering. Along the way there were lots of bodies to account for, and you will read about some of the major, well-known, gangland-style slayings. As Gene Mustain and I detailed in *Murder Machine* (Dutton, 1992), killing is a way of life in La Cosa Nostra, and real stories about it are usually very bloody.

What You'll Find Inside

I'll tell you about various efforts the law made to discover just who and what La Cosa Nostra was. A few chapters will detail some of the major events that brought the Mafia to the public's attention and essentially forced the government to begin making legislative and administrative moves to attack it. I have included some government triumphs, mostly in the 1980s, that at least temporarily have given the feds the upper hand.

You will read about some of the extreme measures gangsters have used to reach for the thrones of Mafia families. There aren't enough pages in any book to detail every battle for control, but I have included some of the conflicts in New York's Gambino and Colombo families that serve as real-life examples of the intrigue, betrayal, and violence involved.

You will learn about mobsters such as Joe Colombo, who courted the media in a briefly successful attempt to cow the government, about hoods who became informers for the government and gave us an insider's view of Mafia life, and about a few major turncoats such as Joe Valachi and Sammy Bull Gravano. Their stories, as well as those from more recent mob defectors including Salvatore "Good Looking Sal" Vitale and Michael "Mikey Scars" DiLeonardo, confirm how treacherous Mafia life is.

After reading this book, it is my hope that you will have a better understanding what the real Mafia *was*, *is*, *did*, and *does*. Although you might still find the Mafia a fascinating subject, I hope you will also realize that there is little honorable about people who lie, cheat, threaten, beat, and murder to get their own way.

A Few More Things About the Book

This book also features extra tidbits called *sidebars*. These asides are designed to supply you with extra information, tips, and cautions. Here's what you'll find:

Mafia Speak

These sidebars give explanations of Mafia practices, often through direct quotes from wiseguys.

Big Shot

These anecdotes provide a few pertinent facts about a mob hit.

Slammer Time

These boxes tell you about mobsters and associates who spent some time in prison.

Fuhgeddaboudit

These short sketches illustrate various examples of Mafia life.

Acknowledgments

This revised edition of *The Complete Idiot's Guide to the Mafia*, and the original in 2001, couldn't have been written without the assistance of Andy Petepiece, an organized crime historian with a voluminous collection of books, magazines, FBI files, and other research material on the subject. A voracious reader with a remarkable memory, Petepiece became intrigued with the Mafia in 1963 when Joe Valachi became the first "made man" to publicly break *omerta*, the La Cosa Nostra code of silence, and describe the inner workings of a secret society of Italian-American criminals that most people know as the Mafia.

I was also aided by my co-author of three books, Gene Mustain; Tom Robbins, a former colleague at the *New York Daily News* who now toils at the *Village Voice*; and numerous others, including many whose work is cited in this book.

In the Alpha family, I thank my prior and current acquisitions editors, Gary Goldstein and Paul Dinas; their editorial assistant, Michelle Vega; and copy editor, Molly Schaller.

A special thank-you to development editor Jennifer Moore, who aided immeasurably in revising and editing the entire first edition, and in helping me design and structure the new material, including the sidebars and margin notes contained in the seven chapters that comprise Part 6, "The New Millennium." Last but not least, I thank production editor Jan Lynn for her patience and professionalism in dealing with me and the entire Alpha team for producing the new edition you have in your hands.

Trademarks

All terms mentioned in this book that are known to be or are suspected of being trademarks or service marks have been appropriately capitalized. Alpha Books and Penguin Group (USA) Inc. cannot attest to the accuracy of this information. Use of a term in this book should not be regarded as affecting the validity of any trademark or service mark.

Part 1

The Organization

When you write a book about the Mafia, the reader has to know who and what you are talking about; otherwise, the material turns out to be gibberish. In this first part, I explain just who these American Mafia guys are so that you don't confuse them with a rock group of the same name.

I'll tell you who the bad guys are, how they became outlaws, what positions they fill, and the rules by which they are supposed to live. Furthermore, you can read about Mafia families that exist or that used to exist in different parts of the United States and Canada, perhaps even in your hometown.

Who Are These Guys?

In This Chapter

♦ Identifying the different Mafia groups

♦ La Cosa Nostra's American roots

♦ The structure of La Cosa Nostra

The word *Mafia* has led to more confusion than the 2000 presidential election. Some scholars claim it's a Sicilian-Arabic word indicating a proud, self-sufficient way of life. Others say it's an acronym for a Sicilian resistance cry that was used against the French invaders of the thirteenth century. Whatever its origin, today the word is used to refer to a wide variety of ethnic organized criminals from the Chinese to the Russians to the so-called Jewish Mafia. The term also has less serious applications. The party animal buddies of Elvis Presley were called the Memphis Mafia. The groupies around President John F. Kennedy and his brother Robert were often labeled the Irish Mafia. In this book, the term *Mafia* refers to Italian or Italian-American organized crime.

In this chapter, I give a brief outline of the four criminal groups commonly called Mafia. Furthermore, you'll get a description of the various positions in a Mafia family, as well as examples.

Which Mafia?

America's La Cosa Nostra and Italy's three major organized crime groups—the Sicilian Mafia, the Camorra, and the Calabrian Mafia—are distinct entities despite their similar structures, the rules they follow, and the illegal activities they pursue.

The Sicilian Mafia

The island of Sicily has had a long and violent history. At various times, armed resistance groups formed to battle the invaders of the moment. Some clans were noble patriots, but others were gangs of criminals. In the mid- to late 1800s, larger groups called "families," often composed of many relatives by blood or marriage, sprang up. These families had similar structures and regulations. And because of these similarities, outsiders wrongly believed that those who followed this way of life, Cosa Nostra, were all one group. Furthermore, it was clearly understood by all that a Mafioso would kill to get his way. The fear factor was a powerful weapon. Few dared to resist. To justify this regular use of force, the Mafia bosses spun the illusion that Mafia members were men of honor, acting only to help others. They created monopolies, both legal and illegal, making money anyway they could, always using threats of violence and death as the primary tools of their trade. This control of the population led to alliances with the major political party, giving the more than 100 families a collective stranglehold on the island.

The last 50 years of the twentieth century brought major changes to the Sicilian Mafia. Having learned how to produce heroin, the Mafiosi were no longer dependent on the skills of French chemists who worked for the Corsican underworld. As the heroin trade exploded around the world, more Sicilian Mafia members began dealing directly with American counterparts and their associates. Eventually, some Sicilian hoods took up permanent residency in the United States and Canada to facilitate the movement of the drugs and the mountains of money it created. These newcomers were responsible to their bosses in Sicily and were often confused with members of the American La Cosa Nostra.

The expanding heroin wealth brought an increase in violence. The more ambitious bosses formed alliances in order to dominate rivals. This led to rounds of killings that periodically roared out of control from the 1960s into the 1990s. Attempts by the Italian government to crack down had only lukewarm political support. With the lack of will obvious to all,

> **Slammer Time**
>
> Sicilian Mafia boss Salvatore "Toto" Riina was able to avoid capture for more than 20 years despite directing a campaign of terror against honest government officials and Mafia rivals. He was finally arrested in January of 1993, convicted, and sentenced to life in prison in June of 1999.

some bosses escalated murderous attacks on anti-Mafia officials hoping to break the government's will altogether. By the end of the twentieth century, however, the wanton killings were taking their toll on Sicilian society. After two anti-Mafia crusaders were killed in bombings that also took the lives of innocent bystanders, the public outcry forced politicians to get serious in their fight against the Mafia. As the century ended, the authorities finally seemed to be making progress. Public pressure, new legislation, and cooperation with law enforcement officials from the United States and other countries were key factors. The Sicilian Mafia remains a serious concern, however.

The Camorra

With roots going back centuries, the Camorra is believed to have solidified during the 1800s in the prisons of the Italian city of Naples. Gradually, as prisoners were released, the gangs' reach extended into the city itself. Today, authorities estimate that there are more than 100 families, the majority based on the Italian mainland. Like Sicilian Mafia families, each has a hierarchical structure with a boss at the apex. He is assisted by various capos who oversee crews of members and associates.

Until around 1970, the Camorra primarily made their money on gambling, loan-sharking, extortion, tobacco smuggling, and political corruption. In the 1970s, many Camorra families moved heavily into the international drug trade and its companion, money-laundering. Many got rich very quickly, but many others perished.

Like the Sicilian Mafia, the Camorra has always been quick to resort to savage outbursts of violence. The expansion into the drug trade escalated killings of rivals and law enforcement officials. This has increased the Italian government's pressure against the Camorra, leading to more arrests, and more members who decide to cooperate, which has led to more arrests, causing a reduction in the organization's power and influence. Nevertheless, the Camorra continues to thrive, although it is the least active of all Italian organized crime groups in the United States.

Fuhgeddaboudit

American oil billionaire John Paul Getty was a victim of a Calabrian Mafia plot in 1973. Members of a clan kidnapped his grandson, J. Paul Getty III, who was living in Italy at the time. At first the elder Getty refused to pay their ransom demand, but when he received delivery of his grandson's ear in the mail, he approved the payoff. No one was ever prosecuted, and none of the $2 million ransom was recovered.

18

The Calabrian Mafia

This version of the Italian Mafia takes its name from its base in the southern province of Calabria. More accurately called the Honored Society, it also goes by the name of 'Ndrangheta. Like its Sicilian cousin, the Calabrian Mafia claims to have roots based on resistance to government oppression. Men of similar thinking merged into what eventually became families with a hierarchical structure, strict rules of behavior, and a vow of secrecy.

Members have been engaged in the regular gamut of criminal activities, including tobacco smuggling, gambling, kidnapping, and extortion. By the 1970s, families were active in the worldwide drug trade, moving both heroin and cocaine. Some members also began specializing in money-laundering as well. To avoid rivalries with other Italian drug gangs, many Calabrian Mafia members set up shop in the United States, Canada, and other countries.

Increasing wealth and more rackets exacerbated the normally high level of paranoia in Calabrian wiseguys, ultimately resulting in more dead bodies and more negative publicity. In the 1990s, the Italian government finally generated the political will to mount offenses against the Calabrian drug kingpins. Nevertheless, the Calabrian Mafia remains a major force.

La Cosa Nostra

From wiretaps and bugs of Italian-American criminals, the FBI learned in the late 1950s and early 1960s that the term "Cosa Nostra" (meaning "our thing") was used to indicate a particular lifestyle these men had sworn to follow. Eventually, the FBI coined the phrase "La Cosa Nostra" to distinguish Italian-American organized crime from its Mafia cousins in Italy. It is grammatically incorrect when translated into Italian, but the label has survived and is commonly used to refer to the American brand of the Mafia. For our purposes in this book, the terms "La Cosa Nostra" (or "LCN") and "Mafia" are interchangeable.

La Cosa Nostra didn't just appear. It evolved in the new circumstances of America, and it continues to evolve. Initially, in the 1890 to 1920 era, they were essentially American carbon copies of Camorra and Sicilian Mafia families as well as numerous Calabrian Mafia cells. Eventually, the purity of each group began

> **Mafia Speak**
>
> The American Mafia has been known by many names. Prior to 1920, it was called the Black Hand after a popular extortion scheme used by Italian criminals. It has also been referred to as Unione Siciliana, which is the name of an organization conceived to aid new Italian immigrants that was eventually corrupted by Mafia members. Neither term is an accurate description of La Cosa Nostra.

to fade into the melting pot of America as new friendships and criminal liaisons developed. Violence also played a role in the blending. For example, in New York City, a prominent Camorra group was decimated by murder convictions and faded from contention. In Chicago, the Camorra group of Johnny Torrio and Al Capone overpowered their Sicilian-American rivals. By the 1930s La Cosa Nostra had emerged, a unique, powerful, Italian-American organized crime group. The American Mafia was born.

In the first half of the twentieth century, some thought Italian crime groups had sent emissaries to establish branches in the new world. However, despite similarity in structure and rules, it appears that American families formed gradually and weren't part of a global plan, even though some Sicilian Mafia members—such as Salvatore Maranzano, a major player in Mafia affairs around 1930—emigrated to America and were inducted into an American family.

Top Dogs

Despite being spread across America, each La Cosa Nostra family has a similar hierarchical structure. It's a format they adopted from the Sicilian Mafia that has lasted for more than 100 years. The following diagram shows the pyramid-type formation.

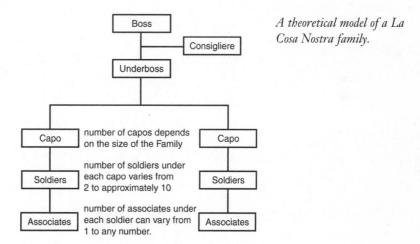

A theoretical model of a La Cosa Nostra family.

The Boss

The boss sits at the apex of the "food chain" of a La Cosa Nostra family. There are three basic ways to become boss, but no matter what system is used, the man perceived to have the most power wins.

In 1931, a show of hands by all the members of Joseph Bonanno's family elevated him to the top position. However, by 1958, such meetings were considered too susceptible to detection by law enforcement, especially in the larger families. Consequently, when John Gotti was elected leader of the Gambino family in 1986, only the capos voted.

When a boss dies of natural causes, the second-in-command—the underboss—often moves to the top. This is what happened in 1959 when a heart attack felled Pittston boss Joseph Barbara. Underboss Russell Bufalino took over.

Two years earlier, Carlo Gambino used another system to take the top spot. He formed alliances with other family leaders and ensured his own elevation by having boss Albert Anastasia killed.

After receiving a long prison sentence, bosses—John Gotti is an obvious exception—are supposed to step down, for the sake of the crime family as well as his own sake. In 1987, Luchese boss Anthony "Tony Ducks" Corallo stepped down after receiving a 100-year sentence. Capo Victor Amuso was elected the new leader. Since then, however, Amuso, and every other convicted Mafia boss—for personal gain, glory or gratification—has retained his position, to the glee of law enforcers. Aging and imprisoned-for-life leaders have throttled their families, rendering them virtually rudderless, by steadfastly refusing to step down, for the good of the surviving gangsters.

"It's the 'me' generation," said one law enforcement official. "The bosses are just like the skippers (capos), the soldiers, the associates and the hangers-on—out for themselves. Whatever loyalty and tradition these mutts had years ago, is long since gone."

A boss spends much of his working time settling disputes. Although a boss is, for all intents and purposes, a dictator, he has to know how to pick his spots, how to play politics. Ruling against a powerful mobster may come back to haunt a boss, and only a very foolish one tries to rule by pure muscle. When a boss is wise and keeps his men faithful, he reaps tremendous benefits through regular tributes from all his capos, who pass a portion of their crew's income up to him. In a 200-member family, that can total millions of dollars a year. Most bosses have been smart enough to invest in legitimate businesses, allowing for a very comfortable lifestyle without problems with the taxman.

The income, prestige, and power make the boss position a much-coveted one. It also makes him a target of ambitious underlings as well as ambitious law enforcement officials.

Big Shot

Family boss is a powerful position, but there are limits, as John Bazzano Sr. learned in 1932. After taking over the Pittsburgh mob, he tried to solidify his power by whacking the rival Volpe brothers. He picked off John, Arthur, and James on July 29, 1932. But brothers Louis and Joseph survived, and soon after, Bazzano was invited to dinner, murdered, and left in the street in a burlap bag.

The Underboss

It is the prerogative of the boss to select an underboss. In Dallas in 1921, Carlo Piranio named his brother Joe as his second in command. In the larger outfits, the choice is more political. Certain strong factions of the family often need to be recognized to maintain some semblance of unity. Salvatore Maranzano, of the Bonanno family, followed this strategy in picking Angelo Caruso in 1930. Carlo Gambino rewarded Joseph Biondo with the underboss seat after they successfully plotted the 1957 murder of boss Albert Anastasia.

Fuhgeddaboudit
Underboss Joe Biondo angered boss Carlo Gambino with his constant womanizing. Gambino felt this openly adulterous behavior reflected badly on the family administration. To make matters worse, Gambino caught Biondo muscling in on a garbage racket in New Jersey without seeking the boss's approval. In June of 1965, Biondo was demoted to soldier, a huge embarrassment, but when weighed against the penalty they meted out to Anastasia, Biondo got off pretty easy.

Not all underbosses have the same power. In 1964, Stefano La Salle, second in command of the 150-member Luchese family, obviously wielded more influence than the underboss of the 12-man San Francisco clan. When the legendary Anthony Accardo was underboss of the Chicago outfit in the mid-1940s, he had tremendous strength. This was due not only to his own considerable abilities but to his closeness to boss Paul Ricca and the fact he was seen as a future boss.

In most families, the underboss arbitrates many of the disputes that arise. Depending on the seriousness of the problem, he might or might not consult with the boss. Some conflicts are immediately bucked up to the boss. In those cases, the underboss usually sits in and offers his opinion. In either event, everyone knows that the ultimate authority rests at the boss level. This sometimes chafes the ego of an ambitious underboss and can lead to problems.

Monetary compensation lands in the underboss's lap in various ways. For example, he might be involved as a partner in some rackets and thus get a cut. In addition, certain capos might pass their envelopes through the underboss on their way to the top. He takes a piece before visiting the boss with the rest. Additionally, the boss may give a slice of some of the family rackets to his underboss. However he makes his illegal money, it is a significant enough amount to make his position one of envy, especially when prestige and the possibility of additional advancement are weighed.

The Consigliere

Most theoretical descriptions of the consigliere position tell of an aged, respected, Mafia veteran who is consulted on a variety of matters. Supposedly, the consigliere is devoid of ambition and thus bases his advice on what is "right" rather than what is in his or the boss's best interest. It is further claimed that this position was created to protect the ordinary member from a capricious boss. Therefore, a consigliere was elected by the membership rather than being appointed by the boss.

Reality is another matter. For the first half of the twentieth century, the names of the consigliere of most families were hard to come by. It wasn't until about 1959 that serious intelligence gathering about La Cosa Nostra really began. During that era, there were some families with an identified consigliere who fit the theoretical description previously outlined. In 1971, however, Colombo family consigliere Joseph Yacovelli directed a murder campaign against renegade mobster Joseph "Crazy Joe" Gallo. Two decades later, a Yacovelli successor, Carmine Sessa, was part of a hit team poised outside the home of the acting boss looking to kill him. There are enough examples of an active, biased consigliere to bring the theoretical model of the more passive role into question. Additionally, electronic surveillance in 1979 caught New England boss Ray Patriarca Jr. talking about appointing his consigliere. So much for an election!

> **Big Shot**
>
> In 1976, Frank "Bomp" Bompensiero was appointed consigliere of the Los Angeles family. This ploy was dreamed up by his boss, who felt that if Bompensiero were promoted, he would relax his guard and be easier to kill. Bompensiero was shot to death on February 10, 1977, after he was lured to a public phone booth where his killers were waiting.

Capos

The boss appoints the capos. The number depends on the size of the family. New York's Gambino family has had more than 20; St Louis had but a handful. Each capo is in charge of a mini-gang or crew of soldiers and associates that can range greatly in size. These men might or might not be based in close proximity. Capo Joe Notaro of the 1960s-era Bonanno family had crewmembers spread throughout New York's five boroughs and New Jersey.

Capos have varying degrees of power. Some are relatives or close friends of the boss, which gives them more influence. A capo with an active crew, producing lots of money, is always respected. Capos who don't produce or who make too many mistakes face an uncertain future. Capo Joe Sferra of the New Jersey family was demoted to soldier and removed from his lucrative union post in June of 1965 after a series of blunders.

In 1984, Salvatore "Salvie" Testa, a once rising Philadelphia capo, suffered a much worse
fate: He ended up with a head full of bullets
after boss Nicodemo "Little Nicky" Scarfo
became suspicious of his loyalty.

A slice of the rackets of his soldiers and associates provides the capo with illegal income.
He, in turn, kicks a portion up to the boss at
regular intervals. Accurate estimates of the
income of an average capo vary greatly and
are difficult to quantify. It's always in a state
of flux, depending on the success and size of
his crew. However, it's safe to say that capo is
a much-coveted, more lucrative position than
soldier or associate.

> **Mafia Speak**
>
> During a court hearing
> in January of 1998, aging Detroit
> capo Vito "Billy Jack" Giacalone
> admitted that the Detroit La Cosa
> Nostra family existed and that he
> was a member. Giacalone
> pleaded guilty to a charge related
> to illegal gambling. The Detroit
> capo and his brother Anthony
> "Tony Jack" Giacalone were sus-
> pects in the 1975 disappearance
> of former Teamster president
> Jimmy Hoffa (see Chapter 33).

The Puppies

All organizations need people to do the grunt work. In La Cosa Nostra, the soldiers
and associates carry out these tasks. Not surprisingly, they are required to pay tribute
to their capo for the privilege of being allowed to operate.

Soldiers

The soldier is the lowest level of formal La Cosa Nostra membership. Becoming a
"made man," however, is a tremendous step up from the associate level. A soldier's
responsibility is to make money and kick a portion up to his capo. Everything else,
including murder, is a means to that end.
Most of his illegal schemes fall through, but
enough had better succeed for him to remain
in favor. Some men are rewarded with induction into La Cosa Nostra for their strong-
arm work but end up being incompetent
when it comes to hustling money. A few
lucky ones inherit successful rackets, but for
most, it is a daily grind to generate income.

> **Fuhgeddaboudit**
>
> Longtime Philadelphia La Cosa
> Nostra member Harry "The
> Hunchback" Riccobene claimed
> he was made a formal member
> of that family when he was only
> 17 years old.

Not all soldiers are created equal. A boss's son, such as Alphonse Persico of the Colombo family, might be a soldier, but all family members and wiseguys from other families know early on that he is being groomed for bigger things. Another soldier might be a strong money earner and report directly to the boss, like Robert "DeeBee" DiBernardo did in the 1980s when Paul Castellano was boss. Others, like Chicago's Phil Alderisio in the 1950s, are respected for their crafty ruthlessness. On the flip side is Colombo soldier Tony "The Gawk" Augello. He blew his brains out when he feared boss Carmine "Junior" Persico was going to kill him for involving son Alphonse in a busted drug deal. Others react to their loss of power by becoming informers.

Soldiers can be virtual brokesters, scrambling to earn enough cash to pay the rent. Far too often, they live high and flirt with the poverty line. Frequently they have to borrow money from other mobsters at usurious or loan shark interest rates. Lawyers regularly eat away at their money when they get arrested, and their earning ability can be thwarted by incarceration or surveillance.

They can also be multimillionaires, either through their own prowess or because they have inherited their fathers' well-established rackets along with their fathers' substantial so-called "legitimate" enterprises.

Associates

Associates are the worker ants of La Cosa Nostra. They engage in regular criminal activity with the blessing of a made member of the Mafia. The key word is *regular*, because there are hundreds of others who have brief criminal partnerships with a soldier but then move on.

Associates come in all shapes, sizes, nationalities, and religions. One might simply be a street guy who hangs around doing odd jobs such as unloading hijacked trucks and shuffling stolen cars to a wrecking yard. Another might be a union delegate who secretly cooperates with the wishes of a particular mob family. Another could be a multimillionaire construction magnate who has allied himself with a mob family because it controls the unions that can make or break his projects. Yet another might have more power than most capos. Murray "The Camel" Humphreys was one of the leaders of the Chicago outfit in the 1950s and 1960s even though he wasn't even eligible to be a formal member. Joseph Watts, a close associate of three successive bosses of the Gambino family from the 1970s through the twenty-first century, made $30,000 a week from his loan-sharking business for the eight years from 1986 through 1994, according to testimony at his July 2001 trial, at which he was convicted of tax fraud. Associates also make up a large number of mob rubout victims because their loyalty is always first to be suspect.

Mafia Speak

There are lawyers who defend mobsters and then there are mob lawyers. The former are respected as vital defenders of the principle of the presumption of innocence until proven guilty. The latter are basically mob groupies who, for some reason, love to bask in glow of the media spotlight shining on their clients. A number of these advocates have crossed the legal line. Some end up behind bars; a few end up in the street with bullet holes in their heads.

Mob associate Joe Watts made $30,000 a week from 1986 until at least 1994 as a Gambino family loan shark.

(Photo courtesy of GangLandNews.com)

Real Life

It would be nice if one could diagram the power structure of a La Cosa Nostra family and then everyone involved in that life adhered to the rules. Unfortunately, the Mafia, like life, is more complicated than that. In many families, the formal structure doesn't do justice to who actually has power, as shown in the following figure. The examples in the following figure are drawn from a variety of families.

A realistic model of a La Cosa Nostra family.

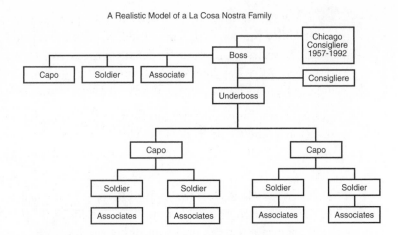

A Realistic Model of a La Cosa Nostra Family

When Paul Castellano was a capo in the Gambino family, his brother-in-law Carlo Gambino was the boss. Paul and Carlo were also cousins. This gave Castellano unlimited access to Gambino and thus more power than the other capos and perhaps as much as underboss, Aniello Dellacroce. On the surface, everyone would have to pretend that Dellacroce was superior to Castellano, but reality raised its head when Gambino named Castellano as his successor, passing over Dellacroce.

In the Chicago family, Gus Alex wasn't a formal member of La Cosa Nostra—his Greek background eliminated him from consideration. Nevertheless, Alex was at the top of the Chicago outfit for decades. His role was critical. He was in charge of the many political connections maintained by the Chicago family. His success in this role and his personal ties with the other major players gave him more power than most capos.

Colombo soldier Ralph Scopo was a key player in a multimillion-dollar labor racketeering scheme in New York City. He controlled a key District Council of the Laborers Union that helped establish a Mafia-led monopoly on major construction jobs in Manhattan. Scopo met regularly with leaders of his own Colombo family and with the heads of three other families who were involved in a club that took a piece of all Manhattan construction jobs over $2 million. As such, he wielded more influence than most capos within his family.

Big Shot

Despite his close working relationships with Mafia bosses, Ralph Scopo was well aware of the fragility of Mafia life. In April of 1984, Scopo was overheard explaining to an associate that Gambino soldier Roy DeMeo had been killed by his own family because they merely suspected that he would not be able to stand up to legal charges that resulted from his stolen car ring.

When Thomas "Tommy Del" DelGiorno was appointed capo in the Philadelphia family of Nicky Scarfo in March of 1986, his power seemed to be growing greatly. However, his excessive drinking and critical comments about his boss put his star in a steep decline. Although he was still a capo, everyone knew he was on the way out. Eventually, DelGiorno recognized this reality himself and became a government witness.

Like DelGiorno, Philadelphia underboss Sal Merlino was a heavy drinker. Although he was a long-time friend of boss Nicky Scarfo, his troubles and perceived treachery led to a decline in his prestige. Finally, Scarfo demoted Merlino to soldier early in 1986.

As these examples show, the power structure of a La Cosa Nostra family is constantly in flux. Every day is a struggle. Each member is trying to hold his position or move up. At the same time, there is always someone coveting his money, position, or influence, or a superior who is suspicious of his ambition.

The Least You Need to Know

- La Cosa Nostra is America's homebred Mafia.
- Each La Cosa Nostra family has a formal structure.
- Formal positions in La Cosa Nostra don't always indicate real power.
- La Cosa Nostra depends on many nonmembers called associates.

Making the Mafia Grade

In This Chapter

- ◆ How to join La Cosa Nostra
- ◆ All about the initiation
- ◆ Rules and regulations
- ◆ Saying hello
- ◆ Money rules

Many street terms are used to describe the process by which a Mafia associate becomes a formal member of La Cosa Nostra, including "being made," "getting your button," and "getting straightened out." To mob wannabes, it's the culmination of a life's dream, like dying and going to heaven.

Who's Eligible?

A candidate must be a man whose father is of Italian heritage, although some families are more strict and require that both parents be of Italian heritage.

Women can never become members of La Cosa Nostra. They are supposed to be kept ignorant of Mafia activities, no matter what their relationship with the made men might be. Furthermore, because women are not to be involved in Mafia affairs, women relatives are to be considered noncombatants in any mob violence. In addition, Mafia women are not supposed to talk to outsiders about anything having to do with their family affairs.

Mafia Speak

Like all Mafia rules, the ones pertaining to women are often broken. Anna Genovese, second wife of Vito Genovese, a New York Mafia boss whose name is used to refer to one of the city's five families, detailed her version of life with the Mafia kingpin in a stunning divorce court hearing in 1953. She even described how she ran a highly lucrative gambling operation—$30,000 a week, she said—for her husband.

Like Father, Like Son

If your father is a member of La Cosa Nostra your chances of getting "made" are much better. If your father is the boss, you're a shoo-in. The following table presents a partial list of La Cosa Nostra bosses whose sons were also inducted.

Boss	Son	Family
Joseph Bonanno	Salvatore "Bill" Bonanno	Bonanno
Carlo Gambino	Thomas Gambino	Gambino
Joseph Barbara	Joseph Barbara Jr.	Pittstown
Raymond Patriarca	Raymond Patriarca Jr.	New England
Joseph Zerilli	Anthony Zerilli	Detroit
Joseph Profaci	Salvatore Profaci	Colombo
Joseph Todaro	Joseph Todaro Jr.	Buffalo
Joseph Lonardo	Angelo Lonardo	Cleveland
Carmine Persico	Alphonse Persico	Colombo
John Gotti	John A. "Junior" Gotti	Gambino
Nicholas Licata	Carlo Licata	Los Angeles
Gaetano "Tommy" Reina	Giacomo Reina	Luchese
Carl Civella	Anthony Civella	Kansas City
Philip Testa	Salvatore Testa	Philadelphia
Santos Trafficante	Santos Trafficante Jr.	Tampa

Of course, many bosses showed better judgment and pointed their sons in more positive directions.

Fuhgeddaboudit

At a meeting of New York Mafia leaders in 1988, John Gotti spoke with pride that he had recently inducted his son John A. "Junior" Gotti into the Gambino crime family. Salvatore "Sammy Bull" Gravano and Anthony "Gaspipe" Casso both reported that Genovese boss Vincent "Chin" Gigante replied that he had seen Junior's name on a list of proposed mobsters that had been passed around and had been surprised. "I don't know why anyone would want to bring his son into the life," said Gigante, whose sons have never become "made men." In Chapter 27, I detail the indictment and conviction of Chin and his unmade son, Andrew.

Blue Chips

The blue-chip prospect is the associate who has proven he can make money. Many hoodlums are ready to kill at the drop of a hat, but few can consistently earn enough money to pass some on to his capo. Undercover FBI agent Joe Pistone infiltrated New York's Bonanno family posing as a jewel thief who went by the name of Donnie Brasco. To ingratiate himself with his mob superiors, Pistone passed envelopes stuffed with cash (unbeknownst to the mobsters, the money was supplied by the FBI) up to mob sponsors Benjamin "Lefty Guns" Ruggiero and Dominick "Sonny Black" Napolitano.

One FBI scheme to make Pistone appear to be a "blue chip" candidate, a guy who would put cash into the crime family's coffers, involved a nightclub in Florida. Tales of the money Pistone and his Mafia sponsors were making got back to Anthony Mirra, a Bonanno soldier who had met Pistone early in his undercover career. Mirra claimed that Pistone, and his rackets, belonged to Mirra. Ruggiero, another soldier, and Napolitano, his mob superior, didn't want to lose the cash that Pistone was sending up to them so they challenged Mirra. Ultimately they won a "sitdown"—a mob-style conflict resolution procedure in which opposing factions meet with a high ranked gangster who serves as judge and jury—that ultimately cost Napolitano his life. When the Bonanno family realized that Pistone was really an undercover FBI agent and had stung them, they held Napolitano responsible and killed him.

Murder Requirement

Besides having the correct lineage, a prospective member must prove himself. Eventually, most will have to take part in a murder, but not necessarily as the triggerman. It is important, however, to be willing to be the shooter.

Joseph "Joe Cago" Valachi, the first Mafioso to testify publicly about the Mafia, explained in October of 1963 how he was recruited as an associate to fight an undeclared war against the forces of Joseph "Joe the Boss" Masseria, a powerful New York City boss in 1930. Valachi proved himself by simply renting an apartment from which his friends could spot their target. His friends were successful in their mission, and Valachi earned induction into what is now called the Luchese family.

Aladena "Jimmy the Weasel" Fratianno claimed that Carlo Licata, son of a future boss, fulfilled the murder requirement by driving the getaway car in a 1950 murder.

In April of 1983, Philadelphia's Charles "Charlie White" Iannece met the rule by suckering Pasquale "Pat the Cat" Spirito, a member who had fallen out of favor with boss Nicodemo "Little Nicky" Scarfo. Iannece tricked Spirito into going for a drive to find another person who was supposedly a target. On a Philadelphia side street, Spirito pulled over and Iannece, from the back seat, fired two shots into Spirito's head.

There is much evidence that this murder requirement has not been applied equally. In his testimony before the U.S. Senate in 1988, former Cleveland underboss Angelo Lonardo said that a prospective member has only to indicate his willingness to kill on behalf of the family. Of course, he was only speaking about the Cleveland family. But Michael Franzese, a turncoat Colombo capo, also claims that he never participated in a killing prior to initiation. Bill Bonanno, son of the legendary boss, Joe Bonanno, gives no details of his involvement in a murder rite either. Vincent "Fish" Cafaro, a Genovese member, also claimed that he was not required to commit a murder before his induction. Although the testimony of Franzese, Bonanno, and Cafaro was self-serving and is suspect, Lonardo's is believable. He had already admitted to several murders and had no reason to claim killing was not necessarily a preinduction requirement.

Making the List

New York City has a unique Mafia situation. With five La Cosa Nostra families based there, it is much easier for interfamily problems to arise than in areas where there is but one Mafia family. To minimize tensions, bosses decided back in 1931 that each of the five families would circulate the names of its proposed new members to the four other families. This prevents inducting an associate who was in serious conflict with someone connected to another family. Families want to avoid such situations because after an associate is "made," family pride requires a defense of him, thus escalating a minor associate-level problem into a family matter. If there are objections to a proposed member, the bosses attempt to straighten out the difficulty. Sometimes this is easily done. Other times, the person is dropped. In rare cases, the associate can be killed if a serious complaint—the candidate had been an informer, for example—is confirmed.

In a 1997 raid on a basement hideaway in a building owned by a young friend of Junior Gotti, authorities found lists of proposed members for the Luchese, Bonanno, and Genovese families. On the sheets were the names of nominees for induction alongside the names and dates of death of members they were replacing. The lists were early 1990s vintage, and why Junior Gotti kept them drove his jailed-for-life father crazy.

"What do you need a list for? I don't understand that," said Gotti, equating it to a man shopping for groceries and then saving the list "for posterity? to show that [he] went shopping one time?"

The following picture shows the Luchese list.

NEW	OLD
PETEY DEL CIOPPO	PHIL ALBERTI - 1987
PATTY TASTA	PETEY BOUATI - 1984
Tommy (RED) ANZALATA	SAM CAVALIERI - 1988
PATTY DeLAROSSO	SALI MILITARI - 1984
Rocco VITULLI	SALLY SHILLITANI - 1985
SANTO GIAMPAPPA	ROSARIO SACCO - 1984
ANTHONY MANGANO	SAL CATUARA - 1985
JOEY (BLUE EYES) COSENTINO	TONY VADALLA - 1986
FRANKIE GIACCOBBE	JIMMY VENTALORO - 1985
TOMMY GELARDO	JOE IANELLO - 1985

The proposed Luchese members, circa 1990, along with the deceased members they would replace.

(Photo courtesy of GangLandNews.com)

The Ceremony

The formal induction of a new member into La Cosa Nostra was shrouded in mystery for half a century. When Joe Valachi publicly testified before a Senate committee in 1963, the reality nearly lived up to the myth.

Get Dressed

When a prospective member's capo tells him to get dressed up, that is the signal that his induction is about to take place. To prepare him for the ceremony, Philadelphia's Nicholas "Nicky Crow" Caramandi related that capo Chuckie Merlino simply said, "Tomorrow's your day." Joe Valachi was told he was going upstate to meet some of the boys and the boss.

Fuhgeddaboudit

The induction ceremony has evolved over the last 100 years, but it is still essentially the same for all American Mafia families except the Chicago Outfit. The Chicago Outfit's key early leaders, including Al Capone, had their roots in Naples and rejected the ritualistic ceremony that originated in Sicily. The Outfit uses no oaths or secret rituals. The leaders simply invite the new member to a formal dinner and introduce him to other members.

Oaths, Blood, and Fire

Mafia members who have become witnesses for the government have given remarkably similar accounts of the induction ceremony. Back in 1917, a member of a Camorra gang revealed its secret induction ritual during a murder trial. Joe Valachi, however, provided the first, and the most famous, description of the oath of allegiance of La Cosa Nostra families. In his 1963 testimony, Valachi told how he was driven, in 1930, to a private house where 40 or so mobsters were gathered, sitting around a large table that was set for dinner.

Valachi was brought to the head of the table and sat beside Salvatore Maranzano, the leader of the group. A gun and a knife were on the table. All the men joined hands while Maranzano repeated some oaths. Next, a paper was burned in Valachi's hands, signifying how his soul would burn if he betrayed the organization. Then the men began a counting ritual that appears to only exist in some families, but that has been used as late as 1989 in Boston. All those present put out one hand with any number of fingers showing. The extended fingers are counted to arrive at a number. Then Maranzano counted around the circle until the number was reached. That person, Joe Bonanno, became the "godfather" (mentor) of Valachi. Bonanno then used a needle to draw a drop of blood from Valachi's trigger finger, symbolizing his birth into the new organization.

Mafia Speak

Contrary to depictions in the movies, the burning of the image of the family's saint (often a tissue is substituted) is not a test of will. The paper is juggled from hand to hand by the new member, and it burns so quickly that no damage is done if he juggles the burning paper. Mobsters don't believe in burning themselves, even a little.

Seventeen years later, in the fall of 1947, Aladena "Jimmy the Weasel" Fratianno was inducted into the Los Angeles family under the sponsorship of Johnny Roselli. This ceremony took place in front of approximately 50 members assembled in a winery. Fratianno's recollection of the ceremony is remarkably similar to Valachi's, except for the burning of the tissue. Fratianno had been inducted decades before he testified about it, and he admittedly was highly nervous during the ceremony, so it's possible he simply forgot the burning.

The most accurate recounting of an initiation doesn't come from the memory of some mob turncoat, but from the FBI tapes of a New England induction ceremony on October 29, 1989. Although the legality of the taping is questioned to this day, the bugging preserved a real induction for posterity.

On that historic day, four inductees were brought, one at a time, into a room of a house in Medford, Massachusetts, where the boss, consigliere, capos, and soldiers were gathered. Consigliere Joseph "JR" Russo ran each ceremony with the aid of capo Biagio DiGiacomo. Each new man was asked if he'd like to join the organization for life. Each said "yes." Then everyone was given a chance to clear up any problems they might have had with the new member or vice versa. This was a mere formality because any real problems would have prevented this person's induction in the first place. Next, an oath was taken in which the new member said he wanted to enter the organization to protect his family and friends. He swore never to divulge the secrets of the group and to obey all orders he received. After the oath, the consigliere used the counting ritual that Valachi described to find a "buddy" for the new man. That person pricked the recruit's finger and drew blood. Then the paper was burned in his hands as he repeated another oath about his soul burning in hell if he betrayed Mafia secrets. The similarity between the FBI taped account and the accounts of informers is striking.

Bargain-Basement Inductions

Joe Valachi thought he got a bargain-basement induction in 1930; it was an abbreviated ceremony with few of the rules explained to him because of the crisis atmosphere brought on by open warfare between families. When Michael Rizzitello was initiated in 1976, however, it made Valachi's ceremony look like a royal wedding. Both the Los Angeles boss and underboss were in jail, so acting boss Louis Tom Dragna was technically in charge. He, consigliere Frank Bompensiero, Rizzitello, and Jimmy "The Weasel" Fratianno sat in a smoke-filled car on some obscure road and performed a quickie induction. Rizzitello uttered the traditional oaths and his finger was pricked, but just like at Fratianno's 1947 ceremony, there was no burning paper. In hindsight though, their roadside location seems like a decent excuse.

Sammy Bull Gravano, then a Gambino family capo, was involved in a unique induction ceremony in 1986. Joe Paruta had been a close associate of Gravano's for decades but had never been seriously considered for membership. He was kept around for his loyalty and his willingness to do anything to please his

> **Fuhgeddaboudit**
>
> When the FBI was performing a sting operation in Cleveland in 1998, they conducted a fake induction ceremony on one of their targets. He was told he was joining New York's Gambino family and fell for it completely! Small wonder the Cleveland family is merely a memory.

bosses. As a Gravano crewmember, he helped carry out several murders, including that of Robert "DeeBee" DiBernardo, a Gambino soldier. For a while in late 1985, Paruta was even a candidate to execute Paul Castellano and key aide Thomas Bilotti in a Brooklyn diner they often frequented. However, by 1986 it was clear that Paruta wasn't going to be doing the Mafia's dirty work for much longer. He was dying of cancer, and the pain was so intense that he asked Gravano to whack him. Instead, Gravano received permission from boss John Gotti to induct Paruta into the family. Gravano and several other capos gathered in Paruta's bedroom and carried out an abbreviated ceremony. Paruta died a month or so later, apparently pleased to have been finally admitted into La Cosa Nostra.

Another quick induction involved George Fresolone, a long-time Philadelphia mob associate. He had been working as an informer for New Jersey state police for some time prior to being made. The Philadelphia family was in turmoil in July of 1990. Boss Nicky Scarfo was in jail, and the family was being led by acting boss Anthony "Tony Buck" Piccolo. Fresolone's sponsor was acting underboss Pasquale "Patty Specs" Martirano, who was dying of cancer. The ceremony was held in the Bronx home of another associate who also was being inducted. Out of respect for Martirano's weakness, the five men were initiated at the same time, and the symbolic gun and knife were kept in a paper bag in case the wife of the homeowner returned unexpectedly.

Eleven years later, Fresolone, secure with a new identity in the federal witness protection program, took aim at fictional New Jersey mobster Tony Soprano and HBO. He charged the cable network and the producers of *The Sopranos* with copyright infringement for depicting an induction ceremony during a 2001 episode that was "word for word, line for line" lifted from Fresolone's book, *Blood Oath* (Simon & Schuster, 1994).

Big Shot

Luchese mob associate Henry Hill recounted a story in which associate Tommy DeSimmone was told he was going to be inducted and to dress up for the affair. Unfortunately for DeSimmone, this was a ploy to lure him to his death for murdering a made member of the Gambino family.

More than 10 years later, Bonanno associate Louis Tuzzio got "dressed up" and told his mother he was going to be either made or killed. He was killed.

No induction compares to the initiation of Michael "Baldy Mike" Spinelli, the toilet bowl mobster. He was found guilty in one of the very low points in La Cosa Nostra history, the attempted rubout of the sister of a turncoat capo, Peter Chiodo. Under orders from his capo, Spinelli and another associate, Dino Basciano, gunned down Patricia Capozzalo as she arrived home after dropping two of her three children off at school. Fortunately, she survived.

Toilet bowl mobster Michael "Baldy Mike" Spinelli was inducted into the Luchese family in a bathroom ceremony in a New York federal lockup in 1993.

(Photo courtesy of GangLandNews.com)

Spinelli used his actions to lobby for induction into the Luchese clan. When underboss Anthony "Gaspipe" Casso was incarcerated with him, Spinelli got his wish. He was inducted into the family in a bathroom ceremony at the Metropolitan Correctional Center in January of 1993. They had no gun and no knife. To make it official, they burned toilet paper and flushed the ashes down the toilet.

The Rules

Once inducted, the new soldier is formally introduced to the administration of the family and other members who are present. He is also told of the existence of other nearby families and their leaders. Another important post-induction ritual is the explanation of the rules that the new member must obey under pain of death.

La Cosa Nostra has these rules to maintain secrecy and to keep members in line. Inevitably, those who flout the rules are disciplined. Often that means death, and there is no appeal process.

Shut Up!

The legend behind the famous *omerta* rule of silence is that the various Italian Mafias were formed to protect their members and families from a cruel, corrupt government. Secrecy, backed by the harshest of sanctions, was necessary to prevent betrayal. Not surprisingly, in North America, in the early decades of the twentieth century, the Mafia adapted this rule to protect the Mafia bosses from legitimate government actions.

Before the advent of electronic surveillance and cooperating witnesses, the leaders of La Cosa Nostra were generally well isolated from the criminal actions of their underlings. If the members could be convinced or intimidated into remaining silent, even if caught, authorities would not be able to convict the top echelons of La Cosa Nostra. Consequently, great emphasis was put on *omerta*, and a boss wouldn't hesitate to make an example of someone as a reminder to everyone of the harsh penalty for disobeying this rule.

Ken Eto wasn't even a formal member of the Chicago Outfit, but he had run gambling operations with their permission for decades. When he was indicted, his past meant nothing. Just the mere suspicion that he might talk made Eto expendable. He was ordered to meet two hoods, John Gattuso and Jay Campise, and then proceed to a meeting with his capo, Vincent Solano. Eto was sitting in the front seat and was instructed to pull into the back parking lot of a restaurant. As soon as the car stopped, he was shot three times in the head. Miraculously, Eto survived. Not surprisingly, he became a government witness. For their incompetence, the two wannabe hit men were shown the proper methods of execution and ended up in the trunk of a car. Eto testified that, according to his experience, his attempted murder would have had to have been approved by his capo and the boss of the family. The death of Gattuso and Campise cut off any possibility of prosecution of those who had ordered the Eto killing.

To the delight of law enforcement officials—and the scorn of many mob bosses—the *omerta* rule has been broken many times. However, with the increased use of electronic surveillance, law enforcement no longer has to rely on members breaking their code of secrecy to get the dirt they need to nab wiseguys. Instead, bugging has often enabled prosecutors to use the boss's own words, or those of another member, to help send the boss to jail.

New Orleans Mafia boss Carlos "Little Man" Marcello was one such victim of his own words. He was ensnared in an FBI sting in 1979 that was part of a labor racketeering investigation called BriLab, short for bribery and labor. Using undercover agents and a con man mob associate who had begun secretly working for the government to lessen an upcoming jail sentence, Marcello was taped carrying on many criminal conversations. On August 4, 1981, Marcello was found guilty of a conspiracy count and later was sentenced to seven years in prison. Three months later, Marcello was convicted of conspiracy to bribe a judge in a case involving the leaders of the Los Angeles family. Once again, the tapes of his conversations were crucial in his defeat. For this conviction, he was sentenced to 10 more years. Marcello spent a number of years incarcerated during which his mental health deteriorated greatly. He won an appeal of the New Orleans case, was released from prison, and passed away in 1993.

Do As I Say!

All members are taught that La Cosa Nostra comes before God, country, and family. An order from a superior must be obeyed without question. Disobedience can mean death. That penalty would be harsh for assembly-line workers at a manufacturing plant, but it is just another day at the office in the world of gangsters. It is the only way a boss can control large groups of men who have clearly demonstrated their lack of respect for rules and who don't hesitate to use violence to get what they want. Only fear could keep such men under some semblance of order.

John Gotti's temper was well known to all who had spent any amount of time around him. Gambino soldier Louis DiBono was pushing the envelope from both ends when he managed to anger both Gotti and underboss Sammy Bull Gravano. DiBono and Gravano had been involved in some business deals that went sour. Gotti summoned the soldier to his headquarters to discuss the matter, but DiBono kept finding excuses not to appear. Gotti was overheard explaining why DiBono was going to get killed. "He didn't rob nothing. Know why he's dying? He's gonna die because he refused to come in when I called."

DiBono was found, shot to death, on October 4, 1990.

La Cosa Nostra taps its associates in much the same way that major league baseball teams promote players from their farm teams. There is ample opportunity for the leaders to see the prospects in action over a number of years. Those who show promise are picked out and given more intensive training. Because sponsors are responsible for their charges, these sponsors take the training very seriously. Few members are going to gamble their lives by recommending an associate who has difficulty following orders.

Associates are told that they must always respond when called by a superior. This point is reiterated and expanded upon during induction. New soldiers are instructed that they must respond to a summons, even if they are at the deathbed of a loved one. Conveniently, this rule can be used when a member is to be killed. If he doesn't come to the meeting, that is a capital offense. If he does respond, he gets whacked anyway. It's a catch-22 for certain!

Obedience in La Cosa Nostra also means that a member must carry out any ordered killing, even if it's a close friend or a personal family relation. Members often play this card to lure a target into a trap.

Joseph "Joe Punge" Pungitore grew up in the Mafia milieu. His father was an associate and then a member of the Philadelphia mob. Boss "Little Nicky" Scarfo had become suspicious of capo Salvatore "Salvie" Testa and ordered his death. The hit teams were having difficulty luring Testa to a place where he could be easily killed, and Scarfo was becoming impatient. Finally, it was decided to bring Testa's best friend in on the murder plot.

On September 14, 1984, Pungitore brought his boyhood friend to an unopened candy shop, where mobster Salvatore "Wayne" Grande shot him in the head and killed him.

> **Fuhgeddaboudit**
>
> Wayne Grande was inducted into the Philadelphia family in June of 1980 by boss Phil "Chicken Man" Testa, the father of the man he would kill four years later. Grande was acquitted of Salvie Testa's murder but was found guilty of federal racketeering charges that included Testa's murder. He was sentenced to 38 years in prison in 1989.

Political Correctness

Every new member is warned that he must show the utmost respect toward the wives and daughters of Mafia members. Although it's not said, new members quickly learn that this rule also applies to the *comares*, or girlfriends, of married Mafiosi. Mafia traditionalists claim this rule demonstrates that mobsters respect women. A spin-off of this so-called respect rule mandates that wiseguys may get involved with sisters and daughters of other mobsters only if their intentions are "honorable." One night stands with the boss's daughter, or sister, are out. An important plus to this rule is it prevents internal problems that are bad for business. Respect, or lack of it, means a great deal to mobsters, and they respond to any insult quickly and harshly. The subject of women is especially touchy. Slights to their honor are insults to all members of their personal family.

Scarfo, the former Philadelphia boss, almost lost his life over a woman when he was a young soldier. In 1977, he and underboss Phil Testa and a few others were discussing the ongoing maneuvering to replace consigliere Joe Rugnetta, who had passed away. During the conversation, which was tape recorded, Scarfo and Testa revealed that Scarfo had once rejected Rugnetta's suggestion that he begin courting the consigliere's daughter and that Testa saved Scarfo's life a number of times when Rugnetta was looking for any kind of excuse to eliminate Scarfo for having insulted his family honor.

Colombo family associate Joseph Cantalupo had a similar close call. In a book about his life, *Body Mike* (1990, written by Tom Renner), Cantalupo recounted taking up with a woman who was considered to be the property of a made man. When confronted by boss Joseph Colombo, Cantalupo told Colombo he didn't know of the mobster's interest in the woman and promised to stop seeing her. This happened twice, and each time he was told to stop, Cantalupo stopped immediately.

No Slapping or Pushing or Shoving or Punching!

Mob rules against slapping, pushing, shoving, and punching Mafia members are attempts to prevent minor disputes between members from escalating into shooting affairs. If they are broken, the combatants are called to a sitdown, where they are read the riot act by a capo. Usually they are forced to shake hands and ordered to forget about the incident. They generally do as they are told but file the insult away for later retribution.

In his 1963 Senate testimony, Joe Valachi told how he broke the rule but was spared any punishment after a sitdown. Valachi, then a member of the Genovese family, was involved in a business relationship with Frank Luciano of the Gambino family. Valachi thought Luciano was stealing from him, and his temper got the best of him. He punched Luciano around. His victim filed a complaint with his capo. At a sitdown, Albert Anastasia, then the boss of what is now called the Gambino family, presided. Anastasia chided Valachi for breaking the rule, but because Luciano had been cheating Valachi, he decided to break up the partnership, which was exactly what Valachi had wanted.

May I?

Mafia soldiers and associates are supposed to get their capo's permission before doing anything. This includes business dealings with other members and traveling outside their home area. Taking a spur of the moment vacation with your wife or girlfriend is not part of a Mafioso's life.

The Mafia's official justification for this rule is to prevent conflicts with rackets or scams of other mobsters. For example, one soldier might organize an armed robbery of a card game without knowing it was under the protection of another family. The rule also makes it more difficult for soldiers to hide any income-producing scam from their capo so they don't have to give him a cut.

This rule can cause problems for soldiers when the proposed scam falls through. This happened to Colombo soldier Jilly Greco when his crew bungled a hijacking and there was no payoff for any of the crew—but even worse, nothing for the capo, according to undercover FBI agent Joe Pistone.

Although the penalty for failing to alert your mob superiors about a moneymaking scam is often death, many associates and members let their greed get the best of them. Anthony "Tony Bender" Strollo was a powerful capo under boss Vito Genovese. His stature increased when Genovese became entangled in a drug conspiracy and was put behind bars. Not in the best of moods because of this, Genovese became very suspicious that Strollo had been engaged in highly lucrative heroin dealing without cutting Genovese in. On April 8, 1962, Strollo left his home for a short errand and hasn't yet returned.

Just Say No to Drugs

One of the most frequently broken rules is the prohibition of drug trafficking. Mob bosses put this rule in place around 1950 when federal drug agents began cracking down on the illicit drug trade. They were afraid they would lose the hidden political and law enforcement support that turned a blind eye to gambling. Furthermore, they didn't want their members receiving lengthy drug sentences that might tempt them to inform.

Despite the rule, many known La Cosa Nostra members have been convicted of drug dealing, so many that it is foolish to list even a few. The way La Cosa Nostra is run strongly suggests the real rule is "Don't get *caught* dealing drugs."

Salutations

Theoretically, only La Cosa Nostra members are supposed to know who the other members are. Accordingly, there is a secret code that alerts a member that he is being introduced to another member. Each new member is instructed on this rule at his induction. The following is an example of a La Cosa Nostra introduction.

Paulie, a veteran member, was present at Jimmy's induction and therefore has formally met Jimmy as a La Cosa Nostra member. A week later, both Paulie and Jimmy are at a wake. Also present is Bobby, who had been inducted years ago and has already been formally introduced to Paulie as a La Cosa Nostra member. This enables Paulie to introduce Jimmy and Bobby to each other as La Cosa Nostra members. He would say, "Jimmy, meet Bobby, he's a friend of ours. Bobby, meet Jimmy, he's a friend of ours." The Italian words *amico nostra* are often used and mean the same thing as "friend of ours."

The Real Rule

When you wash away 100 years of propaganda about honor, respect, and obedience, what becomes very obvious is that the Mafia was and is simply about making and accumulating as much money as possible, by whatever means necessary. Therefore, the real rule in La Cosa Nostra is "Get the money!"

The Least You Need to Know

- Only men with a father of Italian heritage are eligible to be members of La Cosa Nostra.
- With the exception of the Chicago Outfit, all La Cosa Nostra families use a formal ceremony to induct new members.
- Members are expected to follow certain rules.
- Members are expected to make money and share it with their superiors.

Chapter 3

The Mafia's Commission

In This Chapter

- ◆ Defining the Mafia Commission
- ◆ The reasons behind the formation of the Commission
- ◆ Some important Commission rulings

Members of a Mafia family are told that La Cosa Nostra comes first—always. The laws of the nation do not apply to them. Even before they are inducted, members learn that whenever there is a dispute, power invariably carries the day over fairness. It should come as no surprise that many leadership changes occur because of violence. When Prohibition (1920–1933, see Chapter 8), with its vast opportunities for riches, was added to the mix, the life span of a boss became very tenuous. Finally, in 1931, a number of sitting bosses tried to bring stability to their way of life by shifting the dispute-solving mechanism from one person to a group of bosses. This forum would become known as the Commission. In this chapter, I will explain the circumstances leading up to its formation and give examples of how it carries out its mandate.

The Mafia Killing Fields

Life at the top of a Mafia family in New York City is a lucrative but deadly business. Being a boss means being treated with a great deal of respect because everyone associated with a family is required to share part of his illegal income with you. However, being boss means you have to resolve disputes—often over income—between two parties who are angry at each other and feel they are in the right. Ultimately, one person will walk away from the sitdown feeling frustrated and perhaps humiliated, and often a fair bit lighter in the pockets. Plus, in a group of 100 or 200 men, there are always a few whose ambition and ego drive them toward the top, men like John Gotti and the man for whom his crime family was named, Carlo Gambino. When these desires are combined with a feeling of frustration, thoughts turn to being in a position to control one's own destiny. Secretly, this person begins hoping that the boss dies of natural causes, goes to prison, or gets whacked.

A boss in New York doesn't simply have to worry about conflict among his own soldiers, however. There are four other Mafia organizations in the same area and, inevitably, disputes arise with one or more of them. This puts a strong-minded boss in a game with someone whose ego and ambition are as big as his own. Losing at this level can be humiliating because everyone in the Mafia life will know about it sooner or later. Because every boss likes to exercise his power, the temptation to use it is strong. Like decisions made within the family, these interfamily disputes usually result in at least one frustrated loser.

The Boss of Bosses

Prior to 1931, if a dispute between families couldn't be resolved, it either ended in bloodshed or was decided by the boss who was perceived as the most powerful at that time. He was commonly called the "boss of bosses." This respected boss wielded great power and didn't hesitate to use it. This situation frequently led to frustration. The losing boss would be angry that he was subject to the decisions of another person. The "boss of bosses" would be frustrated by the arguments of the losing boss and couldn't help thinking how much easier life would be if a more agreeable leader was on the throne of that family. Both situations could turn ugly very quickly under the right set of circumstances.

Mafia Speak

In the late 1950s, Vito Genovese was at the height of his power, and some called him "the boss of bosses under the table." A decade later, Carlo Gambino had so much influence that he was often referred to as the "boss of bosses."

Shooting Gallery

As they did in cities around the country where Italian immigrants settled, five Mafia families formed in New York on their own around the turn of the twentieth century. Newspaper and police reports reveal violence within growing Italian communities in the New York area, but details are sparse. A serious discussion of this topic has to begin around 1910. Ignazio Lupo and Peter "The Clutch Hand" Morello were related by marriage. In 1909, they formed the nucleus of an extended Morello clan that controlled what we now know as the Genovese family. The following year, they received lengthy prison terms after being convicted of counterfeiting. This set off a series of events that led to more than two decades of continuous intrigue and periodic violence. Many leading members of the five families were killed during this period.

Slammer Time

Lupo and Morello were given 30- and 25-year sentences, respectively, in 1910. In 1922, their sentences were commuted by President Warren Harding. His was a notoriously corrupt administration, which raises interesting questions about how they managed their release. In light of the many pardons President Bill Clinton granted in his final days in office, perhaps John Gotti's reported plan to bribe his way out of prison wasn't so wild or far-fetched an idea as it seemed when first disclosed by a turncoat.

Here's the list of events that went down:

1. Weakened by the jailing of their two leaders, the Morello clan faced many challenges. Over the next few years, Giosue Gallucci surfaced as the most prominent Mafioso. However, he was gunned down in 1915, and the Morellos began to regain their status under brother Nicholas Morello.

2. A Camorra gang began competing with the Morellos and successfully ambushed Nick Morello after conning him into a sitdown. He and a cohort were killed on September 7, 1916.

3. Another Morello man, Giuseppe Veranzano, was killed in a restaurant on October 6, 1916.

4. On May 8, 1922, Vincent Morello, brother of Nick, was murdered, probably by men of rising power Joe "The Boss" Masseria.

5. An attempt was made on the life of Masseria on August 9, 1922.

6. Two days later, Masseria retaliated. Umberto Valenti, an ally of the Morello brothers, was killed after being lured to a meeting.

7. Capo Frankie Yale, a Masseria man, was machine-gunned to death in his car on July 1, 1928.

8. Salvatore "Tata" D'Aquila, whom some suspected in the Valenti killing, was blown away on October 10, 1928.

9. On February 26, 1930, Gaetano "Tommy" Reina, boss of the Luchese family, was shot to death.

10. On May 31, 1930, Detroit mobsters allied with Joe "The Boss" Masseria murdered boss Gaspar Milazzo.

11. Peter "The Clutch Hand" Morello, underboss of Masseria's group, was shot to death on August 15, 1930.

12. The new Luchese boss who replaced Reina, Joseph Pinzolo, was killed in early September of 1930.

13. Al Mineo, who replaced D'Aquila, and his underboss, Steve Ferrigno, were shot to death on November 5, 1930.

14. Joseph "Joe Baker" Catania, a Masseria power, was shot to death on February 3, 1931.

15. On February 6, 1931, Detroit boss Caesar LaMare was murdered in his own home by "friends," a response to the Masseria-sanctioned murder of Milazzo nine months earlier.

16. On April 15, 1931, around 3:30 P.M., Joe Masseria was murdered in a Coney Island restaurant.

17. Sam Monaco, the underboss of the New Jersey family, was killed on September 10, 1931.

18. On September 10, 1931, Salvatore Maranzano was shot to death in his own offices by killers posing as police officers, sent by Charles "Lucky" Luciano.

There were many other killings during this period, brought on in part by the lucrative bootlegging opportunities during the Prohibition era. These killings made every Mafia boss all too aware of his own vulnerability and created a climate in which all the bosses were open to a new system that might prevent problems from deteriorating to the shooting stage—and possible death.

Mafia Speak

After Maranzano's murder, rival hoods floated stories to justify the killing. For instance, they said that Maranzano was hijacking Luciano's liquor trucks and that he was also hijacking truckloads of clothing material. Additionally, Vito Genovese repeated a story that he and Luciano were lucky they struck when they did because Maranzano had hired an independent hood named Vincent "Mad Dog" Coll to murder them the same day. These stories are common in La Cosa Nostra and are usually told to justify actions that are likely to be questioned.

The Board of Directors

Lucky Luciano is credited with the idea of having a group of bosses—rather than just one boss—arbitrate family disputes. There is little evidence to support this theory, but logic strongly suggests that without Luciano, who was on top of the Mafia world at the time, behind the idea, it never would have happened.

Shortly after Maranzano's death, the various La Cosa Nostra bosses met in Chicago to regroup. They formally approved the idea of a Commission at this meeting, although they held preliminary discussions in order to present a common front at the Chicago gathering.

The Mafia leaders decided that the Commission would be composed of seven members: the five New York bosses, Joseph Bonanno, Tommy Gagliano, Lucky Luciano, Vincent Mangano, and Joseph Profaci; the Chicago boss, Al Capone; and the Buffalo boss, Stefano Magaddino. Within a few months, Frank Nitti replaced Capone when Capone's appeal of his tax conviction was denied and he began his 11-year prison term.

Mafia Speak

Best known as Charles "Lucky" Luciano, Lucky Luciano was often called Charlie Lucky. His given name, however, was Salvatore Lucania.

They also decided that the families without seats on the Commission would work through a Commission member to voice their concerns. For example, Chicago represented the Los Angeles, San Francisco, San Jose, Milwaukee, and other families. The Genovese family represented Pittsburgh, Philadelphia, and Cleveland.

Fuhgeddaboudit
In the early 1980s, Anthony "Fat Tony" Salerno represented the Genovese family on the Commission. Salerno's nickname, while not kind, was accurate. During a June 1983 meeting, a capo, acting as a lookout, excitedly reported that he'd seen an FBI agent in the vicinity. The Mafiosi panicked and escaped through a basement window of a restaurant-supply business. Salerno, however, got stuck in the window and had to be pushed and pulled until he was freed, according to turncoat soldier Vincent "Fish" Cafaro.

At the famous Commission trial in 1986, detailed in Chapter 19, Angelo Lonardo, a turncoat Cleveland underboss, left the impression that two former Cleveland bosses had been Commission members during a careless answer to a query from the prosecutor. This was not the case, and Lonardo knew it. He must have misunderstood the question and thought they were asking whether he knew of instances in which a boss from outside New York had sat down with the Commission. He had been present in Miami in the 1930s when the case of his cousin John DeMarco was presented to the Commission by then-Cleveland boss Al Polizzi. In his testimony before a United States Senate committee two years later, Lonardo clearly stated that Cleveland had long been represented on the Commission by the Genovese family. This testimony meshes with the writings of Joe Bonanno, an original Commission member, and other historians.

Despite what has been reported in newspapers, magazines, and books for decades, the infamous 1957 gathering of scores of Mafia leaders from around the country at Apalachin, New York (discussed in Chapter 14) was not a Commission meeting. This was an out of sequence emergency national meeting of La Cosa Nostra one year after a regularly scheduled conclave had taken place in the same upstate New York town. Beginning in 1931, Mafia bosses from across the country met each year to discuss national strategy and to ratify the membership of the Commission for the next five years. The Commission could, and did, meet at other times to discuss pressing problems. The national meeting was something quite different than an ordinary Commission meeting.

The same seven families maintained seats on the Commission for 30 years. However, in response to rancor among other families who believed that the same seven families had held power for so long, the Commission decided at the 1956 national meeting that, starting in 1961, it would add two members. Accordingly, the boss of Detroit, Joseph Zerilli, and the Philadelphia leader, Angelo Bruno, joined the Commission in 1961.

Decision-Making Time

The 1931 national meeting of La Cosa Nostra was held in Chicago. At the gathering, all the bosses were introduced to those in attendance. In effect, this introduction was a public seal of approval of their right to rule. Because all the bosses met only every five years, it became the practice for the Commission to give official approval of a new boss and legitimize his reign shortly after he took over his crime family, with formal introductions being made at the next national meeting.

Blessing the Boss

As the concept of blessing new bosses sank in, it became very important. Anyone contemplating overthrowing a boss had to make sure he legitimized his actions by convincing key members of the Commission that such drastic actions were necessary. The key was that the Commission members were anxious to establish control over leadership changes. They wanted to make it nearly impossible for a renegade faction to shoot their way to the top. Anyone could kill a boss, but to stay alive to profit from such an action was another matter altogether. Not having the Commission behind you was suicidal. The following examples illustrate the Commission's role in king making or breaking.

In 1951, New York underboss Albert Anastasia arranged the murder of his boss, Vincent Mangano. The two had been feuding, each attempting to outflank the other by forming alliances. After Mangano disappeared, Anastasia appeared before the Commission and claimed he acted in self-defense because Mangano was trying to kill him. Frank Costello, then the leader of what is now called the Genovese family, backed Anastasia up. With that support, Anastasia was accepted as boss and thus a Commission member.

Six years later, Anastasia was killed in a plot involving Carlo Gambino and Vito Genovese. The Commission approved Gambino as the new boss, but he was on probation for three years before being accepted officially.

> **Big Shot**
>
> On October 25, 1957, Albert Anastasia was murdered while getting his hair cut. He was hit three times by .38-caliber bullets and once with a .32-caliber. He also suffered a glancing blow from a bullet of indeterminate size. A .38 Colt revolver and a .32 Smith and Wesson long revolver were recovered. No one has ever been charged with the killing.

Powerful New York crime boss Carlo Gambino orchestrated the execution of Albert Anastasia to take over as boss.

(Photo courtesy of New York Daily News*)*

Transcripts of conversations recorded in the office of New Jersey boss Simone "Sam the Plumber" DeCavalcante reveal that the Commission intervened in the affairs of the Pittsburgh family during the reign of John LaRocca. Like Gambino, LaRocca, who had become boss in 1956 when Frank Amato developed health problems, was put on probation. Because Amato remained as consigliere, it is unlikely the predicament involved a serious problem between the two men. The Commission likely acted cautiously in approving a new boss because of problems that occurred two decades earlier with Pittsburgh boss John Bazzano, detailed in Chapter 5.

As I'll detail in Chapter 25, Joe Bonanno, an original Commission member, had difficulties with this ruling body. In 1964, some members believed that Bonanno had conspired to murder some of its members. They gathered enough support and formally deposed Bonanno in 1964 and installed one of his men as new boss.

As discussed in Chapter 5, the history of the Philadelphia family includes the violent murder of two sitting bosses in 1980 and 1981. The killings were not sanctioned by the Commission. In both cases, most plotters were killed, and another key player had to flee to Florida to save his life. Both groups had succeeded in eliminating the boss, but none of the participants enjoyed the spoils.

A slight variation of Commission approval was revealed by Angelo Lonardo when he testified before a U.S. Senate committee. He detailed how capo Jack Licavoli peacefully became the new Cleveland boss when John Scalish died in 1976. According to Lonardo, Licavoli didn't even know he was supposed to travel to New York to introduce himself to Genovese family leaders as a courtesy. (The Genovese family represented Cleveland on the Commission.) Lonardo left the distinct impression that Cleveland elected a new boss without consulting the Commission first, a practice that evolved over the years. Lonardo wasn't part of the administration of the family at this time, however, and he simply might not have been aware of contacts with the Commission.

In 1984, the FBI had legally bugged a social club belonging to Anthony "Fat Tony" Salerno, the acting boss of the Genovese family. One day, they overheard Joe Pieri, from the Buffalo family, seeking advice on a leadership dispute that was escalating there. Salerno told Pieri to deliver some advice to the quarreling mobsters in Buffalo: They were dealing with the "big boys from New York" now. Eventually, the Commission supported Joe Todaro as Buffalo boss. Commission approval was still very important, 53 years after it was formed.

> **Mafia Speak**
>
> On March 21, 1980, Philadelphia boss Angelo Bruno was shot to death while sitting in a car driven by soldier John Stanfa. It was clear that Stanfa hadn't done the shooting, but few believed him when the Sicilian-born Stanfa testified that if he'd seen the killers he "… can push the gas in the car and take off with Mr. Bruno."

Approving Inductions

During the Castellammarese War of 1930 and 1931, many of the New York families recruited new members to strengthen themselves and to have soldiers who were not known by rival hoods. This permitted the new mobsters to move in closer to their enemies to stalk their counterparts and carry out murder assignments. Even if one of the killers was seen and recognized after taking part in a murder, the hope was that he wouldn't be connected to a particular family.

When the Commission was formed in late 1931, all the New York bosses had used such wartime hiring practices. They knew that if one family began inducting new members without consulting the others, problems were sure to arise. To nip such practices in the bud and lessen the likelihood of setting off another war, the Commission decided that the names of all proposed new members would have to be circulated and approved by all five families. If disputes arose, the Commission would make the final decision on the fitness of the proposed mobster to become a "made man."

On October 13, 1963, the illegal bugging of the office of New England boss Ray Patriarca caught a brief discussion concerning the making of a new member in New York City. This happened during the Gallo brothers' revolt against Joe Magliocco, which is discussed in Chapter 24. Any peace attempt between the two factions would have required a sitdown. Only formal members are allowed to take part in these discussions, however, and most of the Gallo loyalists were merely associates and were ineligible to participate. Nicholas Bianco, a Gallo crewmember who was originally from New England, asked Patriarca to arbitrate the dispute. In turn, Patriarca sought and received permission from the Commission to make Bianco. It was also an olive branch to the Gallos, who were pushing to have some of their men formally join the family.

In the late 1970s, the Cleveland family was under assault from a longtime associate. Boss John Scalish had died in 1976, and John Nardi, a Teamster representative, was contemptuous of the new administration led by Jack Licavoli. Nardi had combined with Danny Greene, who led a violent crew of hoodlums who were predominately Irish-Americans. Initially, the feud was restricted to associates of each faction. However, in 1976, Greene and Nardi arranged the killing of underboss Leo Moceri, which increased tensions tremendously. Licavoli and new underboss Angelo Lonardo traveled to New York to discuss the problem with Genovese front boss "Fat Tony" Salerno. Lonardo testified years later that Salerno, obviously after consulting with other Genovese leaders and other New York family bosses such as Paul Castellano, gave them permission to induct the 10 new members they requested. Cleveland knew it couldn't just independently make new members without checking it out with the Commission if it expected to have its support when the going got tough.

> **Fuhgeddaboudit**
>
> A year after being inducted, Bianco deserted the Gallos and joined new boss Joseph Colombo. In 1971, when Colombo was shot and incapacitated, Bianco sought and received permission to transfer to the New England family. In 1991, Bianco became the acting boss of that group. Eventually, he was arrested, indicted, and sentenced to federal prison. He died behind bars.

Deciding Issues

From electronic surveillance, information from Mafia turncoats, and the writings of mobsters, a number of additional areas of Commission dealings have surfaced. The first two are from the autobiography of Joe Bonanno.

District Attorney Thomas Dewey, New York rackets buster, was the scourge of gangsters in the 1930s, so much so that Dutch Schultz, a famous beer baron and numbers kingpin, offered to kill Dewey. This scheme was vetoed by the Mafia powers of the time, and when Schultz vowed to proceed, he was killed. Bonanno claims that Lucky Luciano's close friend, Albert Anastasia, also wanted to whack Dewey and suggested it to the Commission, which was horrified by the idea and turned it down flat.

During the mid-1950s, the Commission was called to decide whether one of its own—Gaetano "Tommy" Lucchese—had violated the rules and deserved to be sanctioned or worse. At the time, Luciano was living in Italy and had been replaced on the Commission by Frank Costello, a fact that didn't sit well with Vito Genovese, Costello's underboss. Genovese had been second in command to Luciano and his natural successor. However, when Luciano was jailed in 1936, Genovese had fled to Italy to avoid legal problems of his own and thus lost out to Costello. When Genovese returned to America, he constantly plotted to gain power. Costello was well aware of Genovese's discontent and was concerned about Vito's alliance with Lucchese, who headed his own family. To counter Genovese, Costello tightened his ties with Albert Anastasia, also a boss. A series of chess moves took place. One involved Costello complaining to the Commission that Lucchese was plotting to kill Anastasia. A serious discussion was held by the Commission members, and Costello urged that a vote be held on the matter. Incredibly, Lucchese admitted the plot, was forgiven by Anastasia, and survived with a mere tsk, tsk.

Big Shot

Baldo Amato and Caesar Bonventre were with Carmine Galante serving as his bodyguards on July 12, 1979, when the wannabe Bonanno boss was blown away as he dined at an outdoor patio at an Italian restaurant in Bushwick, Brooklyn. Ballistic evidence and common sense showed that both took part in the shooting. Amato moved up in the mob world, as did Bonventre, but the latter's glory days ended abruptly in 1984 when he was killed and his body parts ended up in two separate oil drums in New Jersey.

A 1979 Commission meeting concerning widespread discontent and concern about Carmine "Lilo" Galante's efforts to take over the leadership of the Bonanno family had a much more volatile outcome. A number of capos in that family brought the problem before the Commission. A vote was taken to kill Galante, and this edict was carried out in July of the same year. At the famous Commission trial of 1986, Fred DeChristopher, a Colombo associate who hid boss Carmine Persico in his attic while working as an FBI informer, testified that Persico claimed to have voted against killing Galante. Persico was outvoted by the bosses of the Genovese, Gambino, and Luchese families.

For all his faults, John Gotti was politically adept at dealing with the other members of the Commission when he got to the top of the Gambino family. At a Commission meeting in 1988, Gotti was able to persuade the Genovese and Luchese families to accept Victor "Little Vic" Orena as the Colombo family representative at the next national meeting of the Commission. Orena had been selected as acting boss by jailed boss Carmine Persico, and Gotti wanted Orena on the Commission because they were close allies.

Acting Colombo family boss Victor "Little Vic" Orena wanted to make his position permanent; John Gotti liked that idea.

(Photo courtesy of GangLandNews.com)

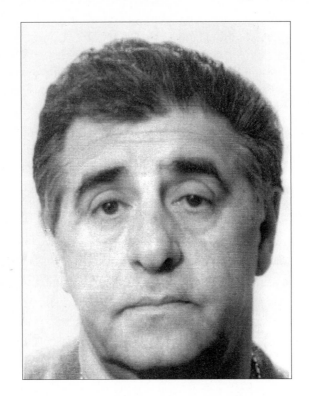

At the next meeting, according to turncoat underboss Salvatore "Sammy Bull" Gravano, Orena was going to support a motion to give a Commission seat back to the Bonanno family. Its leader, Joseph Massino, was a longtime friend of Gotti. With Massino, Orena, and his own vote, Gotti would be in control of the Commission. Alas, Gotti was arrested and jailed before the next meeting. So much for his best-laid plans.

Many Commission meetings during the late 1970s and early 1980s concerned construction problems. Four of the five New York families had cobbled together a system of controlling all Manhattan construction projects over $2 million. With so much money at stake, there were constant squabbles to be resolved. Periodically, the bosses met to straighten things out.

> **Fuhgeddaboudit**
>
> On May 15, 1984, the Commission planned to meet at the Staten Island home of a longshoreman whose wife was the cousin of a top member of the Gambino family. It was a top-secret affair. Only a trusted few knew the time and place, or so they thought. The FBI took pictures of 12 men who either attended the session or drove those who did attend to and from the house, courtesy of a tip from an informer.

Out of Commission

For about 25 years after its inception in 1931, the Commission had the unchallenged last word in the world of La Cosa Nostra. That all began to change, albeit slowly at first, in late 1957.

As I'll discuss in Chapter 14, in November of 1957, a few New York state troopers uncovered a meeting of Mafia bosses from around the country in a tiny town in upstate New York, a few miles west of Binghamton and a few miles north of Pennsylvania. A number of leaders and other mobsters were rounded up. The publicity was tremendous and went on for years as different jurisdictions held hearings and garnered headlines. Mafia leaders were forced to cancel their national meetings, and for the next four years, Commission members were afraid to meet. They were reduced to sending messages back and forth, making their decision-making slower and less forceful.

By the early 1960s, the Commission was consumed by an alleged plot by New York Mafia boss Joseph Bonanno to kill two of its members. A five-year struggle ensued. The Commission declared that Bonanno was no longer the family boss. Bonanno, in turn, rejected their right to make such a judgment, asserting that because the five-year mandate of the Commission ran out in 1961, those claiming to be members of the Commission were really illegal. He argued that because the last uninterrupted national meeting was held in 1956, the Commission mandate theoretically ran out in 1961. No one except Bonanno took this argument seriously.

During the Bonanno problems, the Chicago Outfit's representative began skipping more and more Commission deliberations. The Chicago Outfit cared little about who headed the Bonannos, and it quickly lost interest in traveling to New York for each new Bonanno family development. The net result was a two-headed Commission, with Chicago resolving disputes between families west of them. Chicago and New York maintained regular contact only because of their common interest in the affairs of four major international unions.

As decided at the 1956 national meeting, Detroit boss Joseph Zerilli became a new member in 1961 when the Commission increased from seven to nine members. Zerilli was tightly tied to Joseph Profaci, head of what we now call the Colombo family. Zerilli's son Anthony had married one of Profaci's daughters, as did Anthony Joseph Tocco, the son of a power in the Detroit family and a close friend of Zerilli. But the prestige of being a Commission member quickly wore off for Zerilli. Almost immediately, he was plunged into the Bonanno dispute that threatened to escalate into the type of warfare seen back in the 1930s. In short order, Zerilli began attending fewer and fewer meetings, sending in his vote instead. The Bonanno family turmoil ended in 1968, and as the 1970s unfolded, Zerilli once again started making the trip to New York to attend Commission meetings. However, increased surveillance by law enforcement and declining health caused him to cut back once again. When Zerilli died in late 1977, Detroit lost its Commission seat. This was another step in making the Commission a New York City concern. One of the founding members of the Commission was Buffalo's Stefano Magaddino. Officially, he served from 1931 until his death in 1974. This longevity is unmatched by any other member. Magaddino's health began to fail in the 1970s, and there was less and less reason to call upon him. Carlo Gambino was firmly in control of the five New York families and Philadelphia and thus easily had a quorum. Magaddino became redundant. With his passing, Buffalo lost its seat at the Commission table.

Angelo Bruno, the Philadelphia boss, had become a Commission member when Zerilli did. Bruno was closely allied with Gambino, the rising power in La Cosa Nostra, and Gambino could count on Bruno to back his position. But when Bruno was killed in 1980, Philadelphia lost its Commission seat. This was another step in the "New Yorking" of the Commission.

Bruno's murder and that of Philip "Chicken Man" Testa a year later lessened the prestige of the Commission. One of its primary reasons for being was to decrease, if not eliminate, the unsanctioned killings of bosses. Its mandate had failed in the cases of Bruno and Testa, and try as they did to maintain their clout by killing those responsible for the Philadelphia killings, the Mafia's Board of Directors lost much of its power.

Slammer Time

Sam Giancana was the Chicago Outfit's representative on the Commission from 1956 to mid-1965. In May of 1965, he was granted immunity and was ordered to testify before a federal grand jury. Giancana refused and was jailed for a year. This ended his leadership role in Chicago and on the Commission.

Fuhgeddaboudit

Philip "Chicken Man" Testa, boss of the Philadelphia family, was blown up on March 15, 1981. A year to the day later, the man who helped plan the attack was murdered by Testa's son. Three firecrackers were stuffed in the victim's mouth as a clear sign of why he was killed.

> ### Slammer Time
>
> During the Commission trial, Anthony "Fat Tony" Salerno rejected some friendly healthy eating advice from an FBI agent who gave him a granola bar and suggested he stop eating the Mars and Baby Ruth candy bars he had been munching on. "They are really much better for you, Mr. Salerno. Better than all that chocolate," said the agent. "Who the fuck cares. I'm going to die in the fucking can anyway," said Salerno. He was right. Salerno passed away on July 27, 1992, still in prison.

During this same period, the Bonanno family lost its seat on the Commission. This happened in 1979 when Carmine Galante's reign of the Bonanno family was hotly disputed. The family wasn't unified, and the situation didn't improve even after the Commission-sanctioned murder of Galante in July of 1979. The Bonanno family stock fell even further in 1981 when authorities disclosed that FBI agent Joe Pistone had infiltrated the family. The family wouldn't regain its seat on the Commission until the 1990s when Joe Massino had become boss.

Four years after the bombing murder of Testa, Castellano was killed in Midtown Manhattan. The spectacular murder startled the underworld. There had been no formal sanction of this killing. It had never been brought to the table at a Commission meeting. Nevertheless, within days, everyone in the business had a good idea who was behind the hit. What passed for approval were a wink and a nod from the leaders of the Bonanno and Colombo families. To many, especially the Genovese family, the Castellano murder was unsanctioned, and the perpetrators had to be punished.

The Commission suffered another blow when, in late 1986, three Mafia bosses and five others were convicted of racketeering in the so-called Commission trial. The government was successful in proving that the Commission was an entity and that leaders of the Luchese, Genovese, and Colombo families were guilty of committing two or more illegal activities to further the criminal interests of the Commission. In the government's view, it would have been better to have all five family bosses on trial, but Paul Castellano had been killed, and Bonanno boss Phil Rastelli was on trial for racketeering charges in federal court in Brooklyn. As it was, the entire administration of the Luchese family, the boss and underboss of the Colombo family, the Genovese family's representative on the Commission, and the mobster who coordinated the mob's stranglehold over the city's construction industry were all convicted and sentenced to 100 years in jail. Only three of those seven are still living, serving what are virtual death sentences. The eighth defendant, Anthony "Bruno" Indelicato, a participant in the Galante hit, was released in 1998, but returned to prison for two follow-up stretches for violating parole, the latest in 2004.

During the same era, much of the Chicago Outfit's leadership was convicted in prosecutions revolving around the skimming of some Las Vegas casinos. These cases are covered in Chapter 12. As far as the Commission was concerned, the new Chicago leaders weren't personally acquainted with the rising powers in New York like John Gotti and Vittorio "Vic" Amuso of the Luchese family. When the government began a nationwide offense against mob infiltration of four national unions, there was even less reason for Chicago to reestablish contact with the New York bosses.

In 1992, Gambino family boss John Gotti was sentenced to life in prison, and for the rest of the twentieth century, the Gambino family was represented by his son John A. "Junior" Gotti, his brother Peter Gotti, and various other capos who were part of a family ruling committee. The Colombos spent the first few years of the 1990s fighting amongst themselves. Even when peace was restored, the leadership kept changing due to convictions. Luchese boss Amuso has been in prison since 1991, and this family has been represented by numerous acting bosses, which suggests instability. When Vincent "Chin" Gigante was finally given a 12-year prison sentence late in the decade, the last of the older, experienced New York Mafia leaders was gone.

As the new century unfolded, the Bonannos had regained their Commission seat, and Joe Massino was the only official New York City boss on the street. Other families were represented by acting bosses or committees. I detail the travails of Massino in Chapter 28, and some new mob rackets in Chapter 30. The days of the Commission trying to split the proceeds of a $60-million Teamsters Union pension fund loan are long gone. The group is barely alive. The days of making decisions that affect some 25 active La Cosa Nostra families and literally tens of thousands of others—be they union members or consumers of products whose prices were escalated by Mafia practices—is over.

The Least You Need to Know

- The Commission is a group of La Cosa Nostra bosses.

- Its main purpose is to prevent Mafia disputes from escalating into violence.

- For about 50 years, the Commission had national influence.

- Today, the Commission is basically a New York City enterprise.

Chapter 4

Five Families Carve Up the Big Apple

In This Chapter

- A brief history of each of the five families
- Growing the Bonanno family
- The Colombos make history
- Learning the Luchese past
- Telling Genovese tales of woe
- Discovering the Gambino secrets

In 1931, the Genovese family took its boss out to dinner and gave him a few ounces of lead for dessert. In 1957, the Gambino boss went for a haircut and instead took a few shots to the head and body. Near Christmas 1985, another Gambino boss was anticipating a nice juicy steak but was blown away by automatic pistol fire about 10 feet from his dinner. Such is the world of New York's five Mafia families.

In this chapter, I'll tell you the stories behind these hits and many others as members of the Bonanno, Colombo, Gambino, Genovese, and Luchese families vied for prestige, power, and most of all, money on the streets of the Big Apple.

In my discussion of the five families, I've estimated the number of members of each family. The first figure in the range indicates the largest approximate size, while the second number is the smallest. These figures are from about 1960 to the present. These are rough estimates from a wide variety of sources, including FBI intelligence reports, police estimates, and evidence from turncoat gangsters. For the last 20 years, the FBI has been able to maintain what is believed to be a very accurate accounting of family sizes. Before 1980, however, the estimates are less accurate the further back you go in time.

A Word About Labels

In the early 1900s in New York City, the five families were referred to by the name of the Italian region from which many of their members had emigrated. For example, there was the Castellammarese family and the Villabate family. However, as the families expanded and recruited men from other areas, it became common to use the name of the boss to identify the family. *Omerta*, the rule of silence, was still strong, and for the most part, these names were not public knowledge then and remain a secret today.

Mafia Speak

Because of the massive media attention that John Gotti received when he took over the Gambino crime family, Gotti was on track to become the second mob boss whose notoriety caused people on all sides of the law to use his name as that of the crime family. Less than five years later, however, the swashbuckling Dapper Don was jailed, and, until the new millennium, Joe Colombo was the only Mafia boss whose name had replaced that of the one that came into common usage in 1963. See Chapter 28 for the next name change.

In 1963, a certain standard began to evolve. When Joseph Valachi testified before the U.S. Senate, Deputy Inspector John Shanley of the New York Police Department prepared five large charts to better illustrate the New York criminal organizations that Valachi was talking about. Shanley testified that the information came from the files of the New York police, the Federal Bureau of Narcotics, and the Senate committee. He used the names of the five reigning New York City bosses to indicate the respective La Cosa Nostra families. Four of the five labels are still in use today:

Bonanno, Genovese, Gambino, and Luchese (although the Mafia boss after whom the Luchese family was named spelled his name Lucchese). The Colombo family went through a few changes. Its sitting boss, Joseph Magliocco, had only recently taken over the family and died on December 28, 1963, a few months after Valachi's testimony. Although Magliocco's name was used on the Senate chart, it became the practice to use the name of the previous leader, Joseph Profaci, who had been boss for more than 30 years. In 1970, however, Joseph Colombo, the mobster who replaced Magliocco, became famous. From then on, his name was used to refer to the fifth New York City family.

> **Big Shot**
>
> Paolo Violi was a Bonanno family capo based in Montreal, Canada. In testimony before a Quebec Police Commission inquiry into organized crime, a secret witness claimed Violi led a 1,000-man criminal army. It was a gross overstatement of his real power. Three years later, one of Violi's men fired a shotgun blast into his head, putting the number of men under Violi's control at zero.

The Bonanno Family

Estimated range: 300 to 130 members

This family evolved around the turn of the century in New York City. Initially, it was composed mainly of men whose roots were in the western Sicilian town of Castellammare del Golfo. The Mafia was strong in this area, and it became a way of life for certain people of a wide variety of social and economic backgrounds. An indeterminate number of these "men of honor" took part in the massive Italian immigration to the United States around the turn of the twentieth century. Once here, they continued to follow the practices they had learned in their homeland, including congregating around a leader or father. This Castellammarese group eventually evolved into what we now call the Bonanno family.

The names of the earliest leaders are in dispute. However, in the period from 1915 to 1920, Stefano Magaddino was one of its strong men, a capo or higher. Magaddino was involved in several shootings that were a continuation of a feud that had begun in Castellammare del Golfo. In 1921, Magaddino was implicated in the murder of a rival and moved to Buffalo.

Back in New York, boss Cola Shiro and his men moved quickly into the burgeoning bootleg liquor industry. One of his key wiseguys was Joseph Bonanno, who had illegally immigrated to the United States in 1924. He became a protégé of Salvatore Maranzano, who arrived later from Castellammare del Golfo. Maranzano also became involved in bootlegging.

Maranzano would become a legendary figure in La Cosa Nostra, and his career is detailed in Chapter 18. He took over the family when Shiro stepped down in 1930. After an all-out mob war, Maranzano was proclaimed the victor when his rival, Joseph "Joe the Boss" Masseria, was killed in April 1931. Maranzano held a series of realignment meetings for all La Cosa Nostra bosses, and he was considered the top Mafia power at the time. He had a very short run, however. A few months later, on September 10, 1931, he was whacked by men employed by rival Lucky Luciano.

Fuhgeddaboudit

The authenticity of Lucky Luciano's autobiography, *The Last Testament of Lucky Luciano* (1974) by Martin A. Gosch and Richard I. Hammer, is very, very suspect. For example, the authors claim that the judge who sentenced him to a long jail term secretly visited Lucky in jail and broke down crying, begging forgiveness for sending him to jail. Yeah, right. The authors also claim that Lucky and Vito Genovese had it out in Cuba in 1947 and that Lucky beat the crap out of him. In the book, Lucky also claims that it was stupid to hold the famous 1957 national meeting in Apalachin (see Chapter 14) because it was such a small town. Of course, the authors didn't know when they wrote "his" book that the mob had met there quite safely in 1956. *The Last Testament of Lucky Luciano* is a farce, if not a fraud.

Joe Bonanno was elected to replace Maranzano and began a 33-year reign. His first major activity involved the formation of the Commission that was discussed in Chapter 3. Within two years, Prohibition was over and the family expanded its gambling, loan sharking, and labor rackets. Bonanno claimed that his family contained many men who were involved in legitimate business like he was. However, if they were like him, they used the reputation of the Mafia to help create monopolies and to protect their sphere of business influence, be it a restaurant, corner store, or trucking concern.

Relatively speaking, Bonanno's years were uneventful until the 1950s, when he sent a rising star, Carmine Galante, to Montreal to oversee the Bonanno branch plant there. The Canadian seaport was a wide-open city with many politicians, police, and court officials on the take. Galante and his men used strong-arm methods to extort tribute from major gamblers, nightclubs, pimps, con men, and drug dealers. When a reform movement tried to gain power in a Montreal city election, hoods openly intimidated voters at polling booths. Unfortunately for Galante, the reformers won. Eventually, in 1956, political pressure forced him to leave Canada, but the Bonanno family influence remained through others.

Bonanno's control of his family and the Commission began unraveling by the end of the 1950s. Rivals now headed the Gambino, Genovese, and Luchese families. In addition, his longtime support from cousin Stefano, the boss of the Buffalo family, began to wane. Bonanno was also being pursued by a number of jurisdictions that were conducting inquiries into a variety of matters including the disastrous Mafia meeting at Apalachin in late 1957. Bonanno reacted by adopting a policy of constant movement. This only raised the suspicions of his underworld rivals, who felt that Bonanno had designs on their territories.

In the early 1960s, Bonanno's troubles worsened. He lost the support of the Colombo family when new boss Joe Colombo took over in 1964. This was during an explosion of public interest in the Mafia because of the revelations of informer Joe Valachi, who knew Bonanno and spoke about him. Ominously, Bonanno was being sought by the Commission to explain charges that he plotted to kill Gambino and Lucchese. The government was also trying to subpoena him to appear before a grand jury. On October 21, 1964, Bonanno appeared to be have been kidnapped. That event will be discussed in detail in Chapter 25. Bonanno was deposed by the Commission and was prevented from maintaining control of his family. Sporadic shootings broke out that accomplished little except to generate great publicity. Ultimately, he gave up the losing battle and, in 1968, retired to Tucson, Arizona, where he died in 2002.

> ### Fuhgeddaboudit
>
> In the late 1970s, a national magazine published an article calling Joe Bonanno "The Real Godfather." According to the article, Bonanno was then the most powerful Mafia boss in the nation. In fact, he was no longer even a minor player in the Mafia life. Bonanno, and son Salvatore "Bill" Bonanno, helped keep the myth alive for decades through their own writings.

The Commission chose a former Bonanno friend, Gaspar DiGregorio, to replace Bonanno. The strain of the resulting chaos helped destroy DiGregorio's health. In 1966, he stepped aside for capo Paul Sciacca, who conducted much of the warfare against Bonanno loyalists. By 1970, he, too, was broken by health problems and was replaced by Natale Evola, a longtime capo and an usher at Bonanno's wedding. Evola's reign was short. He died on August 28, 1973, and was replaced by Philip Rastelli three months later.

In January 1974, Carmine Galante was released from prison after serving 12 years for heroin trafficking. Rastelli was tied up with his own legal problems, and Galante moved for the top slot. Immediately, he rekindled his heroin connections, trying to make up for lost time.

Galante's style didn't appeal to many in his family or to other New York leaders. With the Commission's blessing, some capos allied themselves with Galante's closest aides and arranged his murder on July 12, 1979.

Phil Rastelli took back the throne but spent much of his reign behind bars. That led to more disunity, the worst instance of which was the execution of three capos on the same night, May 5, 1981. It was during this period that the family lost its seat on the Commission because they were in constant disarray and so many of its members were involved with narcotics. The fact that undercover FBI agent Joseph Pistone was able to infiltrate the family so well that he was proposed for membership reinforced the Commission's biases that the family was out of control. Pistone's work also destroyed the ascending mob career of capo Dominick "Sonny Black" Napolitano. He had been close to Pistone and paid for this mistake with his life. Rastelli's bad luck also continued. He was found guilty of federal racketeering charges and died of liver cancer on June 26, 1991, while serving a 12-year prison sentence.

Out of this mess emerged Joey Massino. He surrounded himself with loyalists, shut down the Bonanno social clubs, and tried to adopt a more secretive manner of doing business. Under his leadership, the Bonannos regained their seat on the Commission and reasserted themselves in narcotics, labor racketeering, and other criminal enterprises. Massino escaped being indicted in the first years of the twenty-first century, but as I detail in Chapter 28, the bubble burst for him in 2003.

The Colombo Family

Estimated range: 200 to 120 members

Like the Bonanno family, the Colombo family's origins go back to the last decade of the nineteenth century. Its members followed the tradition of their Sicilian homeland and united for common protection and profit. As it did for all criminal groups with any foresight, Prohibition greatly increased the geographical scope of this group, putting them in contact with others of similar interests outside of New York. Evidence of this can be traced to the presence of both the family boss and underboss at a 1928 Cleveland meeting of Sicilian mobsters that was broken up by the police. Boss Joe Profaci and underboss Joseph Magliocco were arrested at a time when authorities had no idea of their important positions, let alone the structure or scope of La Cosa Nostra.

Profaci was one of the smarter Mafia leaders. He established thriving legitimate businesses that enabled him to live an opulent lifestyle despite a few battles with the IRS. He was known as the "Olive Oil King" because a company he owned was the largest importer of olive oil and tomato paste in the United States. As boss of one of the five New York La Cosa Nostra families, Profaci was a charter member of the Commission, formed after the murder of Salvatore Maranzano in September of 1931. For 30 years, Profaci was allied with the dominant group in this body and was unchallenged by any serious dissent from within his family.

Slammer Time

John "Sonny" Franzese, a Colombo capo, was convicted in 1967 of a bank robbery conspiracy that had taken place a decade earlier. Sentenced to 50 years, he began serving his time in 1970. He was released on parole in February of 1979. Since then, he has been in and out of jail numerous times for parole violations. Released at age 87 in January 2004, he remained on parole as this revised edition went to press.

Based mainly in Brooklyn with some Staten Island interests, the Profaci soldiers were involved in gambling, loan sharking, hijacking, labor racketeering, extortion, counterfeiting, and many other criminal pursuits. Furthermore, federal authorities listed Joe Profaci as a major heroin dealer in the 1960s, although he never was personally charged with drug dealing.

Profaci faced the first serious challenge to his leadership when an upstart crew of wiseguys based in the Red Hook section of Brooklyn and headed by Albert, Larry, and Crazy Joe Gallo launched an open revolt, which involved kidnapping, shootings, and murders. These events, known as the Gallo-Profaci war, are detailed in Chapter 24. After experiencing poor health for a long time, Profaci died on June 6, 1962.

Mafia Speak

During the Gallo revolt, Joey Gallo was interviewed as he left a police station after one of many harassment arrests. With a straight face, he told a reporter that he and his friends were big game hunters and that the guns cops found during a raid on his headquarters were for hunting.

Profaci's brother-in-law and longtime underboss, Joe Magliocco, was quickly selected to head the family after Profaci's death. The other New York families weren't too happy about his selection, and the family remained in turmoil. Magliocco took over right before the government trotted out its first Mafia turncoat, Joe Valachi, who promptly named Magliocco as boss of one of New York's five La Cosa Nostra organizations. In a desperate attempt to secure control of his family, Magliocco apparently plotted the killing of his antagonists, Carlo Gambino and Tommy Lucchese, bosses of their own families. It failed, as did Magliocco's heart—he died on December 28, 1963.

Carlo Gambino supported the election of Joe Colombo as the new boss. Initially, Colombo kept a low profile. However, Colombo responded to the arrest of one of his sons by picketing the Manhattan offices of the FBI. In short order, the protest grew exponentially, and soon Colombo was a national figure, heading a quasi–civil rights organization that captured the imagination of many Italian-Americans. All the attention backfired, however, by increasing FBI pressure, which displeased the other bosses.

They urged caution, but Colombo ignored them. He went so far as to appear on national television shows to protest what he described as anti-Italian biases by the FBI. Around the same time, hotheaded Joey Gallo was released from prison and resisted Colombo's leadership. At a Midtown Manhattan rally of Colombo's civil rights organization on June 28, 1971, Colombo was shot and permanently crippled, both physically and mentally. I detail these events in Chapter 17.

With Colombo incapacitated, the logical successor was veteran capo Carmine Persico, but he was unable to formally move to the top slot because of a pending prison sentence. He approved of the elevation of aging capo Thomas DiBella as acting boss. Everyone understood that Persico and his brother Alphonse were the real powers, though. When DiBella's health failed, Carmine, Alphonse, and Gennaro "Jerry Lang" Langella acted in his stead.

By the 1980s, the Persicos had serious legal difficulties, as did many other Colombo members. This was during the great FBI push to cripple La Cosa Nostra across the country. In 1987, Carmine and underboss Gennaro Langella were sentenced to more than 100 years in jail. Alphonse was convicted of federal loan-sharking charges and finally died behind bars after a number of years on the run. Carmine Persico selected capo Victor "Little Vic" Orena to mind the throne. It was clear to most observers—except for Orena—that Persico was planning to install his son Alphonse in the top slot. However, Alphonse, who had been convicted at the same trial as his father, had to complete a prison sentence first.

Alphonse Persico, who followed his father to the top of the Colombo family, might spend the rest of his life in federal prison like his dad.

(Photo courtesy of GangLandNews.com)

By 1990, Orena, with the backing of Gambino boss John Gotti, had begun angling to take permanent control of the family. An unsuccessful attempt was made by Persico loyalists on Orena's life outside his home in June 1991. Although no shots were fired, Orena went into hiding and protested to the other families. A committee of top mobsters from the other families attempted to broker a truce, but this fell apart.

The shooting started in November 1991 when a group of Orena loyalists ambushed capo Greg Scarpa Sr. as he drove home one night. Several passersby were injured in a wild shootout and chase that followed, but Scarpa escaped unhurt. It was a costly debacle, and Scarpa, a controversial gangster who had been a top-echelon FBI informer for more than 30 years, would kill three Orena faction members over the next several months during the bloody Colombo war.

As Orena and Persico loyalists quickly split up into hit teams, a dozen people, including two innocent bystanders, lost their lives in the open warfare that resulted. Finally, authorities applied enough pressure to bring the shootings to a halt. Nearly 100 mobsters and associates were hit with murder and racketeering indictments and were jailed. Some participants cooperated with the law, most notably Carmine Sessa, the family's consigliere and a Persico loyalist. Scores of gangsters from both factions received prison sentences, some for life. In the end, the Persico side won, but many of them will be old and gray before they get out of prison. Many of Orena's men were acquitted, but Orena himself was a big loser. He was convicted of murder and racketeering and is serving a life sentence.

Following his release from prison, Alphonse took over the family and made an outward attempt at unification by naming Orena faction member William "Wild Bill" Cutolo as underboss. However, Cutolo was called to a meeting in May of 1999 and hasn't been seen since. A few months later, Alphonse was arrested on gun charges. He pleaded guilty and received an 18-month sentence. On the eve of his release in early 2001, he was hit with racketeering charges, which I detail in Chapter 31.

> **Slammer Time**
>
> While under house arrest in December of 1992, Colombo capo Greg Scarpa got involved in a shootout a few blocks from his home and lost an eye. He drove himself home, poured himself a scotch, and called police.

The Colombo family has been in near-constant leadership turmoil for the last 40 years. However, the estimated 120-member organization has always managed to survive attacks both from legal authorities and from within. And although their days of playing a key role in the lucrative labor-racketeering enterprises of the famous Concrete Club are over, they still have interests in loan sharking, stock manipulation, and a host of other rackets.

The Gambino Family

Estimated range: 300 to 190 members

Salvatore "Tata" D'Aquila was the first well-known leader of this group. At one time, he was considered the most respected La Cosa Nostra boss in America. By the fall of 1928, however, that respect had pretty much deteriorated. On October 10, 1928, D'Aquila was shot to death while standing next to his car in New York. Tata had opposed the ambitions of Joseph Masseria, the boss of the family we now call the Genovese family. The ascension of Al Mineo as leader and his close association with Masseria suggest strongly that Mineo had a hand in D'Aquila's demise.

Mineo would have only two years to savor his victory. As he was leaving a strategy meeting with Masseria, Mineo and his underboss were shot to death by three men working with Masseria's chief rival, Salvatore Maranzano.

In April of 1931, Masseria was also eliminated. Maranzano backed Frank Scalise as the new boss of the Gambino family. When Maranzano was killed in September of 1931, however, the members of the Gambino family feared that the closeness of Scalise to Maranzano would put their family in disfavor with the new power, Lucky Luciano. They selected Vincent Mangano as boss, beginning two decades of relative peace and stability.

Big Shot

In 1951, Frank Scalise became part of the administration of Albert Anastasia. On June 17, 1957, in a scene that was recreated in the shooting of Vito Corleone in Francis Ford Coppola's *The Godfather*, Scalise was gunned down while buying fruit at a produce store.

For unity purposes, Mangano appointed Albert Anastasia as his underboss. Anastasia was young, violent, ambitious, and close to Luciano. For 20 years, Anastasia remained loyal to Mangano, who had powerful allies of his own. By 1951, however, Anastasia had forged a compact with Frank Costello, then leader of the Genovese family, and felt strong enough to eliminate Mangano and his brother, Philip. On April 19, 1951, Philip was found shot to death in a swampy area of Sheepshead Bay, Brooklyn. Brother Vincent disappeared the same day; his body has never been found. Anastasia was elected boss and was recognized by the Commission.

Carlo Gambino, a member of Anastasia's administration, had ambitions of his own. In addition, he had close ties with Tommy Lucchese, boss of another New York family. Anastasia was weakened when his ally Frank Costello was toppled from power by Vito Genovese. Anastasia was now opposed by two of the five New York families. Worse yet, the remaining two offered little support. On October 25, 1957, as Anastasia sat in a Manhattan hotel barbershop chair with a hot towel over his face waiting for his daily shave, two men pushed aside his barber and shot him to death.

Gambino took over and led the family until his death from heart disease in October 1976. His family was firmly entrenched in many unions and trade associations, enabling him and his family to become rich through labor-racketeering efforts in Manhattan's garment center, on the docks, in construction, in private sanitation, in hotels, and in restaurants. Gambling, loan sharking, and other mob staples provided further income. At one point, Gambino had more than 20 capos leading more than 300 soldiers. He fought off deportation attempts, kept a low profile, and died a millionaire. In the early 1970s, he had friends on the thrones of the Colombo, Bonanno, Genovese, and Luchese families and was considered by many to be the most powerful Mafia boss in the nation.

By 1975, as Gambino's health failed him, his cousin and brother-in-law, Paul Castellano, became acting boss. Underboss Aniello Dellacroce was in prison. In November 1976, a month after Gambino's death, Dellacroce got out of prison and gave his blessing to the selection of Castellano as boss. Castellano was at the helm of a well-oiled money-making machine. By the early 1980s, however, Castellano's personal life had deteriorated. He became more interested in personal wealth and success than in keeping his soldiers happy, and he became entangled in a series of legal problems that made him seem vulnerable. John Gotti, an acting capo based in Ozone Park, Queens, perceived Castellano's vulnerability and plotted to kill him.

Meanwhile, Castellano recognized Gotti's ambition and talked of breaking up his crew. The pretext was that his men had been caught dealing drugs. For a while, longtime family underboss Dellacroce kept both men from acting on their wishes. Once he died, however, both moved their plans ahead. Gotti moved faster. He crafted an alliance with several Gambino capos and orchestrated the spectacular Midtown Manhattan assassination of Castellano and his key aide Thomas Bilotti on December 16, 1985. I detail the Castellano-Bilotti murders and the killing of Albert Anastasia in Chapter 23.

Mafia Speak

John Gotti and Salvatore "Sammy Bull" Gravano watched from across a busy intersection as four designated shooters blew Paul Castellano and Tommy Bilotti away at the height of the evening rush hour during the Christmas shopping season. When the shooting stopped, Gotti calmly drove by the shooting scene. Gravano later testified that he looked down at the very still body of Bilotti and said, "He's gone."

Gotti burst upon the media scene a few weeks later when he showed up for a previously scheduled court appearance in Brooklyn.

The Dapper Don strode into the federal courthouse in Brooklyn wearing a big smile and a $2,000 suit. Asked by reporters if he was now the boss of the Gambino family, Gotti smiled and said, "I'm the boss of my family—my wife and kids at home." Like a skilled politician on the stump, Gotti gently pushed his way through a gaggle of reporters, always smiling broadly for the cameras, until he and a female reporter arrived together at the courtroom door. "I was brought up to hold the door open for ladies," he said with a twinkle in his eye as he grasped the door with his right hand and ushered her in with his left.

In the next four years, the Dapper Don became the Teflon Don as he won three consecutive battles with the law. In 1987, he became the first and only Mafia boss to be acquitted of federal racketeering charges. Later that year, assault charges lodged against him by Queens's prosecutors were dropped when his victim "forgot" who hit him. In 1990, he was acquitted of assault charges in Manhattan and became a folk hero in some quarters.

A darker side was revealed in 1992 when federal prosecutors played a tape recording of a long conversation Gotti had in which he discussed the killings of Gambino mobsters Robert "DeeBee" DiBernardo, Louis Milito, and Louis DiBono. The bodies of DiBernardo and Milito were never found. DiBono was killed in the World Trade Center parking lot on October 4, 1990.

"When DeeBee got whacked, they told me a story," said Gotti. "I was in jail when I whacked him. I knew why it was being done. I done it anyway. I allowed it to be done anyway."

Gotti said he approved Milito's murder because underboss Sammy Bull Gravano, who would later testify against Gotti, had pushed him to it. "I took Sammy's word that he talked behind my back. I took Sammy's word."

As for DiBono, Gotti said, Gravano "wanted permission" to kill DiBono for cheating him in a business deal. "I saw the papers and everything," said Gotti. "He didn't rob nothing. Know why he's dying? He's gonna die because he refused to come in when I called."

The Genovese Family

Estimated range: 400 to 225 members

The Genovese family has long been recognized as one of the most powerful La Cosa Nostra families since the turn of the twentieth century when Ignazio Lupo was the boss. In 1910, he and Peter "The Clutch Hand" Morello were given lengthy prison sentences for a counterfeiting conviction. The extended Morello family continued to control the family under Nicholas Morello, but he was killed in 1916 in warfare with a Camorra gang. Half-brother Ciro Terranova tried to assume control but proved ineffective.

Joseph "Joe the Boss" Masseria rose from the ranks and began asserting himself. Vincent Morello was killed, probably by Masseria forces, on May 8, 1922. So was brother Charles. This brought the Morellos in line behind Masseria. Peter "The Clutch Hand" Morello, released early from his counterfeiting sentence, agreed to become Masseria's underboss and chief strategist. Together, they managed to kill their main rival, Salvatore D'Aquila, the leader of the Gambinos, on October 11, 1928. This left Masseria as the top power in New York City.

As will be detailed in Chapter 22, Masseria apparently tried to overpower the Castellammarese clan and was strongly resisted. Ultimately, his own man, Lucky Luciano, arranged Masseria's killing and ended the war. Luciano continued his coup by having the leader of the Bonannos, Salvatore Maranzano, murdered a few short months later. This was the genesis for the creation of the Commission, which was discussed in Chapter 3.

Luciano ruled for only a few years. In 1936, he was convicted of organizing a prostitution racket and was sentenced to 30 to 50 years. Despite numerous appeals and a consensus that the sentence was outrageously harsh, Luciano languished in prison until February of 1946, when he was released and deported to Italy, winning an early parole for cooperating with a naval intelligence effort to prevent sabotage on the New York waterfront during World War II. In 1947, Luciano traveled to Cuba and met with leading La Cosa Nostra figures. American government pressure forced his return to Italy, however. Despite repeated rumors that he was involved in the heroin trade, nothing was proven. He died in 1962.

Luciano's underboss, Vito Genovese, the logical successor, was facing a murder inquiry and fled to Italy at about the same time that Luciano was incarcerated. Capo Frank Costello took over, first as acting boss and then later as official boss when it became clear that Luciano would never be able to retake the reins. Costello ran a low-key operation, solidifying political and union connections to protect and enable a wide range of rackets and earning the title of the "Prime Minister of Organized Crime."

> **Big Shot**
>
> According to Joe Valachi and Joe Bonanno, Peter "The Clutch Hand" Morello was killed by the Maranzano forces. Some feel Masseria ordered his murder in a continuation of his earlier feud with the Morello clan. The statements of Valachi and Bonanno seem to overpower the evidence that supports the latter theory.

After World War II, the murder case against Genovese fell apart. He chafed under Costello's leadership and plotted to take over. By 1957, Genovese felt he had enough support and made his move on Costello. The gunman, Vincent "Chin" Gigante, only wounded Costello, but he promptly stepped down. A few months later, Genovese was part of the plot to remove Albert Anastasia as crime boss and replace him with Carlo Gambino, a friend. Unfortunately for Genovese, just two years later, he was convicted of narcotics conspiracy and was given a 15-year sentence. He died in jail on February 14, 1969.

For the next dozen or so years, the Genovese family managed to keep the identity of its real boss a secret, even from the leaders of the four other families. Philip "Benny Squint" Lombardo headed the family from 1969 until his death in 1981, but a series of "up front" bosses—Thomas "Tommy Ryan" Eboli, Frank "Funzi" Tieri, and Anthony "Fat Tony" Salerno—dealt with the other families and were carried in FBI files as the family boss. Salerno was convicted as the family boss in the historic Commission case and was sentenced to 100 years in 1987. In reality, however, Vincent "Chin" Gigante took over as boss shortly after Lombardo's death and remains the family's official boss as this revised edition goes to press, serving a 12-year sentence for racketeering, as well as 3-year sentence for obstruction of justice that I detail in Chapter 27. He is due to be released in 2010.

Fuhgeddaboudit

When Vincent "Fish" Cafaro was locked up with Tony Salerno, his mentor of more than 30 years, they argued about money, and Salerno threatened to hit Cafaro with his cane. Cafaro considered this to be an insult, and it was one of his stated reasons for becoming a cooperating witness for the government, helping to clear up the identities of the real family bosses after the death of Vito Genovese.

Essentially, who was the "real" boss is simply an academic question. All of those named played leading roles in the family. They controlled the Fulton Fish Market, the San Gennaro Festival, the Javits Convention Center, large gambling rings, and a major portion of the labor racketeering in Manhattan and parts of New Jersey, along with a host of other illegal enterprises.

For 30 years, Gigante avoided trial by pretending to be mentally ill. He would often walk through Greenwich Village in slippers and a bathrobe, muttering to himself. Following his indictment for racketeering in 1990, he played his crazy act to the hilt, successfully avoiding trial until mid-1997. But the game ended, and he went to trial and was convicted of racketeering. Until his release—he will be 82 when he gets out—a series of tough, experienced capos are expected to act in his stead.

Chin Gigante's crazy act worked for 30 years, but in 1997 he was convicted of racketeering and sentenced to 12 years. In 2003, he admitted faking mental illness and 3 years were added to his prison term.

(Photo courtesy of New York Daily News*)*

The Luchese Family

Estimated range: 175 to 110 members

The Luchese family has been around since the turn of the twentieth century, but the public wasn't aware of its existence until the testimony of Joe Valachi in 1963. He explained that Gaetano "Tommy" Reina was the boss of this family at the start of the Castellammarese War. Reina was 40 years old when he was shot to death on February 26, 1930, as he was leaving a private residence in the Bronx. This killing was apparently part of Joe Masseria's plan to place supporters at the heads of the four other New York City families.

Joe Pinzolo, a man allied to Masseria, succeeded Reina as boss. It was at this time that Valachi, a common street hood, was secretly recruited by Tommy Gagliano, a Reina loyalist. The plan was to bring unknown men into the Gagliano circle and strike back at Pinzolo. Because they were

Big Shot

Tommy Reina's father was a friend of the Morello brothers of the Genovese family. Reina's daughter, Mildred, married Joe Valachi. His son, Giacamo Reina, also became a member of the Luchese family.

new, the theory was that Masseria wouldn't know who was attacking his puppet. On September 5, 1930, Pinzolo was gunned down in a Manhattan office building by one of Gagliano's recruits.

The mobsters loyal to Gagliano allied themselves with Salvatore Maranzano, the leader of the family that would become known as the Bonanno family. Eventually, men within Masseria's camp began to feel that he wasn't going to win the war and that it was time to end hostilities. Masseria was killed in April of 1931. Tommy Gagliano then openly became boss of the Luchese family, aided by the blessing of Maranzano.

Within four months, Gagliano and his underboss, Tommy Lucchese, had deserted Maranzano and took part in a plot to kill him. Their participation was evident because Lucchese was on the scene on September 10, 1931, when Maranzano was killed. The fact that Lucchese wasn't harmed is telling. So, too, was the fact that Gagliano and Lucchese continued in power in the new state of affairs.

> ### Slammer Time
>
> In the early 1960s, Luchese capo John "Big John" Ormento was convicted of a narcotics conspiracy for the fourth time. His fourth conviction was his last. Sentenced to 40 years in prison, he died there in 1974.

The two played an important role in initiating the Commission (see Chapter 3), the establishment of which helped the family maintain stability for decades. Lucchese was personally involved in trucking and production in the garment district, with corresponding influence and control of key Teamsters and Ladies Garment Workers locals, as well as trade associations.

Decades later, when Idelwild Airport (now Kennedy Airport) was opened, the Gaglianos moved in, again using unions and trade associations to create monopolies in trucking, warehousing, hijacking, and assorted other rackets centered at the airport. On Long Island, the Luchese family had its hooks in the garbage industry. It controlled a trade association that set rates, established who had which stop, and kept out competitors through arson, murder, and assorted other mayhem. In New Jersey, the family also ran blue-collar rackets such as gambling, loan sharking, extortion, robbery, and assorted other schemes.

Gagliano died in 1954 and was replaced by Lucchese. Within a few years, his consigliere and three capos were in prison on narcotics charges. Lucchese was embroiled in the Commission's attempt to depose Joe Bonanno (see Chapter 25), and his health was failing. He passed away from cancer on July 13, 1967. Anthony "Tony Ducks" Corallo took over after the brief reign of Carmine "Mr. Gribbs" Tramunti ended with a prison sentence. Corallo was a veteran, low-key mobster who had the misfortune of being bugged, both in the auto that ferried him about and at the headquarters of another boss. He and his entire administration were convicted in the Commission case in 1986. They had led the family for a lucrative decade. Corallo and his under-boss, Salvatore "Tom Mix" Santoro, died in prison in the year 2000.

The next administration, handpicked by Tony Ducks, was a disaster. Vittorio "Vic" Amuso and his underboss, Anthony "Gaspipe" Casso, were totally out of their league when it came to the subtleties of running such a major operation. Their main idea of management was to kill anyone who displeased them in any way. Their secondary plank was to kill anyone whom they thought might displease them. Soon capos and soldiers were running to the government for protection. Both Amuso and Casso ended up with life sentences. For a brief period, Casso looked like he'd landed himself a sweet deal as a cooperating witness, but he blew it with his lies, continued criminal activity, and erratic behavior.

Amuso's handpicked acting boss, capo Joseph "Little Joe" DeFede, took over in the mid-1990s, but his reign was also a disaster. Convicted of racketeering charges, DeFede cooperated in 2002 and helped bring down successor acting boss, Louis "Louie Bagels" Daidone, in 2004, whose fall is described in Chapter 31.

The Least You Need to Know

- The five New York families take their names from bosses from the 1960s.
- Bonanno, Colombo, Gambino, Genovese, and Luchese are the names of the five New York City families.
- The five families have been in existence for 100 years or more.
- The proximity of the five families creates tensions.

Chapter 5

Mafia Families Poison the Northeast

In This Chapter

- Three families plague the Keystone state
- Mafia hunts in Buffalo
- Bad guys nest in the Garden State
- Wiseguys on the loose in New England
- Breaking away in Rochester

For most of the twentieth century, each of the seven La Cosa Nostra families discussed in this chapter, with the possible exception of the Rochester family, were active, powerful organizations. Two, Buffalo and Philadelphia, had bosses who sat on the Commission. One, the Pittsburgh family, was the focus of a congressional investigation into the assassination of President Kennedy. The leaders of two others, the New England and Newark (New Jersey) families, were humiliated by the release of summaries of illegal FBI wiretaps. Another, the northeastern Pennsylvania family known as the Pittstown family, became the focus of a massive investigation following the disappearance of former Teamster president Jimmy Hoffa in 1975. Let's begin this chapter with their story.

The Pittstown Family

This northeastern Pennsylvania–based family can trace its roots back more than 100 years. The family probably was the first to use extortion-type scams, commonly known today as labor racketeering, in the area's coalmines and garment factories. Santo "King of the Night" Volpe was most likely the family's first boss. An immigrant from Sicily, he became a power in several United Mine Workers locals. Using this leverage, Volpe created the classic La Cosa Nostra racket of extorting payoffs from mine owners to avoid labor problems. His members owned two mines that received favorable treatment from miners' locals that the family controlled, giving the family a huge competitive advantage over other coalmines. Volpe also directed the family's bootlegging operations during the Prohibition years of 1920 through 1933. A number of known family members were arrested for liquor distribution, but Volpe was never nailed for bootlegging. In 1933, however, he was implicated in the murder of a Scranton hood that had done excellent work for Volpe, hijacking competitors' liquor trucks just a few years earlier. The murder case fell apart, but Volpe withdrew from power and enjoyed the spoils of his criminal activity with no further contact with the law.

John Sciandra, who also owned a coal business, replaced Volpe shortly after the 1933 murder investigation. The family's union connections made it easier for Sciandra to make a handsome profit. His son Angelo, who stepped into the family business, also had pieces of two different garment-industry companies. Angelo was one of the 58 wiseguys known to have attended the famous 1957 Apalachin Mafia convention that is discussed in Chapter 14.

Around 1940, Joseph Barbara took over the crime family. He was from Castellammare del Golfo, the same village from which Joseph Bonanno had emigrated. The two were good friends, and this helped Barbara's ascension. Like Bonanno, Barbara was a bootlegger who was savvy and tough enough to outwit and overpower both outsiders and greedy underlings who gravitated toward the lucrative business. He also outmaneuvered the law. He was arrested twice on suspicion of murder, but each time the case disintegrated and he was released. Barbara, an ally of Bonanno during the bloody Castellammarese War, was ready for action in 1931, the height of the war. He was driving in New York City with a crew of wiseguys armed with various weapons, including a submachine gun that had been used in a New York murder. Barbara did not own the car, and his fingerprints were not on the weapon, so he was not charged in the incident.

Barbara is most famous for two meetings held at his estate in Apalachin, New York, not far from the Pennsylvania border, in 1956 and 1957. These events will be covered in detail in Chapter 14. Scores of Mafiosi were detained leaving the Barbara grounds when they panicked and ran after seeing state troopers observing them. The resulting publicity and hearings ruined Barbara's lucrative legitimate business connections. His poor health continued to deteriorate, and he passed away on June 17, 1959. Ironically, for years afterward, Barbara was incorrectly labeled a member of the Buffalo family rather than a powerful boss in his own right.

Mafia Speak

Many of the Mafiosi who were detained after leaving Barbara's estate during the national meeting of La Cosa Nostra on November 14, 1957, claimed that they had simply stopped by to visit ailing, longtime friend Joe Barbara. They didn't know the others would be doing the same thing, but once they arrived and saw each other, they hung around and enjoyed themselves, talking about their families and friends and reminiscing about the old country. Right!

The family's next boss was Russell Bufalino. He, too, was Sicilian born and would go on to become semi-famous. By marrying into the family of boss John Sciandra, Bufalino solidified his place in the organization. After Sciandra's death, Bufalino moved up to underboss. The administrative position gave him many new connections with Mafiosi from around the nation. He also inherited and increased business interests in New York City that again brought him into regular contact with powerful men. Although his family was known for gambling, loan sharking, and extortion, it was labor racketeering that gave the family clout and influence and later made Bufalino a target of the FBI.

In 1975, former Teamster president Jimmy Hoffa disappeared. He had been attempting a comeback after a prison term, but the Mafia bosses didn't appreciate his ambitions. In a wide-ranging but ultimately unsuccessful investigation into Hoffa's murder, the FBI thought that Bufalino had played a role in the affair. The FBI was right, according to an account by a close Bufalino associate that was made public in 2004 (for more on the Hoffa murder, see Chapter 33).

The feds put great pressure on Bufalino in the hopes of making one of the main targets in Hoffa's murder become an informer. In August of 1977, he was convicted of extortion and served about three years. It was a bitter pill for the gangster, not so much because he was found guilty of extortion, a noble crime, but because of the person who did it, assistant U.S. attorney Barbara Jones. "It's bad enough being convicted," he moaned. "But did it have to be by a broad?" In the meantime, Los Angeles mobster Aladena "Jimmy the Weasel" Fratianno became the second mobster to publicly break his vow of silence and implicated Bufalino in a murder conspiracy. Bufalino was convicted and eventually went to prison until 1989. When his health declined, the aged boss formally retired. He died in 1994.

Ed Sciandra, a nephew of the family's 1930s leader, became Bufalino's consigliere around 1981. He spent 18 months in jail on a kickback scheme conviction, and after his release he served as acting boss until Bufalino retired in 1989. By 1990, Sciandra was 78 years old, and much of the family's activities were directed by William D'Elia, who had his hands in gambling, extortion, and quasi-legitimate interests in the private sanitation and trucking industries.

The Buffalo Family

This family was ideally situated to be an active participant in the illegal importation of liquor from Ontario, Canada, during Prohibition. Joseph Peter DiCarlo held the family reins in 1920, at the start of Prohibition. His group was engaged in constant combat over the bootleg trade with Calabrian gangsters from Ontario and the Buffalo area. On July 9, 1922, DiCarlo died of natural causes. His death led to the ascension of the family's most influential boss in its history: Stefano Magaddino.

Magaddino was another mobster from Castellammare del Golfo. He arrived in the United States in 1902, settled in New York City, and became a leader of the Castellammarese clan there. The family was involved in gambling and extortion prior to Prohibition. Magaddino had been involved in a feud in Sicily prior to his emigration, and the battle raged on in New York. In August of 1921, Magaddino was arrested on suspicion of ordering the killing of Camillo Caizzo, a mobster from the old country whose body was found in a potato sack in New Jersey. The hit man confessed to the murder and claimed that Magaddino made him do it because Caizzo had killed Magaddino's brother Pietro in Castellammare. Magaddino was never prosecuted in the case. Ultimately, he relocated to Buffalo and took over for the deceased DiCarlo.

Fuhgeddaboudit

When Philadelphia boss Salvatore Sabella was arrested in New Jersey in August of 1931, it was discovered that he was living in the same Brooklyn home that Stefano Magaddino lived in nine years earlier. Both were from Castellammare del Golfo. It could be an extraordinary coincidence, but more likely, it illustrates the close ties that Castellammarese Mafia clans had in the northeastern United States.

Magaddino grew in stature as he became involved in Mafia affairs throughout New York State. He supported the Castellammarese clan in its war with Joe Masseria and became an original member of the Commission in 1931. His family expanded its gambling, loan sharking, and extortion activities after Prohibition and became more deeply involved in labor racketeering. Building on Canadian alliances from the Prohibition era as well establishing new contacts, Buffalo quickly laid claim to southeastern Ontario as its territory for most of the illegal activities. Many Buffalo members got involved in the lucrative heroin trade, using their proximity to the Canadian border to facilitate the movement of drugs. Magaddino had become a power in La Cosa Nostra.

Magaddino's low profile came to an end in 1957 at Apalachin, New York. He avoided detection, but eight of his men were detained. (For a more detailed look at this affair, see Chapter 14.)

A few years later, Magaddino became embroiled in the Bonanno family split (discussed in Chapter 25). Although Joe Bonanno and Magaddino were cousins, their relationship came to an unhappy end when Magaddino supported deposing Bonanno. Carlo Gambino emerged as the big winner from the Bonanno split, and he forged alliances in New York that basically eliminated Magaddino's former influence. Slowly but surely, Magaddino began to fade as an important figure in all but Buffalo Mafia affairs.

Aware of Magaddino's loss of power and failing health, his capos began preparing for the future without him. Soon the once-powerful family splintered into factions, each of which cast about for allies. By the time Magaddino died in 1974, his family was a shell of its former self.

> **Slammer Time**
>
> One of Magaddino's most feared enforcers was Pasquale Natarelli. He received a 16-year sentence in 1967 that eliminated him from leadership contention as Magaddino deteriorated. Natarelli served nine years before being released.

Magaddino's underboss, Sam Pieri, was convicted of a narcotics violation in 1954 and spent the next eight years in prison. As Magaddino's grip loosened on the family, crews aligning with Pieri began feeling their oats and asserting themselves. In 1970, however, Pieri went back to jail, and his crews floundered as Joe Fino stepped up as acting boss. Pieri was released a few years later and attempted to assert control in 1974 by whacking longtime member John Cammillieri. At the time, Pieri's competition came from the crews that lined up with emerging powerhouse capo Joseph Todaro. Members from both factions tried to use their ties to officials of Laborers Local 210, a key plank in the Buffalo family rackets for decades, to gain control of the family.

In 1983, Sam Pieri died and his brother Joe inherited his brother's rackets, but was unable to consolidate his position. In 1984, he sought the support of the Commission during a visit to Anthony "Fat Tony" Salerno of New York's Genovese family, which represented the Buffalo family. Ultimately, the Commission supported Joe Todaro, and he took over the top spot.

Joseph Todaro Jr. now runs the family, which has lost its hold on Laborers Local 210 and has been stung by several federal racketeering prosecutions. Two of their key Ontario members were murdered in 1997 by a hit man working for a Canadian Calabrian clan. There was a brief period when it appeared that a few Buffalo members were making a major move on Las Vegas. It turned out to be just another attempt by some hoods to make money wherever they could. The once-powerful Buffalo family is now a minor player in organized crime.

The Newark Family

This New Jersey group, the model for HBO's hit television show *The Sopranos* (at least in their own minds), has been around since the early 1900s. The family's boss in 1931 was Steven Badami, who had earlier appointed Sam Monaco as his underboss. Like many Mafia leaders of the year, however, Monaco's tenure was short-lived. He was reported missing on September 10, 1931, and was found dead three days later.

Philip "Big Phil" Amari was a controversial leader and an important family player in the 1930s, although his exact relationship to Badami is unclear. He is credited by some with starting the family in the 1930s. Ultimately, he was overthrown in 1957, probably with Commission approval, and was replaced by Nick Delmore. The family was well represented at the Apalachin conference, with the two mobsters who served as family underboss that year, Louis "Fat Lou" Larasso and Frank Majuri, in attendance. Delmore reigned quietly for five years and helped his nephew, Simone "Sam the Plumber" DeCavalcante, move into the top spot in 1962. DeCavalcante, who had been inducted into the family in the 1940s with his father performing the ceremony, would reign for decades.

> **Fuhgeddaboudit**
>
> Sam the Plumber DeCavalcante demonstrated some great footwork as he juggled his wife, his lover secretary, and assorted other paramours while running his Mafia empire. Unfortunately for Sam, his extramarital shenanigans were caught on FBI tapes and presented to the world. Ouch!

This family took on the name DeCavalcante because of a unique set of circumstances seven years later. Sam was tangled up in a court case. His lawyer tried to outsmart the prosecution; the results were disastrous. He had heard rumors that the FBI had illegally bugged Sam's office. He demanded that prosecutors turn over to him any and all transcripts of any electronic surveillance involving DeCavalcante. Lawyer S. M. Franzblau assumed that if they were indeed illegally bugging, the government would try to save face by dropping the charges against Sam instead of revealing its illegal actions. To the shock of the lawyer and DeCavalcante, the government publicly filed thousands of pages of FBI summaries of the bugged conversations in Sam's office. The transcripts were a smash hit for the New York/New Jersey media and were the basis of two books: *Sam the Plumber* (1970) by Henry Zeigler and *The Mafia Talks* (1969) by Joseph Volz and Peter Bridge. Another consequence was that the Newark-based family took on DeCavalcante's name.

In the early 1980s, DeCavalcante moved to Florida, leaving capo John Riggi as acting boss. Riggi continued the legacy of gambling, loan sharking, and labor racketeering. His labor rackets were greatly aided by the fact that, in 1965, DeCavalcante had promoted Riggi to capo and placed him as Business Manager of Local 394 of the Laborers

Union. Riggi's father had held the vital union position earlier. Riggi held on to the union job until 1987, when he stepped up to District Council 30 of the same union. Riggi filled many of the various jobs at the local with his sons and other relatives and friends, which increased his influence and his earnings.

By 1990, Riggi was behind bars, creating much turmoil within the family as members maneuvered for power. Capo Larasso, the former underboss who was at Apalachin, and Riggi's acting boss John D'Amato, were both killed as the family began to behave like *The Sopranos*, the fictional New Jersey family that would capture the attention of television audiences in the United States and abroad during the new millennium. In Chapter 31, I detail the prosecution of virtually the entire family, including Riggi, who at age 78, earned the unenviable distinction of being the oldest Mafia boss to plead guilty to racketeering charges.

New Jersey mobsters rubbed out former acting boss John D'Amato and disposed of his body at a secret mob grave-yard.

(Photo courtesy of GangLandNews.com)

The New England Family

Formed around 1900, this family has had two centers of power: Providence, Rhode Island, and Boston. Like most families, bootlegging provided a steady income for the New England family during the Prohibition era. In 1933, the family expanded its gambling operations and came to dominate that racket in both growing urban areas.

Phil Buccola took over as boss shortly after the Commission was formed. He held this position until he retired in 1954.

Raymond Patriarca of Providence succeeded Buccola as family boss. He proved to be a good choice. The veteran mobster was already respected, and with his new power and intimidating presence, Patriarca tightened his mob's grip on gambling. To achieve this, he teamed up with the Angiulo brothers in Boston who proved to be masters at organizing that racket.

Unfortunately for Patriarca, his reign would be plagued by turmoil. He was illegally bugged by the FBI from 1962 to 1965 and was identified as boss of the family by Joe Valachi in 1963. Four years later, the FBI released transcripts of Patriarca's conversations that ended up in a *Life* magazine profile. In 1968, he was convicted of gambling. From 1970 to 1974, he did time in state prison for a murder conspiracy conviction. For the next six years, Patriarca maintained a firm grip on his family. In December of 1980 and again in March of 1981, he was arrested on murder charges. The murder cases were quickly followed by labor-racketeering charges in Miami. For the next few years, grooming his son Raymond Jr. to take over the reins while expanding his rackets to Miami, he fought off both the authorities and failing health until his death on July 11, 1984.

Slammer Time

Joe Salvati spent 30 years in prison for a crime he had nothing to do with. In 1965, mob informant Joseph Barboza fingered Salvati as a participant in the murder of Boston's Teddy Deegan. Recently released FBI documents from that era reveal that confidential informants had told FBI agents that others had whacked Deegan. This information was never told to the defense or the prosecution during Salvati's trial. On May 3, 2001, after conceding that Salvati was framed, retired FBI agent H. Paul Rico snarled, "What do you want, tears?"

Until the mid-1990s, the prevailing wisdom credited excellent work by FBI agents for all the difficulties Patriarca suffered. They turned violent mob associate Joe Barboza into a successful murder witness against Patriarca and a number of his men. In 1999, however, the bubble burst on decades of abuse of the legal process by a number of heralded FBI agents who had manipulated Barboza's testimony and most likely were aware that they sent a man to prison for a crime he didn't commit.

In 1981, the FBI took out Patriarca's underboss, Gennaro "Jerry" Angiulo. They bugged his office, overheard him admitting numerous crimes, and made a federal racketeering case against him, for which he ultimately received a 45-year sentence. On top of that, Angiulo was found guilty of murder charges and was finished as a mob power.

Ray Patriarca Jr. received the blessing of the Commission and took over the family after his father's death, but the family's unity was gone. Capo Joseph "JR" Russo and the Boston faction that replaced Angiulo and consigliere Larry Zannino (who was also convicted of racketeering) were very suspicious of underboss Billy "Wild Guy" Grasso and Boston soldier Frank "Cadillac Frank" Salemme. Russo feared that Salemme, backed by Grasso, would move in on the rackets of a Russo cohort who was immersed in legal problems. Russo feared that this was only the first move in an effort to push Russo and his friends out.

The Russo faction staged a coup, killing underboss Grasso but only wounding Salemme. Patriarca Jr., despite urgings by his top aides, did not fight back. New York's John Gotti, who was flexing his muscles as a member of the Mafia Commission, prevailed on Russo and Patriarca to reach a peaceful solution. Neither Russo nor Patriarca Jr. could afford to ignore Gotti's warning, and ultimately an uneasy truce was reached.

Russo was appointed consigliere and was given control of the Boston area rackets of the New England family. Looking to expand his clout, Russo moved to induct four new soldiers. Unbeknownst to Russo and Patriarca, mobster informer Sonny Mercurio told the FBI about the induction ceremony. They taped it, leading to convictions of many New England gangsters, including Patriarca Jr., Nicholas Bianco, Russo, and many others.

> ### Fuhgeddaboudit
>
> On October 29, 1989, the hierarchy of New England's La Cosa Nostra family inducted four new members in a basement ceremony at a private home in Medford, Massachusetts, a suburb of Boston. As capo Vincent "The Animal" Ferrara, a Boston College grad with a way with words, was leaving, he said that only the ghost knew what took place that day. It wasn't too much later, however, that everyone knew what the ghost knew—the FBI had bugged the basement and tape-recorded the ceremony.

Nicky Bianco took over as New England boss for a brief period, but he, too, went down under the federal government legal avalanche. He was jailed on December 28, 1991, and died on December 14, 1994.

Frank Salemme recovered from his wounds and took over. He was about the only one still standing after Bianco. The FBI wasted no time in charging him with racketeering, to which Salemme responded by fleeing the state. Captured in 1995 in West Palm Beach, Florida, he pleaded guilty to racketeering charges and was sentenced to 11 years and 4 months in jail. He was released early, in 2003, when, after a truly remarkable period of intrigue and outrage about decades of misdeeds by Boston-area FBI agents, he cooperated with authorities. The episode is detailed in Chapter 32.

The Philadelphia Family

Salvatore Sabella is the first known leader of the Philadelphia family that has been active in Philadelphia and South Jersey since the early 1900s. His reign began around 1920. Sabella oversaw the family's protection, bootlegging, and other rackets, as well as numerous personal businesses, including an oil and cheese store, a candy store, and a café. On May 31, 1927, Sabella and five other Philadelphia wiseguys, including two who would follow Sabella to the top of the family, were arrested for a double murder of two rival hoods on a South Philadelphia street. All would ultimately beat the case.

Sabella moved to New York City around 1930 and, like many area gangsters, was involved in the famous Castellammarese War that is discussed in Chapter 22. In 1931, he was arrested for assault, pleaded guilty, was placed on probation, and stepped down as family boss.

Sabella was replaced by protégé John Avena, who was walking with Sabella when they allegedly shot the two South Philly hoods in 1927. Avena, who ran major bookmaking operations with Jewish gangsters, ran the family rackets for five peaceful years under the aegis of the new Mafia Commission. The tranquility ended in a blaze of gunfire on August 17, 1936, when Avena was shot to death on a Philadelphia street corner by rival gangsters.

Next came Joseph Bruno, who increased the family's gambling activities and enjoyed Commission support until he died of heart disease in a New York hospital on October 22, 1946. Joe Ida, who was allegedly part of the hit team with Sabella and Avena in 1927, replaced Bruno, but Ida was a reluctant boss. He attended the Apalachin conference, became unnerved by the publicity, and retired, returning to Italy.

Mafia Speak

On February 23, 1963, an illegal bug in the home of Genovese mobster Ray DeCarlo caught him and New Jersey boss Simone "Sam the Plumber" DeCavalcante discussing Joseph Ida.

"He used to stay home under the grapevine and read a book," said DeCarlo. "He must love it in Italy 'cause all he ever did in New Brunswick until they made him the boss was read books. He never went no place until they made him the boss. And then he didn't want to go to them meetings at all. He was a quiet man. His pleasure was in reading books. Now in Italy, he must feel right at home."

"He goes back and forth all the time," said DeCavalcante.

Capo Angelo Bruno, no relation to Joe Bruno, took over as leader in 1959 and headed the family for 21 years—what are considered the golden years of the Philadelphia family. Violence was kept to a minimum, and the family was viewed for the most part as harmless gamblers. The family's loan-sharking, extortion, protection rackets, and labor-racketeering scams were carried out with little public awareness. Bruno was personally involved in the lucrative vending machine business, aided by not-too-subtle threats of storeowners who even considered not allowing them in their shops.

In 1970, Bruno refused to testify before the New Jersey State Commission of Investigation and spent nearly three years behind bars. He was released when he developed a bleeding ulcer and then split for Italy when it cleared up. He returned in 1977, ready to face more legal pressure, but not the kind he ultimately got from within.

Big Shot

Nicky Scarfo Jr. wanted to follow in the Mafia footsteps of his gangster father. On Halloween night of 1989, he must have had second thoughts as a hit man pumped anywhere from 7 to 11 shots into him, depending on how many holes were made by the same bullets. He survived, and those second thoughts disappeared.

Much of Bruno's strength came from his close, personal friendship with Carlo Gambino, the powerful New York City Mafia boss. When Gambino died in 1976, Bruno appeared weak to his ambitious consigliere, Anthony "Tony Bananas" Caponigro, who after years of plotting, carried out a coup against Bruno on March 21, 1980, by having him blown away while sitting in a car outside his home. This murder was obviously disastrous for Bruno, but it was the same story for Caponigro and some of his allies.

Caponigro and underboss Philip Testa were summoned to New York by the Commission. It's not certain whether Caponigro wrongly believed he had Commission permission to kill Bruno, whether he pretended to his allies that he believed this, or whether he simply denied having anything to do with the killing. The Commission never announced what Testa said, but it's pretty clear whose account they favored. The Commission backed Testa as boss. Caponigro was tortured and killed, and over the next few months, his allies were whacked one by one.

Mafia Speak

When the mutilated body of Anthony "Tony Bananas" Caponigro was discovered in the trunk of a car, ripped $20 bills were stuffed in his mouth and rectum as a sign of disrespect, a message to other would-be boss killers.

Following Bruno's murder, Testa set out to rejuvenate the family. In the summer of 1980, Testa inducted nine new members, including his son Salvatore. In an attempt to unify the family, he also brought in 66-year-old Anthony Casella and promoted Anthony's brother Peter Casella as underboss. But Peter Casella, a heroin dealer who had spent 17 years in prison for a federal narcotics conviction and felt he was in line to be boss, wasn't happy. Casella had missed out on making millions while in prison, and he was anxious to cash in—now!

Casella and capo Frank Narducci had Testa murdered less than a year after he took over. Chicken Man Testa was blown up on the front porch of his home. It was a stunning development considering what had happened to Caponigro and his friends. Once again, the plot didn't work. The Commission stepped in, determined that Peter Casella and Frank Narducci had killed Testa, and supported consigliere Nicky Scarfo as boss. Casella fled to Florida, where he died of natural causes in October of 1983. Narducci was gunned down by Phil Testa's son Salvatore and mobster Joseph Pungitore on January 7, 1982.

The Nicky Scarfo reign as boss of the Philadelphia family set the stage for its decimation. Scarfo was an activist boss who wanted to exert his power everywhere. Scarfo ordered his men to extract tribute from everyone conducting illegal activities in Philadelphia. Gamblers, drug dealers, hijackers, and anyone else they could find were muscled. He inducted more than 30 new members, nearly a 50-percent turnover in personnel. Many of the new members were young, hot headed, and of questionable intelligence. Paranoia grew rapidly as member turned on member when they saw opportunities to move up the ladder. Scarfo unnerved everyone. He demoted his hard-drinking underboss, broke capos to soldiers, and had members shot for scant reason. Eventually, the chaos collapsed on itself. Several key mobsters became government witnesses, and Scarfo and many of his men were found guilty of numerous charges in a massive racketeering case. Scarfo was given 55 years in May of 1989. This sentence was in addition to the 14 years he received earlier for an extortion conviction.

Big Shot

Nicky Scarfo selected Frank Monte as his first consigliere. His honor and glory were short-lived, however. On May 13, 1982, Monte was whacked by bookie Joseph Pedulla. Monte's mistake was forgetting that brotherly love could be greater than the Mafia blood oath. Ordered by Scarfo to eliminate capo Harry "The Hunchback" Riccobene, Monte reached out to Riccobene's brother Mario. Mario told Harry, Harry called his bookie, and Monte was shot to death in the City of Brotherly Love.

For a short time, Scarfo's consigliere Anthony "Tony Buck" Piccolo tried to carry on as acting boss, but it obviously wasn't working. With the backing of John Gotti, the New York City Gambino boss, John Stanfa became the new official boss. This was a surprise. Stanfa was driving the car in which Angelo Bruno had been killed back in 1980. He was obviously involved, but he had escaped punishment because he wasn't a major player, and he had important friends.

Stanfa's reign would be just as chaotic as Scarfo's. Many young Philadelphia hoods, some of whose fathers were members, rejected Stanfa's right to leadership. He tried to accommodate them by inducting some and appointing others to leadership positions, but tensions continued to escalate. Stanfa was angered at being ignored, and the young kids were recklessly optimistic. A number of murder plots were carried out, some successfully. Eventually, FBI bugging and the testimony of mobsters destroyed Stanfa. By 1994, he was behind bars for life.

Next up was veteran mobster Ralph Natale. He was a long-time labor racketeer but had taken a big fall—17 years—for heroin trafficking. This long stretch in prison saved him from the killings of the Scarfo/Stanfa years, and he was unopposed as the new leader. Natale immediately appointed Joseph "Skinny Joey" Merlino as his under-boss. Merlino was the son of Salvatore Merlino, who had been Nicky Scarfo's first underboss and who had been demoted by Scarfo. Young Merlino was a flashy mobster who captured the attention of the Philadelphia press. When Natale began having parole problems and was returned to jail, Merlino was in the news on an even more regular basis. As always, Mafia guys who bring attention to themselves become targets of every law enforcement agency and prosecutor in the area.

Merlino was stung in 1999 by a capo who had secretly become an FBI informer. He was indicted on murder and racketeering charges. In July 2001, Merlino was acquitted of all the serious crimes in the indictment, including murder and drug dealing, but convicted of gambling and extortion charges. Still, he was sentenced to 14 years in federal prison. He is due out in 2011.

The Pittsburgh Family

Stefano Monastero, who ran several bootleg-supply houses on the north side of town, is the earliest boss of the Pittsburgh family whose identity is known. Like many Mafia bosses of the 1920s, Monastero went out in a blaze of glory but not before he survived several rubout attempts. He was killed outside the Allegheny Hospital on August 4, 1929. His successor, Giuseppe "Joseph" Siragusa, didn't fare much better. Assassins blew him away in his home in the Squirrel Hill section of Pittsburgh on September 13, 1931. An ally of Salvatore Maranzano, Siragusa's killing contributed mightily to the mythical Mafia purge of 40 so-called "moustache Petes," a myth that will be examined in Chapter 22.

John Bazzano followed Siragusa. He was Sicilian but attempted to bring Calabrians and Neopolitans into the family. One overt move in this direction was a partnership with some of the eight Volpe brothers, Calabrians who had a strong base in nearby Wilmerding. The Bazzano/Volpe alliance was headquartered at Bazzano's Roma Coffee Shop.

By 1932, however, tensions rose when the Volpes tried to expand their operations. On July 29, 1932, Bazzano tried to end their ambitions with an ambush at the Roma Coffee Shop. His shooters stormed in, leaving John Volpe dead on the sidewalk outside the front door. Then they blasted Arthur and James Volpe and beat a retreat. It was a brazen act, and few didn't know who was behind it.

Fuhgeddaboudit

Joe Bonanno and others have written about how La Cosa Nostra has deteriorated from its honorable roots. This lamented past included the murder of two bosses in their own homes: Pittsburgh's Joe Siragusa and Detroit's Caesar "Chester" LaMare, who was shot in the back of the head as he entertained two of his men—Joseph Amico and Elmer Macklin. They were acquitted at trial. A sniper must have done it.

Brothers Louis and Joseph Volpe traveled to New York and used their strong connections to lodge a complaint with the Commission. Obviously, they were persuasive because in early August, Bazzano was called to New York to answer the charges. Instead of denying them, he tried to beat the case with a technicality, stating that the Commission didn't have jurisdiction over internal family matters. That didn't go over too well with the Commission. Bazzano never got back to Pittsburgh. His body was found in Brooklyn on August 8, 1932, sewn up in a burlap sack, with 22 stab wounds. He was strangled and his tongue had been cut out.

The next two bosses, Vincent Capizzi, who ruled until about 1937, and Frank Amato, who gave it up in 1956, resigned because of health problems. Little is known about Capizzi, but Amato expanded the family's influence beyond Allegheny County, concentrating mostly on gambling. He stepped down to underboss due to kidney problems. He died in 1973.

John LaRocca succeeded Amato and ruled for nearly 30 years. He devoted considerable energy to the family's bootlegging rackets during the Prohibition era and made a big impact in the family's extensive gambling and loan-sharking operations. LaRocca had politicians, police officers, and other authorities on his payroll. He also had a firm grip on union matters in the region through control of Local 1058 of the Laborers Union. This infiltration wouldn't be shaken until the twenty-first century. LaRocca attended the famous 1957 Apalachin meeting of Mafia leaders. His participation made him a target of a secret FBI intelligence-gathering operation.

Veteran mobster Michael Genovese replaced LaRocca in 1984. The family flexed its muscles and took over gambling interests in Mahoning Valley from the Cleveland family. Overall, however, the family lost membership and power under Genovese because some troops grew old and died; and many others, such as underboss Charles Porter and capo Louis Raucci, were convicted of drug trafficking and sent away for long prison sentences. Porter eventually became a secret informer from behind bars. Capo Lenny Strollo also cooperated, detailing murders and other violence the family used in the Mahoning Valley. Despite all the convictions and informers, Genovese remains free and is still considered the boss as the new century unfolds. However, the latest intelligence has the family on its last legs.

The Rochester Group

For more than 40 years, Rochester was considered a part of the Buffalo family led by Stefano Magaddino. By the late 1960s, however, as Magaddino's hold on his crews began to fade, the family split into a number of factions, and Rochester, long led by brothers Frank and Costenze "Stanley" Valenti, broke away.

By 1970, the Rochester/Valenti group was being referred to by the traditional labels associated with an independent family, although there is no evidence that the Commission approved the formation of a new family. Technicalities aside, the power and influence of mobsters in Rochester, as well as the blood they spilled during a mob war, was real. At least nine killings were connected to a bloody war that raged from 1970 to 1983.

In 1972, a key Valenti capo, William "Billy" Lupo, was killed, and Frank Valenti was nabbed for labor racketeering. Samuel "Red" Russotti took over the top spot, but his reign was a roller-coaster ride that crashed and burned by the end of the decade.

Russotti and five key underlings were convicted of murder in late 1976 and were sentenced to 25 years to life. While jailed, Russotti and his men won a reversal of their convictions when their lawyers showed that the sheriff's office had fabricated evidence against them. They were back in action by January of 1978.

> **Fuhgeddaboudit**
>
> Francesco "Frank" Frassetto served 17 years for taking part in numerous bombings in the Rochester wars. He was released in 1997. Three years later, however, he was again in trouble, charged with attempting to sell a kilo of heroin.

Thomas Didio, however, who had been appointed acting boss when Russotti was sent to prison, kind of liked the idea of acting like a boss and decided to try to hang on to the position, much like New York's Colombo family's acting boss Vic Orena would a decade later. Russotti began an all-out effort to reclaim the family. Six months later, Didio, who had turned to the Valenti faction for help, was blown away in a motel in Victor, New York. Bombings and shootings shocked the city as the two factions fought for control. In 1980, many Russotti and Valenti loyalists were arrested, convicted, and sentenced to long prison terms.

With so many Russotti/Valenti faction members jailed, remnants of the old Didio wing and new insurgents banded together to try to oust Russotti again. He beat back the insurrection, again littering the streets of Rochester with bodies. As often occurs, surviving members of the losing faction began talking to authorities, filling in the details of the violence and the reasons behind it.

In 1984, boss Samuel "Red" Russotti, underboss Richard Marino, consigliere Rene Piccaretto, and capos Joe Rossi and Thomas Marotta were convicted on racketeering charges and given long prison terms. Piccaretto's son Loren moved up to underboss, with Angelo Joseph Amico serving as acting boss. After a short run, they were also convicted by the feds in 1988 and 1989, effectively reducing the family's clout and influence to that of a street gang. The result was likely an inevitable one brought on by the federal onslaught against the mob, but it was probably hastened by the violence of its members against each other.

The Least You Need to Know

- The Buffalo family had the same boss for more than 50 years.

- The Philadelphia family boss sat on the Commission for 19 years.

- Continuous FBI pressure has decimated the leadership of the Newark family.

- The New England family has been virtually destroyed by successful prosecutions.

- The Pittston-based Mafia family is barely alive.

- The Pittsburgh family has been in a steep decline for 20 years.

- Internal discord destroyed the fledgling Rochester family.

Chapter 6

From the Windy City to the City of Angels

In This Chapter

- ◆ Chicago's domination by the Outfit
- ◆ Mile-high Mafia in Colorado
- ◆ Missouri gambles twice with the Mafia
- ◆ Having a beer with the Milwaukee Mafia
- ◆ Going fishing for the San Francisco Mafia
- ◆ Making cheese with the San Jose Mafia
- ◆ Mafia clowns surf Los Angeles

In this chapter, I'll discuss how Al Capone used New York mob connections to rise out of a melting pot of Italian gangsters who had emigrated to Chicago from Naples, Calabria, and Sicily and became the most feared Mafia boss of his generation. I'll also talk about his fall from power and the powerful mobsters who succeeded him as leaders of the powerful Chicago Outfit.

Along the way, I'll also take you to six cities west of the Mississippi whose crime families the Chicago Outfit represented as a charter member of the Mafia's Commission that was formed in 1931.

Gunning for Control over the Windy City

Chicago's first main Italian criminal leader was James "Big Jim" Colosimo, who emigrated from the Italian province of Calabria in 1894. He organized the city's street sweepers and created a political power base for himself in the notoriously corrupt First Ward, the most important area of the city. It had a wide-open, red-light district that was the foundation of the Colosimo empire, which also included saloons and gambling. He opened a high-class restaurant that featured top entertainment, and it became the "in" place to be for both gangsters and high society.

Chicago was also home to Sicilian gangsters. As in New York, these groups were initially formed around blood families and friends from their homeland. The most powerful of the Sicilians were the six Genna brothers. They ran gambling operations, saloons, and an importing firm. In an ongoing attempt to win more political power in the Nineteenth Ward, the Gennas backed Anthony D'Andrea for alderman. He already had considerable political clout because he was president of the Chicago chapter of the Unione Siciliana. This was an honest fraternal organization formed to help new Sicilian immigrants, but it had gradually been taken over by mobsters. It became a powerful instrument to control crime in the Sicilian areas of Chicago and other large cities.

> **Big Shot**
>
> Politics in Chicago has always been a serious business. After Anthony D'Andrea failed to unseat the Nineteenth Ward incumbent for the third consecutive time, his followers gunned down some key supporters of his main opposition. Unfortunately for D'Andrea, the opposition knew where to get guns, too. As he arrived home late on the evening of May 11, 1921, two shotgun blasts ended his presidency of the Unione Siciliana, his political career, and his life.

D'Andrea was executed, and the Gennas lost their quest for an elected official in their control. Despite this setback, the Genna brothers continued to prosper. They organized the home production of liquor and became serious competitors of an Irish-American gang led by Dion O'Banion. The two groups hijacked each other's trucks and used violence to move their products. Both had political support that protected them from most police actions, but in 1925, the O'Banions killed brothers Angelo and Antonio Genna, and the police killed a third, Michael "Mike the Devil" Genna. The three others fled the city.

By this time, Colosimo's organization had been taken over by an ambitious underling, his nephew John Torrio, who orchestrated the murder of Big Jim in his own restaurant on May 11, 1920. Torrio had come to Chicago from New York, and he organized and expanded his uncle's interests. Big Jim became comfortable, however, and when he decided against the lucrative liquor-distribution opportunities posed by Prohibition, Torrio killed him. Torrio tried to forge working relationships with other bootleg gangs, but double-dealings and violence ruled. In 1924, for example, O'Banion sold his share in an illegal brewery to Torrio and then tipped off the cops, who raided the place, costing Torrio a bundle of cash. Six months later, on November 10, 1924, O'Banion was gunned down in his flower shop. Two months later, O'Banion's gang ambushed Torrio, who survived but decided to get out of town. He left the organization under the control of a young Al Capone.

Mafia Speak

Naples, Italy, was home to the Camorra crime families. Because Torrio, Capone, and other leaders in the Chicago Outfit were of Neapolitan background, the Outfit wasn't accepted by the Sicilian Cosa Nostra world until 1931.

One early step Capone made was to push his Sicilian *paesano* Antonio Lombardo as the new president of the Chicago chapter of the Unione Siciliana. Because Capone was Neapolitan, he was ineligible for membership in the Sicilian society. His support of Lombardo angered Joseph Aiello, head of his own Mafia family and a former ally of the Genna brothers. To meet the Capone challenge, Aiello teamed up with the O'Banions. He succeeded in killing Lombardo and his successor, Pasquale Lolordo, and became president of the Unione Siciliana's Chicago chapter. But he never got Capone.

Aiello had strong allies in Gaspar Milazzo and Stefano Magaddino, bosses of the families in Detroit and Buffalo, respectively. With this backing, a meeting was arranged with Joe Masseria, the New York leader. Aiello asked for Masseria's support against Capone. This didn't go over well, and the two bosses parted on bad terms. According to Joe Bonanno, this was a key incident in the start of the Castellammarese War, which is discussed in detail in Chapter 22. When a key Masseria strategist, underboss Peter "The Clutch Hand" Morello, was killed in August of 1930, Masseria needed a closer alliance with Chicago's Capone. Consequently, Masseria recognized Capone as the boss of his own family within the sphere of La Cosa Nostra. It was a no brainer, considering Capone's strength.

Capone had ended the threat of the O'Banions by massacring seven members and associates on Valentine's Day of 1929. On October 23, 1930, he overpowered the last Sicilian resistance to his reign when Joe Aiello was ambushed and killed. After Joe Masseria, his New York ally, was shot to death in April of 1931, Capone hosted a gathering of La Cosa Nostra leaders. At this function, Salvatore Maranzano formally accepted Capone by introducing him as boss of the sole Chicago family. There was little else Maranzano could do, of course. Capone was one of the most powerful mob bosses, with or without Maranzano's blessing. The introduction sent a signal to those who were thinking of opposing Capone that they weren't going to find any allies among the Maranzano followers. A few months later, when Maranzano was killed, Capone agreed to become a member of the new La Cosa Nostra Commission.

Capone, however, would have a short run. After numerous complaints about Capone and crime in Chicago, the federal government instituted a full-court press against him and his organization. Eliot Ness, made famous by *The Untouchables* television show of the 1950s and the 1987 movie starring Kevin Costner as Ness and Robert DeNiro as Capone, played a key role in attacking Capone's beer supplies. This tremendous loss of income hurt his ability to pay off police and politicians. The IRS finished off Capone. In the fall of 1931, he was found guilty of income tax violations and was sentenced to 11 years. He was in prison until November 1939, when he was released due to deteriorating mental health. He died on January 25, 1947.

> **Fuhgeddaboudit**
>
> After Capone's deadly rival Hymie Weiss was killed, Capone held a press conference and said, "I'm sorry Hymie was killed, but I didn't have anything to do with it." Right, Al!

Frank "The Enforcer" Nitti, a long-time member of the Capone organization, replaced Capone. Gambling and labor racketeering became the main source of revenue of the Chicago Outfit as the glory days of Prohibition ended in 1933. Unfortunately for Nitti, a very lucrative scheme to extort money from major motion picture studios fell apart and led to indictments of him and other Chicago leaders. On March 19, 1943, Nitti killed himself, despondent at the prospect of going to jail and frightened and embarrassed by the way other gangsters would react to his handling of the extortion fiasco.

Chicago Outfit boss Al Capone said he was a businessman. "My rackets are run along strict American lines."

(Photo courtesy of GangLandNews.com)

Nitti might have been only a front boss during the last years of his reign, with underboss Paul "The Waiter" Ricca being the real power. In any event, Ricca became the formal leader after Nitti's suicide. Ricca served three years for the movie studio scheme but remained in firm control, using Anthony "Big Tuna" Accardo to carry orders to his men from the federal prison in Leavenworth, Kansas. Some say that Accardo was the real boss and only consulted with Ricca, but it really didn't matter who was No. 1 and who was No. 2. The gangsters were the closest of friends, and until Ricca died, they ran the Chicago Outfit.

Under Accardo, the Outfit was heavily involved in labor racketeering, gambling, loan sharking, and assorted extortion rackets. Drug dealing was not sanctioned. Accardo, unlike many Mafia leaders throughout history, was serious about this rule.

> **Slammer Time**
>
> Paul Ricca was sentenced to 10 years in prison for an elaborate extortion attempt involving the major film studios in Hollywood. Despite a long criminal record and a reputation for violence, he and the other major Chicago powers convicted with him were paroled after three years. Nothing untoward was ever proved, but rumors of payoffs to important national figures continue to this day.

In 1957, Accardo stepped aside for Momo Salvatore Giancana, who used the name Sam "Mooney" Giancana. The change in leadership proved to be a lucky break for Accardo and a big mistake for Giancana. The discovery of the 1957 Mafia conclave at Apalachin, New York (which is discussed in Chapter 14), prodded the FBI into a major effort against organized crime. Politicians and news organizations were clamoring to know who these men were, and the FBI didn't know. This infuriated FBI director J. Edgar Hoover. He instituted the Top Hoodlum program, which was designed to identify the top 10 hoods in each major city. To achieve this goal, the FBI installed secret, illegal bugs at meeting places where Giancana met to talk strategy with his top gangsters.

The FBI often learned many of Giancana's future moves even before his men did. The G-Men harassed him constantly—at his home, at his so-called offices, and even on the golf course, where FBI agents would often tee up after him and lob drives into his group. They drove him nuts. He went to a friendly judge and got an injunction that kept the agents a block away from his home and office and a foursome behind him on the golf course. In one bugged conversation, Giancana's underboss Frank "Strongy" Ferrara was heard complaining, "I tell you, those guys are driving him goofy. He's not making the right decisions."

In 1963, after informer Joe Valachi made his big splash, media interest in the Mafia skyrocketed. Giancana was right in the middle. The FBI fed dirt about Giancana to news organizations, and Giancana added to the frenzy by dating Phyllis McGuire, a member of the McGuire Sisters, a top female singing group of the era. Finally, in June of 1965, when he refused to testify before a grand jury after receiving immunity, he was jailed. When he was released a year later, Accardo ordered him to retire. Giancana moved to Mexico until 1974, when he was expelled. Aging and in poor health, Giancana returned to Chicago, an unhappy and beaten man. He became expendable. His former friends thought he might begin talking to the authorities, so on June 18, 1975, Giancana was shot to death in the basement of his Oak Park home by one of his closest friends, most likely Dominic "Butch" Blasi.

During the first few years of Giancana's forced exile, mobsters Sam Battaglia, Phil Alderisio, and John "Jackie" Cerone served as bosses of the Chicago Outfit. Each was convicted and sent to prison. Finally, in 1971, some stability was achieved when Accardo selected Joseph Aiuppa to be the front boss. The Outfit continued its involvement in gambling, extortion, loan sharking, and labor racketeering that was fueled by political corruption. The Family's connections to the Teamsters Union, arguably its biggest source of power and influence, led to the downfall; Aiuppa, Cerone, and several others were convicted and sent to prison. This will be further detailed in Chapter 12. Aiuppa and Cerone were released 10 years later and died soon after.

The next front boss was Joseph Ferriola. He was a strong leader who had the respect of his men, but he died of cancer in 1989. Samuel "Wings" Carlisi took over, but by this time, the real power of the Chicago Outfit, Anthony Accardo, was in failing health. His participation had decreased dramatically, and he died on May 27, 1992. Many say that Accardo was the all-time, most powerful La Cosa Nostra boss. Four years after Accardo's death, Carlisi was convicted and jailed. He died early in 1997. Carlisi aide John DiFronzo was convicted in the same case but won an appeal and was released. He became the formal boss, although some experts said Joseph "Joey the Clown" Lombardo was the real power in the late 1990s.

> **Mafia Speak**
>
> The Chicago Outfit also oversaw the affairs of the small families in Madison, Wisconsin; Rockford, Illinois; and Springfield, Illinois. Some say the groups were never independent families, but factions of the Chicago Outfit. Whatever they once were, they are all now defunct.

In November 2003, Windy City wiseguy James "Little Jimmy" Marcello, who was convicted of racketeering with Carlisi in 1996, was released from prison, and at age 60, the veteran but relatively youthful gangster was viewed as the Outfit's main man. But the FBI, which had kept its ears tuned to his conversations on prison telephones, quickly put him on notice. In early 2004, as part of a racketeering investigation designed to send him back to prison, they raided a business he controlled.

Like other big-city La Cosa Nostra families, the Chicago Outfit has been hurt tremendously by the FBI's major effort against the Mafia. The Outfit's control over corrupt union officials in the International Brotherhood of Teamsters Locals and the International Laborers Union of America has been substantially reduced, as have skimming opportunities at Las Vegas casinos. Nevertheless, the Outfit remains a powerful organization. Despite its legal setbacks, the Chicago Outfit remains a serious concern of law enforcement.

Putting Denver on the Mafia Map

The public first became aware of a Denver Mafia connection when James "Black Jim" Colletti was detained at Apalachin, New York, in 1957. Colletti was one of the many mobsters who panicked and tried to escape on foot after spotting troopers outside Joe Barbara's Apalachin estate, and he was found walking down a side road. From then on, Colletti's facade as a legitimate businessman was over.

Investigators quickly learned that Colletti was in the cheese business with Joe Bonanno, the powerful New York boss and charter member of the Mafia Commission. They also learned that he had stayed at a Newark, New Jersey, hotel controlled by Bonanno for three days prior to the Apalachin fiasco. For a time, Colletti was wrongly believed to be a member of the Bonanno family. Colletti, however, was the leader of a small, independent La Cosa Nostra family, which, like New England, had two seats of power: Denver and Pueblo, Colorado.

The origins of the family go back to the start of Prohibition in 1920 and probably a few years before that, perhaps to the turn of the century.

Like most Mafia families, the Colorado groups were very active in bootlegging during the Prohibition era. They had the turf wars and body counts to prove it. In a battle between Pueblo-based Peter Carlino and Denver's Giuseppe "Joe" Roma, Carlino and a brother were gunned down, and it appeared that Roma was secure as the top man in Denver. He had moved there from New York City and spent three years in jail, starting in 1925, for alcohol and drug violations. Upon his release, he moved to the top, probably killing the Carlino brothers on the way. However, he was killed on February 18, 1933.

Slammer Time

The major bootlegger of Pueblo, Colorado, Peter Carlino, was jailed for arson in 1931. His chief rival, Denver's Joe Roma, put up the bond to free Carlino. Whether this was a peaceful interlude in their violent conflict or a ploy to get Carlino loose so that he could be killed has been debated for decades. It's safe to say that Carlino couldn't have done any worse if he had stayed in jail. He was killed shortly after being released.

Despite the notoriety and adverse publicity surrounding the Apalachin meeting, Colletti, with help from his brother, Vincenzo, led the Colorado family for a dozen more years, stepping down in 1969. Joseph "Scotty" Spinuzzi took over until his death on September 6, 1975. Eugene Smaldone then replaced Spinuzzi.

Eugene, Clarence, and Clyde Smaldone were part of the Colorado family's liquor-distribution business during the Prohibition days. Known as Checkers, Chauncey, and Flip Flop, respectively, the brothers later turned their skills to gambling and loan sharking, rackets that became their staples for decades. They also tried to maintain a veneer of respectability and operated an Italian restaurant in Denver. After more than half a century of plunder, the Smaldones were snared by the federal government's onslaught against the Mafia that began in earnest in the late 1970s. On December 6, 1982, boss Eugene Smaldone, underboss Clarence Smaldone, and consigliere Paul Villano were convicted of extortion, tax evasion, and other charges. Eugene died in 1992, and for all intents and purposes, Colorado's La Cosa Nostra family died with him.

Making History in Kansas City

John Lazia, a dapper, darkly handsome nightclub owner, is the first known boss of the Kansas City family, which, like all of the American Mafia clans, began forming around the turn of the twentieth century. The gangster, who changed his surname from Lazzio, controlled soft drink concessions, operated a dog track, and during the booming days of Prohibition, was appointed leader of the North Side Democratic Club.

Like other Mafia leaders during the Prohibition era, Lazia had important connections to politicians, the police, and the judiciary. So complete was his control that, if you called the police, there was a 50-50 chance John Lazia would answer the phone. Lazia went one better than most others in the political arena as well: He could deliver votes. Machine politics was alive and kicking in that western Missouri city, and Lazia played the game well.

From his headquarters at the Democratic Club in the First Ward, he ran his gambling, loan-sharking, and bootlegging businesses with an iron hand. He went too far, according-ing to the prevailing wisdom, when he engineered the Union Station massacre on June 17, 1933, an incident in which four lawmen were gunned down while transporting a hood to another jurisdiction. The slaughter helped destroy Lazia's political connections. His legal problems mounted. He was arrested on tax charges, was released on bail, and on July 10, 1934, was machine-gunned to death as he stepped out of his car. No one was ever charged with his murder.

> **Big Shot**
>
> When Johnny Lazia, Kansas City's top gangster/politician, was gunned down by machine gun in the summer of 1934, he was with his wife. Luckily, she wasn't hit. This is the old, so-called "honorable" era of La Cosa Nostra that many have lamented.

The man who was driving Lazia's car on the night of his killing, Charles Carrollo, took over Lazia's rackets. For the short term, he appeared to have inherited the politi-cal mantel as well. However, Carrollo went the way of Al Capone, being convicted of income tax evasion in October of 1939. He was deported in 1954.

Another gangster/politician, Charles Binaggio, was the next leader. Like his predeces-sors, Binaggio knew the importance of political connections, and he concentrated on protecting and improving them through the Democratic Club. Unfortunately for Binaggio, some people didn't like the way he did business. They walked into the club headquarters on April 6, 1950, and put four bullets into his head.

Anthony Gizzo, long involved in gambling, replaced Binaggio but only lasted three years before dying in 1953.

Following Gizzo were Nicholas and Carl Civella. In 1957, Nick Civella reportedly used a phone at an establishment a short distance from the state police roadblock in Apalachin, New York, and he achieved notoriety as a likely attendee of the mob conclave. Despite the publicity this affair created, Civella avoided serious legal problems through the 1960s. Like all his predecessors, Civella was involved in politics, running a political club that had a great deal of influence.

Nick Civella also had his hooks into Roy Williams, a regional Teamsters Union official with great power. As is detailed in Chapter 12, Civella used this connection to financial advantage in a Las Vegas scam. However, the pressure was building on Civella in the 1970s. He was convicted of bookmaking and went down on a bribery charge involving the Teamsters and Las Vegas. When the Las Vegas skim racket was finally exposed, Nick was charged but was dying of cancer. He passed away on March 12, 1983.

Fuhgeddaboudit

Kansas City Teamsters Union leader Roy Williams became the president of the International Brotherhood of Teamsters Union due to the support of Mafia boss Nick Civella. After he was elected, Williams told Civella that he no longer needed the $1,500 a month he was receiving for helping orchestrate a huge Teamster Pension Fund loan for the mob. Of course, Williams was now going to be making over $100,000 a year with an unlimited expense account.

Carl Civella replaced his brother Nick but was convicted in the Las Vegas casino case in 1984. He died in prison on October 1, 1994. Underboss Carl "Tuffy" DeLuna went away for 30 years. William Cammisano Sr. became the acting boss but was convicted in 1990 and died five years later. Carl's son, Anthony "Tony Ripe" Civella, also acted as boss but was in and out of jail from 1984 until 1996. The Kansas City family that once influenced the national affairs of the Teamsters Union and had connections with mob leaders from around the country is history.

Running Rackets in Milwaukee

The Milwaukee family was always small and operated within the orbit of the Chicago Outfit. Its roots go back to the early 1900s, but no Milwaukee boss has ever played an important role in the national affairs of the Mafia. In 1921, Peter Guardalabene took over from his father, Vito, who died of natural causes. Peter resigned in favor of Joe Amato. Amato died on March 28, 1927.

Joseph Vallone was boss from 1927 until about 1949, when he resigned. The next leader was Sam Ferrara, whose reign was an unhappy one that led to his ouster in 1952. The next family boss, John Alioto, was at the top for nine years. There was no sign of him or any of his men at the big Mafia meeting at Apalachin, New York, in 1957. Four years later, in late 1961, Alioto stepped down in favor of his son-in-law, Frank Balistrieri.

Thanks to a multifamily manipulation of the Teamsters Union Central States Pension Fund, Balistrieri began receiving skimmed money from a number of Las Vegas casinos. (These events are explained in Chapter 12.) A few years later, he was snared by FBI undercover agent Joe Pistone and ultimately was convicted of racketeering charges stemming from his control over the vending machine business in Milwaukee. The case demonstrated that the Milwaukee family was subservient to the Chicago Outfit and had to receive permission from it to deal with the New York hoods with whom Pistone was running at the time. FBI reports also indicate that the Milwaukee family had influence in the produce market and several local labor unions.

> **Fuhgeddaboudit**
>
> In 2001, Benedetta Balistrieri, daughter of the late Milwaukee boss Frank Balistrieri, went to court in a dispute over family assets with brother Joseph. Both gave newspaper interviews. Benedetta claimed Joe was living high on assets hidden by their father. Joe said she was "pathetic." Their father must be turning over in his grave.

In July of 1984, Balistrieri was given a 13-year sentence for using extortion and other racketeering tactics in his vending machine operation. He also was convicted in the Las Vegas skim case. Due to ill health, he was released after seven years. He died in 1993. A few members soldiered on, but for all intents and purposes, the small Milwaukee family was done.

Making News in the Bay Area

The San Francisco family has always been a minor league operation compared to even the medium-size La Cosa Nostra organizations. By design and default, the family remained small throughout its life.

Its first known leader was Francesco "Frank" Lanza, who guided the family during the Prohibition era and died on June 14, 1937. Anthony Lima succeeded Lanza, remaining in power for 16 years until he was jailed for grand theft. Michael Abati replaced Lima, but he either missed the Apalachin, New York, meeting in 1957 when many Mafia leaders met, or managed to avoid any links to the mob conclave.

James Lanza, son of the family's first known boss, was registered at a hotel some 50 miles away with some other Mafia bosses who were caught. James Lanza took over the family in 1961 after Abati was deported by immigration authorities.

Lanza had the misfortune of being family boss when the public's interest in the Mafia was heightened in the aftermath of the Apalachin meeting. National magazines published his picture and listed him as the San Francisco boss. The FBI provided information to the press—both *Life* and *Look* magazines profiled Lanza—from thousands of hours of taped conversations it made from an illegal bug it installed in Lanza's office from 1960 to 1965.

In addition, the media was very interested in Joseph Alioto, the popular San Francisco mayor of that period. He was a rising star on the national political stage, and his background was carefully examined. In what Alioto, and many others, felt was a smear attempt, *Look* magazine linked the mayor to six Mafia members, including Lanza. Alioto's resulting legal suit drew even more attention to him and Lanza.

In his autobiography, Jimmy "The Weasel" Fratianno said he reported to Lanza in 1973 when he moved to San Francisco after his release from prison. Lanza wanted no part of Fratianno and complained about the Weasel's presence in the Bay Area. A few years later, when Fratianno heard rumors that he was on a hit list, one of the charges was that he was bringing too much attention to the existence of the Mafia in San Francisco.

Today, the San Francisco family is considered defunct.

Getting Organized in San Jose

This is another small, West Coast family that is known more for the few times some of its members made the national media than for what it actually did.

The first known boss was Onofrio Sciortino, who led the family until his death on September 10, 1959. He was not present at the 1957 Mafia meeting in Apalachin, New York, but there is evidence that Joseph Cerrito, the next boss, was in the area. It is not clear whether Cerrito was representing Sciortino or whether he had already taken over the formal reins of the family.

The Apalachin affair brought Cerrito to the attention of the FBI, and they began tailing him. In 1964, he was observed by Italian police meeting in Palermo, Sicily, with Frank Garofalo, a former underboss of New York City Mafia leader Joe Bonanno. This was during Bonanno's fight to retain leadership of his family. Speculation was that Cerrito was consulting with Garofalo to try to bring the crisis to a peaceful end.

Three years later, *Life* magazine published a two-part series on La Cosa Nostra and named Cerrito as a Mafia boss. He filed a $7 million libel suit. *Life* pulled out all the stops, and its ace crime reporter Sandy Smith wrote a feature article that amplified Cerrito's organized crime links. He didn't have a criminal record at the time, but that didn't stop Smith, with the help of FBI sources, from detailing a failed extortion scheme that Cerrito's men attempted. He ended his piece by saying "Genial Joe Cerrito, shoeshine and all, is a gangster."

Ten years later, a botched murder revealed more of the family affairs. On October 11, 1977, the body of Peter Catelli was found in the trunk of a car in San Francisco. Also in the trunk was Orlando Catelli, father of Peter. Despite being shot in the head at close range, Orlando was still alive. He said he and his son had been summoned to a cheese factory owned by Angelo Marino, a capo who had inherited a hugely successful business founded by his father.

Orlando testified that Marino's son Salvatore killed Peter Catelli and then shot Orlando in the head. He added that he pretended to be dead as the Marinos and their cohorts stuffed the Catellis into the trunk of a car and left it at San Francisco Airport, where police rescued Orlando after passersby heard screaming and pounding from inside the trunk.

The case played out in court over the next 15 years. Angelo Marino was convicted, released when he won an appeal, and then died. Son Sal Marino was convicted, released after winning an appeal, and then faced retrial on lesser charges, which meant little in terms of prison time. Meanwhile, Joe Cerrito died on September 8, 1978, shortly after the Marino mess began.

Today, the San Jose family is basically defunct despite the presence of a few made men still moving around, albeit very slowly.

> **Fuhgeddaboudit**
>
> As Salvatore Marino battled the law over the murder of Peter Catelli over the years, he was also involved in a bitter fight with his three sisters over the fate of the cheese company that dear old dad founded. Salvatore sued his three sisters to overturn the sale of his father's cheese business, which was sold for $11.5 million in 1986.

Meeting the Mob in St. Louis

Like so many other cities during Prohibition, St. Louis was the scene of numerous bloody murders as rival gangs battled for domination. Vito Giannola, the first known St. Louis family La Cosa Nostra boss, was among the many gangs trying to get rich through bootlegging along the Mississippi River.

St. Louis was one of three Mafia families that didn't have any known representatives at the infamous Mafia gathering at Apalachin, New York, in 1957. (The others were Chicago and Milwaukee.) The best-known boss of the St. Louis family was Anthony Giordano, who received national exposure during the 1960s following the Apalachin convention and the defection of Joe Valachi. Giordano's family was heavily involved in the mob's staples: illegal gambling, loan-sharking, and extortion rackets. Giordano also had sway over several locals of the Laborers International Union of North America. This provided legitimate income, perks, and the leverage needed for labor racketeering.

Giordano, like other bosses, was pictured in a two-part *Life* magazine series in 1967. He was a target of the FBI and, in 1972, was convicted of having a hidden interest in the Frontier Hotel and Casino in Las Vegas. The case also exposed the relationship Giordano had with the Detroit family, which acquired a seat on the Mafia's Commission in 1961 in the person of boss Joe Zerilli.

Giordano was a politically savvy boss whose associations with other major Mafia powers created the impression that he had much more power and influence than he actually did. When he died from cancer in 1980, reality began to replace myth.

Matthew "Mike" Trupiano Jr., a nephew of Giordano, had been pulled along for decades by his uncle's power. He had been placed in Local 110 of the Laborers Union and served for years as president of the local.

When Trupiano was promoted to boss with the approval of the Chicago Outfit, he became an instant target for the FBI's national push against the mob. Plagued by ill health, Trupiano and his small family were investigated throughout the decade. The prize was control of the unions, and the feds were eager to take it away.

In the early 1990s, Trupiano was charged with conducting an illegal gambling operation and with labor racketeering, including the embezzlement of union benefit funds.

The embezzlement charges were dropped, but Trupiano spent more than two years in prison on the gambling conviction. He also lost his union office in a 1992 election. After his prison sentence, Trupiano's health continued to fail. He died on October 22, 1997. The St. Louis Mafia had been on life support for more than a decade. With Trupiano's death, the switch was finally turned off.

Mickey Mousing in the City of Angels

The most powerful Los Angeles boss was Anthony Rizzoti, better known as Jack Dragna. During Prohibition, Dragna followed the lead of the big-city families in the east and created a supposedly benevolent organization for his own purposes. Dragna's vehicle was called the Italian Protective League, and its vice president was Joe "Iron Man" Ardizonne. He was Dragna's boss until he disappeared on October 15, 1931. Not surprisingly, Dragna, the chief beneficiary of Ardizonne's departure, was always suspected of the deed. There is little doubt (really, no doubt) that Dragna was responsible. Ardizonne's rubout was likely a Commission-sanctioned hit, because other Mafia leaders accepted Dragna as boss.

Gambling and loan sharking were the main rackets of Dragna's family, and like gangsters everywhere, Dragna used political and police corruption as his keys to success. Dragna, who had set the tone when he took over, was also willing to use violence (and the threat of it) to muscle in on independent bookmakers and take a piece of their action. For years, Dragna coveted the lucrative bookmaking operation of Mickey Cohen, an independent Jewish gangster, and tried to kill him several times. He failed each time, though he did rub out several Cohen bodyguards and enforcers along the way with shotgun ambushes and bombings. Additionally, Dragna also got a cut of the Chicago Outfit's national wire service that provided the results of horse races, which were the big moneymaker for bookies of that era.

On February 23, 1956, Dragna was found dead in a motel room. The family was taken over by lawyer Frank Desimone, who was one of two lawyer/bosses of a La Cosa Nostra family. (The other is discussed in Chapter 7.) Desimone's supposedly honest life was exposed when he was detained with scores of Mafia bosses at the infamous mob conclave at Apalachin, New York, in November of 1957. His underboss, Simone Scozzari, who was also there, was put under intense scrutiny and eventually deported as an undesirable alien in 1962. Desimone's reign also received unwanted notoriety when soldier John Stompanato Jr. was killed in a domestic dispute with his lover, the beautiful movie star Lana Turner, in 1958.

Stompanato was a ruggedly handsome, charismatic ex-Marine who had drifted into the criminal life on the West Coast. He was occasionally seen around gangster Mickey Cohen and was often referred to as one of his bodyguards.

Gangsters love women, and Stompanato was no exception. Early in 1958, he wooed Turner with flowers and cards, and they soon began a torrid, tumultuous relationship. She was no stranger to turmoil. Besides having a booming acting career with hits like *The Postman Always Rings Twice* and *Peyton Place*, Turner had a drinking problem that was exacerbated by a man problem. Before her life ended, she had been married eight times and had many lovers. Stompanato might have been the worst.

According to Turner and her daughter, Cheryl Crane, Stompanato would get physical when things didn't go his way. On April 4, 1958, he was allegedly beating up on Turner when the 14-year-old Crane came into their bedroom and drove a kitchen knife into his midsection. Stompanato went down and soon died. After a sensational trial, the killing was ruled a justifiable homicide.

Later in that same year, Anthony Mirabile, a capo from San Diego, was killed in an apparent botched robbery in which he resisted.

Nick Licata became boss after the death of Desimone on August 4, 1967. He ruled for seven years before dying on October 19, 1974.

The next administration was decimated by mobster-turned-informer Aladena "Jimmy the Weasel" Fratianno, who also did lots of damage to gangsters in New York, Chicago, Pennsylvania, and San Francisco. A small-time hood but a proficient killer, he was "made" by the Los Angeles family in 1947, transferred to Chicago in 1960, and transferred back to Los Angeles in 1975. Fratianno spent a lot of time in jail, always frustrated by his lack of stature and money. In 1973, after completing another term in prison, Fratianno became an FBI informer in return for miniscule amounts of money. Unbeknownst to him, one of his best friends, Frank "Bomp" Bompensiero, was doing the same thing.

In 1975, boss Dominic Brooklier and underboss Samuel Sciortino were sentenced to relatively short prison terms, 20 and 18 months, respectively. Louis Tom Dragna, the nephew of the former boss, was given the acting boss position. Worried about Bompensiero, Dragna asked Fratianno to help him in some activities. Fratianno jumped at the chance and managed a transfer back from the Windy City. The Weasel began moving about the country in his endless quest to make money, passing himself off as acting boss of Los Angeles, making deals, making money, and making the FBI happy with information about powerful mobsters from Chicago, New York, Pennsylvania, and Los Angeles.

It's hard to believe Fratianno didn't realize that the family's real boss would find out about the Weasel's activities even though he was in prison. In any event, Brooklier learned of Fratianno's schemes, put out a contract on him, and the Weasel ran to the FBI for protection, agreeing to become the second made mobster to break the vow of silence and testify against his friends.

Big Shot

L.A. boss Dominic Brooklier didn't like Frank "Bomp" Bompensiero in part, at least, because he felt Bompensiero didn't give him the respect he deserved. To fix that, back in 1977, Brooklier lured Bompensiero to a phone booth to take a call. Waiting for him was Thomas Ricciardi, a wannabe mobster from New York looking to make his bones in tinsel town. Ricciardi blew Bompensiero away and was inducted into the Los Angeles family as a reward. He dropped dead of a heart attack soon after.

The Los Angeles family tried to regroup under the leadership of Peter Milano and his underboss brother, Carmen. Like gangsters all over the country, however, they too went down in the nationwide FBI drive to decimate the mob. In May of 1988, Peter was sentenced to six years for racketeering; his brother got two years. Capo Michael Rizzitello received four years. Nearly a decade later, Carmine Milano was nailed in another FBI investigation that included the killing of a Las Vegas associate of the Chicago Outfit. Milano thought about cooperating but changed his mind. To his extreme embarrassment, however, an FBI interview with Milano was released after he changed his mind. Eventually, Milano received less than three years for racketeering. The Los Angeles family, long known as the "Mickey Mouse Mafia," was history.

The Least You Need to Know

- The Chicago Outfit remains united and strong.
- A Las Vegas Casino skim discovery decimated the Kansas City family.
- You can find beer but no Mafia family in Milwaukee.
- Only stories remain of the tiny San Francisco family.
- The cheese company has been sold and the Mafia family is long gone from San Jose.
- What remained of the St. Louis Mafia died with boss Matthew "Mike" Trupiano Jr. in 1997.
- The Los Angeles "Mickey Mouse Mafia" has faded away.

Chapter 7

Mafia Up North, Mafia Down South

In This Chapter

- Gangsters battle over beer and unions in Cleveland
- Discovering the Dallas Mafia
- Motor city Mafia drives long and hard
- The Mafia parties in Mardi Gras land
- The Trafficantes tie up Tampa

One of the great Mafia stories involved a future Cleveland underboss using his mommy to lure a hated rival to his death. Another fascinating mob tale featured the longtime New Orleans boss being unceremoniously bundled onto a plane by immigration agents and dropped off in far away Guatemala in a surprise quickie deportation. In Florida, the FBI scored a huge coup when one of its undercover agents shook hands with the Mafia boss of Tampa. In Detroit, a famous former Teamster president was taken for his last ride in a story that continues to fascinate crime buffs.

In this chapter, I'll tell these stories and many others that involve Mafia families from Cleveland, Dallas, Detroit, New Orleans, and Tampa. You'll get to know some of the more famous bosses and how some of them met their untimely ends. It's an easy ride, and we'll look for the missing Jimmy Hoffa while we truck along.

The Cleveland Family

Joseph Lonardo was the first known Mafia boss of Cleveland. He and his brothers had several legitimate businesses, including one that sold corn sugar—a key ingredient for people who distilled home-brewed liquor during the Prohibition years. The end product was sold to Lonardo men, who retailed liquor at a handsome profit. On October 13, 1927, Lonardo and his brother John were ambushed and killed in a barbershop, which was owned by the family that would take over the Cleveland crime family.

Angelo "Big Ange" Lonardo, the son of Joseph, testified 50 years later that he believed that Salvatore "Black Sam" Todaro, who had managed the Lonardo sugar refineries before leaving in a dispute and joining up with family rival Joseph Porrello, had murdered his father and then taken over as boss. Two years later, Angelo avenged his father by shooting Todaro to death in front of the Porrello warehouse on June 11, 1929. Todaro's execution set off another round of violence. Angelo's uncle, Frank Lonardo, was shot to death four months later in a downtown barbershop.

> **Big Shot**
>
> Angelo Lonardo and his cousin John DeMarco killed a mobster they knew as Doctor Romano because they believed he helped plot the murder of Angelo's father. DeMarco told Angelo they had permission to kill Romano from mob power Frank Milano. After the deed was done, however, Milano denied any prior knowledge of the murder. Whether DeMarco lied about receiving permission or Milano lied when he denied prior knowledge is up for debate. Eventually, new boss Al Polizzi convinced the Commission to spare DeMarco.

New boss Joseph Porrello didn't fare much better than the previous bosses. He was gunned down in Frank Milano's restaurant on July 5, 1930. Milano, the leader of the so-called Mayfield Road Mob, rose to prominence as the Porrellos were killed off. After a short but successful run, Milano left Cleveland and moved to Mexico in 1935, one of the few Mafia bosses who voluntarily walked away from a leadership position. Alfred "Big Al" Polizzi then took over.

One of the key factors in the long-term success of the Cleveland family was its association with Jewish gangsters. Moe Dalitz is the best known. In 1947, Dalitz invested in the construction of a new hotel/casino in Las Vegas. To prevent other Mafia families from muscling in, Dalitz gave the Cleveland Mafia leaders a piece of the action. Their payments were skimmed off the top, in cash, to avoid problems with the tax people. The partnership between Dalitz and the Cleveland family began prior to the Las Vegas endeavor and lasted into the 1980s.

In the mid-1940s, flush with cash, Polizzi semi retired to Florida, leaving capo John Scalish in charge. In 1957, Scalish was stopped and identified as he left the Apalachin meeting, giving him unwanted national prominence. His use of a car registered to the Buckeye Cigarette Service of Cleveland also alerted the law about his participation in a long-running vending machine monopoly in Ohio. Scalish became the focus of numerous investigations and a target of a secret FBI intelligence-gathering operation. He was investigated but never charged.

By the mid-1970s, even before the national push by federal authorities against the Mafia, the Cleveland family was on its last legs. A generation of Cleveland mob powers had died. Scalish died in 1976, underboss Anthony Milano in 1978, consigliere John DeMarco in 1972, and capo Frank Brancato in 1973. With no new blood waiting in the wings to take over—there were few inductees in the prior three decades—the family was growing old. Aging capo James "Jack White" Licavoli took over as the handpicked choice of the dying Scalish.

Mafia Speak

James Licavoli's nickname was "Jack White." He got the name because of his dark complexion.

Licavoli inherited a slice of the skim from the Las Vegas hotels and casinos. This came about because Cleveland associate, Teamsters Union International vice president William "Bill the Plug" Presser, had helped win a huge Teamster Central States Pension Fund loan for the Argent Corporation, which operated four casinos (see Chapter 12). Licavoli soon faced a rebellion from some longtime associates of the family who felt they were being left out of the action.

John Nardi, secretary/treasurer of Teamsters Local 410, was contemptuous of Licavoli and his administration. A relative of former boss Frank Milano and underboss Tony Milano and also a member of a Teamsters Joint Council that represented several locals, Nardi ignored orders from Licavoli and his underboss Leo "Lips" Moceri. To strengthen his position, Nardi allied himself with swashbuckling Irish gangster Danny Greene, who had his own gang of toughs. In August 1976, Moceri disappeared, no doubt at the hands of Nardi and/or Greene, and a shooting war broke out. On May 17, 1977,

Nardi was killed by a bomb that blew up in a car parked next to his. "It didn't hurt," he said in a final act of defiance moments before he died. Several months later, on October 6, 1977, Greene was blown up by a bomb as he left his dentist and got to his car. The mob planted the bomb in a nearby car after he arrived at the dentist's office. These bombing deaths were the beginning of the end of the Cleveland Mafia.

Key participants in the war, including Angelo Lonardo, became government witnesses. Turncoat California hood Jimmy "The Weasel" Fratianno, who had spent years in Cleveland, filled in many details about the Cleveland situation. Boss Jack Licavoli died behind bars on November 24, 1985. Capos John Calandra, Thomas Sinito, and Joe Gallo and numerous soldiers and associates were given lengthy prison terms.

John "Peanuts" Tronolone, although based in Florida, tried to carry on, but he was an ineffective leader who faced many legal problems until his death in 1991. By this time, there really were few men to lead. The FBI also convicted Joseph "Joe Loose" Iacobacci in 1996. He was referred to as the acting boss, but this was a label used to make his conviction seem more important than he really was.

> **Slammer Time**
>
> When Angelo Lonardo was given a life sentence for drug dealing, he found that he missed his family terribly. Hence, he said, he made a deal with the government to become a witness against his lifelong friends. The thought of getting out of jail probably had something to do with his decision.

Along with the convictions, death, and defections, the loss of the family's influence over the Teamsters Union made running the Cleveland family much less appealing than before. Even when Jackie Presser succeeded his late father William as Teamsters Union powerhouse, it was all a house of cards. The mob had lost control of the Central States Pension Fund goldmine, and it faced two decades of increasing government pressure to eliminate the Mafia's influence over the Teamsters Union. The days of the Cleveland family being part of a criminal empire with national significance were long gone.

The Dallas Family

The Dallas family was always small. It had little national impact unless you believe the Mafia was behind the assassination of President John F. Kennedy. According to FBI documents, the first Dallas boss was Carlo Piranio, a bookmaker who gravitated toward bootlegging during Prohibition. Piranio ran a close-knit family, and his brother Joseph replaced Carlo when he died on February 20, 1930.

Joe Piranio had one of the longer reigns as a La Cosa Nostra boss. He lasted until 1956, when he reportedly committed suicide due to ill health. Under his stewardship, the family was heavily involved in gambling and moved into the heroin trade. Dallas was home to many non-Mafia gambling syndicates, so clearly the Mafia didn't control gambling. However, they were connected to the strong New Orleans family that ran race wire services that provided vital information to bookies in the decades before sports betting became a national rage.

Joe Piranio's successor, Joseph Francis Civello, would achieve the most notoriety of any Dallas Mafia boss. Born in Port Allen, Louisiana, in 1902, Civello was convicted of a Federal drug violation in 1928. He relocated to Dallas, where he operated Civello's Fine Foods and Liquor. A year after he became boss, he was detained at the famous 1957 Mafia gathering in Apalachin, New York. He shared a hotel room with the San Jose underboss. In the next suite were the bosses of Los Angeles and San Francisco. Civello was convicted of obstruction of justice for failing to adequately explain his presence at Apalachin and was sentenced to five years in federal prison. An appeals court overturned the conviction, but Civello's status as a Mafia boss was firmly established.

> **Big Shot**
>
> Dallas boss Joseph Piranio wasn't the only Mafia leader to take his own life. Chicago boss Frank Nitti shot himself after being indicted in 1943. Ailing and aging New England Mafia power Frank Cucchiara killed himself at age 79—moments after he killed his wife of 52 years.

Through the 1960s, Civello's power and influence, like that of many other La Cosa Nostra bosses, was greatly inflated by a media that fed the public's fascination with the Mafia. The FBI gave friendly writers material culled from illegal bugs and informers, and this information was invariably exaggerated. In 1967, Civello was pictured with many other Mafia bosses in a two-part *Life* magazine story on La Cosa Nostra. By this time, Civello was fading fast. He died on January 17, 1970. What little there was left of his family soon followed him.

Civello's career was given new life less than a decade later. A congressional investigation into the Kennedy assassination began looking into the possibility that the Mafia was behind Kennedy's murder. If this were the case, the Dallas boss obviously would have had to be involved. An FBI interview with Civello surfaced in which he admitted knowing Jack Ruby, the Dallas nightclub owner who killed Lee Harvey Oswald, the alleged assassin of President Kennedy. Civello had told the FBI he met Ruby a few times, the last time in 1957. A connection between Ruby and the Mafia was critical to those who fancied this conspiracy theory. Consequently, Civello's name has become known to a new generation of conspiracy lovers. By the way, I give no credence to any Kennedy assassination conspiracy theory that includes the Mafia.

The Detroit Family

There is much evidence of shootings, killings, and other Detroit Mafia activity in the early 1900s, but the first family boss whose identity has been firmly established was Salvatore "Sam" Catalonette. Catalonette took over in 1920 after years of rubouts and other violence that began in 1913.

The following year, Gaspar Milazzo, a Castellammarese immigrant from New York City, began to flex his muscles in the lucrative bootlegging industry. Milazzo arrived in the Motor City after he became a suspect in a Prohibition-era murder in the Big Apple in 1921.

Milazzo's Eastside organization included some tough, seasoned gangsters, men like Peter and Thomas "Yonnie" Licavoli, Joe Zerilli, William Tocco, Leo and Joseph Moceri, and Joseph "Scarface Joe" Bommarito. They controlled the smuggling of liquor into the East side of Detroit from Canada, which was just across the Detroit River.

It's unclear exactly when Milazzo took over the reigns of the family, but he certainly was on top by February of 1930, when Catalonette died after a bout with pneumonia. In any event, by the late 1920s, Milazzo had become entangled in a conflict involving mobsters in Chicago and New York. Milazzo made the mistake of supporting a Chicago enemy of New York boss Joe Masseria. On May 31, 1930, Milazzo was lured to a fish market, where he was shot and killed by a Detroit crew led by Caesar "Chester" LaMare, who had been one of Catalonette's top lieutenants.

It's no surprise that LaMare became the next boss. Surprisingly, though, cops arrested two LaMare loyalists—Joseph Amico and Joseph Locano—for the murder. Both were acquitted at trial.

LaMare had been active in the bootlegging trade for years. He ran a very popular Eastside speakeasy, Venice Café, along with a couple of other up-and-coming wiseguys, Angelo Meli and Leo Cellura. He was influential and smart enough to make deals with Harry Bennett, the notorious right-hand man of auto-making giant Henry Ford. LaMare ended up with a Ford dealership, Crescent Motor Sales, and the fruit concession for food wagons at the huge River Rouge Plant. Unfortunately for LaMare, his lucrative run would be very short.

On February 6, 1931, LaMare was at home celebrating a moneymaking deal with Ford. Among the party animals taking part were Joe Amico and Elmer Macklin. Macklin allegedly put two bullets into the side of the boss's head while the others had his attention. Once again, the alleged killers were acquitted at trial. In less than two years, Joe Amico became the only mobster in history to be tried and acquitted of the murders of two successive Mafia bosses.

Fuhgeddaboudit

After Chester LaMare was killed, Harry Bennett, a secretive power in the Ford Motor Company, recognized the new strength of capo Peter Licavoli. He gave jobs in the Ford service department to a number of Licavoli men. When Licavoli tried to get them a raise, however, Bennett fired them all. Not long afterward, Licavoli retaliated. Bennett's car was run off the road in an attempt to kill him. He survived, and no one was ever charged in the incident.

LaMare's killing began a 70-year reign by Joseph Zerilli and his relatives. One of the key elements in this lengthy tenure was the unity of the Zerilli family in running the Detroit family. Zerilli and key capos William "Black Bill" Tocco, Peter Licavoli, and Scarface Joe Bommarito all had their roots in Terrasina, Sicily, a small town near Palermo. The sons and relatives of Zerilli and Tocco replaced their elders and kept the power within the personal family structure through the 1990s.

 **Big Shot**

For every wannabe wiseguy who makes it to the top, there is often a brother or relative who paid the ultimate price. Capo William "Black Bill" Tocco went on to a long and successful career in the Detroit Mafia, occasionally filling in as acting boss. He died of natural causes in 1972. His brother Joseph was shot to death in 1938 in the endless fighting that erupted between rival gangs regularly during the post-Prohibition era.

In addition to the usual mob staples of bookmaking and loan sharking, the Detroit family was heavily mixed up in labor-racketeering schemes involving the burgeoning auto industry and the International Brotherhood of Teamsters. Detroit was home to Jimmy Hoffa, the powerful Teamsters Union president who was tightly tied to capo Anthony "Tony Jack" Giacalone. Hoffa also had key contacts in the Chicago Outfit. The support of the Chicago and Detroit families assured Hoffa the backing of La Cosa Nostra families around the nation. This support gave Hoffa the presidency of the Teamsters Union and gave the Mafia families a firmer grip on local labor rackets and the huge Teamsters Central States Pension Fund (see Chapters 12 and 20).

In 1956, at a national meeting of Mafia bosses, the participants decided that, in 1961, two more members would get seats on the Mafia Commission. Joe Zerilli was selected because of his longevity as a Mafia boss, his connection to Jimmy Hoffa, and his personal relations to sitting Commission member Joe Profaci.

Like many Mafia leaders, Zerilli and the other members of his Detroit family received a great deal of publicity after Joe Valachi testified before a Senate committee in 1963.

However, this didn't translate into criminal problems for Zerilli. He and many of his capo/relatives had many legitimate businesses, and they were able to ride out the notoriety as FBI propaganda without substance. They lived in exclusive neighborhoods with a comfortable lifestyle and had many influential friends and acquaintances.

In 1975, the Detroit family came under the most law enforcement pressure it had felt up to that point. Former Teamsters president Jimmy Hoffa had been convicted of jury tampering and was released from prison. He was—very foolishly, as it turned out—desperately trying to return to power against the wishes of some powerful Mafia leaders.

Jimmy Hoffa in a September 1974 photo, nine months before he disappeared on his way to meet Detroit mobster Tony Jack Giacalone.

(Photo courtesy of New York Daily News*)*

On July 30, 1975, Hoffa was last seen outside the Machus Red Fox restaurant just outside Detroit, getting ready to meet his friend, capo Anthony "Tony Jack" Giacalone. "TG—2pm—Red Fox," read a note on his desk. At 2:30, Hoffa called his wife wondering where Tony was. Minutes later, Hoffa was spotted getting into a car; he has never been seen again. Members of the Detroit Mafia and Charles "Chuckie" O'Brien, whom Hoffa had considered an adopted son, were immediately suspected, but despite intense investigations, no one has ever been charged in his killing. Tony Giacalone would later spend time in prison for income tax evasion, a crime that was uncovered because of the Hoffa inquiries.

Anthony Zerilli, the son of boss Joe Zerilli, was also questioned about Hoffa's disappearance, but nothing came of it. Anthony had been convicted in 1972 of a racketeering conspiracy for attempting to conceal a hidden interest in the Frontier Hotel and Casino in Las Vegas, in a scheme that took place prior to the 1967 sale of the Frontier to billionaire Howard Hughes. Also convicted were longtime Detroit capo Michael "Big Mike" Polizzi and St. Louis boss Anthony Giordano. All were sentenced to four years and served about two and a half.

Slammer Time

Michael "Big Mike" Polizzi was a leading capo in the Detroit Mafia. While preparing to go to prison in 1972, Big Mike told his son Angelo that the mob would regularly drop off an envelope with cash for the Polizzi family while he was incarcerated. Big Mike's wife denied she ever received money this way, but when Angelo became a government witness in the early 1990s, he detailed regular payments during the entire time his father was away.

The 1970s brought a number of leadership changes. In 1972, Black Bill Tocco died. Five years later, boss Joe Zerilli passed away, and in 1979, underboss John Priziola died at age 84. All three died of natural causes while free men, events that became rare for Mafia leaders as the twentieth century wound down. These deaths left openings for a new generation of eager replacements who had taken a different route to get there than the wiseguys they replaced. For example, the family's next leaders, boss Jack Tocco and underboss Anthony Zerilli, were college graduates.

Like many other Mafia families, the Detroit family declined in size and influence over the next 15 years. Many of its leaders were wealthy with little need and no desire to jeopardize their futures to make a few more bucks. They were also wise enough to see the increased federal pressure coming and were eager to avoid attention. They continued their bookmaking and loan-sharking activities, but their control over labor racketeering and other rackets declined.

In 1990, boss Jack Tocco made his biggest mistake. He agreed to let two young mobster relatives apply pressure to several independent bookies to try and get a piece of their action. Unfortunately for the Mafiosi, the FBI had bugged their cars and taped many conversations about illegal activities. In 1996, Tocco, underboss Anthony Zerilli, and many others were hit with racketeering charges that included a 30-year conspiracy to control gambling in Detroit and to obtain hidden interests in Las Vegas casinos. Authorities had high hopes that the charges might lead some older members to talk to avoid prison. Of prime interest was the mysterious disappearance of Jimmy Hoffa in 1975.

Things broke badly for the government, however, even though it won. Jack Tocco was convicted of racketeering and extortion, but was given a lenient one-year-and-one-day sentence. The government appealed, noting that strict sentencing guidelines called for much greater time and that, if anything, Tocco deserved more time, not less. The government prevailed, and in May of 2000, Tocco was resentenced to 34 months, receiving credit for the year he had already served. Despite the added time, Tocco kept his mouth shut. He never said a word about the disappearance of Jimmy Hoffa and was released from prison in late 2001. That same year, Chuckie O'Brien was identified as a key suspect in an FBI investigation into the murder. Using sophisticated DNA testing, the FBI determined that Hoffa had been in a car belonging to Giacalone's son and that it was driven by O'Brien the day that Hoffa disappeared, something O'Brien has consistently denied. (In Chapter 33, I discuss the reputed tell-all account of the killing by Frank "The Irishman" Sheeran, the former president of Teamsters Local 326 in Wilmington, Delaware, and the involvement of Russell Bufalino, the former boss of the Northeastern Pennsylvania.)

With most of its leaders infirm or dead, the Detroit La Cosa Nostra family is but a shell of its former self.

The New Orleans Family

Around 1890, New Orleans became the supposed capital of American Mafia activity because of a series of related incidents between two groups, the Matrangas and the Provenzanos. Both were battling for the right to unload ships carrying fruit. The Provenzanos had a monopoly on this business for years, but then the Matrangas pushed their way in. This contest, which led to bloodshed, has been incorrectly explained as a Camorra/Mafia rivalry. Neither family had emigrated from the Italian mainland city of Naples, the home of the Camorra. In fact, both groups knew each other from their Sicilian hometown.

Fuhgeddaboudit
The New Orleans rivalry between two groups from the same Sicilian hometown is similar to that of the Lonardos and Porrellos that was detailed earlier in this chapter. Another version of a hometown rivalry continuing in America involves Stefano Magaddino and the Bucceletas of the Sicilian town of Castellammare del Golfo. The summary of the Buffalo family in Chapter 5 has an outline of this story.

By 1888, the Matrangas had taken over the dock preserve of the Provenzanos. The prevailing wisdom is that the Matrangas (the forerunners of the Mafia family that Carlos Marcello, the well-known New Orleans Mafia boss, headed in the 1960s) used threats of violence and violence itself to accomplish this end. Obviously, they had to have done something persuasive to push out a long-established company. Things heated up two years later. On May 5, 1890, half a dozen Provenzano loyalists ambushed five Matrangas after they finished unloading a boat. When the shooting ceased, three Matranga workers, including Anthony Matranga, brother of boss Charles Matranga, were shot and seriously wounded. The attackers escaped. Later, six Provenzano crew-members, including Peter and Joseph Provenzano, were arrested. They were found guilty, but the convictions were thrown out, and they were acquitted at a second trial, largely because several New Orleans cops testified as defense witnesses and provided alibis for some of the Provenzano defendants.

On October 15, 1890, David Hennessy, a young New Orleans police chief, was gunned down as he returned home late at night. He couldn't identify any of the men who shot him. However, before he died the following day, he said, "The dagos shot me." For the investigators, it was an easy leap to conclude that the perpetrators were members of the Matranga group, since Hennessy was being paid off by the Provenzanos and had sided with them in the feud with the Matrangas.

Charles Matranga and 18 family members and associates were charged with Hennessy's murder. On March 13, 1891, six of nine defendants, including Matranga, were acquitted. The jury couldn't reach a verdict on the other three. Many local officials and businessmen saw this as a travesty of justice. Rumors spread that jurors had been bribed. A deep sense of frustration was waiting for a spark to ignite it as all 19 defendants, including the six who had been acquitted, remained housed in the city jail.

On March 14, a large group estimated at 5,000 to 20,000 strong, protested the verdicts. Aroused and led by local businessmen, the crowd stormed the jail and killed 11 Italian immigrants. One was shot to death and then hanged; the others were lynched and then sprayed with bullets. The cold-blooded, indiscriminate murders—three of the dead had been acquitted, three had received a mistrial, and five were awaiting trial—still remains one of the darkest, most shameful episodes of American vigilantism gone mad more than 100 years later.

There is disagreement over the leadership of the New Orleans family from 1891 until 1922. Many believe Charles Matranga remained as boss and retired then.

After Matranga stepped down, Corrado Giacona took over the New Orleans family and led it until his natural death on July 25, 1944, a very long run for Mafia bosses of that era. As you have seen in Chapters 5, 6, and 7, many Mafia leaders were killed during bootlegging wars in the Prohibition era.

Frank Todaro took over from Giacona but only ruled for a few months before dying. He was replaced by longtime member Sylvestro Carollo, who inherited a piece of the lucrative slot-machine racket that New York Mafia boss Frank Costello introduced to New Orleans during the previous regime. Costello's New Orleans representative, Phillip "Dandy Phil" Kastel, opened a large gambling house in Jefferson Parish, and a minor piece of the operation went to then up-and-coming capo, Carlos Marcello.

The gambling joints prospered with the help of large regular payoffs to the notoriously corrupt local and state politicians and the equally corrupt police officials. Unfortunately for Carollo, his past came back to haunt him in 1947. With two convictions and allegations that he was a major criminal power, U.S. immigration officials deported him on April 30, 1947. This left the leadership of the family open to Carlos Marcello.

During his long reign, Marcello had problems with all three branches of the United States government. In 1951, he was subpoenaed to testify before a U.S. Senate Committee investigating organized crime's involvement in interstate commerce. In 1959, he was subpoenaed to testify before a Senate committee investigating corruption in the labor movement. As Marcello did eight years earlier, he invoked his Fifth Amendment privilege against self-incrimination, this time to questions posed by a young Robert Kennedy. The issue of deportation was raised, but not acted on, until two years later.

Mafia Speak

In 1966, Marcello was enjoying a lovely dinner at La Stella, an Italian restaurant in Queens, New York, when he was rudely interrupted by police. Marcello's meeting with New York bosses Carlo Gambino and Joe Colombo and others caused a mini media frenzy in New York, with stories and pictures in several newspapers. When Marcello returned to New Orleans, he wasn't in a happy mood. He let his fists do the talking when approached by an FBI agent. Worse yet, a cameraman was there to record his big swing.

Early in 1961, Robert Kennedy, now attorney general in the administration of President John F. Kennedy, took aggressive action and summarily deported Marcello to Guatemala. Eventually, Marcello made his way back to the United States and was able to fend off any further deportations. This Kennedy/Marcello conflict would give conspiracy fans some support for the claim that Marcello was behind the murder of President Kennedy in 1963.

Marcello also survived numerous national magazine stories that portrayed him as a Mafia boss. The articles had little impact on his rackets. The common theme was that Louisiana politics had been corrupt for decades, and Marcello was simply pulling the right strings to protect his Mafia activities. In the late 1970s, however, things got worse. The Mafia and Marcello emerged as prime suspects in the assassinations of President Kennedy and Martin Luther King Jr. when a Congressional Committee reopened probes of both killings.

Fuhgeddaboudit

Some conspiracy buffs believe the Mafia executed President Kennedy in an elaborate plot that also involved the murder of the alleged assassin by a Mafia contract killer, Jack Ruby. In July of 1979, Joe Campisi of Dallas was secretly taped by the FBI discussing a media story about this plot with Marcello. Campisi, who had known Ruby, said, "… you wouldn't know Jack Ruby if the fuck was to, uh, crawl in your room."

Around the same time, Marcello was seduced by a con man working for the FBI into some serious criminal acts that were caught on tape. Marcello was overheard talking about obtaining insurance contracts through payoffs. To add to his misery, he also bit on a scam to bribe a judge involved in a trial of major members of the Los Angeles family. Marcello was convicted in both cases. In 1982, he received 7 years for the insurance scheme and another 10 years for conspiring to bribe the California judge. Marcello's mental health deteriorated in prison. He was released early and died in 1993.

Marcello's relatives were unable or unwilling to carry on without his leadership. Anthony Carollo, son of former boss Sylvestro Carollo, attempted to regroup, but he and underboss Frank Gagliano were convicted of racketeering in 1996.

There is still crime and corruption in New Orleans, but no longer is an all-powerful Mafia family there directing it.

The Tampa Family

The Tampa family was just as quick as every other La Cosa Nostra family around the country to recognize and seize on the lucrative bootlegging opportunities that arrived in 1920, courtesy of U.S. lawmakers.

Although the national media attention focused on illegal liquor distribution in New York and Chicago, Tampa was also a hotbed of the activity and violence associated with the 13-year goldmine of opportunities for criminals. Tampa's proximity to Cuba and the Bahamas made smuggling a fairly simple matter. A number of family members and associates had arrest records for bootlegging activities, including Tampa mobsters Gaetano "Joe" Mistretta and Angelo Bedami.

Tampa wiseguys, including Bedami's sons Ciro and Joseph, were involved in labor rackets on the Tampa docks and armed robbery crews, but the Tampa family's primary interests were in gambling. They didn't simply set up card games and bookie joints and wait for business to arrive. The family muscled into virtually every independent gambling operation that cropped up. Like Mafia families everywhere, Tampa felt it had a proprietary right to all games of chance in the area. They moved in on other illegal activities every chance they could.

Some independents simply caved in at the least hint of violence, figuring they could still make a living while sharing a piece of the action. Others needed a show of force. A few, like Bob Wall, a major independent gambler who refused to knuckle under, paid the ultimate price. In 1955, he was found dead, stabbed to death in the bathtub of his home. No one was ever charged in the killing.

Ignacio Antinori and sons Paul and Joseph were trailblazers in the lucrative drug trade, supplying heroin that was refined in France and then smuggled to the United States through Cuba to Kansas City mobsters who had links to other mob drug traffickers across the country. In a drug dispute, Ignacio was blown away—he received several shotgun blasts to the head—on October 23, 1940, at the Palm Garden Inn in Tampa.

In 1943, sons Paul and Joseph were convicted of drug dealing and were sentenced to four years in prison in a Kansas City case that established the Tampa family as major drug dealers in the files of the Bureau of Narcotics and Dangerous Drugs, the forerunner of the Drug Enforcement Administration. The Antinoris—Joe was later killed at the Boston Bar in the Latin quarter section of Tampa—were fingered as suppliers of the heroin by Carl Carramusa, a low-level Kansas City crewmember. Two Kansas City and two St. Louis mobsters were also convicted in the case.

In June 1945, as his daughter looked on in horror, Carramusa was shot to death as he changed a flat tire in front of his Chicago home—a familiar scenario that mobsters have used since shortly after Henry Ford invented the Model T.

The Tampa family also had lucrative business interests in Cuba in the 1940s, primarily through Santos Trafficante Sr., who operated casinos on the Caribbean island 90 miles off Florida. Trafficante took over as family boss in 1950, following the death of his predecessor, James Lumia, who was shot to death on June 5, 1950. Trafficante Sr., who died of natural causes on August 11, 1954, was replaced by son Santos Jr.

Junior had been running legal casinos in Cuba since 1946 but moved back and forth between Havana and Tampa, earning the support of other capos when his father died.

In 1957, Trafficante became a national figure when he was identified as taking part in the famous Mafia meeting at Apalachin, New York. During the Valachi hearings in the fall of 1963, Trafficante's picture was atop the chart depicting the organizational structure of the Tampa family. In 1966, he was seated next to New Orleans boss Carlos Marcello when cops interrupted a dinner party at La Stella restaurant in Queens. He was also one of the Mafia chieftains profiled by *Life* magazine later in the same decade.

In 1975, Trafficante received more unwelcome publicity. He was linked to the Kennedy assassination, primarily because of his admitted role in a CIA plot to kill Cuban leader Fidel Castro in the early 1960s. No evidence suggests that any mobsters ever did anything other than talk about murdering Castro. Nevertheless, the fact that Trafficante was involved in the CIA plot certainly warranted further inquiries. Nothing of substance was ever discovered that would prove Trafficante's involvement in an anti-Kennedy conspiracy.

> **Slammer Time**
>
> Santos Trafficante Jr. was in Cuba when revolutionary Fidel Castro took over the government in 1959. Many people, including a number of gamblers/businessmen like Trafficante Jr., were thrown in jail. Their accommodations were pleasant enough. Trafficante said they were in a minimum-security prison, had excellent visiting privileges, and had a great rapport with the prison guards.

The 1980s saw Trafficante become a top target of a nationwide push against the Mafia by the FBI. He was lured into an FBI sting and gave his permission to set up bingo halls in his territory. Trafficante was also charged with looting union benefit funds. By then, however, Trafficante was running out of steam, and his health was failing. When he died on March 17, 1987, he had finished a long career as a La Cosa Nostra boss without hardly ever being seriously inconvenienced.

Vince LoScalzo replaced Trafficante and retained Frank Diecidue as underboss. Diecidue passed away in October of 1994, further symbolizing the evolution of the Tampa family from a powerhouse to a minor league operation.

The Least You Need to Know

- Cleveland's powerful Mafia family is only a memory.

- According to the FBI, the Dallas family no longer exists.

- The government has crippled the Detroit family.

- The Mardi Gras continues, but the New Orleans family is gone.

- You won't find an active Mafia family in Tampa.

Part 2

Mafia at Work

Like most people, Mafia guys have to make a buck. The trouble is they don't like to work for it. That leaves a variety of illegal and semi-illegal activities that a mob member or associate can plumb to make enough cash to support his personal family and his mistress and still have enough left over to keep his mob superiors happy. The latter is the most important concern.

Although I talk about a variety of mob moneymakers, you must keep in mind that Mafia guys have fertile imaginations. They see possibilities to turn an illegal buck where most ordinary citizens see a parking spot. Sawing off the heads of parking meters for the change they contain is not beneath a Mafioso, if he is not too tired. I'll also give you some examples of more lucrative scams in which the hoods ply their trade.

Chapter 8

The Mob Loves Prohibition

In This Chapter

◆ Mafiosi milk their own communities

◆ The reasons behind Prohibition

◆ Gangsters supply illegal liquor

◆ Prohibition produces unforeseen consequences

The United States received a massive influx of immigrants from southern Italy between 1880 and 1914. The overwhelming majority settled in the nation's growing urban centers. Many were uneducated, poor, and spoke only Italian or Sicilian. They also found themselves living in locations where earlier immigrants, mostly Irish and Germans, had taken control of local governments by the judicious use of machine-type politics. Most government jobs and contracts for a wide range of goods and services went to others. Finding themselves on the outside in their new country, many Italians held the belief that governments were corrupt and not to be trusted. Despite this, only a tiny fraction of the new immigrants turned to crime.

In this chapter, you will read of the activities that Italian criminals engaged in before Prohibition began in 1920. Then the main focus will be to explain why the United States banned the use of alcohol and how La Cosa Nostra families and members reacted to the golden opportunities presented by this historic social experiment.

Making Money with Local Rackets

Like other immigrants, Italians tended to group together in ethnic neighborhoods, where they found comfort in common languages and customs. Another reason for this settling style was the availability of affordable housing for the mostly poor newcomers. Although there were positives in these enclaves, they provided a fertile ground for those who were determined to engage in criminal activities by victimizing their *paesanos*.

The Black Hand

The Black Hand was an extortion method, not an organization. A target would receive a note, often sent through the mail, demanding money. The request was backed by threats of injury or death to the victim or his family. Sometimes the extortion was a multi-step affair, but the essentials were similar. Although the practice was widespread, few threats were reported to the police. Some became public knowledge when a reluctant target received a reminder in the form of a bomb blast or some other violent act that police couldn't ignore.

Mafia Speak

In 1903, a New York newspaper coined the term **Black Hand** in a story about an extortion attempt of an Italian businessman who received a letter signed, *Mano Nera* (which means Black Hand). It became common, but incorrect, to use the term to refer to the Mafia.

Italians around the nation were plagued by Black Hand extortions. New York, with its large Italian population, had the most reported cases, but Chicago, Cleveland, Kansas City, Philadelphia, Pittsburgh, and others also had many incidents. Public pressure from the publicity surrounding the hard-to-ignore bombings caused some communities to respond. This was unlike the normal practice of laughing off problems among immigrants. The best-known response took place in 1904, when the New York police department formed an Italian squad headed by Detective-Lieutenant Joseph Petrosino.

Black Hand extortions also plagued hard-working members of Italian communities throughout Canada in the early 1900s. There is no "proof beyond a reasonable doubt" that these activities were carried out by members of secret Mafia-type organizations, but there is little doubt among historians—and no doubt by the author of this book—that Black Hand extortions perpetuated against Italian immigrants were Mafia activities by secret Italian-only organized crime networks. These networks were forerunners of the gangsters who formed a Mafia Commission in 1931 and those who were rousted by state troopers in Apalachin, New York, in 1957.

> ### Big Shot
>
> Detective Petrosino was a vocal and fearless investigator. After five years of investigating Italian-on-Italian crime, Police Commissioner Thomas Bingham sent Petrosino to Sicily to work with Italian officials to gather information about New York criminals believed to have records in Italy that would allow them to be deported. In early 1909, his trip was big news in English- and Italian-language newspapers. Unfortunately, his fact-finding trip angered Italian criminals on both sides of the Atlantic. On March 12, 1909, Petrosino was gunned down in the streets of Palermo. Sicilian Mafioso Don Vito Cascio Ferro was arrested, but the charges were later dropped for lack of evidence. No one was ever convicted of the crime.

Counterfeiting

Counterfeiting was linked to the Mafia at the 1909 New York trial of Ignazio Lupo. He was related by marriage to Peter "The Clutch Hand" Morello, a leader of what became the Genovese family. Lupo and Morello were convicted of running a ring that imported counterfeit American money from Italy. Lupo received a stunning 30-year sentence, and it seemed he would die behind bars. However, President Warren Harding commuted Lupo's and Morello's sentences after 12 years. His was a notoriously corrupt administration, but the pardon might be a better indication of the political and financial strength of the Morello clan. Then again, it might not.

There were other counterfeiting activities in Chicago, Boston, Cleveland, and New Orleans that involved mobsters and their associates after the turn of the century. However, Lupo's 30-year sentence had the desired deterrent effect, pushing mobsters away from counterfeiting and toward criminal activity that was treated less harshly by law enforcement.

> ### Slammer Time
>
> Anthony Milano was a legendary La Cosa Nostra figure, serving as Cleveland family underboss for 31 years, from 1945 to 1976. Earlier, his brother Frank was family boss for five years, from 1930 to 1935. In 1984, Anthony's son Peter took over the Los Angeles family, serving as boss into the twenty-first century. Nearly a century earlier, Anthony Milano served a prison term for counterfeiting, starting in 1911.

Prostitution

The world's oldest profession was booming in most American cities from 1900 to 1920. Different districts were well known for whore houses that mobsters in virtually every family ran pretty openly, with the acquiescence of police and politicians on the take. The Mafia didn't have a monopoly on these lucrative operations, but they ran many. Most "made men," however, weren't directly involved in prostitution because it was viewed as low class, not a respectable business befitting a mobster. Extorting a weekly cut from brothels, however, was honorable and was permitted by the Mafia code. In the 1930s, Lucky Luciano and Al Capone would be tied directly to whore houses, but there is no doubt that made members derived income from prostitution, one way or another, in the early 1900s.

Gambling

Today, legal gambling is a gigantic moneymaker for local and state governments everywhere, attracting millions of players. It is an activity that goes back thousands of years in many cultures. It is no surprise that the Mafia saw the vast moneymaking opportunities in bookmaking and other gambling within Italian communities at the turn of the century.

Card games of all kinds were very common. They required few materials and could be held in backrooms of stores, social clubs, and barbershops. Although it isn't illegal to gamble socially by playing cards or other games, most states outlaw gambling businesses that charge a fee for those who play. It is a service, however, that the Mafia and other organized crime groups have long provided, most often by "cutting" the game or taking a slice of each pot for the "house."

Big Shot

Playing cards could be dangerous for your health, especially if you were a Mafia boss named Joe. New York's Joseph Masseria and Cleveland's Joseph Lonardo and Joseph Porrello all were blown away with cards on the table.

A lottery ran in most Italian neighborhoods. It was a simple game requiring little money to play. In its most basic form, a bettor tried to guess which three-digit number would be the number of the day and would place a bet on his hunch. This number would come from some widely circulated daily number that was supposed to be beyond manipulation.

In 1921, a suspect in a New Jersey murder case told the police that the Castellammarese group had been using violence for the previous seven years to take over the Italian lottery in their section of New York City. They must have achieved their goal because longtime Mafia boss Joe Bonanno wrote that he inherited the rights to that lottery when he replaced murdered boss Salvatore Maranzano in 1931.

Most major cities had extensive gambling operations run by non-Italians. These were highly organized and relied on an ingrained system of corruption for protection from police raids. Much later in the century, powerful Mafia families began moving in on these independent bookies, numbers bankers, and gaming-house entrepreneurs.

Monopolies

Creating and maintaining monopolies has always been a common business practice used by the Mafia. Many mobsters were engaged in small businesses that would gain a great advantage if competition were eliminated.

In discussing the New Orleans family in Chapter 7, I detailed the bloody battle between the Provenzanos and Matrangas to control the unloading of ships carrying fruit. In New York, Ciro "The Artichoke King" Terranova, a relative of Ignazio Lupo, who was often called "Lupo the Wolf," earned his nickname around 1910 by controlling much of the market in that commodity. Other families tried to monopolize perishables like vegetables and ice in the years before refrigerators became a common item. The physical nature of these products made them easy targets for pressure tactics because they would spoil or melt.

Wherever they could, mobsters also attempted to control other services and products that were run in small operations. Cleaning establishments, stores, bakeries, newspaper stands, and the like were easy prey for serious men who weren't opposed to using violence to achieve their goals.

Targeting victims who were suspicious of the police and who had difficulty with English made the mobsters' job easier. Italian criminals didn't invent these tactics, but they used them to perfection.

Mafia Speak

Contrary to the accepted rules of the Mafia, both the Matrangas and the Provenzanos made statements to the police and testified against each other in court. Perhaps neither group contained Mafia members. More likely, each decided to violate the rules because the other faction did.

Petty Crime

The records of many La Cosa Nostra members who grew up in the pre-Prohibition era show arrests for common street crimes such as robberies, burglaries, bank holdups, and muggings. Michael "Trigger Mike" Coppola, a well-known Genovese family mobster in the 1950s who retired in Miami, had a rap sheet that began at age 14 and included 13 arrests for homicide, grand larceny, and robbery from 1914 to 1928. Frank Costello went on to lead the Genovese family, but young Frank was arrested for armed robbery (first in 1908 and again in 1912) in cases that were thrown out. In 1915, Costello served 10 months for carrying a concealed weapon, a handgun.

New York Mafia boss Frank Costello, the "Prime Minister of Organized Crime," served 10 months in jail on a weapons rap in 1915.

(Photo courtesy of GangLandNews.com)

Why Prohibition?

On January 16, 1920, Prohibition, a national experiment to legislate morality, went into effect. From that day on, it was illegal to manufacture, transport, or sell liquor in the United States. The Volstead Act, the enforcement arm of the Eighteenth Amendment, was put into law the next day.

Fuhgeddaboudit
Armed hoods began stealing stored liquor weeks before the start of Prohibition. Within weeks of its implementation, three Prohibition agents were arrested for aiding bootleggers.

Support for Prohibition had been growing for decades. America was undergoing a dramatic evolution before 1920, and for some, this was unsettling. Mass immigration was changing the face of a predominately Anglo-Saxon Protestant nation into one with a wider variety of cultures and values. The fact that most newcomers lived in the same neighborhoods in ethnic enclaves, where they followed many of the practices from their homelands, helped create a "them vs. us" attitude among the established classes.

At the same time, an industrial revolution was changing rural America into an urban nation. With growing cities came increased corruption, more crime, and wide-open red-light districts with gambling dens, saloons, and whore houses. For some, liquor removed the self-control that was necessary to avoid these other vices. The thinking was that John Barleycorn was the root of all evil, and if you could ban liquor, the other problems would decline as well. It seemed like a nice, simple solution.

The obvious flaw with Prohibition was that too many people wanted to drink. They were willing to deal with those who would provide the product even though it was illegal. This flouting of the intent of the law by millions made it easy for the local cop to ignore blatant bootlegging. Because police officer positions were often patronage appointments, key political leaders could easily transfer or fire those zealots who interfered with the illegal liquor trade. Furthermore, prosecutors and judges could easily affect the outcome of cases that got to court. Unfriendly judges and prosecutors could be worked around by controlling their assignments or removing them at the next election. The authorities knew that there would be no great outcry if Volstead Act violations were not pursued and punished. In addition, the federal government hired only a few thousand Prohibition agents, and many were patronage appointments with little training or screening. The bottom line: The great demand for liquor combined with an already corrupt political system meant that Prohibition was doomed before it began.

Where Did the Liquor Come From?

Most televised accounts of Prohibition show boats racing across the water with a load of illegal liquor and the inevitable shot of a speakeasy door with the small hatch that allowed the doorman to control who was permitted entrance. Although these depictions are real, they are misleading in that the truth was much more complicated.

In Stock

When Prohibition began in 1920, the existing liquor didn't simply disappear. It was stored in warehouses and was the first source of illegal liquor. Some was moved onto the black market through misleading paperwork. Some was claimed to have been destroyed or diverted for industrial use. Other amounts were simply stolen by thieves or armed robbers. The problem—for bootleggers—was that this was a limited supply and only a short-term solution.

Mafia Speak

"Is the doctor in?" took on a new meaning during Prohibition. A provision of the Volstead Act permitted doctors to write prescriptions for the medicinal use of alcohol. Some physicians abused this to their own financial benefit.

Homebrew

Many Italians liked to produce their own wine. It was an easy step to begin making liquor, especially if there was a ready market for the product. Prohibition created that demand. Contrary to what some have written, homebrew was not a stopgap measure between the time when the stored, "real" liquor ran out and when serious smuggling of foreign liquor began. On the contrary, homebrew remained a vital part of the illegal liquor trade until Prohibition ended in 1933. It was a practice that was carried out in many homes of every ethnic background, but in the Italian enclaves in major cities, the Mafia organized many of the operations.

In Chicago, the Unione Siciliana, a supposedly benevolent organization with more than 30,000 members, controlled the homebrew market in the Taylor Street district of the West Side. Originally, the Sicilian Genna brothers would sell the stills and ingredients to Italian residents and pay them for their finished product. The still operator had no choice in the matter. If he was going to distill liquor in his own home for sale, he was going to deal with the Unione Siciliana, and that meant dealing with the Gennas.

In Cleveland, the Lonardo and the Porrello families were both involved in the corn sugar business. This was a key ingredient of homebrew that was sold along with small, one-gallon stills to Italian-Americans in the Woodland district. The final product was sold to the Lonardos or Porrellos.

Fuhgeddaboudit
Running your own still was an easy way to make money. It was also dangerous. For example, in December of 1925, Joe Bonanno's partner and boyhood buddy Giovanno Romano perished when a basement still exploded and burned him to a crisp. In Cleveland, in October of 1927, a hidden 50-gallon operating still in the attic of Cleveland mobster John Porrello's house exploded and caught fire. Porrello wasn't injured, but the blast caused him grief. He was arrested for operating an illegal still.

The national president of the Unione Siciliana, Brooklyn's Frankie Yale, cornered a large segment of the homebrew output in his area. New York's Salvatore Maranzano was also a major bootlegger. His men not only collected liquor produced in small home stills in neighborhoods controlled by his family, they also ran larger stills in the countrysides of New York and Pennsylvania.

Maranzano was also allied with Giuseppe "Joe" Siragusa, the Pittsburgh family boss. Siragusa was called the "Yeast Baron" of Allegheny County because of his business of selling yeast to home brewers of beer. Both men got out of the bootlegging business two years before Prohibition ended, not because they saw the end coming but because they didn't. Both were blown away in September 1931, as part of the violence that was commonplace in the Prohibition era.

Joe Roma, boss of Colorado's La Cosa Nostra family, also controlled the production of homebrew in the "Little Italy" section of Denver.

There are many other instances of Mafia members being involved in homebrew production in other American and Canadian cities, including Rocco Perri of Hamilton, who was "Canada's Al Capone" during the Prohibition era. Perri is featured in Chapter 26.

Imports

Importing liquor from Canada, Europe, and Central America was a lucrative part of Prohibition. Everyone seemed to benefit from these enterprises. The foreign liquor companies gained a huge increase in business, the shippers had steady work, the U.S. Coast Guard got more manpower and new equipment, some Coast Guard members supplemented their salaries with bribes, and local police officers did likewise to ignore the landing of liquor. The obvious downside was that people were killed, public officials were corrupted, and the government lost huge amounts of potential tax income.

Canada was a primary exporter of liquor. Its miles of common border with the United States made it practically impossible to stop the inflow of spirits. And despite having its own forms of Prohibition at various times, it wasn't illegal for Canadian firms to export liquor and beer to the United States until mid-1930. The purchaser would simply have to pay a tax and obtain an export permit from customs officials. Then it was just a matter of getting the goods across the border by car, truck, train, or boat. There were periodic spectacular busts, but most loads got through.

On the East Coast of Canada, the tiny island of St. Pierre became well known as a staging area for booze from Europe and Canada. Other ships would anchor directly off the coasts of large American cities, and smaller vessels would go out to retrieve the cargo. Groups with the right connections could dock in the harbor to unload. New York and Boston weren't the only U.S. cities that received goods this way. Smuggling took place all around the American land mass. Cuba and the Bahamas were notorious centers of the illegal liquor trade.

Criminals being what they are, many couldn't resist the temptation to doctor the so-called real booze coming in from Canada and Europe to increase their profits. They produced counterfeit labels and rebottled liquor, often diluted with industrial alcohol that supposedly had the poisons removed. Contrary to legend, it wasn't just the homebrew liquor that could be dangerous to drink.

The United States was well aware that bootleggers were importing liquor from Canada and Europe. Officials applied diplomatic pressure, but the smugglers always found a way around the new roadblocks. They could hardly resist, when a case of liquor purchased in Canada for $30 to $50 would fetch three times that amount in New York.

Fuhgeddaboudit

Anthony Cornero was a San Francisco cab driver in 1922 when he decided that quenching people's thirst was more rewarding than driving them to work. He started with small boats and sailing ships that serviced clubs from San Francisco to Los Angeles. In 1926, he had a huge supply ship that was seized by Prohibition agents off the coast. Cornero fled overseas but returned in 1929 and served two years in prison.

Illegal Breweries and Distilleries

Large quantities of bootleg liquor were processed at illegal distilleries. In these plants, denatured alcohol would be distilled a second time to remove the poisonous materials that had been added for its intended purpose. Success was spotty, and there were many reports of illnesses and deaths. Other ingredients were added to try to give the appearance and taste of legitimate brands, again with varying success.

Illegal breweries gained in importance as Prohibition moved into the late 1920s and early 1930s. Owners of mothballed breweries leased or sold their facilities to those willing to flout the law. Familiar Genovese family gangsters Gerardo Catena, Vito Genovese, and Willie Moretti all invested in a number of breweries in New Jersey.

 Big Shot

Future New Jersey boss Nick Delmore brought at least one Garden State brewery into a large combine of beer-production facilities that dominated the East Coast. At one point, he went into hiding after the shooting death of a Prohibition agent in the brewery. When the heat died down, he returned.

The Al Capone organization in Chicago had many distilleries and breweries. Some were existing facilities brought back on line; others were new permanent plants or large stills that were still small enough to be periodically moved.

Capone's notorious status as Public Enemy No. 1 caused the Treasury Department to dispatch a special nine-man squad of Prohibition agents, headed by the legendary Eliot Ness, to zero in on the transplanted Brooklyn gangster. Ness, lionized by Robert Stack in the 1960s hit television series *The Untouchables*, hammered and harassed Capone. When Capone finally went down in 1931, however, it was for tax evasion.

The Consequences of Prohibition

Prohibition ended in December of 1933 when the Twenty-First Amendment was ratified by the states. Obviously, the 13-year experiment in morality would have profound effects on society. Few of the results, however, were predicted by either the advocates of or those opposed to the "noble experiment."

Violence

Thousands of deaths during the Prohibition era can be tied to the bootleg trade between 1920 and 1933. Historians have estimated that more than 1,000 people were killed in the Chicago area alone. Those numbers might be excessive, but the following examples show that the killing was widespread and lasted throughout the 13 years before repeal:

◆ **1920, Chicago** Boss James "Big Jim" Colosimo was gunned down in his restaurant by his own men because he resisted taking advantage of the opportunities presented by Prohibition.

◆ **1922, Niagara Falls** Dominic Scaroni, a major bootlegger from Guelph, Ontario, took three to the head after attending a banquet with other Canadian bootleggers.

◆ **1924, Cleveland** Joe Rosen, a minor league bootlegger, was shot-gunned to death in a dispute involving liquor.

◆ **1926, Chicago** Hymie Weiss, a bootleg rival to Al Capone, was mowed down with machine gun fire in the street.

◆ **1928, New York** Frank "Frankie Yale" Uale, president of the national Unione Siciliane and a major bootlegger, was machine-gunned to death while driving his roadster.

◆ **1930, New Orleans** William Bailey, a major bootlegger, was murdered.

◆ **1932, Pittsburgh** Three bootlegger brothers, John, Arthur, and James Volpe, were gunned down and killed.

◆ **1933, Denver** Boss Joe Roma, controller of that city's homebrew production, was blown away in a power struggle.

Mafia Speak

Al Capone let his shotguns and Thompson machine-guns do the talking for him on Valentine's Day in 1929. Seven members and associates of the rival Bugs Moran gang were mowed down in a garage while awaiting the arrival of contraband liquor. By chance, Moran avoided the massacre and reacted by saying, "Only Capone kills like that!"

Corruption

To enforce the Volstead Act, Congress created the Prohibition Bureau. It had fewer than 2,500 agents in the field for the entire United States. Poorly trained, they worked for salaries of less than $3,000, which did little for their motivation. The turnover was great, and many reportedly went to work for those they were supposed to be arresting. Corruption was rampant in many police forces, and the Prohibition Bureau was no different, with more than 10 percent of its agents fired for taking bribes. Many men who took their jobs seriously paid with their lives. About 100 agents were killed in the line of duty.

During this period, thousands of speakeasies operated openly and were usually jammed with customers. A relative few were padlocked. Obviously, local police didn't want to close them all down. It would not have been popular. It would have cut off the flow of bribes into police stations, state police barracks, district attorneys offices, and political clubs. It is impossible to gauge how many law enforcement officials were on the take, but the widespread breaking of the Volstead Act simply could not have taken place on such a grand scale without massive corruption.

Fuhgeddaboudit
Elmer Irey was the chief of the Internal Revenue Service Enforcement Branch, the unit that succeeded in bringing down Chicago's Al Capone. Irey had a low opinion of Prohibition agents. He was quoted as calling them "hacks, hangers-on, and highwaymen." According to Professor Howard Abadinsky, Irey complained that one agent had worked on a garbage truck before getting his job, adding, "He worked three months as an agent and then took a six-month leave so that he and his wife could tour Europe."

Consolidation and Growth

Prohibition changed the face of the nation. It also fueled the rise of the Mafia across the country. The very nature of Prohibition increased contact between the various families around the nation. Contraband liquor was constantly on the move, and it's not surprising that the Italian organized crime groups would deal with others of similar beliefs and ethnic background whenever they could. To be sure, they dealt with other ethnic groups, including Jewish and Irish hoods, but for the most part, they dealt with each other. Chicago's Al Capone dealt with his longtime friend Frankie Yale from Brooklyn. The Zerillis from Detroit helped supply the Milano clan in Cleveland. Buffalo's Stefano Magaddino was friendly with Joe Barbara from the Scranton area.

Handling this massive amount of liquor and beer required increased manpower. So, too, did the fighting with other bootleg gangs. Joe Valachi, who would later reveal many Mafia secrets as a government informer, was recruited for just this purpose. Although there were many killings, the net result was a substantial increase in the size of many La Cosa Nostra families.

In 1931, relations among the more than 20 Mafia families were formalized by the establishment of the Commission. Many had been connected earlier through personal friendships—New York's Joe Profaci and Detroit's Joe Zerilli, for example. Others had been acquainted by their membership in the Unione Siciliana. But the formation of the Commission gave a structure to family relationships that would last until near the end of the twentieth century.

> **Slammer Time**
>
> Thomas "Yonnie" Licavoli, brother of longtime Detroit Mafia power Pete Licavoli, did not get to enjoy the fruits of their bootlegging successes. He was convicted of the murder of rival Toledo bootlegger Jack Kennedy in 1934 and spent the next 37 years in prison. He died two years later, in the fall of 1973.

Certainly, the fast-moving events of Prohibition provided many lessons for young Mafia members. The need to organize trucking, rent buildings, purchase equipment, and find competent brewers, distillers, and accountants certainly improved their management skills. They also learned early on that using men of ethnic backgrounds other than Italian was useful. Members had to be Italian, but La Cosa Nostra would, from Prohibition on, have many valuable associates who were not Italian.

Prohibition greatly improved the economic circumstances of many leaders of Mafia families. Much of the hierarchy that emerged had been of modest means a few years earlier. For example, Joe Bonanno details how he used money from his criminal activities to open legitimate businesses, including two garment enterprises, a funeral home, a laundry, and a cheese company. He doesn't mention it, but he also took over bootlegging interests of the murdered Salvatore Maranzano. Prohibition still had more than a year of life left when he took over—plenty of time to cash in. There were similar stories involving other Mafiosi around the country.

The Least You Need to Know

- Prohibition lasted from 1920 to 1933.

- The ban on liquor was widely flouted.

- Bootlegging relied on widespread corruption.

- La Cosa Nostra members were heavily involved in the illegal liquor trade.

Gambling Makes Mobsters Smile

In This Chapter

- The Mafia's main gambling operations
- How the Mafia protects these rackets
- What loan sharking is and how it works

Gambling is one of the best, most consistent moneymakers for La Cosa Nostra. From before Prohibition to the present day, wagering has always been a part of Mafia life. It is an activity that rarely offends the ordinary citizen, so there is little public pressure on authorities to stop it. If estimates are correct, millions of people wager billions of dollars a year, one way or another. What surprises most is that legal wagering hasn't eliminated its illegal counterpart. In this chapter, I will examine some of the different forms of illegal gambling and explain why they have been such durable moneymakers for the mob.

Playing Numbers

Numbers is one of the simplest and cheapest games to play. Mafia members make money from this racket in two main ways: owning all or a piece of a numbers operation or extorting a cut of an independent numbers business.

Numbers comes in many varieties, but an explanation of one version will suffice for our purposes. A player picks a three-digit number from 000 to 999. On a wager of $1, if his selection is correct, the bettor gets $600, a 600-to-1 payoff. In the past, a host of methods were used to pick the winning number, including methods that could be manipulated. Numbers became very popular around 1920 when operators began using a system for picking the winning number that was seen to be out of their control and not susceptible to being fixed.

Several methods were used in different cities, but the common denominator was its presumed honesty and the fact that it was printed in the daily newspapers. The number was often the last three digits of the total mutual handle at a racetrack. Because these results were printed in the newspaper, it was easy for players to know if they'd won, and it added to the sense that the game was honest.

Mafia Speak

When a Mafia wiseguy says he "did a number" on a guy, it has nothing to do with the gambling activity called numbers. But then again, it might. "Doing a number" usually means beating up someone, and that sometimes happens when the gambler hasn't paid off gambling debts!

Prior to the advent of state lotteries (New Hampshire was the first in 1964), numbers was the only game in town for the poor bettor. Early in the last century, a nickel was a common bet. For the very destitute, wagers on a single-digit number were available for less money and obviously a lower payoff.

John Gotti looks like a Dapper Don on Dec. 13, 1990, as he arrives at Brooklyn Federal Court for arraignment on racketeering and murder charges that doomed him to die in federal prison.

(Photo courtesy of New York Daily News)

Fuhgeddaboudit

In 1981, five years before John Gotti became boss of New York's Gambino family, he was a soldier who usually bet $1,000—"a dime"—on horse races. On May 20, however, he hunch-bet $500—"a nickel"—on a horse whose name he liked, John Q. Arab.

"That's all?" said the surprised bookie.

"That's all," said Gotti. "I ain't going crazy no more."

Numbers survive today for several reasons. Betting on credit is one. Hope springs eternal, and it's easy to phone in a bet. And if you win, no tax money is withheld. That appeals to a lot of gamblers. Finally, the odds in illegal numbers are often better than in the legal game.

How does the operator make money? By having the odds in his favor and by balancing his books. Let's assume he gets only one bet of $1 on the number 123. The odds on that number coming up are 1,000 to 1. The operator, commonly called the banker, has a great shot at keeping the player's money. Now let's assume he has 1,000 bettors, and each bets $1 dollar on a different number from 000 to 999. Obviously, one winner collects $600, and the banker, after paying out the winning $600, has a $400 profit.

But bettors don't cooperate that much. A bunch of them might bet on the same number for some reason. Let's assume 20 players each bet $1 on number 222. If that number hits, the banker has to pay out $600 to each of the 20 players for a total of $12,000. If he only had $2,000 in losing bets, he would have to come up with $10,000 to pay off the winners. Obviously, this situation can bust a bank very quickly, so steps are taken to prevent this from happening.

Mafia Speak

In Philadelphia, when a La Cosa Nostra boss orders his men to extort money from the independent illegal numbers operators, it's called "the elbow." Nicholas "Nicky the Crow" Caramandi, a turncoat Philadelphia member, told how the family received $10,000 up front and $300 a week from a numbers operator when he and friends applied "the elbow."

As bets come in during the day, the banker's men chart the numbers being bet. In the previous example, the banker, seeing that number 222 is getting heavy play, phones another banker and bets $18 on number 222. This insurance policy is called the "layoff." If number 222 is the winner, the banker uses the $10,800 he "won" from his layoff bookie to help him pay the 20 players who bet that number for a total of $12,000. The cash he takes in on other numbers is his. Watching the incoming bets and using a proper layoff makes it a lucrative business rather than a gamble. In recent years, many numbers banks have lowered their odds to 500 to 1; on "hot" numbers like 714 and others with a 1 in the middle, they're lowered to 450 to 1.

Betting on Sports

By far, sports betting accounts for the most illegal wagering action today. Very rough estimates in the tens of billions of dollars are bandied about as the annual amount wagered. Numbers and sports-betting amounts are often combined in these estimates.

As in numbers, some mob guys make money by owning the operation or by being partners with the bookie. Others leave the details to independent operators and take a cut for giving them the privilege of taking bets and for "protecting" them from other mob predators. This is simply extorting money from someone who can't run to the police. The Mafia's reputation of not being afraid to use violence greatly aids the collection of a street tax.

This type of extortion effort brought down the Detroit family in the late 1990s. Soldier Nove Tocco received permission to shakedown independent gamblers who hadn't been paying for the right to run gambling in Detroit. The FBI taped some of his attempts and subsequently filed charges against him and a group of his superiors, including boss Jack Tocco.

Fuhgeddaboudit
When police raid gambling joints, written records are important evidence to win convictions at trial. To counter this, gamblers often use water-soluble paper. At the first sign of a raid, the betting slips are dropped into a garbage can of water so they will dissolve. The downside is that the records of the gamblers' bets are gone, but mob bookies often use this to their benefit—and to the detriment of their customers—by telling only the players who claim they have won about the raid. They tell the winners that all bets were off but collect from the losers if they can.

In areas of the country where there is no Mafia presence, mob bookies are occasionally the power behind local operators through layoff betting and related services.

The Line

The bookmaker's ideal situation is to have an equal amount of money bet on each team. In this case, the bookie earns a 10 percent surcharge from the losing bettors because gamblers are required to wager $110 in order to win $100 in most cases. Let's use the Dallas Cowboys and Cleveland Browns football teams as an example. The bookie has

$100 bet on Dallas and an equal amount wagered on Cleveland. If Dallas wins, the bookie uses the $100 of the $110 bet on Cleveland to pay off the person who bet on Dallas. The 10 percent surcharge on losing bets is for the bookie's expenses and profit.

It's never quite that simple, however. If Dallas were viewed as the better team, more people would likely wager on them. To try and balance the action, bookies establish what is called a "betting line." For example, the experts might give gamblers who take Cleveland an imaginary six points to start the game. That line is published as Cleveland +6 or Dallas –6. Dallas has to beat Cleveland by more than six points for Cowboy bettors to win their bets.

Bookmakers fluctuate the line during the week when, despite the handicap or because of it, one team has much more support than the other. This is an attempt to balance the books and make a profit no matter which team wins.

The Layoff

As in numbers, sports bookmakers lay off bets to protect themselves from having too much money on one team. One might call another bookmaker and wager enough to soften the blow if the heavily supported team wins. In turn, the layoff bookie will even hedge his own bets by calling yet another large bookie somewhere else in the country.

> **Big Shot**
>
> Gilbert "The Brain" Beckley of Newport, Kentucky, was one of the biggest layoff bookies in North America in the 1950s and 1960s. His operation spanned many states, and he was connected with major La Cosa Nostra figures in New York and New Jersey. Unfortunately for Beckley, in 1966, the FBI made a case against him. He was convicted of interstate gambling and was sentenced to 10 years. Worse yet, while free on appeal in 1970, Beckley disappeared. The FBI believes he was knocked off by mob bosses who feared he was about to talk.

Controlling the Machines

Americans love to gamble with machines. I'll let the armchair psychiatrists and psychologists among you try to figure out why. It is estimated that 50 percent of the take in legal casinos is from slot machines. Early on, Frank Costello, a major New York La Cosa Nostra power, realized that there were vast riches to be made and cashed in on slot machines in the 1930s.

The Early Days

In the late 1920s, Costello placed slot machines around the city of New York. After some difficulties with honest cops enforcing antigambling laws, Costello added a gimmick to avoid legal problems. When the player dropped a nickel and pulled the handle, a candy mint dropped out, turning the slot machine into a sort of vending machine. If three identical objects showed on the machine, fake coins called slugs would be ejected. These could then be exchanged for cash.

After a very lucrative run with the so-called "one-armed bandits," which obviously couldn't lose because there was no way for them to give out more money than they took in, a change in the city's mayoralty ended Costello's New York slot machine enterprise. Some machines were confiscated by the new reform administration of Mayor Fiorello LaGuardia, so Costello moved them to the more hospitable climate of Louisiana.

> **Fuhgeddaboudit**
>
> Mob turncoat Joe Valachi never rose above the rank of soldier, but he had 20 slot machines that grossed about $2,500 per week during the post-Prohibition depression era in the 1930s, according to biographer Peter Maas.

> **Slammer Time**
>
> According to mob turncoat George Fresolone, Philadelphia associate Carmen Ricci was paying boss Nicky Scarfo $4,000 a week for the right to place his video gambling machines in the Philadelphia family's area. In the mid-1980s Scarfo was sent to jail. Before long, Ricci was only paying $1,000 a week. Nicky needed a "Get out of Jail" card.

Slot machines did require servicing, and there were problems with the racket. Collectors were required to empty the machines, which were relatively expensive, often broke down, and needed repair. They were also vulnerable to seizure, costing the owner his investment and weekly income. To safeguard them, mobsters had to make payoffs to police and politicians, cutting into the profit margin. Nevertheless, slot machines were always a part of the illegal gambling scene, but were not the major players that they are today in video machine form.

Video Poker

Video poker is one of the fastest-growing illegal gambling games. A wide variety of machines are now in use, but a description of an early version gives a clear picture as to how the system works.

The machine is similar to the banking machines that are common today. They have a video screen and buttons to manipulate what is on that screen. They are in bars, restaurants, and backrooms of other locations that have regular patrons who aren't likely to run to the police.

The machines and their locations vary, but they all operate pretty much the same way. In a bar, a customer might give the bartender $20 to start. The bartender punches in a secret code to register 20 points on the video screen. The player then tries to beat the machine by getting the best possible poker hand. In a "draw poker" game, the player is able to keep the five cards that are shown on the screen or replace one to four of them by pushing a button. The player gains or loses points depending how good his hand is. Let's imagine that after playing for one hour he has 40 points on the screen. The bartender is called, sees the points, and punches in a code that sets the points back to zero. He gives the player $40 for the accumulated points. More often, however, the player does poorly and loses, eventually reducing his points to zero, ending the game unless he gives the bartender more money.

How does the mob make money from this? Often it owns the machine and places it in a bar by agreeing to give the bar owner a percentage of the profits, sometimes half. If the machine earns $1,000 by week's end, the bar owner has made himself $500 for doing very little. Indeed, the presence of the machine might increase his customer base. The Mafia owner of the machine has also made $500. With a modest 10 machines around the city, that's $5,000 a week in income.

It's not quite that simple, though. Because the machines are illegal, they can be confiscated before they've paid back the original investment. A trusted associate, always hard to find, visits each machine and uses a secret code to find out how much it won. Associates, who by definition are schemers like their mob superiors, have been known to skim some of the money for themselves. It's a dangerous game that can lead to the culprit being found dead in a trunk.

These illegal machines are found all over the country. Where there is a strong La Cosa Nostra family, the builder of the machines usually finds himself making some kind of secret deal with a senior member so that his machines can be sold and placed in that area.

Building the Clubs

In the days before legal casino gambling, Las Vegas–style casinos were set up in many locations around the country. Many were built on a grand scale with elegant dining and top-notch entertainment to go along with the gambling.

Some of the more famous clubs were run by Jewish gangsters who had a La Cosa Nostra partner to prevent other hoods from moving in on them. During the 1930s, Meyer Lansky, in partnership with mobsters Frank Costello and Joseph "Joe Adonis" Doto, ran the very successful Piping Rock club at Saratoga Springs in New York.

After World War II, Lansky, mobster Vincent "Jimmy Blue Eyes" Alo, and others reopened the luxurious Colonial Inn in Hallendale, Florida. Like the Piping Rock, the Colonial Inn featured various types of wagering, good food, and great entertainment.

A continuing problem for the clubs was their reliance on political influence and law enforcement leaders who were often routed from office in periodic reform movements. The frequent cleanups of gambling establishments convinced Mafia leaders to look to Cuba, the Caribbean isle 90 miles off the Florida coast.

Jimmy Blue Eyes Alo was a Genovese capo and close buddy of Meyer Lansky.

(Photo courtesy of GangLandNews.com)

Gambling had been legal in Cuba for decades when Santos Trafficante Jr. of the Tampa family began operating a casino there in 1946. Things really opened up after Fulgencio Batista took over the government in a 1952 coup. Within a few years, there was a hotel/casino boom with many American mobsters as investors. Meyer Lansky built the luxurious Riviera with friend and partner Jimmy Alo as an investor. A Trafficante syndicate opened the Capri, and Cleveland's family associate Moe Dalitz was involved in the National. Powerful Pittsburgh family capos Samuel and Gabriel "Kelly" Mannarino had a piece of the Sans Souci club.

Obviously, Batista didn't let the mobsters run these casinos out of the goodness of his heart. He, his family, and his friends were the beneficiaries of a variety of methods to channel casino money their way. The mobsters took care of themselves as well. Many of these scams involving Las Vegas casinos are discussed in Chapter 12.

There is an expression that all good things must come to an end, and they did for the Mafia and their partners in Cuba. The decades of corruption led to an internal collapse of the Batista regime and the ascension of the forces of Fidel Castro in January of 1959. Among other changes, Castro closed down the casinos. A month later, they were allowed to reopen, but the magic was gone. A few months later, Castro decided that casinos didn't fit into his new Cuba, and the investments of the Trafficantes, Mannarinos, and other assorted Mafiosi and their associates were lost. To say the least, they weren't happy campers.

Big Shot

In 1960, after prodding by CIA Director Allen Dulles, the Eisenhower administration plotted a secret invasion of Cuba by an army of Cuban exiles. The plan, funded by the CIA, was to assassinate Cuban leader Fidel Castro. Mafioso Johnny Roselli was approached by former FBI supervisor Robert Maheu to determine whether Roselli and his boss would be interested in undertaking this job. Mafia bosses Santos Trafficante Jr. and Sam Giancana eventually met with CIA operatives, but they never did much besides listen. This sordid story led to a multitude of conspiracy theories putting the mob, Castro, or both in the middle of the 1963 assassination of President Kennedy. Castro was said to have responded to the attempts on his life by having Kennedy killed; the Mafia's so-called motives stemmed from brother Robert Kennedy's efforts against them as attorney general.

Collecting the Payoff

None of the illegal gambling operations described in this chapter can operate on a long-term basis without protection from both legal authorities and other hoods. These threats are dealt with differently.

Anthony Trombino and Anthony Brancato really should have known better. The two Tonys had the bad habit of including men with Mafia connections among their stick-up victims. By the summer of 1951, when Jimmy "The Weasel" Fratianno complained that the Tonys had muscled a bookie friend, Los Angeles boss Jack Dragna had had enough. Dragna gave "The Weasel" permission to whack them. On August 6, 1951, Fratianno dangled the prospect of a robbery in front of the two hoods. When the two Tonys drove to the agreed meeting spot, Fratianno and Charlie "Charlie Bats" Battaglia slid into the rear seat and blew their brains out.

During the same era, Montreal was a hotbed of wide-open gambling, prostitution, and violence. In addition, some of the continent's major layoff bookies moved there to avoid heat from the Kefauver hearings. (For more details on these proceedings, see Chapter 14.) Montreal's most powerful criminal syndicate was led by a Bonanno family crew headed then by capo Carmine "Lilo" Galante. A reform movement had been gaining strength in reaction to the widespread mob activity and the lack of response to it by police and elected officials. As a municipal election approached in October of 1954, the hoods looked to ensure reelection of their compliant political friends. It didn't work, and the reform party swept into power.

Shortly after the election, police raided the Montreal home of Bonanno associate Frank Petrula. Ironically, the impetus for the raid had nothing to do with the election or gambling. However, in their search, the police found a payoff list. It included politicians and media that the hoods were trying to manipulate to reelect the political party that had protected them for years. The Mafia had made more than $100,000 in contributions, a technique the mob often uses to protect its gambling operations. In 1954 in Montreal, it didn't work. But it wasn't for lack of effort.

Big Shot

After the police discovered a payoff list in Frank Petrula's home in 1954, his reputation began to wane. The Royal Canadian Mounted Police was onto him and so were prosecutors. Three years later, he developed serious tax problems. Then his problems got much worse. He disappeared and was never seen again. No one thinks he fled. Politician Jean-Pierre Charbonneau wrote that "underworld rumors suggested that Petrula had been executed by his former partners."

In February of 1999, former Mahoning County Sheriff's Captain John Chicase pleaded guilty to corruption charges involving helping protect the Pittsburgh Mafia's gambling operation in the Youngstown, Ohio, area. He also testified that Sheriff Phil Chance was on the take. Chance was sentenced to five years in prison for a variety of charges, including helping Lenny Strollo, the Pittsburgh Mafia overseer of the Mahoning Valley.

Joseph "Bayonne Joe" Zicarelli was a Bonanno soldier based in New Jersey. In June of 1960, the Bayonne police were parked outside his gambling establishments, putting quite a dent in his operations. This upset Bayonne Joe to no end. So he did what every good American does when things aren't going properly: He complained to his congressman. The congressman was Neil Gallagher. Unbeknownst to him and the mobster, the FBI was listening in on one of the many illegal bugs it had up at the time. After several calls to Gallagher's home and office, Bayonne Joe finally reached him on June 21, 1960, and lodged his complaint. Four days later, after Gallagher "got hold of a friend" who "got hold of the little guy in Jersey City," Gallagher was able to assure his constituent not to worry any longer.

> *Gallagher:* "I got hold of those people, and there will be no further problem."
>
> *Bayonne Joe:* "I hope so because they are ruining me."
>
> *G:* "They damn well better not."
>
> *BJ:* "They are doing a job on me like as never done before."
>
> *G:* "I laced into them."

> **Slammer Time**
>
> Congressman Neil Gallagher had a difficult time staying out of trouble. In the early 1970s, Gallagher went to prison as just another disgraced politician. More than 20 years later, he was looking at more prison time for bank and tax fraud. On September 6, 1995, Gallagher pleaded guilty to these charges and went to prison a second time.

In the 1940s, the Broward County, Florida, casinos of Meyer Lansky and Mafioso Jimmy Alo were under the protection of Sheriff Walter Clark. He was openly pro-gambling but carried things to extremes by having his deputies escort the night's take from the casino to the bank. Clark also had a tough time explaining how he accumulated a very comfortable net worth on a sheriff's salary.

A 1984 federal investigation into police corruption in Philadelphia led to charges against a number of cops for accepting payoffs to protect video gambling. It was estimated that 16 cops took more than $350,000 in payoffs over three and a half years.

The stories of payoffs to protect gambling interests are endless. Experienced hoods and politicians disguise them as political contributions from a front organization or funnel cash to a relative or some other third party.

Rooting out corruption is a difficult task. It's difficult to get a conviction without a taped conversation in which the politician is heard accepting the money from the mobster. With increased focus and efforts in official corruption cases, however, prosecutors have been able to use the testimony of mob turncoats to win convictions of public officials much more frequently.

The focus and energy of most law enforcement agencies today, however, is on violent crime, extortion, labor racketeering, and drug dealing. Gambling, once the focus of the FBI and local and state organized crime squads in the 1960s, generally receives attention as a part of a larger racketeering-type investigation of a Mafia family.

Bringing in the Loan Sharks

Mafia guys love loan sharking. Although it's not gambling, it's often a result of gambling. Loan sharking requires three things: money, a reputation for violence, and a borrower who can't get money from a bank or other financial institution because his credit rating is poor or nonexistent. Not all Mafiosi have money, but many do, and those who don't know where to get it. When it is finally loaned to the cash-starved recipients, La Cosa Nostra's reputation—built up over 100 years—for using violence has customers usually paying off their loans at extremely exorbitant rates.

> ### Fuhgeddaboudit
>
> One of the first mob associates who turned against his Mafia friends was Vincent Teresa from Boston. His importance was vastly overrated, and he told many exaggerated tales. Among those was how his fellow hoods stole $4 million from him including a mythical $100,000 in loan-shark money.

Loan sharks make tremendous amounts of money. Longtime Gambino family associate Joseph Watts earned a cool $12 million between 1986 and 1994, according to onetime Gambino soldier Dominick "Fat Dom" Borghese, who picked up $30,000 a week in payments from a slew of Watts customers during those years.

Most loan sharks charge customers anywhere from two to five points a week in interest on the unpaid balance of the loan. For example, if a customer borrowed $1,000 on a Friday at five points a week, the following Friday he would pay a $50 "vig" to keep the cash another week or pay it off with a $1,050 payment. If he kept it six months—forking over 50 bucks in interest each week for 26 weeks—before paying off the loan, he would pay $1,300 in interest on his $1,000 loan.

Small loans, say $100, are usually six-payment affairs in which a customer makes weekly payments of $20 to satisfy a $100 loan. Some loan sharks take $4 at the front end. His customers make eight weekly payments of $15, paying back $120 for a $96 loan. A loan shark's most generous rates are more than double the legal interest rate of 25 percent per year. His average rates are about 150 percent a year.

The Least You Need to Know

♦ Illegal gambling is a La Cosa Nostra moneymaker.

♦ There are many forms of illegal gambling.

♦ Police and political corruption are important to protect illegal gambling.

♦ Mob loan sharks charge exorbitant interest rates.

Chapter 10

The Mafia Puts the Squeeze on Unions

In This Chapter

- ◆ Why mobsters love the union framework
- ◆ Using voting scams to favor the Mafia
- ◆ Exploiting union power
- ◆ Filling union posts with Mafia friends
- ◆ Using violence to control the union
- ◆ Listening in on the mob

In 1978, Peter Vaira, then chief of the Chicago Strike Force, submitted a paper to the White House on organized crime and organized labor. He declared that four large unions—the International Brotherhood of Teamsters (IBT), the Laborers International Union of North America (LIUNA), the Hotel Employees and Restaurant Employees International Union (HERE), and the International Longshoremen's Association (ILA)—were controlled by La Cosa Nostra.

By using the Teamsters Union as an example, I demonstrate some of the ways in which La Cosa Nostra gained and retained control of all four unions. The schemes and scams were similar. This chapter shows how La Cosa Nostra used its influence over the unions to make money at the expense of millions of honest union workers.

The Teamster Structure

To understand how La Cosa Nostra makes money from labor racketeering, I look first at the International Brotherhood of Teamsters, the powerful labor union that had more than 2 million members in 1976.

Slammer Time
The Teamsters Union third international president, Dave Beck, served time for larceny and income tax evasion. Jimmy Hoffa, the fourth president, was jailed for jury tampering and embezzling union funds. The sixth president, Roy Williams, was convicted of bribery conspiracy and became a government witness to avoid prison. Jackie Presser, president number seven, was under indictment for embezzling union funds when he died. Ron Carey, the great hope of reformers, was thrown out of office in 1997 for illegal election practices. Indicted for lying to a federal grand jury about these practices, Carey was acquitted of all criminal charges in October 2001.

Formed in 1903, the original Teamsters Union members drove teams of horses that pulled delivery wagons filled with cargo. It achieved national clout in 1933 when it began to organize workers in the emerging long-haul trucking industry. The union represents many employees, including drivers, helpers, loaders, hi-lo drivers, and other platform workers. The union's power at one time was such that its president's support would be courted by candidates for president of the United States. Unfortunately, the Teamster history is filled with tales of corruption on an unbelievable scale.

The Teamsters Union has about 800 locals throughout the United States and Canada. Each local is simply a group of workers engaged in a similar type of activity, usually in the same geographic area. For example, Teamster Local 295 is based at John F. Kennedy Airport in New York. Its 2,000 members include drivers, helpers, and others in the trucking industry. Members of each local elect leaders, including a president, vice president, secretary/treasurer, recording secretary, and trustees.

The president of a local isn't always the most important official. Often, it's a business agent or other officer with a lesser-sounding title designed to deflect attention from investigators. Between the local and the international president are myriad union bodies such as joint councils, conferences, and executive boards. Each is made up of many officials, often local officers, earning a second salary for little or no work who pretty much serve at the pleasure of the international president. The Teamsters president has been said to have about as many jobs to hand out as the president of the United States.

> ### Fuhgeddaboudit
>
> Before Roy Williams's brief reign as Teamsters president, he was a long-serving vice president who received salaries and expenses for many union posts, including president of Local 41, president of Joint Council 56, president of the Missouri-Kansas Conference, recording secretary of the Central Conference, vice president of the Teamsters, and a general organizer of the Teamsters. This brought him $111,381 in 1973. How could he perform all these jobs? The simple answer is he didn't have to. After receiving a long prison sentence for a 1983 bribery conviction, Williams became a government witness and admitted he was a puppet of Kansas City boss Nick Civella.

Elections

Every three years, all local members are eligible to vote for each of the local officers and trustees. Participation by 50 percent of the members is considered a good turnout. Mobsters parlayed their violent reputations and the membership's general apathy to muscle their way into leadership positions in numerous locals. Once entrenched, it seemed for decades that even an atom bomb wouldn't dislodge them. The executives of each local become delegates to joint councils that oversee locals in a geographic area. It was important for the mob to control this process. If the leader of a member local wasn't cooperating with the hidden arrangements that the Mafia favored, the president of the joint council could apply great pressure in a variety of forms. Members could be transferred. Picket lines of the local could be ignored by other Teamsters, meaning that other unions would follow suit. Worse, the local's administration could be suspended and replaced by a handpicked trustee. The joint councils also sent delegates to the general convention every five years. These delegates voted for the members of the general executive board.

The general executive board is elected for a five-year term by delegates at a national convention. For La Cosa Nostra, the beauty of this electoral system was how easily it could be manipulated. Each family muscled into control of a number of locals. From that base, they powered their way to control many joint councils. The salaried international employees who were delegates would be looking for clear signs as to whom La Cosa Nostra was backing for general president. When they got the word, they voted with blind loyalty to retain the union jobs they enjoyed at the pleasure of the president.

Mafia Speak _____

On April 15, 1988, former Cleveland underboss Angelo Lonardo told a Senate committee that he had conferred with Mafia bosses from Chicago, New York, and Kansas City to determine a new general president for the Teamsters in 1981. According to Lonardo, Kansas City boss, "Nick Civella was interested in Roy Williams running because he controlled Roy Williams." The delegates got the word and elected Williams, even though he was under indictment at the time.

Cleveland underboss Angelo Lonardo earned his freedom by testifying against Mafia bosses from New York and the Midwest.

(Photo courtesy of GangLandNews.com)

The Union Money Machine

For a Mafia member or associate, controlling a union local is like having your own little goldmine. Not only was there a nice salary as president, there also were paychecks for his six friends who served on the administration. Then there's the hired help. Inevitably, family members filled positions like secretary or receptionist. A cousin's company might have the contract to clean the offices, an uncle the one to cut the grass and plow the snow. They'd be sure to bring nice envelopes filled with cash each Christmas.

> ### Fuhgeddaboudit
>
> Thomas and Joseph Gambino, sons of the famous Mafia boss Carlo Gambino, had huge trucking interests in New York's garment center. Charged with crimes that could have meant 15 years in prison, they agreed in 1992 to sell their companies and pay a fine of $12 million. Thomas, a capo in the Gambino family, was reportedly worth more than $100 million dollars at that time.

The fringe benefits were also great. Leased cars were obtained, of course, from a car dealer who would show his appreciation through kickbacks and other perks. Often, when the lease for the car was up, the union man would purchase it at a price far below market value. Expense accounts were large for nonexistent expenses, meals, and entertainment. The scams were endless—a few hundred here, a thousand there. It all added up to something worth killing over. Best of all, the president got to make the rules. None of his executives were going to vote against him, knowing that it would mean the end of their ride on the gravy train, maybe even death.

> ### Slammer Time
>
> John Cody was the president of Teamsters Local 282. He paid $200,000 a year to the leaders of the Gambino family for the privilege of heading this local. In 1982, he was convicted and later jailed for extorting several companies at his mercy. His successor, Robert Sasso, was also convicted of racketeering and jailed a decade later.

Controlling the local meant that you had big-time muscle. For example, a midsize regional trucking company might be doing nicely, operating without union labor. Let's assume this saved him $800,000 a year in salaries and benefits. At the first appearance of a Teamster organizer, the company owner would nearly have a stroke. When you add in the always-present fear factor, it's easy to see why our CEO would quickly agree to pay $50,000 a year, under the table, to be able to continue to operate union-free.

Even if a company was already unionized, there's a payday for the crooked union official. For a payoff, he could negotiate a new contract that didn't cost the company as much as it should. This is called a "sweetheart" contract.

Another great way to make money is to secretly own a company engaged in the same type of business in which you control a union. These Mafia companies would operate without a union or with a "paper" union with few benefits to its workers. Obviously, this would allow the company to make low bids to win contracts that legitimate firms couldn't compete with. It was in this manner that mob trucking firms came to dominate the transportation in New York City's garment industry.

Beginning in the 1970s, the Gambino family controlled Teamsters Local 282 in New York. Members of this local drove concrete trucks that serviced building sites in Manhattan. This small local could easily bring multimillion-dollar construction projects to a dead halt, costing the developer hundreds of thousands of dollars. A simple scheme would have been for the developers to make payments to the local president to ensure that there were no union problems with the concrete truck drivers, but controlling this local provided much greater opportunities than that.

The Colombo family controlled Local 6A of the Laborers Union. These workers placed the concrete that was delivered by members of Teamsters Local 282. Under soldier Ralph Scopo, the Colombo family also controlled the district council of the Laborers Union of which Local 282 was a member. This gave them a stranglehold over subcontractors who used concrete. A subcontractor with union/mob connections would pay Scopo to ensure he got certain jobs.

In the 1970s, the Gambino and Colombo families cooperated with each other and maintained a firm grip over the delivery and placement of concrete in Manhattan. The extortion payments from the builders and subcontractors were immense, but it got better than that.

Through a family associate, the Genovese clan gained control of some of the major concrete-supply companies in Manhattan. The Genoveses worked hand in glove with the Gambino and Colombo families to perfect a scheme that rewarded them all. Any builder, contractor, or subcontractor that resisted purchasing its concrete from the Genovese family's companies would quickly come around when concrete began to arrive late at a job site courtesy of Teamsters Local 282 or when the Laborers Local 6A workers refused to handle it after it finally arrived. Contractors quickly got the message. The Genovese-blessed concrete companies paid $3 a cubic yard to four New York La Cosa Nostra bosses for the right to maintain this monopoly.

Through its control of two building trade unions and concrete-supply companies, the Mafia controlled the vital construction industry in Manhattan into the 1980s. It was an unbelievable display of La Cosa Nostra power. The Colombo family extorted 1 percent of all contracts under $1 million. The four families on the Commission—Gambino, Luchese, Colombo, and Genovese—split a 2-percent kickback on all jobs from $2 to $5 million. All projects over $5 million belonged to the Genovese family.

Direct Mafia Control

A trusted Mafia associate placed in charge of a particular union local would always be sure to pass along a sizeable envelope of cash to his La Cosa Nostra sponsor on a regular basis. The local president would also make sure that a number of Mafia members, relatives, or associates benefited from his position in the form of jobs, contracts, or the best perk of all, the no-show job.

There are many examples of made members of La Cosa Nostra holding important union positions. This was more common before the FBI began to gather information about the Mafia in earnest in the 1970s and 1980s. Public exposure as a La Cosa Nostra member, however, didn't deter some labor leaders who doubled as mobsters.

In 1980, Matthew "Mike" Trupiano Jr. replaced his uncle as boss of the St. Louis family. His "honest" job was as an official of Local 110 of the Laborers Union, where his wife worked as an office employee. Trupiano's consigliere Anthony "Nino" Parrino was vice president of Local 682 of the Teamsters Union. According to FBI documents, Bob Sansone, president of Local 682, answered to his nominal subordinate Parrino.

For decades, Laborers Local 210 of Buffalo was notorious for its mob affiliations. In 1999, the Justice Department claimed that Buffalo family underboss Joseph Todaro Jr., who essentially runs the family for his aging dad, who remained the official boss in late 2001, consigliere Leonard Falcone, and soldiers Joseph Pieri, John Pieri, Joe Rosato, and John Catanzaro were among the many mobsters who held positions in Local 210.

Mafia Speak

In the late 1960s, a Dallas general contractor was having a terrible time trying to construct a new federal building in Buffalo. Laborers Local 210 workers were driving him crazy with absenteeism, lateness, leaving early, gambling onsite, working at a slow pace, and so on. Finally, after talking to some Local 210 officials, the general contractor hired John Cammillieri to kick things into line. Cammillieri tacked up a list of "get to work" orders that were promptly obeyed. The reason? Cammillieri was a capo in the Buffalo family, and the workers knew it.

Anthony Scotto was president of Local 1814 of the International Longshoremans Association. He inherited this position when his father-in-law, Anthony "Tough Tony" Anastasio, died. Scotto, a capo in the Gambino Family, was considered so powerful that presidents and governors courted him. Former New York Governor Hugh Carey testified as a character witness for him, but in 1979, Scotto was convicted of extorting payoffs from company officials. He was sentenced to five years and ultimately served three years in prison.

Late Chicago capo Vincent Solano ran Local 1 of the Laborers Union from 1977 until his death in 1992. Vice president Sal Gruttadauro and recording secretary Frank LeMonte were also members of the Chicago Outfit. While riding herd over laborers, Solano also had time to supervise a huge gambling empire, an extensive extortion racket, and a vending machine monopoly, according to testimony by former Outfit associate Ken Eto.

New Jersey boss John Riggi was business manager of Laborers Local 394 for 21 years despite the fact he was a known La Cosa Nostra member. In 1992, Riggi pleaded guilty to extortion and bribery in connection with his union position and was sentenced to 12 years in prison.

Luchese soldier Peter "Jocko" Vario was also vice president of Local 66 of the Laborers Union. He was convicted in 1990 of labor racketeering and sharing the proceeds with family boss Vittorio Amuso. Vario served about four years and lost his union post.

Labor Union Violence

With La Cosa Nostra, violence always looms on the horizon. It occurs often in Mafia dealings with unions. The following examples illustrate just how deadly Mafia/union activities can be.

The most famous case of all involves the disappearance of Teamsters general president Jimmy Hoffa in 1975. Hoffa was declared dead seven years later. This story is detailed in Chapter 7.

Fuhgeddaboudit

One of the worst books ever written about organized crime was *Contract Killer* by Donald "Tony the Greek" Frankos (1992). In it, he makes a series of pathetic claims, including the assertion that he personally killed Jimmy Hoffa. Frankos says the fact that he was in prison when it happened doesn't put the lie to his story. He purchased a secret pass to do the hit. Right!

Theodore Maritas was the powerful head of the Laborers district council for the New York City carpentry locals in the late 1970s. Influential in city politics, his support was always sought by Democratic party office seekers. None of that helped him in 1981 when the Genovese family, which had worked with him to extort payoffs from contractors, decided to kill him when it appeared that he might cooperate with the feds. His body has never been found, but like Hoffa, he was declared dead years later.

Elmer Alton "Al" Bramlet was president of the Culinary Workers Union in Las Vegas. The union and its workers are vital to the operation of casino restaurants and hotels. Obviously, Bramlet wasn't. In March 1977, he was under investigation for irregularities in his local's benefit funds when he disappeared. No one has seen him since.

In 1980, John McCullough, president of Roofers Union Local 30, was trying to organize the workers in the growing casino industry in Atlantic City. Unfortunately for McCullough, Local 54 of the Hotel Employees and Restaurant Employees Union was trying to accomplish the same thing—and they were backed by Philadelphia Mafia boss Phil Testa. McCullough was shot to death in the kitchen of his home by a street punk who claimed he had been working for two Philadelphia mob associates. They were found guilty, but years later the convictions were overturned.

John O'Connor was the business agent for Local 608 of the United Brotherhood of Carpenters and Joiners in New York. In May of 1986, he was shot in his buttocks in the lobby of his union's office building by members of the Westies, an Irish-American gang based on the West Side of Manhattan. Despite tape recordings and testimony that the shooting was ordered by John Gotti because O'Connor's men had trashed a Gambino soldier's restaurant that had been built with nonunion labor, Gotti was acquitted.

Union Talk

Mobsters are well aware of the dangers that can arise if their Mafia bosses suspect that the feds are about to indict an underling, as a Colombo construction specialist, soldier Ralph Scopo, was overheard explaining to an associate on August 5, 1984:

> "Now I get indicted and they're afraid …. The only guy they got to worry about is me. If I open my mouth, they're dead. So to kill the case—Bango!" said Scopo as he folded his fingers into the shape of a gun and clicked his trigger finger.

Scopo knew that his bosses would kill him in an instant, despite all the money he had made for them, if they even suspected he would talk. Ralph Scopo didn't meet the fate he feared, but he was convicted of racketeering in the historic Commission case, was sentenced to 100 years in prison, and died behind bars.

Big Shot _____

Buffalo capo John Cammillieri wanted some steady income as an executive of Local 210 of the Laborers Union. Boss Sam Pieri didn't think that was a good idea. After Cammillieri complained, however, Pieri reconsidered, and in May of 1974, he decided to present him with a special gift on his 64th birthday—several ounces of lead behind the ears and in the chest.

Sentenced to 100 years for labor racketeering, Colombo family soldier Ralph Scopo died in federal prison.

(Photo courtesy of GangLandNews.com)

In Chapters 12 and 20, you'll find further discussions of the mob/union connections, in particular, the manipulation of their huge pension funds and how the government has attempted to remove the influence of La Cosa Nostra from the four major international unions.

The Least You Need to Know

◆ The way four major unions were organized helped the Mafia gain and retain control of them.

◆ The mob easily manipulated elections of higher union officials in these four unions.

◆ The Mafia used their control of the unions to extort money.

◆ Made members of La Cosa Nostra held powerful positions in the four major unions.

◆ The Mafia used violence to achieve and maintain their control of these unions.

◆ Mafia members and associates involved in union affairs feared being suspected of being an informer.

Chapter 11

Dealing Drugs

In This Chapter

- ◆ The La Cosa Nostra drug rule
- ◆ Federal drug laws
- ◆ The Mafia antidrug law was a sham

La Cosa Nostra's stand on drugs has been a hotly debated subject for more than 50 years. In this chapter, I examine testimony about the no-drug rule from Mafia members and look at the evolution of federal drug laws to see if there is a connection between them. Next, I'll examine several cases to show that, although there might have been such a rule in place, it has often been ignored, until today. In the Mafia, the quest for money overrides everything else.

The Mafia Drug Ban

Joseph Bonanno, the longtime New York City Mafia boss, had his autobiography published in 1983. In it, he claims, "My Tradition outlaws narcotics." If Bonanno were being honest, the ban on narcotics would predate the formation of the Mafia Commission in 1931. But that's not borne out by history.

Fifteen years earlier, on June 26, 1916, Charles "Lucky" Luciano pleaded guilty to possessing a small amount of heroin. He served a year in prison. The Mafia boss, who would make *Time* magazine's Top 20 list of the country's most influential business leaders of the twentieth century, started out as a low-level drug dealer.

Bonanno ignores narcotics during his account of the formation of Mafia's Commission, but he mentions that at the 1956 national meeting, the issue was discussed because so many families were becoming involved in the lucrative trade. The Mafia leadership was going to readdress the issue at the infamous 1957 meeting at Apalachin that was cut short by the New York state police.

Famous mob turncoat Joe Valachi testified at the McClellan Senate hearings that, in 1948, Mafia boss Frank Costello prohibited Genovese soldiers from engaging in narcotics trafficking. "After Anastasia died in 1957, all families were notified—no narcotics," added Valachi.

When Jimmy "The Weasel" Fratianno was inducted into the Los Angeles family in the fall of 1947, he was warned to stay away from drug dealing or face death. Cleveland underboss Angelo Lonardo also testified that he was told of a no-drug rule when he was "made" in the late 1940s.

Fuhgeddaboudit

In Colombia in the 1990s, the government gave farmers money to not grow the coca plant, from which cocaine is derived, as an inducement to get the country out of the drug-dealing trade. In Chicago in 1957, according to Joe Valachi, the Outfit banned dealing in narcotics and paid all Chicago drug-dealing soldiers a $200-per-week allowance to subsidize the loss of earnings from the outlawed narcotics business.

Many mobsters who defected in the 1980s and 1990s confirmed that their inductions included the no-drug-dealing rule. These mobsters include Vincent "Fish" Cafaro of the Genovese family, Michael Franzese of the Colombo family, and Nicholas "Nicky the Crow" Caramandi of the Philadelphia family.

These examples, and a host of others from a wide assortment of La Cosa Nostra members who were separated by space and time, confirm to my satisfaction that many families had a rule against drug dealing. When it began, how many—if any—families enforced the rule over the last 100 years is in doubt. Of course, the real issue is whether this ban was just a sham. It was.

The Federal Drug Laws

In 1919, the U.S. Supreme Court upheld the 1914 Harrison Act that banned the sale of opium, coca, and their derivatives to all except medical professionals. In 1951, Congress passed the Boggs Act, which tightened drug penalties and was a controversial response to the increase in heroin use after World War II.

Five years after the Boggs Act, Congress passed the Narcotics Control Act in which the penalties were ratcheted up again. Probation, parole, and suspended sentences were eliminated. A first trafficking offense brought a mandatory minimum of five years in prison. A second offense had a mandatory minimum of 10 years and a maximum of 40 years.

Big Shot _____

Colombo soldier Anthony "Tony the Gawk" Augello was so afraid of being killed after he was indicted on drug charges in May 1983 that he committed suicide in a telephone booth rather than attend a meeting from which he would not return. For Augello, the mob ban on drug dealing was real.

The passage of these harsh laws in 1951 and 1956 brought the question of drugs to the discussion table at the 1956 and 1957 national meetings of La Cosa Nostra. Morality had nothing to do with it. The concern was that sentences would now be so lengthy that it was too dangerous for bosses to permit underlings to deal drugs because they might talk if they were caught.

Today, a federal conviction for possessing a kilogram of heroin, with intent to distribute it, results in a mandatory 10-year minimum sentence. A third conviction earns life without parole.

Close-Ups of Some Drug Boys

In his autobiography, Bonanno presented an honorable picture of the mobster way of life. His mythology claims that drug dealing was beneath a real man of honor. This statement is a joke when compared to the evidence. In the following sections, I discuss mobsters who were convicted of narcotics offenses while holding top-level positions and mobsters who would later gain promotions despite drug convictions.

Joe Piney Armone

Joseph "Joe Piney" Armone had a lengthy career in the Gambino family. He and his brother Steve were dealing drugs in the 1950s. The Armones operated under the wing of Joseph Biondo, who became underboss when Carlo Gambino took over the family in 1957. Both Steve and Joe Armone registered federal narcotics convictions. Joe Piney served five years and yet emerged to rise within the family. In Chapter 23, I discuss the Armones' roles in getting Gambino to the top of his family.

> **Mafia Speak**
>
> On December 12, 1989, the FBI was secretly taping John Gotti as he spoke to Frank Locascio in an apartment above Gotti's social club. Gotti recounted how he and Armone used to discuss Mafia business that they were not supposed to talk about—drugs. "I didn't know what I'm talking about, he didn't know what he was talking about. So, he won't know that I don't know what I'm talking about," said Gotti. Armone, who was convicted of racketeering in 1988, never got a chance to explain his position. He died in prison in 1992.

During Paul Castellano's reign as boss, Armone was promoted to capo and had the ear of his leader despite his narcotics record. When John Gotti began plotting against Castellano in 1985, Armone became a part of the conspiracy. In 1986, when underboss Frank DeCicco was blown up by a bomb, Gotti promoted Armone to underboss. A year or so later, Armone was convicted of racketeering and went to prison. Gotti reshuffled his administration and made Armone consigliere. Armone's long-standing involvement in drug dealing didn't hinder him from rising near the top of his family. The no-drug rule seemed irrelevant here.

And for all the pronouncements by lawyers and other mouthpieces that John Gotti despised drugs, he selected four drug dealers to be the designated shooters for the December 16, 1985, killing of Paul Castellano.

Vito Genovese

Vito Genovese is a legendary American Mafia figure. His name lives on through its use as the official name of the New York Mafia family that he led in the 1950s. Genovese rose through the ranks and was appointed underboss by Charles "Lucky" Luciano when he took power in 1931.

In the 1950s, Genovese confronted Joe Valachi about his drug dealing. Genovese's ultimate rejoinder to Valachi illustrates the mentality that Mafia chieftains had about their no-drug rule. The confrontation came after Anthony "Tony Bender" Strollo, Valachi's capo, had muscled into one of Valachi's heroin transactions and forced him to give up $20,000 to help Genovese pay off a debt. Not too much later, after Strollo had given Genovese the $20,000, Genovese summoned Valachi and asked him if he was dealing in drugs. Valachi, who knew lying to his boss would be much worse than admitting how he earned the cash he had forked over to him, confirmed this. Genovese said simply, "You know you ain't supposed to fool with it. Well, don't do it again." So much for the Mafia antidrug law.

Slammer Time

In 1959, Vito Genovese was convicted of heroin conspiracy in the company of serious drug dealers. Luchese capo John Ormento, future Bonanno boss Natale Evola, and Rocco Mazzie of the Gambino family were all convicted as part of the same narcotics enterprise. So was Genovese's successor during the last two decades of the twentieth century, Vincent "Chin" Gigante. Genovese died in prison. Gigante served four years, and as soon as he got out, he began a crazy act—walking the streets of Greenwich Village in his pajamas—that kept him out of prison until 1997.

In 1959, Genovese was sentenced to 15 years in prison for heroin trafficking. It was a stunning development. The government was rarely able to convict Mafia bosses of serious charges. Some criminals and law enforcement officials believed Genovese was set up for conviction in a plot by other Mafia leaders. Although possible, there is little evidence to support this hypothesis.

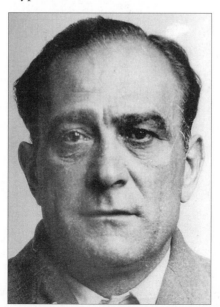

New York Mafia boss Vito Genovese died in federal prison doing time for heroin trafficking.

(Photo courtesy of GangLandNews.com)

Carmine "Lilo" Galante

Carmine Galante, a convicted Bonanno family drug dealer, is the proof that puts the lie to Joe Bonanno's claim that he was against drug dealing. Galante was born in New York City, but his roots were in Castellammare del Golfo in Sicily, as were Joe Bonanno's. Galante's father had emigrated around the turn of the century, and this background earned Lilo the attention of Bonanno, who was decidedly inclined toward people from his own hometown.

Fuhgeddaboudit
While Carmine Galante was serving a prison sentence in Sing Sing Prison in 1931, he was labeled a psychopath. Galante's later exploits would confirm that assessment.

In 1953, Bonanno sent Galante to Montreal to take charge of the family interests in that Canadian city. Around this time, many large layoff bookies fled to Canada to avoid the heat generated by the U.S. Senate hearings on gambling held by Senator Estes Kefauver. In Montreal, Galante was right in the center of a main transit point for the so-called French Connection heroin being smuggled from France to the United States.

By April 1956, Galante had brought too much attention to himself, and he was deported from Canada. A few months later, he was arrested near Apalachin, New York, where La Cosa Nostra had been holding a national meeting. In typical Galante style, he had lost his license for driving offenses and presented one in the name of Joseph "Joe Beck" DiPalermo, a fellow drug dealer in the Luchese family. This led to Galante's arrest for driving without a license.

Mafia Speak

The term "French Connection" is an oversimplification of the heroin trafficking in the 1945 to 1970 era. Sicilian Mafia members and associates obtained the raw material for heroin and opium from the Turks. For the most part, the opium was refined in laboratories in Marseilles and was processed into heroin by French chemists. Traffickers from both sides of the Atlantic would transport the heroin to the United States and Canada. There were many variations of this route, but the French Connection name was catchy, especially after a movie of the same name was made in 1971.

Around this time, Bonanno appointed Galante as his new underboss when Frank Garofalo stepped down. Galante wouldn't have gotten the No. 2 spot if he hadn't been kicking money up to Bonanno. It defies basic logic and common sense for Bonanno not to have known he was receiving money from the proceeds of drug dealing.

Bonanno took no action against Galante because his underboss was too tough and had too many friends, and Bonanno was very happy about all the cash he was earning thanks to the prowess of the cigar-chomping Galante. If Joe Bonanno didn't know that Galante was dealing in drugs in the 1950s, he was the only one.

In 1959, Galante was indicted in two major heroin conspiracies. After three years of legal proceedings that included a mistrial caused when the foreman of the jury mysteriously fell down a flight of stairs, Galante was found guilty on June 25, 1962, and was sentenced to 20 years in prison.

> ### Fuhgeddaboudit
>
> Bill Bonanno, the son of Mafia boss Joe Bonanno, wrote in his book, *Bound by Honor* (St. Martin's Press, 1999), that he was stunned by his father's lack of action once it became known that Galante was indicted for drug dealing. The younger Bonanno wrote, "My father's reactions to these drug arrests, and particularly to Galante's, remains a puzzle to me to this day." To most others, the answer was obvious.

Galante spent the next 12 years in prison. On January 24, 1974, he was released and immediately went back to work. Bonanno had been deposed by the Commission and Philip "Rusty" Rastelli was now family boss. Galante flexed his muscles with a view toward taking over the family. Some key aides, including Caesar Bonventre and Salvatore Catalano, were heavily involved in narcotics. Their connections were through Montreal, where a Sicilian wing of the family was firmly entrenched. The Bonannos were now massively involved in heroin trafficking. There wasn't even a pretense of obeying the no-drug rule.

When Nicky "The Crow" Caramandi turned on the Philadelphia family, he detailed his induction. Among the rules outlined by boss Nicodemo "Little Nicky" Scarfo was his version of the Mafia's no-drug policy. Scarfo said you couldn't deal drugs, but you could lend money to drug dealers, shake them down for a cut of their money, and steal from them. Scarfo might not have realized it, but he was summing up nearly 50 years of La Cosa Nostra drug policy. It was okay for members to make money off drug dealing. The key was not to get caught *and* to make sure you kicked some money upstairs to your superiors.

Despite the so-called ban, drug dealing infested the higher ranks of the Pittsburgh family. On October 29, 1990, underboss Charles "Chuckie" Porter and senior capo Louis Raucci were found guilty of a multicount indictment that included possessing cocaine and conspiracy to distribute it. Porter received a 28-year sentence; Raucci was hit with 27 years. Within a year, Porter began secretly informing to get his sentence reduced. Porter got out in December of 2000; Raucci died behind bars in 1995.

Bonanno mobster Carmine Galante earned millions of dollars as a heroin merchant.

(Photo courtesy of GangLandNews.com)

Canadian-based members of La Cosa Nostra followed in Galante's footsteps when it came to drug dealing. Nicolo "Nick" Rizzuto, the Bonanno capo in Montreal since 1978, was arrested for possession and trafficking of cocaine on February 8, 1988, in Venezuela where he had a second home. He spent almost five years in prison there and returned to Montreal in 1993. Further west in Niagara Falls, Ontario, Carmen Barillaro, a Buffalo family soldier, was heavily involved in drugs. His record included convictions for conspiracy to traffic in a narcotic, conspiracy to import a narcotic, and counseling to commit murder that involved drugs. Barillaro got out of the drug business for good on July 23, 1997, when he was shot to death in Niagara Falls, Canada, by Calabrian mob rivals.

Philadelphia boss Ralph Natale (1994–1999) was a convicted drug dealer who was nabbed by the feds in June of 1999 and was charged with operating a methamphetamine-distribution ring. Facing what would be a life sentence for the 64-year-old gangster, Natale rolled over and became a government witness against underboss Joseph "Skinny Joey" Merlino. In his plea agreement, Natale admitted to seven murders, five attempted murders, drug trafficking, and other crimes. Not only was Natale the first La Cosa Nostra boss in history to testify, he was also the first to admit to drug dealing.

The Least You Need to Know

- La Cosa Nostra had a no-drug rule.
- The no-drug rule has been widely ignored.
- Prominent Mafiosi benefited from drug dealing.
- Tough drug laws have turned many mobsters into defectors.

La Cosa Nostra Builds Las Vegas

In This Chapter

- ◆ Gambling in Las Vegas
- ◆ Mafia members are secret partners in Las Vegas
- ◆ The importance of Teamster money
- ◆ Mobsters get paid first in Las Vegas
- ◆ The goldmine goes bust for the mob

Las Vegas was a huge moneymaker for La Cosa Nostra. For decades, it was rumored that the mob controlled this Nevada city, with longtime Mafia associate Ben "Bugsy" Siegel being the man most responsible for its growth.

In this chapter, I explore the development of Las Vegas gambling palaces and discuss ways in which La Cosa Nostra milked as much money as possible from this unique American city. I also look at how the golden goose got cooked and how the Mafia boys were kicked out of the penthouses and now walk with the rest of the suckers, er, customers.

The Beginning

In 1931, Nevada legalized wide-open gambling and helped set the stage for the Las Vegas phenomenon. The legislation was an obvious attempt to increase the general revenues of the state, which had limited legal gambling by 1900. Today, it is apparent that neither Las Vegas nor Nevada could exist without income from gambling. More than 50 years ago, quite a few people saw it coming and recognized that gambling was going to stay. From then on, the major question was who was going to make the most money from the Las Vegas experience.

Besides the legalization of gambling, Las Vegas received three other huge boosts starting in 1931—an abundance of jobs, water, and electricity—courtesy of the construction of the gigantic Hoover Dam. Nevada also simplified its divorce laws that same year. Unhappy spouses from California and elsewhere would set up shop in Las Vegas and Reno for the required six-week waiting period. Not surprisingly, they filled some of their spare time by doing a little gambling.

Fuhgeddaboudit

In popular literature and the movies, Bugsy Siegel is often credited with being the father of Las Vegas. It's one of many organized crime myths, and it collapses under scrutiny. Although they were of a different style than Siegel's famous Flamingo Hotel, the El Rancho and the Frontier were luxurious hotel/casinos on the Las Vegas Strip at least five years before Siegel's opulent hotel/casino. What's more, the Flamingo was the idea of entrepreneur Billy Wilkerson. Siegel only came aboard after Wilkerson ran out of money.

In 1941, the famous Las Vegas Strip began to take shape along Highway 91 leading out of town toward Los Angeles. That year, the El Rancho Vegas opened at an estimated cost of $450,000, followed soon afterward by the Frontier in October of 1942. Both had pools and air conditioning, big lures for gamblers and weary travelers. El Rancho started with 63 rooms. The Last Frontier had 107. The mob had nothing to do with the beginnings of either hotel.

The history of the Flamingo Hotel and Casino is intriguing, but it was mainly an operation of Jewish gamblers such as Siegel, Meyer Lansky, Moe Sedway, and Dave Berman. Frank Costello was rumored to have put money into it, but unlike the others, his name never appeared on any of the many legal documents associated with the hotel. It was the Lansky group's money that Siegel was mismanaging, and it is likely that these men had Siegel murdered on June 20, 1947, despite the mythical stories of the La Cosa Nostra Commission debating his fate in Havana, Cuba, months prior to his death.

Meyer Lansky had a big piece of the action in Las Vegas.

(Photo courtesy of GangLandNews.com)

The eventual success of the Flamingo spurred already existing interest in the construction of hotel/casinos on the Las Vegas Strip. Like the Flamingo, two of the next projects suffered from poor financing. In 1948, the Thunderbird opened for business, helped along by secret financing from Meyer Lansky after the original investors ran out of funds. San Diego entrepreneur Wilbur Clark began building the Desert Inn in 1946, but financial problems forced Clark to turn to a Cleveland group led by Dalitz and secretly backed by the Cleveland family. They purchased 74 percent of the company and completed the project in 1950.

Evidence of the Mafia's involvement in Las Vegas came to light when the Tropicana Hotel and Casino opened. In 1957, New York Mafia boss Frank Costello invested money in the new Tropicana that was the dream of Ben Jaffe and Charles Baron. When Costello was shot by Vincent "Chin" Gigante on May 2, 1957, police found a piece of

Mafia Speak

In 1988, Cleveland underboss Angelo Lonardo confirmed 30-year-old rumors about the Desert Inn. He said that shortly after it began operating on April 24, 1950, the ownership group led by Moe Dalitz gave a piece of the place to Cleveland family leaders Al Polizzi and Frank Milano. This was to "protect" Dalitz and company from being muscled by other Mafia families.

Big Shot _____

Frank Costello might be the only Mafia boss to do jail time because he survived a rubout attempt. When he was wounded in 1957, he was called before a grand jury that was looking into his attempted murder. Costello refused to testify and was given 30 days for contempt. He was released after 15.

paper in his suit jacket when he was taken to the hospital. On it was written "gross casino wins, 4-27-57, $651,284."

The "gross casino wins" note in Costello's pocket was written by the Tropicana's manager, Lou Lederer, and the amount was the Tropicana receipts for that April day. Clearly, Costello had a financial interest in the casino. Costello's longtime partner, Dandy Phil Kastel, had applied to be the casino's original manager but was denied a license because of his criminal associations.

The Loans

Building a competitive hotel/casino on the Las Vegas Strip strained the financial resources of most entrepreneurs, causing many to seek funds from others. Because many new investors wanted to remain anonymous, rumors of hidden mob influence were spreading along the Strip almost immediately.

This type of murky ownership made it difficult to obtain loans from banks and other legitimate financial institutions. Some bank loans were made, but generally they were exceptions that proved the rule. One notable exception was a 1951 $1 million loan by the Bank of Las Vegas to build the Sahara.

In 1960, the Teamsters Central States Pension Fund had more than $100 million, and the total was growing. A few years earlier, President Jimmy Hoffa realized he could put that money to good use—if not for his members, certainly for himself—and had begun making loans of pension funds. He and a few other powerful Teamster leaders controlled it. On paper, the fund was administered by trustees appointed by both the union and owners, but the owners had no interest in bucking what the Teamster leadership wanted. After all, it wasn't the owners' money. Most pension funds used experienced insurance companies to invest their money, but the trustees decided where the pension fund money went. Hoffa and the other Teamster leaders were suddenly the most important bankers money could buy.

The fund's first Las Vegas hotel/casino loan, in 1960, went to a group that had taken over the Stardust Hotel and Casino project that had been floundering under the ownership of Tony Cornero. The company was sold to Rella Factor, wife of Jack "The Barber" Factor, who knew Moe Dalitz and his group were running the Desert Inn. The Pension Fund gave the new owners a loan of $8 million. Almost immediately, rumors began that secret payments were going to Chicago. The Chicago Outfit was said to have arranged the Teamsters loan and was allowed to place key men in positions in the casino so that they could skim cash that would be sent back to Chicago.

Teamster loans also went to companies building new gambling resorts, including Caesar's Palace and the Aladdin in 1966 and an expanded Circus Circus in 1972. The modern facilities created a demand for loans from some existing gambling complexes that were trying to stay competitive with the new arrivals. Among those receiving Teamsters money for refurbishing were the Dunes and the Fremont. By 1975, under pressure from the federal government, the Teamsters stopped lending money to new Las Vegas enterprises. It had been quite a run.

> ### Fuhgeddaboudit
>
> Illegal FBI bugs revealed that, in the early 1960s, Chicago boss Sam Giancana made frequent trips to Las Vegas to pick up the Outfit's share of the skim. Like many CEOs, Giancana liked to combine business with pleasure. His girlfriend, Phyllis McGuire, often performed there with the famous McGuire Sisters singing group.

The Skim

Most skimming at Las Vegas casinos was done with the knowledge and complicity of the casino operators. The purpose was to generate cash that could be funneled to assorted silent partners, including mobsters, police, and elected officials who were on the take.

When a Mafia boss used his influence with the Teamsters Union to obtain a Pension Fund loan for a new or existing Las Vegas hotel/casino, he also expected to be able to place his own men in charge of the casino. This was so that cash could be skimmed off the top without the knowledge of the IRS, the FBI, or the Nevada Gaming Commission.

La Cosa Nostra bosses who facilitated Teamster loans often earned hundreds of thousands of dollars in kickbacks from the successful applicants.

For our purposes, a skim is quite different than unauthorized stealing by an employee or a customer. Both of these are constant concerns to the owners and gaming officials but are not part of this discussion.

> ### Big Shot
>
> Edward "Marty" Buccieri was a Chicago Outfit member who knew entrepreneur Allan Glick. Buccieri felt he had been helpful in Glick's successful application for a $62 million Teamsters Pension Fund loan. Buccieri confronted Glick about receiving some gratitude for the aid. Glick's more powerful mob friends thought Buccieri's muscle move was in very poor taste. He was killed shortly thereafter.

Cash

At each casino gaming table, a method was developed to skim off the money that came in the form of currency. Near the employee in charge is a slot in the tabletop that leads to a box suspended under the playing surface. When a player purchases chips, the bills are recorded by hidden cameras above the table and then are pushed through the slot into the drop box by a plastic device shaped like a huge credit card with a handle. Periodically, security people collect the drop boxes and replace them with empty ones. They take the full boxes to the cashier's cage, where the cash is sorted, counted, and recorded. At each stage, there is paperwork to try to eliminate stealing and to present a paper trail.

In a skim operation, cash is taken out of the drop boxes before it is counted. Casino employees—sometimes security guards, more often cashiers—have to be in on the crime. Whether it occurs before or after the money reaches the cashier's cage, cash is taken from the drop boxes and is placed aside where it can be collected by someone higher up in the scam's chain of command. The participants are well-placed, highly trusted, well-paid employees who are expected to keep quiet about the practice, obviously. Problems occur when the skimmers are so tempted that they skim from the skim—a very dangerous affair for the skimmer.

Fill Slips

This method leaves a paper trail and is used less frequently. All games (except for slot machines) are played with chips that can be bought at a table but not redeemed there. To cash in, a player takes his chips to a cashier, who redeems them. This necessitates a steady influx of chips to the tables to replace those that players take away.

When needed, the person in charge of the game signals to his superior, and they both sign a request form, called a "fill slip," for more chips. Three copies are taken to a cashier, who signs it and turns over the requested number of chips. He keeps a copy, and the other two are sent back along with the chips. One copy is pushed into the drop box, and the chips are put to use.

The fill slip lets the tax people or the owner balance the books. If the count in the cashier's cage is down $5,000, the fill slip from the cashier should show where it went and should be verified by the other copy in the drop box.

Mafia Speak

In March 1975, Argent owner Allan Glick claimed Kansas City boss Nick Civella said the following to him, "You owe us $1.2 million. I want that paid in cash. In addition to that, we own part of your corporation, and you're to do nothing to interfere."

To use the fill-slip skim, the two signed request forms from the table and the floor man are brought to the cashier. He pockets all three copies, and no chips are handed over. He then places a copy of the fill slip into the correct table box when it is collected. Once that is done, he removes in cash whatever amount in chips was on the slip. On paper, it looks like the chips were legitimately delivered to the table and won by customers. On paper, imaginary winners have the money. In reality, the skimmers have it. Obviously, a lot of employees have to be in on this scam, and others have to pretend not to notice what is going on.

Slot Machine Skim

This is a tough way to skim simply because of the weight of the coins. The most famous slot machine skim took place at the four casinos owned by Argent Corporation in the 1980s. Because there are so many coins, they are weighed instead of counted to determine the dollar value. By using the weight of the coins, one could arrive at a money total for the coins. In the Argent case, the skimmers simply monkeyed with the scale to indicate less money than was really on the scale and pocketed the extra coins.

The difficulty with this method was transporting tens of thousands of dollars in coins. This required a complicated system that employed many people. Essentially, though, the skimmers set up other coin exchanges on the floor of the casino. Slot machine players would come over and exchange bills for coins. The bills would then be easily carried away by the skimmers and their accomplices.

> **Mafia Speak**
>
> Cleveland underboss Angelo Lonardo testified that his family was receiving approximately $40,000 per month from the Argent skim.

> **Mafia Speak**
>
> In his 1988 testimony before a Senate committee, Angelo Lonardo explained, "When a dispute arose in regards to the distribution of the skim between Milwaukee and Kansas City, Chicago settled the dispute and began receiving 25 percent of the skim. Chicago settled the dispute since Milwaukee and Kansas City answer to Chicago ..."

The Bugs

FBI bugs planted in Las Vegas and other cities after the 1957 Apalachin convention gave authorities additional intelligence about the gambling mecca that was growing in the Nevada desert.

According to late FBI agent Bill Roemer, an FBI bug in Chicago disclosed that the Chicago Outfit had made a deal with the Moe Dalitz group to share in all their Las Vegas operations, including the Desert Inn, the Riviera, and the Fremont in downtown Las Vegas.

In his book, Roemer said the FBI followed the skim money as it was delivered to various secret partners around the nation. They learned that La Cosa Nostra bosses Ray Patriarca of New England, Carlos Marcello of New Orleans, Anthony Giordano of St. Louis, John Scalish of Cleveland, and Anthony "Fat Tony" Salerno of New York's Genovese family were getting a cut of the skim from Las Vegas hotels.

Some of the FBI's illegally obtained information was leaked to select journalists including *Life* magazine's Sandy Smith. In one article, he listed the following monthly skim amounts between 1960 and 1965: the Genovese family, $50,000; the Chicago Outfit, $65,000 plus; Cleveland's John Scalish, $52,000. Meyer Lansky and his partners took in $80,000. This was serious money.

An FBI bug in the executive offices of the Fremont Hotel picked up owner Ed Levinson giving an associate some insight into the depth and breadth of the Fremont skim: "You can't steal $100,000 a month and pay dividends. If you steal $50,000? Well, maybe …" Ironically, the Fremont bug was discovered by casino employees, and Levinson used its illegality to blunt legal charges that might have been lodged against him and his organization.

The Strawman

In 1978, the FBI stumbled into another ongoing skim operation involving the Tropicana Hotel and Casino and the Kansas City family. Through the use of legal electronic surveillance, they overheard numerous discussions about Las Vegas, including one among boss Nick Civella, underboss Carl DeLuna, and two Tropicana executives who were in charge of skimming, Joe Agosto and Carl Thomas.

Robert B. Davenport, the special agent in charge of the Kansas City office of the FBI, told a U.S. Senate Committee that the FBI code-named the investigation the "Strawman Case" because the listed owners of many Las Vegas casinos were really nominees, or "strawmen," to conceal the fact that the real operators were the Kansas City, Chicago, and Cleveland Mafia families.

On November 5, 1981, Nick Civella, Carl DeLuna, consigliere Carlo Civella, Joe Agosto, Carl Thomas, and others were indicted for the Tropicana skimming operation. The evidence included $80,000 in skim money that the FBI seized, part of the $280,000 that the men were charged with skimming. By the summer of 1982, the whole crew had been convicted. The prosecution was greatly aided by the testimony of Agosto, who rolled over on his mob friends. Agosto, whose real name had been Vincenzo Pianetti, assumed the identity of an Italian businessman who died in 1951. Soon after he helped convict his Tropicana cohorts, with his conscience clear, Pianetti/Agosto died of natural causes.

The Tropicana investigation led to the discovery of an even larger skimming operation involving four Argent Corporation casinos—the Fremont, the Marina, the Stardust, and the Hacienda.

Allan Glick, a San Diego entrepreneur, had used some sophisticated financial paper-work to obtain loans to purchase the Hacienda Hotel and Casino in 1972. A few years later, Glick worked his way into bidding for Recrion Corporation, which controlled the Stardust and Fremont hotels. As indicated earlier, the Chicago mob was already into these properties, so Glick's bidding attracted a lot of mob interest.

Eventually, Glick was introduced to Milwaukee family boss Frank Balistrieri, who knew a key loan official at the Central States Pension Fund and helped Glick with the loan. For further support, Balistrieri called on the Kansas City family, which controlled another Teamster with Pension Fund influence. Later still, Glick was told he needed help from the Cleveland family, giving Glick three Mafia partners looking for a piece of the action. Eventually, the Chicago Outfit got involved and Glick had four partners.

Glick's euphoria over his loans and purchases didn't last long. He was in way over his head, dealing with people who would shoot him in a minute if he didn't dance to their tune. The four bosses had no idea how the casino operated, nor did they care. Their only concern was getting their cuts, and that they did for several years.

On May 22, 1981, the feds disclosed another seamy Las Vegas mob scheme, this one involving the Chicago Outfit and Teamsters international president of the moment, Roy Williams. The key evidence came from a bug the FBI planted in the office of longtime Chicago associate Allen Dorfman, a liaison between the Teamsters and the Chicago

Mafia Speak

Kansas City underboss Carl DeLuna showed casino owner Allan Glick who was really in charge of Glick's four hotels in an April 25, 1978, meeting. "He informed me that it was their desire to have me sell (the casinos) immediately," said Glick, adding that DeLuna also made a veiled threat against Glick's family if he didn't comply. Glick sold.

Slammer Time

Tropicana co-owner Deil Otto Gustafson was also involved in the Kansas City skim. He was convicted of a $4 million fraud in 1983. Twelve years later, he pleaded guilty to trying to hide the proceeds of a $34 million judgment from the sale of the Tropicana.

Outfit. For years, Dorfman was the man to see about getting a loan from the Central States Pension Fund. The FBI bug in his office picked up evidence that Dorfman and Chicago Outfit capo Joseph "Joey the Clown" Lombardo had conspired to bribe U.S. Senator Howard Cannon. They were hoping the Nevada senator would scuttle deregulation of the trucking industry that would hurt Teamster power. The payoff was to be undeveloped Las Vegas land that would be sold dirt-cheap to a group that included Cannon. The senator was never charged in the scam. The case was a big blow to La Cosa Nostra. Roy Williams cooperated and detailed a long career as a stooge of the Kansas City family. Tough-talking Dorfman got a head full of bullets as he walked through a Chicago parking lot. The Outfit felt his tough-guy image was a sham and that Dorfman would become a federal witness to escape a prison term. His murder ended that possibility.

In 1986, the other shoe of the Strawman case stomped on the leaders of the Chicago, Milwaukee, and Kansas City families. Bosses Joseph Aiuppa, Frank Balistrieri, and Carl Civella received lengthy prison sentences for skimming from the Argent empire. Powerful Cleveland Teamsters official and mob associate Milton "Maishe" Rockman also went down. Cleveland underboss Lonardo, Argent owner Allan Glick, skimmer Carl Thomas, and Teamster president Roy Williams helped corroborate the evidence gathered by the FBI bugs to sink the Mafia bosses.

The End

With the convictions in the Argent skim case, the Mafia's golden age in Las Vegas was over. There was no master plan, just a bunch of guys making money for nearly 40 years in a state that made Men of the Year out of former bootleggers. The first group went in with bankrolls, friends, and acquaintances and tried to build a hotel/casino that would attract customers. Most of the early entrepreneurs had been involved in illegal gambling operations elsewhere and knew how to skim off money. The fact that they could run legal gambling operations seemed unbelievable to them and to other gamblers who went to Las Vegas and tried to make their own luck.

From 1946 until 1959, different La Cosa Nostra families became silent partners in various casinos started by others. Mobsters like Frank Costello earned a piece of the skim because they invested their money in an enterprise. There was no corporation-like Mafia deciding to invest its money in Las Vegas. Each boss made his own decision as opportunity knocked. Leaders like Jack Dragna of Los Angeles and Joe Profaci of New York never were in on any skims. They either declined or never had the opportunity to invest in a casino. For 13 years, Mafia bosses who did get a chance to invest needed to have the money to do so.

> **Big Shot** _____
>
> Although a little bit of a man, Chicago's Anthony "Tony the Ant" Spilotro was a loud-mouth who threw around a lot of weight in Las Vegas. His job was to make sure the Chicago Outfit's wishes were carried out. That meant making sure the skim money kept coming. He did, but eventually his bosses became unhappy with the job he was doing. On June 14, 1986, Tony and his brother went to a meeting, were severely beaten, and then were buried alive in a shallow grave in Morocco, Indiana. Nine days later, authorities dug him up, but the Ant's lips were sealed forever.

That changed in 1959 when Jimmy Hoffa decided to start lending Central States Pension Fund money for Las Vegas enterprises. The Pension Fund had nearly unlimited amounts of money, so Mafia bosses no longer had to put up their own money. All they had to do was use their influence with key Teamsters, influence that they already had through rackets they had been running for decades. The Mafia bosses worked together to ensure loans for each other, and they all benefited. Entrepreneurs who were looking to build or buy a casino had to let the mob place people in key posts in the corporation to get the needed Teamster loans.

Federal government pressure closed the door on mob loans from the Central States Pension Fund in 1977. The days of backroom deals are now over. With the successful prosecutions of mobsters, the general financial community became much more receptive to loaning money to Las Vegas entrepreneurs. Investors no longer have to make secret deals with wiseguys who would kill them if they caused trouble. By all accounts, La Cosa Nostra is no longer a factor in any major casinos. There will always be mob guys on the prowl in Las Vegas, but they are now just like all the other hoods, trying to pull petty scams rather than raking off millions in skim money. It is quite a change.

> **Slammer Time**
>
> St. Louis boss Anthony Giordano and Detroit capos Anthony Zerilli and Michael Polizzi spent a few years in prison after they were convicted in 1972 of having a hidden interest in the Frontier Hotel and Casino in the 1960s. The skim ended when the hotel was sold to billionaire Howard Hughes in 1967.

The Least You Need to Know

- Mafia members invested in Las Vegas in the 1950s.

- Mob investments were paid off through skimming.

- Mafia influence over the Teamsters Pension Fund got the mob inside some casinos.

- Teamster reforms and prosecutions eliminated Mafia influence in Las Vegas.

Chapter 13

No End to Mob Rackets

In This Chapter

- ◆ Making a buck off fraud
- ◆ Stocks and bonds
- ◆ Avoiding the gas tax
- ◆ A piece of the porno
- ◆ Mafia food

Members and associates of La Cosa Nostra have long used just about every method they could dream up to turn an illegal buck. They will steal cars, rob banks, and extort money from other thieves as well as from legitimate businessmen and women. They will hijack truckloads of jeans and sell them to a discount clothing store for 25 cents on the dollar. They will peddle fake credit cards, making sure to save a couple for themselves to go out on the town. Some of the more forward-thinking of them will set up 1-900 phone lines that peddle phone sex for a price.

This chapter looks at some proven moneymakers for Mafia crews. Few made the wiseguys rich, but the trick is always to make a few hundred here, a few hundred there, and the odd $5,000 somewhere else whenever you can. Oh yeah, and if you are associated with the mob, make sure you share what you made with your superior.

Fraud

Some definitions of fraud are deceit, trickery, and cheating. Who better to pull off this type of crime than a man who pretends to be an honest citizen but in reality has sworn a secret oath to an organization that plots to kill people—including members of the group—as a way of life. La Cosa Nostra members and associates love fraud. Here are a few ways they use it to make a few bucks instead of working.

Fuhgeddaboudit

One of the many scams mobsters ran at the huge Westchester Premiere Theater in Tarrytown, New York, in the 1970s involved theater seating. The hoods had a section of seats that wasn't on the building's blueprints. All the money that came in from the sale of these seats—and there were many sellouts for Frank Sinatra concerts—was quickly and safely skimmed by the Gambino and Colombo families.

The Bust Out

The trick is to gain control of an established business that has a credit line with various suppliers. Failing that, a new business can be set up and then credit slowly acquired with your potential commercial victims.

After a credit line is firmly established, wiseguys place large orders from every supplier they can find. If it's a bar, they might order two or three times the usual supply of liquor, wine, and beer and tell the salesmen that they are hosting a special party with lots of guests expected. Perhaps they'll order a few large TV sets as well as some new tables and chairs to replace the older ones.

They then sell all these goods at a fraction of the usual price or ship them to other quasi-legitimate operations that the wiseguy controls. However he liquidates, the entire sales are pure profit because the wiseguy has no plans to pay anything for them. Obviously, it's important to move the goods quickly.

Slammer Time

Roy DeMeo was a psychopath who was a soldier in the Gambino family. As Gene Mustain and I wrote in our book *Murder Machine* (1992), DeMeo's crew made millions in stolen cars and drug dealing. Along the way, they killed some 75 people (that I was able to document) before the entire enterprise blew up. DeMeo ended up dead in the trunk of his car, and three crew members were convicted of racketeering and murder and are spending the rest of their lives in prison.

Before the bills come due, the wiseguy closes the business down and removes all the stock. As suppliers try to figure out what happened, the gangster makes himself scarce and hopes the creditors write off their bills as bad debts or give them to a bill collector who won't be able to find him. If the collector does pursue the case, a few threats might convince the collector to report back that he couldn't locate the missing owner. The worst that generally happens is that a supplier files a civil suit, a minor problem because the paper trail is difficult to follow. Usually, the supplier gives it up and moves on.

Difficulties can occur for a known mobster who is a target of the FBI or a police-organized crime squad. He might be pursued in a criminal fraud case in the hopes of getting him to secretly talk to avoid jail time. Mafia guys usually don't talk unless they are being squeezed.

Luchese soldier John "Johnny Dio" Dioguardi did a prison stint for a bust-out operation. In 1964, he took over a meat business, Consumer Kosher Provisions, and ran it into bankruptcy. The government alleged that Dioguardi had secretly transferred $33,000 worth of assets to a new company and left his creditors holding $300,000 in unpaid bills. Dioguardi was convicted and received five years for this scam.

Earler, Dioguardi earned kudos from the mob for an even bigger fraud. He helped Jimmy Hoffa win the Teamster presidency by setting up some fake Teamster locals in New York. Fictitious delegates from these "locals" voted for Hoffa, assuring Hoffa the coveted top spot.

Credit Cards

One of the better-known Mafia credit card frauds involved a well known wiseguy, Salvatore "Bill" Bonanno, son of the former boss of the New York family that still bears his name. It occurred in 1968, as his father was making a futile attempt to regain control of the family. As more and more of his soldiers and capos defected under pressure from the Mafia Commission, the elder Bonanno's income dried up. So did son Bill's.

Bill Bonanno began to use a credit card belonging to a mob associate. Bonanno signed the cardholder's name as he traveled across country with two companions. He used the card to pay for dinners and drinks, often picking up the tab for others. On March 11, 1968, Bonanno was confronted by a store owner while trying to use the card to buy clothing in Tucson, Arizona. He was indicted for fraud in December 1968.

Born with a "silver spoon in his mouth," Bill Bonanno was nailed for credit card fraud.

(Courtesy of GangLandNews.com)

Bonanno went to trial in November 1969 on charges of conspiracy, mail fraud, and perjury. The latter charge was a result of his testimony before a grand jury investigating the matter.

Bonanno claimed that family member Hank Perrone had given him the card and had said the man whose name was on the card had given him permission to use it. Perrone was unable to back up this story because he was killed on the day Bonanno was arrested. On the stand, however, the owner of the card denied giving permission to Perrone or Bonanno, claiming that the card was extorted from him.

Other government witnesses blew Bonanno's case out of the water. The jury found him guilty of all charges, and Bonanno served about three years in the can for it.

Henry Hill, a Luchese family associate, told some credit card–scam stories to author Nicholas Pileggi, who used them in his book *Wiseguy* (Simon & Schuster, 1985). His buddies knew a bank employee who gave them duplicates of credit cards that were about to be mailed out. She would tell them the credit limit, too. Hill and his cronies would go to a businessman they knew and make as many purchases as possible under the credit limit. Then they sold the items for whatever they could get. The storekeeper didn't lose out because he had received approval for the purchases.

Stocks and Bonds

The simplest version of this scam involves buying stock at a low price and then using corrupt brokers to "pump" up the value by using high-pressure tactics to get others to buy. The buy orders drive the price up even though nothing has happened to justify the increased value of the stock. When the hoods think the price is as high as they can get it, they "dump" their shares at a healthy profit. As the wiseguys unload the stock, the price comes tumbling down, never to rebound.

In 1997, Genovese family capo Rosario Gangi and Bonanno capo Frank Lino were part of a large conspiracy that drove up the price of HealthTech International stock using corrupt brokers and the president of the company. When they sold their shares, Gangi, Lino, and others made $1.3 million in this classic "pump and dump" scam, prosecutors said.

Turncoat New England mob associate Vincent "The Fat Man" Teresa said he once received $200,000 in bonds that had been stolen from a major Wall Street brokerage firm. He used phony identification to cash the bonds with the cooperation of a bribable bank employee. Teresa claims his man was able to cash half of the bonds, with Teresa getting $80,000 and his accomplices splitting $20,000.

Slammer Time

Vincent "The Fat Man" Teresa was one of the first famous mob informants. He also cooperated in the writing of two books about his life and appeared before Senate hearings and on national television. He went into the federal Witness Protection Program but had a difficult time. In October of 1982, Teresa was found guilty of conspiracy to import cocaine in the state of Washington, where he had been living for about four years as Charles Cantino.

In 1958, Pittsburgh capo Samuel "Sam" Mannarino, Montreal-based Bonanno soldier Giuseppe "Pep" Cotroni, and a Chicago financier teamed up to wangle an $87,000 loan from a Swiss bank by posting bonds stolen from a bank in the small, eastern Ontario town of Brockville. The bonds were part of an estimated $9 million in cash, jewels, and securities that were stolen from safe deposit boxes at the Brockville Trust Company on May 3.

Mannarino, who had been a partner of Tampa boss Santos Trafficante in the Sans Souci Casino in Cuba, had a connection with the Chicago financier. The Pittsburgh capo introduced him to Cotroni, who gave $140,000 in bonds to the financier. The windy city operative flew to Switzerland and got an $87,500 loan using the bonds as collateral. The FBI caught on to the scam and nabbed Cotroni and Mannarino.

Many East Coast La Cosa Nostra families had a rule against dealing in stolen or counterfeit bonds. Mobsters felt that, like counterfeiting, these were federal violations that would bring too much attention from the FBI. The practice was supposed to be avoided. But, like drug dealing, it wasn't!

Fuhgeddaboudit
FBI documents about the Brockville Trust heist indicate that Mannarino intended to use the proceeds to help finance Fidel Castro's revolution in 1959. It sounds far-fetched, but a year earlier, four Mannarino associates were arrested for trying to transport two .50 caliber machineguns and 121 rifles to Castro. The FBI speculated that Mannarino hoped that Castro would be so grateful for the funding that he would give Mannarino exclusive rights to operate casinos in Cuba.

Gas Scams

During World War II, the U.S. government limited the use of gasoline and issued ration vouchers and stamps that were used to buy gas. This annoyed everyone. It cut the profits of gas station owners, frustrated motorists, and provided an opportunity for wiseguys to make lots of bucks.

Many mobsters, including up-and-coming capo Carlo Gambino, made small fortunes buying bulk quantities of stolen gas-ration stamps from thieves and selling them to soldiers or close associates who peddled the stamps to gas station owners for a profit. Armed with ration stamps, the station owner would sell gasoline at twice the price to gas-starved motorists and then turn the ration stamps into the Office of Price Administration to purchase more gasoline from the major oil companies.

A more modern gasoline scam swept the East Coast in the early 1980s. At that time, gas stations were required to remit the various fuel taxes to the state and federal governments. In New York State, the owners could delay for up to a year before authorities would get serious about collecting. Crooked gasoline wholesalers grasped this concept and began taking over as many gas stations as they could, hiding the true ownership in a maze of endless paperwork. They offered lower prices, attracted customers, and simply pocketed all the proceeds, ignoring the tax responsibilities. After six months to a year, they'd close up shop, keeping all the tax money. Pretty soon, they figured out an easier way to achieve the same end. They'd simply form a new corporation and sell the existing station to it without altering the appearance of the gas station.

Slammer Time
Lawrence "Fat Larry" Iorizzo was one of the biggest gasoline tax scam artists of the 1980s. Convicted on various fraud and tax charges in April of 1984, Iorizzo fled to Panama and was promptly thrown into prison by dictator Manuel Noriega. When he was sent back to the United States a few months later, Iorizzo didn't take too kindly to his U.S. prison accommodations either, so he began cooperating against his mob friends including Colombo capo Michael Franzese.

Many crooked gasoline entrepreneurs turned to La Cosa Nostra members for protection from other Mafia family extortionists. This is how Michael Franzese of the Colombo family made millions of dollars before he was indicted, pleaded guilty, and cooperated with the feds. Franzese, son of Colombo capo John "Sonny" Franzese, has declined the services of the Witness Protection Program and has been living fairly openly in Southern California, where he coaches a Little League baseball team.

Colombo capo Michael Franzese, who made millions in bootleg gasoline scams, now coaches Little League baseball.

(Courtesy of GangLandNews.com)

Gambino family associate Gennaro "Jimmy Sweats" Dellamonica is a sucker. He pleaded guilty to extortion in 1997 in a sting operation in which the FBI set up shop as a gasoline supplier and refused to pay protection to various La Cosa Nostra families. In an attempt to squeeze the FBI guys, Dellamonica and some friends visited a firm that purchased fuel from the secret FBI gas business and slapped the owner around to get him to stop buying from the FBI's company.

Pornography

Many La Cosa Nostra mobsters have been involved in pornography in one form or another. It would be a great exaggeration to say that the Mafia controls the smut business or even a large part of it. The business is too big for that to happen. Nevertheless, the Mafia makes big bucks off sex.

In the 1970s, Bonanno capo Michael "Mickey Z" Zaffarano was a major player in the porn industry. He had offices in Hollywood and Manhattan and was president of a nationwide chain of adult theatres called Pussycat Cinemas. In 1979, he was under investigation by state authorities in New York and California, but the FBI got to him first. They caught him in a sting operation and knocked him out of business for good on Valentine's Day in 1979. As G-men were putting the cuffs on him, he dropped dead of a heart attack.

Robert "DeeBee" DiBernardo was another major porn dealer whose life came to a quick end. John Gotti didn't pull the trigger, but as he explained loudly and clearly on a tape recording at his 1992 murder and racketeering trial, he sentenced DeeBee to die in 1986.

"When DeeBee got whacked, they told me a story," said Gotti in a conversation with consigliere Frank Locascio. "I was in jail when I whacked him. I knew why it was being done. I done it anyway. I allowed it to be done."

Big Shot

From the witness stand, turncoat underboss Salvatore "Sammy Bull" Gravano gave a detailed description of how he lured DiBernardo to his construction company office to talk business over a drink and how crewmember Joe Paruta shot DeeBee twice in the back of the head with a silenced .22.

In the 1970s and early 1980s, DiBernardo was the mob muscle in Star Distributors of New York City. It produced and distributed films, books, and magazines to theaters and adult bookstores across the nation. He was only a soldier, but he reported directly to boss Paul Castellano, kicking a portion of his large porn income to him. DeeBee often complained that Castellano looked down on him because of the source of the money but nevertheless took the porno money. DiBernardo was one of the first to join Gotti's plot to kill Castellano and was one of the first killed by Gotti.

The Colombo family also made lots of cash in the soft- and hard-core porn indus-tries. In the days before videotape, there were hundreds of small, coin-operated machines in Manhattan's Times Square that showed short loops of 8mm porno films that were under the control of capo John "Sonny" Franzese. Anthony and Joseph Peraino, whose old man Giuseppe was a Profaci family soldier who was whacked in 1931, processed the films and distributed them all over the East Coast.

The Peraino family produced the blockbuster porn film *Deep Throat*, which, because of the huge amount of money it made, brought about copycat versions made by other families look-ing to cash in. Soon wildly inaccurate stories reported that the Mafia controlled 90 percent of the porn industry. The bottom line is that mobsters gravitated to the business, and many made lots of money. Some were partners of pornographers, some owned buildings that housed adult stores, and others muscled in on film labs and distribution of videotapes, but the Mafia had no monopoly in the world of porn.

> **Fuhgeddaboudit**
>
> Linda Lovelace was the first porn star to make the big time. She appeared in the legendary film *Deep Throat*, which made tens of millions of dollars. Later, she wrote a book—*Ordeal*—in which she claimed she earned a pit-tance for her work and made the movie because guys were point-ing guns at her while she frol-icked and carried on with others.

Meat and Potatoes

Expo 67, the 1967 World's Fair, was held in Montreal, Quebec, Canada. The pavil-ions and displays were spectacular. Their location on manmade islands in the St. Lawrence River only added to the glamour. Millions of visitors consumed tons of hot dogs, hamburgers, pizza, and sausages. If they knew what they were eating, they would have brown-bagged it instead!

Nearly a decade later, the province conducted hearings and learned that one Mafia-connected meat salvager sold more than 400,000 pounds of meat from dead, dying, or sick animals to retailers who sold it at Expo 67. The meat had been sprinkled with charcoal to designate it as unfit for human consumption, but the dealers simply sliced off the first inch of meat to get rid of the charcoal.

Vincenzo "Vic" Cotroni, whose brother Giuseppe was involved in the Brockville Trust caper, was a Bonanno capo who functioned as the Mafia boss of Montreal. He also was president of Reggio Foods, a major supplier of meat and groceries. One of Cotroni's managers testified that, during an eight-year period, he bought 1,500 pounds of tainted meat a week to make pepperoni and sausages. He testified that he sold about two tons of this meat to a company owned by William Obront, a major Montreal Mafia associate.

As I have said, the real rule of La Cosa Nostra is to get the money in any way possible. Mobsters have used just about any method imaginable. Some have even been known to operate legitimate businesses!

In Chapter 30, I detail some new schemes that wiseguys have pursued into the new millennium.

The Least You Need to Know

- ◆ Fraud is a moneymaking favorite for the Mafia.
- ◆ Mobsters are adept at exploiting government bureaucracy.
- ◆ The Mafia never had a stranglehold on the porn industry.
- ◆ Wiseguys will do nearly anything to make money.

Part 3

America Opens Its Eyes

For more than half a century, the American Mafia was an elusive entity. It was talked about in vague terms and was feared in some areas, although not many really knew just what they were afraid of. The unknown is always scary.

By the 1950s, by accident and sometimes by design, the shape of the mysterious Mafia, also known as La Cosa Nostra, began to emerge. Over the decades, it became apparent that Mafia mopes were pretty ordinary humans, except they were willing to kill so they wouldn't have to go to work. Ironically, some innocents placed an honorable mantle on these thugs and created a myth about noble men, struggling against great odds to protect their personal families and friends from evil outsiders. It took a while for North Americans to see through that charade.

14

Mobsters Come Out of the Closet

In This Chapter

- ◆ The Salvation Army and the mobster
- ◆ A senator seeks and gets attention
- ◆ The Big BBQ in Apalachin, New York

In the early part of the twentieth century, the public knew there were gangsters, crooked politicians, cops on the take, and hack judges. They just didn't know how it all fit together. That began to change in the late 1940s.

Newspapers began running stories that revealed what appeared to be a secret government, pulling the strings behind the scenes with the aid of a corrupt political system. Americans love to be scared, and the organization that began to emerge took on a shape larger than life, one that created fear in many a law-abiding citizen. In this chapter, I will take a look at some of the events that brought the Mafia into the public eye and will explain how myth became the 1950s reality.

Mob Chieftain Joins the Salvation Army

John Gotti was the first Mafia boss to become a major public figure who didn't pretend to be anything but a hood. Some of his predecessors were just as well known, but in contrast to Gotti, they pretended to be upstanding businessmen, worthy of being with, and a member of the upper crust of society. Frank Costello was one of these individuals.

Mafia Speak

Half a century before fictional New Jersey Mafia boss Tony Soprano began visiting a shrink on the HBO award-winning television series *The Sopranos*, Frank Costello was seeing a psychiatrist regularly. For more than two years starting in 1947, Costello received psychiatric counseling from Dr. Richard Hoffman, according to *Uncle Frank* (Drake Publishers, 1973), a biography by former *New York Post* reporter Leonard Katz. Costello wasn't too happy that Hoffman revealed their relationship, but he took no action against the Manhattan doctor.

Costello was born in Italy but grew up on the mean streets of New York City. By the mid-1930s, he was acting boss of one of the city's five La Cosa Nostra families—and was thus one of the most powerful men in the area. He considered himself to be a diplomat among killers and lived up to his expectations by forging business and social contacts with all levels of society. His charisma came from his wallet and the votes he could turn out for the machine politicians of Tammany Hall.

Tammany Hall was a social organization that became, for all intents and purposes, the Democratic Party apparatus in New York City. This was before welfare and the birth of unemployment benefits. Tammany Hall would pass out gifts to the downtrodden in return for votes. There were no widespread civil service exams, and thousands of municipal jobs were handed out on a patronage basis. New jobholders would be expected to support the Democratic Party with votes and dollars.

The system was ripe for corruption. The man dispensing the firefighting jobs would demand a kickback for his support. A lawyer looking to become a judge would have to prove his willingness to bend the rules for friends, and on, and on. It was a system that was made for La Cosa Nostra. It had the money that attracted politicians, and it could control blocks of votes through its union connections. Frank Costello was a perfect fit for the social environment of the moment. He and his Mafia friends didn't create this milieu; they simply took advantage of it.

In 1949, the Salvation Army in New York City asked Costello to help its annual campaign to raise funds for all its good works. On the advice of his lawyer, George Wolf, Costello agreed to help. The veteran lawyer felt it was a great opportunity for Costello to earn some positive points while raising money for a good cause.

Costello sent out invitations for a $100-a-plate dinner at the famous Copacabana Night Club, long said to be part of Costello's portfolio. Costello agreed to pick up all the expenses, and the Salvation Army would get all the profits.

Costello threw caution to the wind. He invited the Manhattan borough president, a congressman, seven judges, and a host of politicians, including Tammany Hall leader Carmine DeSapio. They came and hobnobbed with numerous gangsters, including Vito Genovese. Everyone had a great time until the evening ended and partygoers were mobbed by photographers and reporters.

The January 24, 1949, affair found judges and politicians ducking for cover and making excuses about their appearance at a dinner hosted by the notorious Costello. Some said they had no idea Costello was involved, even though his name was on the invitation. Salvation Army director C. Frank Cramer said simply, "We'll take anyone's money to further our good work. The money paid by the 150 guests isn't necessarily Costello's."

"It was a lovely affair," said Mrs. Howard Chandler Christie, wife of a well-known painter at the time. "And I never met so many judges in my life."

For those paying attention, however, the dinner showed a link between politicians, the judiciary, and gangsters. It was a story that would be replayed in 14 cities in the near future.

Frank Costello raised money for the Salvation Army in 1949. By 1951, he was Public Enemy No. 1.

(Courtesy of GangLandNews.com)

Fuhgeddaboudit

On August 24, 1943, New York police were listening in on a wiretap on the phone of Frank Costello in the hope of getting a lead on the killers of controversial Italian news-man Carlo Tresca. Unexpectedly, they overheard Magistrate Thomas Aurelio thanking Frank Costello for supporting Aurelio's nomination for a New York Supreme Court judge-ship: "I want to assure you of my loyalty for all you have done; it's undying." Aurelio went on to a prestigious career, but the conversation clearly showed Costello's political influence.

Mobsters Go to Washington

In 1950, the U.S. Senate formed a special five-member committee to investigate organized crime in interstate commerce. Its chair would be Estes Kefauver, a first-term Democratic senator from Tennessee. He had lobbied hard for this committee and succeeded in May 1950 with the passage of Senate Resolution 202. His stated goals were to increase support for local police officers and to pass legislation that would hamper interstate crime. In a relatively short time, Kefauver would be a house-hold name, which many believe was his number-one goal.

Big Shot

Frank Costello's underboss in 1951, Willie Moretti, was in failing mental health and had been for some time. His old friends were very worried that he might accidentally reveal mob secrets, before the Kefauver Committee in the spring of 1951 confirmed their concerns. On October 4, 1951, Moretti went into a New Jersey restaurant to meet some friends and was shot to death. His killing forced boss Frank Costello to appoint a rival, Vito Genovese, as underboss. Six years later, Genovese would send Vincent "Chin" Gigante out to take a shot at Costello.

The Kefauver Committee was a traveling road show that hit 14 cities and provided grist for newspaper headlines for months. Witnesses would be grilled in so-called fact-finding missions, but the process was really an attempt to convince the public that the mobsters who controlled gambling were nefarious crime lords threatening to destroy America.

Many key witnesses, including Joseph "Joe Adonis" Doto of the Genovese clan, Albert Anastasia, and Chicago Outfit boss Anthony Accardo, refused to answer numerous questions on the grounds that they might tend to incriminate themselves. Their refusals created the obvious impression that they were all bad guys who were part of a secret criminal group. For example, when New Orleans boss Carlos Marcello refused to say whether he had attended a May 5, 1947, meeting of hoodlums, it gave the impression that he had. The committee could, and did, create demons out of those who refused to answer simply due to the nature and tone of the questions asked.

The road show passed through Miami, Tampa, Chicago, St. Louis, Kansas City, Las Vegas, Los Angeles, New Orleans, Philadelphia, Cleveland, San Francisco, Detroit, and Newark, en route to a conclusion in New York. The witnesses can be broken into four main groups—bad guys, crooked law enforcement officers, shady politicians, and good guys. As Frank Costello, one of the last of the 600 plus witnesses, took the stand in the grand finale, an estimated 20 million Americans paid close attention to the fast-growing national phenomenon on another fast-growing American phenomenon, national television.

During the Kefauver hearings, the ultimate bad guy was New York boss Frank Costello. The senator and the gangster had gotten off to a rocky start in executive session on February 13, 1951. Kefauver got angry when Costello playfully scolded Kefauver as news photographers took pictures at the end of the session. Soon after, the committee released an interim report that labeled Costello as the number-one hood.

> **Slammer Time**
>
> Genovese capo "Joe Adonis" Doto was a casualty of the Kefauver Committee. After appearing, he became a big-time target, was convicted of gambling charges in New Jersey, and was deported on January 3, 1956, when it was discovered he had never become an American citizen.

> **Big Shot**
>
> On September 25, 1950, Acting Chicago Police Captain Bill Drury was shot to death as he parked his car a day before he was to appear before the Kefauver Committee. The best guess is that Outfit boss Anthony Accardo was unsure what Drury was going to say and decided to silence him forever. No one was ever charged with the killing.

On March 13, 1951, Costello was due for his long-awaited public appearance on a stage that was under construction for more than a year. A national TV audience was waiting with bated breath to see the nation's number-one bad man. He didn't disappoint, even though lawyer George Wolf got the committee to agree to televise only his client's hands, not his face. His five o'clock shadow created the perfect image of a Hollywood gangster, but TV viewers only heard his raspy voice and saw his writhing fingers as he fended off questions that showed Costello as the ultimate string-pulling gangster.

Unlike other hoods, Costello foolishly tried to parry the thrusts of the committee members. At one point, he walked out, claiming his throat was sore. This only added to the drama. Ultimately he returned but, in the end, left as the bad guy Kefauver intended to expose.

Chicago Police Captain Dan "Tubbo" Gilbert, who held various positions in a 30-year career and had often been accused of being corrupt, was one of many corrupt cops who testified when the Kefauver show rolled into Chicago. On October 17, 1950, when he was asked in an executive session about his failure to arrest major hoods despite the more than 100 murders they committed, Gilbert said the mobsters were so good at murder that they never left a trace for him and his men to find. His response to a query about his vast net worth was also weak: "The failure of human nature is that we are prone to believe evil about our fellow man and especially about a peace officer." Excerpts of his testimony were leaked and published a few days before the November elections, and Gilbert lost a bid to become Cook County sheriff.

The role of the shady politician was played by various characters around the nation, but in New York, the part was taken by Bill O'Dwyer, a former mayor and district attorney who was, at the time of the hearings, the U.S. ambassador to Mexico.

O'Dwyer had become famous prosecuting Louis "Lepke" Buchalter, a notorious 1930s garment center gangster who was convicted of murder and then executed. O'Dwyer's March 1951 appearance at the Kefauver hearings was disastrous for him, however. The committee disclosed that O'Dwyer had visited the apartment of Frank Costello in 1942 and had failed to prosecute big fish Mafia hoods like Albert Anastasia.

One of the most suspicious events probed by the Kefauver Committee was the death of informer Abe Reles on November 12, 1941. The notorious killer was being protected by a squad of police at the Half Moon Hotel in Coney Island when he went out a sixth floor window and fell to his death. O'Dwyer promoted the leader of the police detail to Captain. To many, it seemed that the two had arranged or permitted Reles's death to spare Anastasia.

Mafia Speak

In 1951, Dominick Montiglio was 7 years old and playing in his grandfather's Bensonhurst, Brooklyn home as his uncle watched the televised Kefauver hearings. When Reles's death came up, his uncle, Gambino soldier Anthony "Nino" Gaggi, cried out in glee, "The canary could sing, but he couldn't fly," as Gene Mustain and I wrote in *Murder Machine* (Dutton, 1992).

What had the Kefauver hearings accomplished in their 15-month, 14-city odyssey? They succeeded in linking—in the public's mind—gambling, the Mafia, and crooked politicians in a vast national conspiracy that threatened to undermine the legitimate institutions of the United States. There was no question that there were hoods in each major city the hearings visited. There was no question that there were crooked politicians in each location the committee sat. There was no question that there was illegal gambling in each of these places. There was no question that the hoods' gambling couldn't go on without the cooperation of the crooked politicians and the police.

There was no question that there were connections between hoods in each of these locales. There was a question, however, as to whether this all added up to a vast, organized conspiracy. With hindsight, we now know it didn't, but an event in late 1957 sure made it look like it did.

The Big BBQ (Apalachin, New York)

November 14, which arrives each year a few days after Veteran's Day, is Operation Room Nurse Day, a rather ordinary day that begins a week of rather mundane days. November 15 is National Clean Out Your Refrigerator Day, November 16 is Button Day, November 17 is Take a Hike Day, November 18 is Occult Day, November 19 is Have a Bad Day Day, and November 20 is Absurdity Day.

It's a fitting lineup because on November 14, 1957, a watershed event in the history of organized crime in America took place at a large stone house in the tiny upstate New York town of Apalachin, a few miles west of Binghamton and a few miles north of the Pennsylvania state line. Call it Apalachin Day.

At a right angle to the road, the handsome house sits atop a sloping hill with a huge matching stone garage, a rear patio, a barbecue pit, and a guesthouse. In front of the garage is parking for up to 15 full-size cars. In 1957, scores of top mobsters—fish out of water in this idyllic serenity—were oblivious to the calamity that was about to befall them.

For more than a year, New York state trooper Edgar Croswell had been keeping an eye on the owner of the sprawling 58-acre estate, Joseph Barbara, a wealthy businessman who owned a nearby Canada Dry bottling plant. Croswell had become suspicious of Barbara after learning the identity of a houseguest who gave cops phony identification after being pulled over for speeding. The speeder turned out to be notorious drug dealer Carmine Galante. When Croswell learned that other out-of-town criminals had also been in the area at that time, he stored it away for future reference.

Slammer Time

The genesis for Apalachin Day came on October 19, 1956, when Bonanno family underboss Carmine Galante was stopped for speeding near Binghamton on his way home after a national meeting of La Cosa Nostra at Barbara's house. When Galante, whose driver's license had been suspended on June 20 of that year, gave cops a phony one, he was arrested and sentenced to 30 days. In the aftermath of the incident, however, local authorities were pressured to give Galante a free ride on the relatively minor traffic infraction. This piqued the curiosity of Sergeant Edgar Croswell, and when he heard that Galante had been to Barbara's house, the trooper made a mental note to pay closer attention to the rich, but shady, businessman.

As November 1957 rolled around, Croswell's eyes were wide open when it came to the mysterious Barbara, whose secluded home provided privacy but also allowed police to get close without being seen.

On November 13, 1957, Croswell and his partner, Vincent Vasisko, learned that Barbara's son was booking rooms at a nearby motel. They checked out Barbara's home and spotted several out-of-state license plates. That night, the troopers and two U.S. Treasury Department agents took down all the license plate numbers.

The next morning, even more cars had parked on the garage apron and adjoining field. As they were taking down the tags of the newly arrived cars—big, shiny, late-model Cadillacs and Lincolns—they were spotted and all hell broke loose. About a dozen nattily dressed men in dark suits, fedoras, and pointy-toed shoes—including a Dapper Don of the era, Joseph Bonanno—dashed into the woods.

"If they stood still, nobody would have touched them," a 74-year-old Vasisko recalled 43 years later in an interview with the Associated Press. "We would have just gone home. All the (police) cars had to do is patrol the roads. They had to come out sooner or later. You see a guy in a silk suit and a white fedora, you say, 'He doesn't belong in the woods!'"

Others, including Vito Genovese and his underboss Gerardo Catena, Barbara's Mafia boss Russell Bufalino, Philadelphia boss Joseph Ida, and others, climbed into their cars and tried to speed away. Croswell set up a roadblock at the base of the hill on the one road leaving Barbara's estate. Any car trying to get to Route 17 had to pass the barricade. With police reinforcements from surrounding towns, the troopers brought the occupants of the cars stopped at the roadblock—and the men seen running through the woods—to the state police station at Vestal, a few miles away. Each man was asked to identify himself. Croswell had no cause to fingerprint and photograph them, but he and his small band of lawmen took down names, 58 in all.

Fuhgeddaboudit

Authorities found no evidence linking several Mafia bosses—who should have been there—or their representatives to the conclave. These included Chicago's Sam Giancana, Anthony Giordano of St. Louis, and John Alioto of Milwaukee. Some might have stayed in Barbara's home until the next day or perhaps planned to arrive later in the day and cancelled when they saw or heard about the fiasco.

Croswell quickly determined that he had a group of ex-cons from around the nation, many with long arrest records. The authorities, however, who knew little about the structure of the Mafia, didn't know they had more than 10 bosses and many under-bosses, capos, and soldiers. The exact number of Mafiosi who were at Barbara's house has never been determined.

From informants and electronic surveillance, it has been well established that drug dealing and turmoil in New York topped the Apalachin agenda. The feds had begun cracking down on heroin smugglers—Mafia bosses Bonanno and Genovese, to name just two, were heavily involved—and some leaders felt the cash wasn't worth the heat. In New York, new bosses of two families, Vito Genovese (who had been elevated after the May 1957 shooting of Frank Costello) and Carlo Gambino (who took over fol-lowing the barbershop execution of Albert Anastasia in October), were being intro-duced as new members of the Commission. Anastasia's underboss, Frank Scalise, had been whacked earlier in 1957, and the architects wanted to assure the others that the bloodletting was over.

Many gangsters, including Gambino, Joe Profaci, and Paul Castellano, said they had gone to wish Barbara a speedy recovery from health problems he had. A notable exception was John Montana, who until then was known as an upstanding business-man from Buffalo. Montana said he had car problems while driving nearby and had stopped at the Barbara house to find a mechanic. To his surprise, Barbara was hosting a convention of some sort—on November 13, Barbara had picked up a $432.81 order of steaks and other meat staples at Armour & Company in Binghamton—which broke into panic when cops arrived. Looking to avoid the confusion, Montana went for a walk in the woods and was detained by police, a victim of innocent circumstances. For 26 years, his story was the most ludicrous explanation of anyone who was there.

Mafia Speak

"I have a reservation," was the rallying cry of mobsters coming to town for the Big Barbecue at Joe Barbara's house. Pittsburgh Mafia boss John LaRocca and under-boss Michael Genovese had one at the Arlington Hotel in Binghamton, as did Vito Genovese and Kansas City boss and capo Nick Civella and Joe Filardo. Cleveland boss John Scalish, consigliere John DeMarco, and capo Charles Montana had them at the Parkway Motel, as did Buffalo capos James LaDuca and Roy Carlisi. Carlo Gambino and family capos Paul Castellano and Armand Rava, as well as Genovese consigliere Mike Miranda, had them at the Wright Hotel in Kirkwood. Bonanno capo Natale Evola and New Jersey underboss Louis Larasso and capo Frank Majuri had them in Binghamton at the Carleton Hotel. Genovese capo Charles Chiri, Gambino consigliere Joseph Riccobono, capo Carmine "The Doctor" Lombardozzi, and New England capo Frank Cucchiara had reservations at the Dell Motel.

Joe Bonanno wrested the title away in 1983, claiming in his autobiography that he had simply been in the area to discuss a number of issues with cousin Stefano Magaddino, Mafia boss of Buffalo. They met in a small town near Apalachin. When the fiasco happened, two of his men were hunting in the area, accidentally drove across the Barbara property, and were nabbed by cops who wrongly thought they were his guests. One was carrying Bonanno's driver's license and, to make matters worse, had no identification of his own and was identified as Joe Bonanno. That was why Bonanno was listed as an attendee of the Apalachin meeting. Right, Joe!

Fuhgeddaboudit

Not all Apalachin attendees arrived by car. At 10:59 A.M. on November 13, 1957, five men deplaned from Mohawk Airlines Flight 211 from Newark, New Jersey. According to authorities, they were Joe Bonanno, his former underboss John Bonventre, capo Tony Riela, Colorado boss James Colletti, and Frank Zito, boss of a tiny Springfield, Illinois, family that many believe was a satellite of the Chicago Outfit.

The publicity that followed—and the years of hearings and investigations—exposed many of the men as gangsters rather than the simple businessmen they pretended to be. The real damage to La Cosa Nostra, however, came from the embarrassment it caused the FBI and its director, J. Edgar Hoover. When the story broke, elected officials wanted to know who the men were and what they were doing. The FBI had little to offer, but to Hoover's chagrin, the rival Bureau of Narcotics and Dangerous Drugs under Harry Anslinger had piles of documents on many participants, and they trotted them out at the various hearings and press conferences that followed.

Hoover reacted with characteristic anger and energy. He ordered a massive intelligence-gathering operation—the Top Hoodlum Program—in each major city. Each resident agent in charge was to identify and provide information on the top 10 hoods in his jurisdiction. The FBI's mob-informant program, which decades later would result in myriad abuses and indiscretions, moved into high gear.

FBI agents began massive illegal bugging operations against mobsters in Chicago, Newark, Boston, Providence, San Francisco, and Philadelphia. The electronic surveillance could not be used in court, but it helped the FBI figure out who and what the American Mafia was all about.

Grand juries were convened in New York, Newark, and Tioga County, where Apalachin is located. Hoods scattered and got sick as they attempted to avoid testifying. It looked as if a few honest cops had discovered the evil, criminal Mafia that the Kefauver Committee had been talking about. It was, once again, a great show and a wonderful opportunity for the media and the politicians.

For the Mafia, the status quo would never return. Costello's Salvation Army charity dinner, the Kefauver hearings, the Apalachin fiasco, and subsequent events established La Cosa Nostra as big-time bad guys for the rest of the century. They were part of a well-oiled organization with a national agenda on gambling and narcotics. In reality, it was much more complicated than that, as later chapters detail.

Meanwhile, the Barbara estate remains largely as it was then. The vegetation has grown, and a subdivision now covers the bottom of the hill and its slopes. Other houses have been built on the crest of the hill, but the stone garage and the field where a bunch of Detroit's luxury gas guzzlers were parked on the apron while their middle-aged owners ran through the woods are still intact. There is no sign, but if you're in the area and stop to ask old timers who were there in 1957 (and young residents who weren't), they will give you directions to Apalachin's "Mafia house."

Ask anyone in the upstate New York town of Apalachin, and they'll show you the Mafia house where scores of top gangsters met in 1957.

(Courtesy of GangLandNews.com)

The Least You Need To Know

- The Mafia emerged as the nation's bad guys in the 1950s.

- Many politicians appeared to be in with the Mafia.

- The Kefauver hearings reinforced this perception.

- The discovery of 58 Italian-American hoods at Apalachin, New York, on November 14, 1957, firmed up the concept.

- Reality was much more complex than what the public perceived.

The Mafia Starts to Feel the Heat

In This Chapter

- ◆ Another senator asks questions
- ◆ Attorney General Robert Kennedy steps in
- ◆ Joe Valachi breaks down

On January 30, 1957, the U.S. Senate formed the Senate Select Committee on Improper Activities in the Labor or Management Field. Dubbed the Rackets Committee, it came about when the Permanent Sub-committee on Investigations, chaired by Senator John McClellan, discovered that Teamsters Union reports to federal agencies were inaccurate. McClellan felt that a close look into labor and management operations was necessary but was beyond the scope of his committee. After a political compromise, the Rackets Committee was created.

In this chapter, I look at this committee and what it accomplished. In addition, Robert Kennedy's tenure as attorney general in his brother's administration will be examined as it pertains to La Cosa Nostra. I also will discuss the impact of the first public Mafia turncoat, Joseph Valachi.

Labor Pains

In 1956, several U.S. senators began to take notice and question what appeared to be widespread corruption in the labor movement. After some discussion, the Senate created a Select Committee on Improper Activities in the Labor or Management Field to investigate numerous allegations and issue a full report to the Senate. Senator John McClellan, a Democrat from Arkansas, chaired what became known as the Rackets Committee. Robert Kennedy was retained as chief counsel.

Mafia Speak

Chicago mobster Louis Romano, one-time president of Local 278 of the Chicago Bartenders and Beverage Dispensers Union, was an enforcer for Frank Nitti with a reputation as a stone-cold killer. During the Rackets Committee hearings, as Robert Kennedy grilled him about a large number of murders he allegedly committed, Romano replied, "Why don't you go and dig up all the dead ones in the graveyard and ask if I shot them!"

In March of 1957, the committee showed it was serious when it zeroed in on its first target, Teamster president Dave Beck. Kennedy grilled him about $320,000 that disappeared from the union's treasury and made its way into his bank accounts. Beck was so badly battered that he resigned his position. Ultimately, he served two and a half years in prison for embezzlement. Rumors persist that ambitious Teamsters vice president Jimmy Hoffa fed some of the incriminating evidence to the Senate investigators.

Slammer Time

In 1959, Dave Beck was sentenced to five years for tax evasion and falsifying union tax forms. This sentence was later cut in half. After serving his time, Beck returned to his hometown of Seattle and operated four parking lots. Beck remained defiant to the end, which came in 1993 at the age of 99.

Beck's resignation put Jimmy Hoffa on the hot seat. Kennedy made Hoffa his new main target, and the two put on quite a show. They developed a real animosity that lasted for a decade. They hurled insults at each other during Hoffa's appearances and took pot shots at each other in the press.

During Hoffa's appearances before the Rackets Committee, Kennedy used information gleaned from a Hoffa crony who worked for the committee as an informer and exposed many links that Hoffa and the Teamsters Union had with some pretty unsavory wiseguys.

Jimmy Hoffa answers tough questions in 1961.

(Courtesy of New York Daily News*)*

One of the worst was Anthony "Tony Ducks" Corallo of New York, whose record included prison stints for robbery and drug dealing. He had been involved with other unions, but Kennedy focused on charges that Corallo, an official of Teamsters Local 239, stole nearly $70,000 from the local by placing dead men on the payroll. When confronted about this and other allegations, Corallo invoked the Fifth Amendment.

Slammer Time
Tony Ducks Corallo spent a lifetime on the other side of the law. In 1962, he got two years for bribing a New York State Supreme Court justice, and in 1968, he received four years for bribing a city official to win construction contracts. In 1987, after he had risen to boss of the Luchese family and was a member of the Commission, Corallo was hit with a 100-year sentence for his racketeering conviction in the Commission case. He died in prison on August 23, 2000.

The discovery of the national meeting of La Cosa Nostra at Apalachin was a dream come true for Kennedy and the Rackets Committee. On June 30, 1958, the Rackets Committee began an investigation into the gathering. Kennedy hoped to squeeze

Apalachin attendees to expose the mob's infiltration of the labor movement. He expressed concern that the Mafia was pouring its ill-gotten gains into legitimate businesses to give themselves a cover for continuing Mafia activities.

The committee subpoenaed numerous witnesses to testify about Apalachin, including nine mobsters who attended the affair. As it had at the Kefauver hearings, the Bureau of Narcotics provided the lion's share of the Mafia information that the committee obtained. This time, it was narcotics agent Martin Pera whose testimony suggested that the Mafia was an international narcotics-trafficking organization and that some of the Apalachin guests were part of it.

In May of 1958, Robert Kennedy asked the Chicago office of the FBI to locate witnesses and provide evidence about them and their activities to the Rackets Committee. While J. Edgar Hoover's FBI knew little about La Cosa Nostra in 1957, the Top Hoodlum program he instituted right after Apalachin—each office had to identify the top 10 hoods in its area—paid off. Hoover directed the committee to major Chicago players like Anthony Accardo, Joey Aiuppa, Charles "Chuckie English" Ingrassia, and Sam Giancana.

Big Shot

Chuckie English had nothing to say to the Rackets Committee when he was called. He invoked the Fifth Amendment 56 times. He talked too much one July night in 1963, however. He told FBI agent Bill Roemer that "[Giancana] says if Kennedy wants to talk to him he knows who to go through," referring to Frank Sinatra, who was a friend of the Kennedys and Giancana. Years later, in 1988, English's talking got him into the biggest trouble there is. His criticism of then-boss Joe Ferriola got him killed.

Chicago mobster Joseph Glimco appeared before the committee four times, refusing to answer a total of 152 questions.

The Rackets Committee got no answers from Glimco, but it introduced evidence that he, through his control of Teamsters Local 777, extorted kickbacks from taxi drivers who belonged to the local. Glimco also received payoffs from an insurance company that handled the local's health and welfare plan. Glimco was 5'4", but his prowess with a gun—he was acquitted of one murder and suspected in many more—and his status as a member of the Outfit made Hoffa very reluctant to oust the corrupt union official.

Hoffa also had powerful wiseguy friends in Ohio. Cleveland family associate Nunzio Louis "Babe" Triscaro was president of Local 436 of the Excavation Drivers Union and vice president of Ohio Joint Council 41. He was the second most powerful Teamster in the state. Committee investigator Walter Sheridan called Triscaro the "liaison" between the Ohio Teamsters and the underworld. On September 17, 1958, Triscaro refused to answer any questions about kickbacks and sweetheart deals as the Rackets Committee introduced evidence that his family owned three gravel companies that employed nonunion help.

Mafia Speak

According to late FBI agent Bill Roemer, Glimco and powerful Outfit associate Murray Humphreys were overheard on an illegal bug discussing that Hoffa was very quick to provide them with favors whenever they needed one.

When the Rackets Committee ended its run in 1960—after 270 days of hearings and 1,526 witnesses—it had linked Teamsters officials with corruption that the union is still trying to shake more than 40 years later. Hoffa was exposed as a criminal—he would eventually be convicted and jailed—not an honest union leader. The Rackets Committee also suggested that the mystical Mafia was a factor in labor corruption, but just exactly who and what this Mafia was would have to wait for a few more years. In the meantime, the Rackets Committee chief counsel would have an opportunity to go after Hoffa and his friends from a much stronger position of power.

Attorney General RFK

On December 29, 1960, president elect John F. Kennedy confirmed rumors that began shortly after his election and named brother Robert as attorney general. This appointment made Jimmy Hoffa and many of his mobster friends very nervous. Little did they know that the damage had begun a year earlier.

J. Edgar Hoover's Top Hoodlum program—initiated in the wake of Apalachin—was in high gear. On July 29, 1959, the Chicago office of the FBI placed an illegal bug in a building where top Chicago hoods gathered.

Fuhgeddaboudit

In the early 1960s, the FBI used material from the many illegal bugs they had placed in Mafia hangouts to drive mobsters crazy. For example, on June 3, 1963, a bug placed in a funeral home in Niagara Falls, New York, overheard Buffalo boss Stefano Magaddino complaining, "They know everybody's name. They know who's boss. They know who is on the Commission."

On the first day, they heard an earful about crooked cops and politicians. The FBI fed information from this and other illegal FBI buggings around the country to FBI headquarters in Washington, which passed it on to Attorney General RFK.

When Robert Kennedy became Attorney General in 1961, he read hundreds of reports on the nation's major mobsters. He visited FBI offices, including the one in Chicago, where he got a briefing on the Chicago Outfit. He listened to a tape of a crooked alderman discussing, with two other police officers, the killing of a third, troublesome vice squad officer who wasn't being cooperative with the bad guys, according to FBI agent Bill Roemer.

Kennedy also rearranged Justice Department resources to better combat what he called "The Enemy Within." More than 40 lawyers were added to the Justice Department section on organized crime. Satellite offices were opened in New York and Chicago. FBI Director J. Edgar Hoover was encouraged to strengthen the FBI's commitment against La Cosa Nostra, and he responded by pouring incredible numbers of agents into that field. For example, the Chicago organized crime unit went from 5 to 70 agents almost overnight.

Mafia Speak

According to author Dwight Smith, the *New York Times* carried between 5 and 11 stories on the Mafia before Joe Valachi testified before a Senate committee in 1963. After that, the number of Mafia articles jumped dramatically. In 1967, for example, there were 148 stories on that subject.

Fuhgeddaboudit

Carlos Marcello wasn't the only La Cosa Nostra boss the government had trouble deporting. Carlo Gambino was ordered to be deported in the 1940s and nothing happened. After the Apalachin fiasco in 1957, the INS renewed attempts to deport him. Gambino fought these off using claims of heart disease and other ailments. Despite his heart problems, Gambino managed to generate enough energy to run one of the two largest families in the United States for 19 years.

In early 1961, Robert Kennedy decided to show everyone—the mob, the public, and J. Edgar Hoover—that he was a tough guy. New Orleans Mafia boss Carlos Marcello paid the price. On April 4, 1961, Marcello reported to the immigration authorities as required because of his alien status. To his surprise, he was handcuffed, read a deportation order, and hustled to the airport and onto a flight to Guatemala, which Marcello had falsely claimed was his home. The brazen move by the Immigration and Naturalization Services had Kennedy's support. Marcello was denied his constitutional rights and common courtesies usually afforded even the most heinous criminals. He wasn't permitted to call his family nor his lawyer. He wasn't allowed to pack a bag or a toothbrush. The high-handed move was eventually overturned by the courts, and Marcello made his way back into the United States, where he spent the rest of his life successfully fighting off deportation orders, partly because no country was willing to accept him.

Attorney General Kennedy also waged an undeclared war against Hoover, who had been used to being treated with deference by attorneys general and presidents alike. In the JFK administration, Hoover, for the first time in his career, had no direct access to the president. He worked through his superior, RFK.

During his four years in office, Kennedy succeeded in passing legislation that hindered gambling, but these new laws were not a significant blow against La Cosa Nostra. His Justice Department won a conviction of Jimmy Hoffa for jury tampering and misuse of union funds—a major accomplishment that did little, however, to remove Mafia influence from that union. Several major La Cosa Nostra drug traffickers like Carmine Galante and John Ormento were convicted and jailed, but they were replaced and the Mafia kept on trucking. Kennedy had made a major effort to cripple the most powerful organized crime group but failed to strike a mortal blow. Indeed, many families enjoyed two more decades of prosperity.

Joe Valachi

In early 1930, Joe Valachi was a common street criminal when he was recruited into the crime family formerly led by Tommy Reina, who had been killed by an insurgent faction supported by Joe "The Boss" Masseria. The Reina loyalists pretended to accept their new leader, Joseph Pinzolo, but secretly plotted to remove him. Valachi was part of this plan.

The Reina loyalists, led by Thomas Gagliano, killed Pinzolo as planned in September 1930, and Valachi was made a formal member of the Gagliano family. After drifting for a time toward the clan now called the Bonanno family, Valachi joined the family then led by Charles "Lucky" Luciano, later to be headed by Vito Genovese and become known by his name.

For the next 30 years, Valachi was a typical mob soldier. He earned a living through various rackets, including extortion, numbers, selling stolen goods, selling gas-ration stamps during World War II, and drug dealing. The last would be his downfall.

Turncoat Genovese soldier Joe Valachi as he looked in his heyday during a 1933 arrest.

(Courtesy of GangLandNews.com)

Mafia Speak

On April 8, 1962, Anthony Strollo left his house and was never seen again. Without admitting anything, Vito Genovese said he had only Strollo's best interests in mind when he ordered him killed, Genovese told Valachi when they discussed Strollo's disappearance in the Atlanta federal prison. "It's the best thing," said Genovese, "Tony couldn't take it (prison) like you and I."

In May 1959, Valachi learned he was going to be arrested for narcotics trafficking and fled. He was grabbed in November, was released on $25,000 bail, and ran away again. He must have known that prison would be hell. Eventually, he was arrested again and convicted of heroin trafficking. Sentenced to 15 years on June 3, 1960, he arrived at Atlanta Federal Penitentiary to a frosty reception from boss Vito Genovese, who had gotten there four months earlier for his own drug problems, a heroin-conspiracy conviction.

Genovese believed one of his capos, Anthony "Tony Bender" Strollo, was secretly dealing drugs and not sharing his profits with the boss. Because Valachi was in Strollo's crew and had been caught dealing heroin, Genovese looked on Valachi as a traitor.

A year later, in December 1961, Valachi was convicted in another drug case and sentenced to 20 years. He returned to the Atlanta prison in March 1962, accompanied by rumors that he was an informer—in fact he was, although not about fellow wiseguys—and Genovese believed them.

Valachi began to fear for his life and had himself placed in solitary confinement. When he refused to reveal the reason for his request, however, Valachi was returned to the general jail population. He tried unsuccessfully to contact family boss Tommy Lucchese, a friend of Valachi's wife, as well as a Bureau of Narcotics official for help. On June 22, 1962, Valachi's nerves cracked. He bludgeoned to death an inmate who resembled drug dealer Joseph "Joe Beck" DiPalermo, a man Valachi thought Genovese had commissioned to kill him.

> **Big Shot**
>
> Joe Valachi became a government informer in the summer of 1962 after he killed a fellow inmate at the Atlanta Federal Penitentiary. Valachi thought the man was a hit man sent by Vito Genovese. Valachi described his life in La Cosa Nostra and provided details about many major rubouts, including Mafia bosses Al Mineo, Joe Pinzolo, Joe Masseria, Salvatore Maranzano, and Albert Anastasia. Although his information was mostly an oral history passed on by others and was not usable in court, his insight provided a better understanding of La Cosa Nostra history.

A few weeks later, after then–Manhattan U.S. attorney Robert Morgenthau was contacted, Valachi agreed to cooperate in return for protection. On July 17, he pleaded guilty to second-degree murder and was transferred to New York to be debriefed by the Bureau of Narcotics.

Valachi was reluctant to speak to the drug agency that had put him where he was, so the feds brought in a fresh face. On September 8, 1962, FBI agent James Flynn coaxed Valachi into spilling his guts about his life in the mob.

> **Big Shot**
>
> Buffalo family soldier Albert Agueci, a cohort of Valachi's, made lots of money trafficking in heroin, for him and his crime family. In 1961, he was arrested on narcotics-conspiracy charges and became incensed when boss Stefano Magaddino didn't furnish any money for bail. To raise bail money, his wife sold their Toronto home. When he got out, Agueci, who had shared his drug profits with his boss, ripped Magaddino for being a tightwad, according to an FBI bug. A month later, on November 23, 1961, Agueci's body—he was tortured and slain—was found on a farm near Rochester.

"Joe, let's stop fooling around," said Flynn, according to *The Valachi Papers* (Putnam, 1968) by Peter Maas. "I want to talk about the organization by name, rank, and serial number. What's the name? Is it Mafia?"

"No, it's not Mafia," said Valachi. "That's the expression the outside uses."

"We know a lot more than you think," said Flynn, who had a wealth of information on La Cosa Nostra from the FBI's many illegal bugs and informants they had cultivated. "Now I'll give you the first part. You give me the rest. It's Cosa!"

"Cosa Nostra! So you know about it," said Valachi, after staring blankly at Flynn for nearly a minute.

After Flynn turned him on, Valachi was never turned off until he died in 1971 in a federal prison in El Paso, Texas. He filled in many gaps in the FBI's knowledge of the Mafia. His accounts complemented thousands of hours of taped conversations the FBI had listened to the previous three years. He detailed the structure—boss, underboss, capo, soldier, and associate—and the role of the Commission. He gave excellent estimates of the sizes of the Genovese and Gambino families and others he knew about. He described the induction ceremony and the rules they lived by and died for. He detailed murders of bosses going back three decades and gave insight about many significant events.

In addition, Valachi was a great public relations tool. In September and October of 1963, he appeared before a nationally televised session of the McClellan Committee. Through his public testimony, authorities were able to describe the structure, personalities, and rackets of La Cosa Nostra. He was a real-life gangster who put flesh and bones on an organization that, until then, many claimed was merely a rumor and gossip in newspaper and magazine stories. His appearance was a bombshell and made the Mafia big news.

Four decades later, it still is.

The Least You Need to Know

- Senate hearings linked the Mafia to unions.
- Teamster Jimmy Hoffa was linked with hoodlums.
- Robert Kennedy made serious efforts to curb the mob.
- Individual Mafia members were jailed in the 1960s.
- La Cosa Nostra began to feel some heat during the 1960s.

Chapter 16

Falling in Love with the Mafia

In This Chapter

♦ The FBI releases mob information to the media

♦ *LIFE* magazine profiles La Cosa Nostra

♦ *The Godfather* turns mobsters into romantic heroes

♦ *Goodfellas* sets the story straight

Telling stories about La Cosa Nostra became big business in the late 1960s. Much of this was inspired by the appearance of mob turncoat Joe Valachi in the fall of 1963 at nationally televised sessions of the McClellan hearings.

The public was very interested in the Mafia, and the government felt compelled to do something about their concerns. A presidential commission was formed, and it issued a report in 1967 that named the Mafia as the vital core of organized crime. This report led to numerous news stories including some in *LIFE* magazine.

In this chapter, I will look at some of the *LIFE* stories to illustrate the national interest in La Cosa Nostra. In addition, I will review two classic mob movies that captured huge audiences to see whether the reel Mafia depicted on the big screen was an accurate portrayal of real mob life.

Life in the Magazines

Joe Valachi's televised appearance set off more than a decade of news stories about the Mafia. *LIFE* magazine was a frontrunner in this coverage with daring stories that were obviously based on FBI material. It is widely known that writer Sandy Smith was fed confidential information by FBI agent Bill Roemer and others while working as a journalist in Chicago. Smith took his sources with him to *LIFE* magazine.

In September of 1967, *LIFE* produced a three-part series about the Mafia. One part featured a map of the United States with pictures of 24 La Cosa Nostra bosses surrounding it. On the map were cartoon depictions of the many rackets in which mobsters were involved. A dotted line showed the known routes of couriers who moved skim money from Las Vegas to various hidden partners around the United States. At the top of the map were pictures of the eight bosses who sat on the Commission at the time. At the bottom, next to Florida, was a picture of famous mob associate Meyer Lansky.

> **Slammer Time**
>
> According to author Peter Maas, Valachi penned his own autobiography after his Senate testimony. Ultimately, political pressure from Italian-American groups coerced the Department of Justice to rescind its previous permission to publish it. Maas eventually wrote a third-person account, *The Valachi Papers*, an invaluable addition to the understanding of La Cosa Nostra, published in 1968.

> **Fuhgeddaboudit**
>
> Gaetano "Corky" Vastola is a DeCavalcante family member with extensive interests in the music business. He played golf with Sammy Davis Jr. and promoted concerts for Ray Charles and Aretha Franklin. He was a part owner of Roulette Records and the listed songwriter of many top 1950s and 1960s tunes—including the doo-wop classic by the Valentines, "Lily Maebelle," and the Cleftones' "You Baby You"—earning royalties for his "work" while serving 10 years for extortion from 1988 to 1998.

The text contained a very good description of La Cosa Nostra. It accurately portrayed the 24 families as "semi-independent" organizations that "vary widely in size and their importance in the rackets." Smith accurately stated that some bosses, such as Carlos Marcello of New Orleans and Raymond Patriarca of New England, although they did not sit on the Commission, were just as or more powerful than some who did. He also noted mob movement into "legitimate" business such as banking and the music industry.

The complete *LIFE* magazine package gave the impression that La Cosa Nostra was all-powerful in the world of crime. The pictures of the bosses on the outer edges of a map of the United States filled with mob activities made it appear as if they controlled the entire country. With the comment, "Most Americans are just not aware of the extent of its influence," *LIFE* placed the Mafia into the "enemy within" category described by Robert Kennedy.

DeCavalcante soldier Corky Vastola had contacts with entertainers and record companies.

(Courtesy of GangLandNews.com)

The story was essentially accurate but incomplete. It left the impression that organized crime *was* La Cosa Nostra, when reality was much more complicated. *LIFE* noted that the mob, "has been able to insinuate itself into the core of society," but ignored the many non-Mafia organized crime groups that worked independently, sporadically, or regularly with mobsters. La Cosa Nostra was part of organized crime—a major part at that—but not all of it.

LIFE also made the controversial charge that the mob made "widespread attempts to corrupt—or at least to use—individual athletes and coaches of high reputation." To illustrate that, *LIFE* wrote that all-time NBA basketball great Bob Cousy had admitted being a friend of Genovese capo Francesco "Skiball" Scibelli, a major gambling figure in New England. *LIFE* gave no evidence that the Boston Celtic was aware of Scibelli's organized crime membership—and none ever surfaced later—but the article cast suspicion on Cousy that was likely unwarranted and unfair.

Mafia Speak

Like many people, mobsters love celebrities, including those from the sports world. In 1998, Colombo family soldier Dominick "Donny Shacks" Montemarano befriended Cade McNown, then a star quarterback at UCLA. Montemarano accompanied McNown and his family to New York for the Heisman Trophy dinner and gave them a tour of the Big Apple. From past practice, we can assume Montemarano had larceny on his mind. As it turned out, however, news of Montemarano's friendship with McNown and other football players surfaced early, before the veteran gangster had a chance to pull off any scams, according to the FBI, which investigated and cleared McNown of any wrongdoing.

The important point is that the *LIFE* article created the impression that gambling was the exclusive territory of La Cosa Nostra and that there was much "fixing" of games. In reality, however, many people were involved—and still are—in illegal gambling who were not Mafia members or associates. In certain areas, many large bookies did cut the local Mafia power in for a slice of the profits, but the United States is a big country, and many bookies were not dominated by the mob. The doomsday scenario *LIFE* expressed that mob attempts at fixing would threaten public confidence in the honesty of sports never came about, even with the revelation of a number of successful fix attempts. *LIFE* succeeded in magnifying a genuine concern far beyond reality.

Fuhgeddaboudit

In 1970, respected crime writer Nicholas Pileggi made a rare mistake. He wrote an article in *New York* magazine titled "The Decline and Fall of the Mafia" that was at least two decades premature. Pileggi's mistake pales in comparison to his true-crime Mafia books, *Wiseguy* (Simon & Schuster, 1985) and *Casino*, (Simon & Schuster, 1995), which were adapted for the big screen as *Goodfellas*, discussed later in this chapter, and *Casino*.

New Orleans boss Carlos Marcello received much attention from *LIFE* magazine that painted him as a powerful mobster who should be feared. In 1967, it said Marcello "controlled the state of Louisiana—with little interference from local public officials or police, and indeed often with their help."

On April 10, 1970, *LIFE* revisited Louisiana and claimed that Marcello's control was stronger than ever. He was growing rich on loans and other favors from the state government, friends and associates were in key positions of power, and nothing was being done to challenge his illegal activities, *LIFE* said. It was a damning, accurate picture of Marcello that made the Mafia look big, bad, and booming.

The Godfather Romanticizes the Mafia

While the nation was flooded in the 1960s with testimony, television reports, newspaper stories, and magazine articles about the Mafia, at least one man kept his wits about him.

Mario Puzo was a struggling writer from a large, poor family from Hell's Kitchen in Manhattan. In middle age, he had written two novels that received critical praise but were not financial successes. His publisher suggested a novel about La Cosa Nostra, a subject Puzo had touched on briefly in his second book. Puzo finished the manuscript in July of 1968. Earlier, desperate for cash, Puzo sold the movie rights for a $12,500 option payment.

On March 15, 1972, the movie *The Godfather* was released. It had a huge, ready-made audience, including people who had read the novel and millions of others who had lived through the previous 15 years—from Apalachin to Valachi to the birth of the Italian-American Civil Rights League and the shooting of Mafia boss Joseph Colombo in 1971. The movie was a giant success, grossing more than $26 million in the first month. *The Godfather*'s fabulous profits and the film's artistic merit have nothing to do with reality, however.

Mafia Speak

In *The Godfather*, Don Corleone was petitioned by undertaker Amerigo Bonasera to kill two men who had beaten his daughter. Corleone is not pleased with Bonasera, for he had never shown him any respect before. As a sign of his debt, Corleone required Bonasera to refer to him as "Godfather." In real life, this term has rarely, if ever, been heard on FBI bugs or in street talk.

The film opens with an elaborate wedding reception at the estate of Don Corleone. Affairs like this were not uncommon in the years prior to Apalachin. One of the largest wedding celebrations was the one for Bill Bonanno, son of New York boss Joe Bonanno, and Rosalie Profaci, niece of New York boss Joe Profaci. About 3,000 guests attended the reception at the Hotel Astor in New York City in August of 1956. Years later, Rosalie Bonanno wrote that thousands of flowers were flown in from California specifically for her wedding, and entertainment was provided by Tony Bennett and the Four Lads. The expression "Mafia wedding" has a basis in fact.

In the movie, a Frank Sinatra–like character, Johnny Fontaine, makes a much-appreciated visit to the wedding reception. The oft-repeated tale of how Sinatra achieved his freedom from a contract with bandleader Tommy Dorsey is used in the movie. The real-life rumor was that powerful mobster Willie Moretti stuck a gun in the bandleader's mouth and urged him to give Sinatra his release. Although Sinatra did have friendships with mobsters, author Kitty Kelley, no Sinatra fan, researched this story and discovered that it was myth. After he released Sinatra, Dorsey made a disparaging remark about Sinatra and his gun-toting friends. The legend rose from this snide comment. Although Sinatra might have deserved criticism for consorting with known hoods, these falsehoods only cheapened the legitimacy of the complaints. One of the most spectacular scenes in *The Godfather* has to do with the intimidation of a studio head so that Johnny Fontaine would be given a prize movie role. Kitty Kelley also demolishes this myth in her book, *His Way*, and shows that Sinatra gained the role, Anthony Maggio in *From Here to Eternity*, by legitimate means.

Slammer Time

The Chicago Outfit used clout to secure the presidency of the International Alliance of Theatrical Stage Employees (IATSE) for one of its associates in 1934. This union included the projectionists in movie theaters that were big business during this era. From this position of strength, the Outfit extorted millions from major Hollywood studios including MGM, Twentieth Century Fox, and RKO. In 1943, the scam was exposed, and major Outfit leaders, including boss Paul Ricca, were sent to prison.

In the movie, Don Corleone's consigliere, Tom Haden, was kidnapped by rival mobsters, reminiscent of the snatching of five leading members of the Joe Profaci family by the Gallo gang in 1961. Like Haden, the Profaci men were eventually released.

One of the most famous scenes in *The Godfather* was the killing of bodyguard Luca Brasi. He went into a deserted bar to discuss Mafia business with mob rivals. They double-crossed Brasi and strangled him in a horrific scene. This scene was similar to the attempted murder of Larry Gallo in the Sahara Lounge in Brooklyn on August 20, 1961. He, too, had been lured to his near death by treacherous rivals.

The shooting of Don Corleone as he buys fruit is a copy of the June 17, 1956, real-life murder of Frank Scalice, who was buying fruit when he was approached by two men and gunned down. Unlike the Godfather, Scalice did not survive.

In the movie, after killing Luca Brasi, mob rivals try to intimidate the Corleones by sending Brasi's bulletproof vest to them with a dead fish inside. This is a mob legend that reportedly happened to the Gallo brothers' version of Luca Brasi, Joseph "Joe Jelly" Gioelli. After Gioelli disappeared, his suit coat with a dead fish inside was thrown out of a car near a Gallo haunt, according to a book by Raymond Martin, an inspector in South Brooklyn in the early 1960s.

The Godfather concludes with a violent settling of accounts by Don Michael Corleone. Among those killed are the heads of the five families of New York on the same day. Puzo might have based this on a rumored plan by Joe Bonanno to get rid of rival New York leaders Tommy Lucchese and Carlo Gambino in the early 1960s. Gambino made those allegations against Bonanno to oust him as boss of his family in 1964.

Big Shot _____

Michael Corleone, in *The Godfather*, makes a major move on a number of Las Vegas casinos, including one run by mercurial Moe Green, an obvious takeoff on the legendary Ben "Bugsy" Siegel of Flamingo Hotel fame. Siegel was shot to death on June 20, 1947, in Los Angeles, whereas the movie character Moe Green was killed in a casino health club while getting a rubdown. Both had an eye shot out.

Despite the many similarities between real life and scenes in an entertaining movie, *The Godfather* has little in common with the way real-life gangsters operate. *The Godfather* depicted a family that resorted to violence only to defend itself. It didn't show their musclemen pounding a poor degenerate gambler who was behind on his loan-shark payment or mobsters torching a restaurant or garbage truck of an extortion victim. There is no blue-collar worker shot to death after killing a son of a gangster in a tragic car accident.

I enjoyed the movie, but after years of covering the Mafia, I feel *The Godfather*—and its two sequels, a trilogy of mythmaking and entertainment—failed to capture the reality of day-to-day Mafia life. The daily routine involves grit, grime, self-interest, lying, cheating, backstabbing, pettiness, spontaneous violence, stupidity, betrayal, and many other acts that conjure up the idea of killers without honor who will do almost anything to make a buck.

> **Fuhgeddaboudit**
>
> Henry Hill, subject of the movie *Goodfellas*, has had a roller coaster life since he left the world of the Mafia. He has battled drug and alcohol problems, has gotten divorced, was convicted of drug dealing and got a free pass, went to jail, and has appeared on numerous TV shows in various states of sobriety. In 2001, he set a new standard for turncoat mobster by creating his own website!

Goodfellas Gets It Right

Nicholas Pileggi is a talented writer with extensive experience writing about La Cosa Nostra. His best-selling books on the Mafia, *Casino* (Simon & Schuster, 1995) and *Wiseguy* (Simon & Schuster, 1985), were both made into hit movies. *Goodfellas*, starring Ray Liotta, Robert DeNiro, Paul Sorvino, and Joe Pesci, is, in my opinion, the best depiction of real Mafia life yet filmed.

Goodfellas tells the story of longtime Luchese family associate Henry Hill. It captures the essence of daily life in and around street-level associates as they grind out a living in the orbit of capo Paulie Cicero, whose real-life counterpart was Paul Vario.

As the movie begins, Hill, just approaching his teens, is attracted to and lured into "the life" by the wealth of the mobsters and their disdain for any laws except their own. This part of the film nicely captures a few of the lures that bring street kids into the Mafia milieu. It also says a lot about the hoods who exploit impressionable kids instead of kicking them in the rear end and sending them on their way.

Without using much dialogue, *Goodfellas* accurately depicts the corruption that existed during the first two decades of Hill's work with the Mafia. Beat cops take bribes of cash, liquor, and cigarettes to ignore truck hijackings by Jimmy Conway's crew, in real life Jimmy "The Gent" Burke. Mere facial expressions are used to suggest that the crew's lawyer has a long-standing, questionable relationship with the judge who presides over Hill's first court case. You see prison guards on the take, jailed Mafia-connected hoods feasting on Italian delicacies, and a prison guard being paid to ignore Hill's prison drug dealing.

We know that this corruption is based on reality. In the 1980s, the FBI conducted an extensive sting operation to uncover wrongdoing in the Cook County, Illinois Circuit Court System. Eight judges and 34 attorneys were among those convicted of various corruption offenses. A fiasco in which onetime Luchese family turncoat Anthony "Gaspipe" Casso and others enjoyed sex, drugs, and other favors while they were behind bars, shows that bribery is alive and well within the prison system.

Slammer Time

Colombo acting boss Victor "Little Vic" Orena, Gambino capos Nicholas "Little Nick" Corozzo and Leonard DiMaria, and other Mafiosi were enjoying Italian gourmet delicacies, fine wine, and booze while they were incarcerated at the Metropolitan Detention Center in Brooklyn in 1996. Many corrections officers lost their jobs, and some were convicted and jailed, including Anthony Martinez. Martinez was so enamored of the wiseguy life, he was tape-recorded saying he wanted to change his name to Martino so he could be "made."

Pileggi also does a nice job showing how truck hijacking was carried out at Kennedy Airport. The Luchese family had the upper hand there through their control of Teamsters Locals 295 and 851. A major benefit was knowing which trucks were carrying valuable cargoes. In addition, if the driver cooperated with the hoods, his job would be protected by the union. Jimmy Conway also needed the approval of Luchese capo Paul Cicero to engage in airport hijackings. The movie shows the not-too-subtle intimidation tactic that hijackers use to assure silence by truck drivers, taking their driver's license with their name and address.

Another important point that *Goodfellas* gets across is that no crime is too big or too small to commit. The hoods pull off a daring $6-million predawn robbery at Kennedy Airport and sell untaxed cigarettes from the trunk of a car.

Goodfellas also captures the duplicity of married life in the mob. Many have regular girlfriends for whom they set up apartments and buy expensive jewelry and furs. Some wives are suspicious, but most turn a blind eye to it. Others get more aggressive like Hill's wife Karen did in the movie. In real life, FBI bugs often catch Mafia hoods leading double lives. The famous Pizza Connection case revealed that Giuseppe Ganci not only had an affair with a girlfriend but with her best friend as well. Of course, the girlfriend was also cheating on Ganci, so fuhgeddaboudit. This is Mafia life.

> **Fuhgeddaboudit**
>
> According to Ralph Blumenthal in his book, *Last Days of the Sicilians*, Giuseppe Ganci, a key player in a major heroin network involving the Bonanno family, was diagnosed with lung cancer in 1983. It didn't change his routine. On the same day he got the bad news, he continued his heroin dealing. A few days later, he took on a second girlfriend.

Violence is present in both *The Godfather* and *Goodfellas*, but the latter captures the reality of Mafia life much better. There is a scene in which the Conway crew is sitting around drinking and playing cards. Within minutes, a joke turns violent, and a simple-minded mob gofer gets a chest full of bullets. Another scene involves the killing of a Gambino family member. He starts out teasing "Tommy" and is battered, stabbed, and shot to death in a gory real-life depiction of mob violence. Six months later, the crew digs up the body when they fear it will be discovered. Again, this is mob life in which drunken hoods end up killing another hood in a bloody, messy slaughter. Senseless, stupid, and real!

Both movies are excellent entertainment. Both depict real-life situations in La Cosa Nostra, but *The Godfather* makes the hoods too noble. In *The Godfather Part II*, the mob guys were darker, more evil. The violence was messier, the cameras lingered on it longer, and it was more realistic. *Goodfellas* got it right the first time. After *Goodfellas*, few would want to follow in Henry Hill's footsteps.

The Least You Need to Know

- After 1963, the Mafia received a lot of media attention.
- The *Godfather* trilogy is excellent entertainment but doesn't really reflect what the mob is about.
- The movie *Goodfellas* captured real Mafia life.

Chapter 17

Lights, Camera, Action for a Mafia Star

In This Chapter

- ◆ A Mafia boss learns to love fame
- ◆ Italian-American political power
- ◆ Italian-Americans are betrayed
- ◆ The imposter is removed

One of the strangest eras in La Cosa Nostra history blazed across the national stage from mid-1970 until the end of June 1971. A young New York Mafia boss's temper got the best of him, and he and some 30 friends began picketing the FBI. They claimed the agency was prejudiced against Italian-Americans and was using its power unfairly.

The protest caught the imagination of many of the millions of Italian-Americans who rallied to the professed cause of the Mafia boss. Within a month, the Italian-American Civil Rights League was formed and began flexing its newfound political muscle. It was an incredible tale with a Hollywood ending. I tell that story in this chapter and briefly analyze the phenomenon that propelled a Mafia hood to the cover of *Time* magazine.

Enter Joe Colombo

One of New York's five Mafia families is named after a man whose father and a female acquaintance ended up strangled in the back of a car. Joe Colombo was a young man in 1938 when father Anthony Colombo was found dead. Nevertheless, he chose a path that would bring about his own death and the incarceration of three sons.

After his father's murder, Joe Colombo quit school and got a job. He joined the Coast Guard during World War II but received a medical discharge for mental problems. Then he began his life as a petty criminal in Brooklyn. By the late 1950s, Colombo had earned numerous arrests for gambling but managed to avoid any serious arrest or jail time because he became a made man in the Profaci family.

By the time Profaci died from natural causes on June 6, 1962, Colombo was a powerful capo. When acting boss Joe Magliocco conceived a plan to murder two rival bosses to solidify his position, Colombo alerted targets Carlo Gambino and Tommy Lucchese of the plot. Magliocco was hauled before the Commission and was told to call a new election.

Fuhgeddaboudit
The Italian-American Civil Rights League named Mafia boss Joe Colombo "Man of the Year" in 1971. The testimonial dinner in his honor had to be moved up two days because the Man of the Year was scheduled to go to prison on the day he was originally scheduled to receive the award!

On December 28, 1963, Magliocco died of natural causes and Colombo, backed by Lucchese and Gambino, was selected as boss a few days later. At the relatively young age of 41, in January 1964, Colombo became the leader of one of the most powerful criminal organizations in America.

Colombo's new position attracted the attention of the FBI, the New York City police, and the IRS. He was called before a grand jury in 1966 that was looking into the mob's infiltration of legitimate businesses. When the gang boss refused to testify, he was sentenced to 30 days.

Mafia Speak

They weren't Felix Unger and Oscar Madison, but Bill Bonanno and Joe Magliocco became a Mafia odd couple in June of 1963. The son of family boss Joe Bonanno and the wannabe boss of the Profaci family began living together at Magliocco's East Islip, Long Island, home as Bonanno and wife Rosalie attempted to reconcile their failing marriage. Bonanno and Magliocco shared more than his 12-acre estate. That September, the Commission told Magliocco, who was called on the carpet for plotting to kill two Mafia bosses, to step aside and go away quietly—or else. A year later, the Commission would give Bonanno's old man the same order.

Colombo tried to present a legitimate front as a real estate salesman for Cantalupo Realty in Bensonhurst, Brooklyn. Owner Anthony Cantalupo was a longtime associate of Gambino and a boyhood friend of Colombo. The Mafia boss lived in a luxurious home in the Dyker Heights section of Brooklyn, where he and his wife raised five children. Colombo also had a beautiful estate in the country and drove a new Cadillac every year. His lifestyle appeared way beyond his means, and the IRS got onto the young boss.

Fuhgeddaboudit

John Gotti was called the "Dapper Don" because of his attention to his personal dress. His Armani suits, pocket hankies, and matching ties were his trademark as he pranced through Little Italy during his heyday. Two decades before, Joe Colombo maintained an apartment for the sole purpose of holding his extensive clothes collection, according to Joe Cantalupo, who had a desk next to Colombo's in his father's office. Colombo would change suits three times a day and made sure to wear a pinky ring that matched his outfit. He wore $1,000 suits and $500 shoes.

In 1966, Colombo applied for a real estate broker's license that required him to disclose his net worth and other personal matters. By doing this, Colombo opened himself up to public scrutiny, including an IRS investigation. No doubt the FBI, which knew Colombo was a Mafia boss, helped get the IRS started. The Real Estate Board hearings resulted in much unwanted publicity for Colombo and his associates.

On September 22, 1966, Joe Colombo was one of 13 La Cosa Nostra leaders arrested while dining in New York's La Stella restaurant. Among the group were Mafia powers such as Carlo Gambino, Carlos Marcello, and Santos Trafficante. Although one enterprising police officer had the foresight to note the seating arrangements (which meant nothing), the topics of conversation have never been revealed.

In January of 1970, Colombo was hauled before another grand jury, one investigating the disappearance of Salvatore "Sally D" D'Ambrosio. At the same time, hearings on Colombo's broker's license were taking place. Ultimately, he was indicted for income tax evasion and perjury for lying on his broker's license application form.

The Italian-American Civil Rights League

On April 30, 1970, Joseph Colombo Jr. was arrested and charged with melting down coins for their silver content that was worth more than the face value of the coins. It was a minor case that was part of the pressure tactics the FBI used against the elder Colombo. He lost his cool and ordered his men to picket the FBI's Manhattan headquarters, claiming they had framed his young son to get at him.

A week later, Colombo formed the Italian-American Civil Rights League, appointed a number of mob associates as captains, and told them to organize relatives and friends and get them into the league. Using the demonstrations as a rallying point, the idea caught fire, and tens of thousands of Italian-Americans mailed in a $10 membership fee. The league was a phenomenal success. Celebrities and politicians quickly jumped on the bandwagon.

Joe Colombo leads demonstration in front of the New York FBI headquarters on June 9, 1970.

(Courtesy of New York Daily News*)*

Mafia Speak

Joe Colombo wasn't a man of the year to Simone "Sam the Plumber" DeCavalcante. On October 16, 1964, the New Jersey boss was discussing Colombo's ascension to boss of the Profaci family with underboss Frank Majuri. "He sold out his own outfit," and he "sits like a baby next to Carlo (Gambino) all the time," said DeCavalcante. "He (Colombo) was a bust-out guy all his life."

On June 29, 1970, an estimated 50,000 people, including many elected officials, attended the Mafia boss's rally at Columbus Circle in Manhattan. The Mob-controlled unions helped shut down the docks so that its members could attend. Similarly, many businesses in Italian neighborhoods closed their doors as a sign of solidarity (or good sense). The rally was a spectacular success. Joe Colombo was a political force in the nation's largest city.

Colombo used his powerful influence over his soldiers—and the strong feelings of many Italian-Americans that they faced ethnic discrimination—to fuel the Italian-American Civil Rights League to power. Mafia boss Joe Colombo was perpetuating a gigantic fraud, but the media loved it. The incongruity of a Mafia boss being a civil rights leader was a fascinating story. It made great copy, and Colombo did what he could to keep it going. He posed for pictures, he gave interviews, and he was a guest on the Dick Cavett show.

The support Colombo received from the masses clouded the judgment of some weak-willed, politically connected law enforcement officials, including one who would later be convicted of corruption charges. U.S. attorney general John Mitchell announced that the Justice Department and the FBI would no longer use the terms "Mafia" and "La Cosa Nostra." New York governor Nelson Rockefeller issued the same edict for various departments in the Empire State.

In March of 1971, Colombo was sentenced to one to two and a half years in prison for lying on his real estate broker's license five years earlier. However, he won a postponement of his sentence while he appealed his conviction.

Colombo had the league name him "Man of the Year" and hold a black-tie affair to honor him in May of 1971. It was an example of self-praise that made the giant ego of John Gotti pale in comparison. Guest after guest came to the microphone to praise Colombo, failing to mention, of course, his membership in La Cosa Nostra. Asked about Colombo's underworld activities, one partygoer told *Time* magazine, "If Joe's guilty of all they say, they ought to make him secretary of state at least because he is too smart for them to prove anything."

> **Fuhgeddaboudit**
>
> In a famous case of folding under pressure, Al Ruddy, producer of *The Godfather*, announced at a press conference called by the Italian-American Civil Rights League in March 1971 that the terms "Mafia" and "La Cosa Nostra" would not be used in his movie. Ruddy's defenders claim the words were not in the movie script anyway, and thus Ruddy had achieved League support without giving up anything.

The Shooting

Joe Colombo and the Italian-American Civil Rights League accused the FBI of investigating and harassing Colombo, his son, and others solely because they were Italian-Americans. He claimed that, like other civil rights activists, he was unfairly targeted, investigated, and persecuted by the FBI. The trouble for Colombo was that he was different than other civil rights leaders the FBI had investigated over the years. For example, Martin Luther King Jr. rose to national prominence in the 1960s and was targeted by the FBI. The FBI investigated him nearly to death. Eventually, though, the G-men backed off. Unlike King, however, Joe Colombo was a fraud and the FBI knew it. They went at Colombo and his friends despite his rising political strength.

On December 16, 1970, the FBI's surveillance of Colombo paid off. While arresting Colombo soldier Rocco Miraglia, FBI agents seized a briefcase that turned out to be a major embarrassment for Colombo. The briefcase contained a list of first names or nicknames and dollar amounts. Colombo, who had been with Miraglia when he was arrested, was called before a federal grand jury and was asked about the list. Instead of taking the Fifth Amendment, Colombo testified that the names were people who raised money for his civil rights league. "Carl" was Carlo Gambino, and the 30,000 beside it represented $30,000 he raised. The testimony didn't go over well with the powerful family boss.

By the time June of 1971 rolled around, it was apparent there would be no Mafia solidarity on Unity Day, the day of the Italian-American Civil Rights League's second rally. Unlike the previous year, Gambino disapproved. Longshoremen had to work, Mafia-connected businesses stayed open, and some public officials were becoming uneasy about being affiliated with the Mafia leader.

Also fomenting trouble was renegade Colombo soldier Joey Gallo, who had come close to capturing the family throne back in the early 1960s with his brothers. Gallo had gone to prison for nine years. Released that February, Gallo stirred up trouble by questioning Colombo's leadership.

The Gallo brothers were streetwise veterans of Mafia intrigue. Gallo learned that mob leaders like Gambino and Thomas "Tommy Ryan" Eboli of the Genovese family frowned on Colombo's political activities. The Gallos were also close to then Genovese capo Vincent "Chin" Gigante. Joey Gallo was labeled crazy, but he was a wily, cunning gangster who saw a chance to return his crew to prominence, and he knew the fall of Colombo would facilitate that.

On June 28, 1971, a street hustler at the second and last annual rally of the Italian-American Civil Rights League gunned down pseudo–civil rights leader Joe Colombo. Gunman Jerome Johnson got press credentials from the League and approached Colombo before he got to the stage, firing three shots from an automatic pistol into Colombo's head.

Police wrestled Johnson to the ground. A Colombo associate pulled a pistol and killed him with three shots in the back while the cops were restraining him.

The crowd quickly dissipated, although some made a feeble attempt to continue the festival. Although its members didn't know it then, the League was as dead as Jerome Johnson.

Joe Colombo is rushed to the hospital after being gunned down at the Italian-American Civil Rights League Rally on June 28, 1971.

(Courtesy of New York Daily News*)*

Gallo immediately emerged as the number-one suspect because of his well-known animosity toward Colombo. The theory was strengthened because Johnson was black and Gallo was said to have made alliances with black inmates in prison and was reputed to have some black associates in his crew.

After weeks of public speculation by police and elected officials about Colombo's shooting and the execution of Johnson, police questioned brothers Joey and Albert Gallo, Carlo Gambino, and others about it. It was a futile exercise, but authorities felt it was necessary to show the public that cops had pulled out all the stops in their investigation. After a few weeks, it became fairly obvious that neither Joey Gallo nor Gambino was behind the hit. There were no links between Johnson and Gallo, and there were no links between Gallo and the Colombo loyalist who killed Johnson. Johnson was likely deranged and acting on his own.

Mafia Speak

According to Peter "Pete the Greek" Diapoulos, he and Albert "Kid Blast" Gallo met with Genovese capo Vincent "Chin" Gigante not long after the Colombo shooting. Gallo and Diapoulos admitted to Gigante that the Gallos had been trying to kill Colombo but had nothing to do with the Johnson shooting. A few years later, Albert Gallo and some of his men switched and joined the Genovese family.

Although Colombo had fallen out of favor with Gambino, there is no way Gambino would have authorized the Colombo shooting in such a public way by such a loose cannon. Far too much could go wrong. If he had wanted to kill Colombo, he would have simply called him to a meeting from which he never would have returned.

The bottom line is that the best evidence indicates that Johnson killed Colombo for his own demented reasons. There is no evidence to indicate a conspiracy involving Johnson with Gallo or Gambino. Johnson was another in a long line of nuts who exploded on the public consciousness with a cowardly act. Had he lived, you can be sure that along the way, he would have claimed that Gallo, Gambino, or both had hired him. We were spared that nonsense when the Colombo associate fired three bullets into him.

> **Big Shot**
>
> Joe Colombo wasn't the only Mafioso to be gunned down while attending a celebration. In Chicago, on May 7, 1929, Al Capone invited three of his men—Albert Anselmi, John Scalise, and Joseph Guinta—to a banquet at Cicero's Hawthorne Inn. Before the night was over, the three were beaten and shot to death for alleged disloyalty to Capone.

The Aftermath

Shortly after Colombo's shooting, it became apparent that he was going to be severely handicapped both mentally and physically. He was no longer a factor in his family and realignment began. The situation was complicated because powerful capo Carmine "Junior" Persico was in prison for a hijacking conviction. As outlined in the Colombo family history in Chapter 4, others stood in for Persico until he was freed.

Joe Colombo Jr. was ultimately acquitted of the coin-smelting charges, and he and brothers Anthony and Vincent were relegated to minor-league status. In 1985, they were indicted along with 19 others in a massive racketeering case. On June 10, 1986, the brothers pleaded guilty. Anthony was sentenced to 14 years and was ordered to turn over $500,000 to the government. His brothers each received five years. In 2004, more than 10 years after he was released from prison, Anthony was indicted again on racketeering charges, along with the youngest Colombo son, Christopher (see Chapter 30).

> **Mafia Speak**
>
> In 1975, turncoat associate Joe Cantalupo visited Colombo at his home to find out the status of Colombo's physical and mental state for the FBI. "He was a vegetable ... just a vegetable," Cantalupo later wrote.

Joey Gallo didn't live too long after the Colombo shooting. When he continued to ruffle feathers, family leaders obtained Commission approval to take Gallo out. On April 7, 1972, Gallo was blown away as he dined in Little Italy at Umberto's Clam House with relatives and friends (see Chapter 33).

Colombo lived another six years, dying in 1978. His career as a mob boss had been spectacular but short.

Slammer Time
In 1985, the associate suspected of killing Jerome Johnson, Philip "Chubby" Rossillo, was arrested with Colombo's three sons on racketeering charges. The indictment cost him several years in prison and almost caused him to miss a very important wedding—his own. When a judge refused to let him and his bride-to-be get married in a federal lockup, she kicked up a fuss and got another judge to sign an order permitting it. So on November 14, 1985, Chubby and Sherry Rossillo tied the knot in a simple ceremony at the Metropolitan Correctional Center in Manhattan.

As for the league, it collapsed nearly as fast as it rose. Like the Unione Siciliana early in the twentieth century, the Italian-American Civil Rights League, with stated goals to aid Italian-Americans, betrayed the trust that thousands of honest citizens had placed in its leaders.

The Least You Need to Know

♦ Joe Colombo was a Mafia boss who pretended to be a civil rights leader.

♦ Colombo inspired many thousands of honest Italian-Americans to join his organization.

♦ For a short time, Colombo had political power.

♦ After Colombo was shot in 1971, his civil rights organization died.

Part 4

La Cosa Nostra Starts Its Fall

Weakening the Mafia didn't happen overnight. Sporadic efforts were made to attack certain individuals within La Cosa Nostra and its affiliates, but these successes proved to be only temporary. A more coordinated attack was needed.

In this section, I explain how the government finally got its act together. Its agencies identified their targets and drafted a number of means, legal and illegal, that served to cripple La Cosa Nostra. Along the way, there were good and bad guys on the supposedly good guys' side. It was an interesting journey.

Chapter 18

Big Brother Gets Serious

In This Chapter

◆ Listening in on the mob

◆ Approved electronic surveillance pays dividends

◆ The mob meets RICO

◆ How the Federal Witness Protection Program works

There are often times when we all wish we were a fly on the wall and could listen in on certain conversations. Part of this chapter is about that fly. In 1968, law enforcement agencies were given the authority to listen in on mobsters as they did business. I'll look at how that came about and the results of that legislation.

Besides electronic surveillance, the Federal Witness Protection Program was important in combating organized crime. I'll take a look at that program along with the famous Racketeer Influenced and Corrupt Organizations (RICO) Act that all Mafia members fear.

Many other factors were instrumental in the war against the mob, including increased resources from President Ronald Reagan's administration, a Justice Department reorganization, and a focus on long-term investigations by the FBI.

Electronic Muddle

During Prohibition, authorities often used wiretaps to gather evidence on major bootleggers. Roy Olmstead was convicted of running a large illegal-liquor operation and appealed the use of evidence obtained by electronic surveillance without a warrant. In 1928, the U.S. Supreme Court ruled against him. The justices felt that Olmstead's Fourth Amendment rights were not violated because there had been no trespassing in his home. The agents had simply tapped the phone line outside his residence.

Fuhgeddaboudit
One of the best stories about electronic surveillance involves a Florida businessman who was caught in an illegal operation and agreed to wear a tape recorder while he dealt with Mafia associates trying to move in on the Miami docks. At one point, Joey Teitlebaum's recorder slipped and fell on the floor. Before the stunned hood could react, Teitlebaum yelled in horror that the pacemaker for his heart had dropped, picked it up, and raced out of the building.

In 1934, however, Congress passed the Federal Communications Act that prohibited the interception and divulgence of material gathered from wiretaps. As a result, in 1937, the high court made several rulings that banned the use of evidence from electronic surveillance. In 1939, Attorney General Robert Jackson cited the Supreme Court rulings and prohibited the FBI from using wiretaps.

During World War II, however, FBI Director J. Edgar Hoover pressured and persuaded President Franklin Delano Roosevelt to permit electronic surveillance against foreign agents. FDR issued a directive permitting this activity with the understanding that the information would not leave the government. The FBI was also required to keep a record of its activities in this area.

Big Shot

Joseph "Joey Chang" Ciancaglini Jr. was underboss of the Philadelphia family led by John Stanfa in the 1990s. On March 2, 1993, he and a waitress had just opened his luncheonette when three men raced in and opened fire. The shouts and screams were picked up on an FBI microphone, and the silhouettes of the hit men entering and leaving were caught by an FBI surveillance camera mounted outside the building. Unfortunately, the quality of the picture was poor, and the shooters couldn't be identified.

After FDR died in 1945, Hoover convinced President Harry S. Truman to expand the national security limits of wiretapping to include domestic security and/or situations in which human life was in jeopardy. This was a significant change, one that later led to the illegal electronic surveillance of La Cosa Nostra.

During this period, Hoover also implemented ways to hide the fact that the FBI was conducting electronic surveillance. Intercepted material was kept in separate files and would often be designated as coming from a confidential source rather than electronic means.

With this background, it is not surprising that Hoover turned to bugs and wiretaps when he was embarrassed by the lack of information the FBI had about the attendees of the Apalachin meeting. Along with other intelligence methods, Hoover instructed his agents to place bugs in Mafia haunts, knowing the material could never be used in court.

In the summer of 1959, the FBI bugged the headquarters of the Chicago Outfit and was soon sending valuable La Cosa Nostra intelligence to its Washington headquarters. Soon after, other bugs were monitoring the San Francisco boss, a major Pittsburgh capo, the Philadelphia boss, the New England boss, Las Vegas casinos, and other suspected organized crime leaders.

> **Mafia Speak**
>
> In the fall of 1959, FBI agents overheard Chicago Outfit boss Sam Giancana tell consigliere Tony Accardo about a Commission meeting he had just attended in New York. He also mentioned that Joe Bonanno had "planted a flag" in Arizona where he had bought a home. Accardo, who also served as boss and underboss during his years at the top of the Outfit, wasn't happy with Bonanno's unilateral expansion of his territory.

In 1965, President Johnson pulled the plug on this activity unless Hoover obtained written approval from the attorney general. LBJ also placed a 180-day limit on the eavesdropping. Hoover supposedly ordered all the bugs removed. Two years later, a Presidential Task Force on Organized Crime recommended the legalization of electronic surveillance as part of major federal legislation designed to combat the Mafia.

The Omnibus Crime Control and Safe Streets Act (1968)

The Omnibus Crime Control and Safe Streets Act gave the law enforcement community new and powerful tools to use in the fight against organized crime. Title III of the act permitted electronic surveillance by law enforcement agencies under strict conditions. Title III would turn out to be a critical component of the government's attack on La Cosa Nostra in the 1980s.

In filing an application under Title III, a law enforcement officer must demonstrate that all other intelligence-gathering alternatives have been exhausted and that electronic means is a last resort. It can only be used in regard to certain crimes that there is probable cause to believe the subject is committing or has committed. Some of these crimes are bribery, kidnapping, robbery, murder, extortion, fraud, drug dealing, and conspiracy to commit any of those crimes. There must be probable cause that information concerning one or more of these offenses will be obtained by the bug or wiretap. Finally, the location or telephone being placed under electronic surveillance must have been used in criminal activity and be likely to be used again in criminal activity.

Fuhgeddaboudit

On January 8, 1985, Luchese boss Anthony "Tony Ducks" Corallo was overheard making one of the biggest self-delusional statements by a mobster. By then, it was common knowledge that Corallo had been intercepted on a bug that had been placed in a Jaguar that ferried him around town. Anthony "Fat Tony" Salerno, front boss of the Genovese family, asked if Corallo was in trouble with the car. "I shouldn't be ...," said Corallo, who ended up getting 100 years based partly on evidence from the car bug!

To show probable cause, the law enforcement agent uses information from confidential sources, other electronic surveillance, and any other intelligence that tends to show that criminal activity has, is, or will take place. In the FBI, a superior has to approve the application before Justice Department lawyers file it with a judge. After it is ordered by the judge, the agency has 30 days to wiretap or bug the target. After 30 days, authorities must obtain an extension or shut down the electronic surveillance.

To prevent abuses like those by the FBI in the 1960s and 1970s, an outline of each application for electronic surveillance must be made to Congress each year.

Mafia Speak

According to George Anastasia in *Mob Father* (Pinnacle Books, 1993), Philadelphia mobster Thomas "Tommy Del" DelGiorno knew he was in deep trouble when cops played a recording of a conversation between two of DelGiorno's friends. Asked if DelGiorno was in danger of being whacked, Salvatore "Wayne" Grande replied, "Ain't nothing going to happen to him ... yet." DelGiorno cooperated with authorities soon after hearing this tape.

Legal Electronic Surveillance in Action

Legal electronic surveillance played a large role in many major Mafia prosecutions. I will examine one and will also demonstrate that tape-recording words is one thing, being able to hear and understand them is another.

Jerry Angiulo

Early in 1981, the FBI got approval from a federal judge to bug the headquarters of Gennaro "Jerry" Angiulo, underboss of the New England family. Ten days later, after three failed attempts, an FBI special operations team broke into the club in the North End, an Italian enclave in Boston, and planted the bugs. They picked up conversations and sent them to a nearby relay station. From there, they were transmitted to another location, where FBI agents monitored and tape-recorded them for possible use at trial.

Big Shot _____

In 1981, the FBI bugged the headquarters of New England capo Lawrence Zannino, and quickly overheard him say who killed one of the first famous mob turncoats, Joseph "The Animal" Barboza. It was Joseph "JR" Russo, then a soldier and later an underboss, who traveled to San Francisco and killed the man who had helped send both the boss and underboss of the New England family to prison.

After listening to months of conversations about mob doings—including gambling, loan sharking, and murder—the FBI conducted a follow-up probe and obtained a racketeering indictment of Angiulo; his brothers Frank, Donato, and Michael; and other crewmembers on September 19, 1983. The FBI also prevented two rubouts by warning targets whom were marked for death. After a long trial, the Angiulos were convicted. Jerry received 45 years and a demotion to soldier. Brothers Frank and Danny got 25 and 20 years, respectively. Michael, convicted of gambling, got three years. Thanks to Title III, the Angiulos were through.

What Did He Say?

One of the most important rules for law enforcement "black bag" break-in artists who plant bugs is this: Don't get caught! You might alert the target that the law is on to him or, worse, get shot. Another problem is background noise from refrigerators, radios, televisions, and air conditioners that overwhelm the pertinent conversations that the agents are after. The spoken words can often be enhanced, and the background sounds can be wiped out through technology, but these techniques usually result in defense charges that the tapes have been altered and are not reliable at all. These tactics were partly responsible for two mistrials in the drug-trafficking trials of Gambino soldiers Gene Gotti and John Carneglia in the late 1980s. Both men were convicted at their third trial in 1989 and were sentenced to 50 years.

Fuhgeddaboudit

After the FBI bugged the palatial Staten Island home of Gambino boss Paul Castellano on March 18, 1983, they encountered technical difficulties that were rectified by wizards from the FBI's technical side. The techies used sophisticated equipment to drown out a radio station and hone in on conversations from the kitchen, where Castellano and his top aides would meet to discuss family affairs, according to FBI agent Jules Bonavolonta in his book, *The Good Guys*.

Another problem is deciphering what the hell the Mafiosi are talking about. Wiseguys have known each other for decades and don't need to recap ongoing matters for the "late tuners in" the way a baseball announcer might.

Fat Tony Salerno gets an earful outside his bugged Palma Boys Social Club in 1984.

(Courtesy of GangLandNews.com)

The following is a conversation recorded on December 12, 1984, in the Palma Boys Social Club in Manhattan, a headquarters for apparent Genovese boss Anthony "Fat Tony" Salerno. He is telling Luchese boss Anthony "Tony Ducks" Corallo about an internal Genovese family problem that led to Salerno ordering one of his men to chase away another guy if he ever came around. I pick up Salerno's tale at this point.

> **Salerno:** ... Well, sure enough he goes down there, and this guy gives him a whack ... this kid goes to his mother, his brother goes to Ben. He sends that wiseguy ... to knock that fucking Carmine's head off.
>
> I come in on a Monday, he's telling me the story. I said, "Ben, hey, why the fuck, you, you put me on ... you gave me a fucking job over here, do you want me to take care of it or don't you? ...
>
> **Corallo:** But does he reason with him?
>
> **Salerno:** No.
>
> **Corallo:** Did you reason with him?
>
> **Salerno:** He, he just lets you know about it. He just lets you know about it. I don't know what to do. I swear I don't. I tried the first time I ever had an argument with him. So fucking disgusted with myself. I said, "Well, we gotta live with this guy." Yeah, I told him.
>
> **Corallo:** You can't do that, see, you gonna, you gonna let this run from here downtown, is that what you want to do? ... You wanna, you wanna say, "I throwed the fucking thing out." You want it, and you have to run downtown when you want something done?
>
> **Salerno:** No, I'll retire, I don't need that.
>
> **Corallo:** I know you'll retire. I know you'll retire.
>
> **Salerno:** Fuck that shit. I won't take orders from the guy.

Mafia Speak

Multimillionaire Mafia boss Paul Castellano was viewed by many contemporaries as a cheapskate who constantly whined about money, as this June 23, 1983, conversation between Luchese capo Salvatore Avellino and boss Anthony Corallo demonstrates. Avellino said he got word that Castellano wanted to meet with them. Corallo sarcastically wondered why, "Is everybody robbing him?"

It took two years for the feds to discover the very important significance of this conversation. On the surface, it sounds as if Salerno was angry with "Ben" for butting into a decision he had made. Salerno also threatened to retire and declared he would no longer be taking any orders "from the guy."

In September of 1986, Salerno protégé Vincent "Fish" Cafaro became an informer. In debriefings, written statements, and testimony before a Senate committee on April 29, 1988, Cafaro revealed what amounted to staggering information about the Genovese family that was unknown not only by law enforcement but by many mobsters as well.

Salerno was not really the Genovese boss but a "front" boss for real boss Philip "Benny Squint" Lombardo, who retired in 1981 and was succeeded for a brief period of time by Salerno. Later that year, however, Salerno had a minor stroke, and Vincent "Chin" Gigante took over as boss with Salerno continuing as "front boss" until 1984. Unfortunately for Salerno, he was arrested, tried, and convicted of being the Genovese boss in the famous 1986 Commission trial and was sentenced to 100 years.

Fat Tony Salerno gets hit with racketeering charges in the Mafia Commission case in February 1985.

(Courtesy of New York Daily News*)*

With Cafaro's insight, the conversation between Salerno and Corallo makes much more sense. Salerno is angry with Philip "Benny Squint" Lombardo ("Ben") and Gigante (the "downtown" reference) for second-guessing him after giving him "a job to do," a reference to Salerno acting as the "front boss." Finally, the tape clearly demonstrates that Salerno had never been too impressed by Lombardo, was tired of his own no-win role, and would "retire" if things don't change.

The tape recording and Cafaro's account bolsters the notion—shared by the FBI and this author—that the Genovese family was led for decades by a gangster whose identity became known only after he died.

Fuhgeddaboudit

In his testimony before the Senate, Genovese soldier Vincent "Fish" Cafaro shone a light on an amazing Genovese family secret that wasn't known or revealed by the family's only other cooperating witness, Joe Valachi. "In the 1960s, when Vito Genovese went to jail, he had turned over control of our brugad [family] to … Phillip Lombardo, also known as Ben or Benny Squint. Lombardo wanted to stay in the background … Over the years, Tommy Ryan (Thomas Eboli), then Eli Zaccardi, then Funzi Tieri, and finally Fat Tony fronted as bosses of the family …"

The Organized Crime Control Act (1970)

Two key items were crucial in the war on organized crime. One is the famous RICO law, an acronym for Racketeer Influenced and Corrupt Organizations Act. A program to protect government witnesses was the second. Both had teething problems that took years to sort out, but in general, they have proven their worth in cases involving La Cosa Nostra.

The RICO Law

RICO has been so effective against La Cosa Nostra that authorities in Canada and Italy have written similar laws to combat organized crime. Essentially, the RICO laws enabled federal prosecutors to attack entire Mafia families through the introduction of two new ideas, "criminal enterprise" and "pattern of racketeering." A "criminal enterprise" was any group of people whose purpose was to engage in a "pattern of racketeering"—defined as any two violations of state or federal laws from a list of 32 crimes, including murder, extortion, bribery, mail fraud, and gambling. One of the crimes had to have been committed within the previous 5 years, but the second could have been committed within the prior 10 years, essentially giving authorities 15 years to prosecute crimes under the RICO statutes. For example, a gangster who extorted a trucking company and shared the money with superiors in 1996 and was also part of an illegal gambling operation in 1987 that was headed by the same superiors could be found guilty of racketeering.

Mafia Speak

In his book *The Good Guys* (Simon & Schuster, 1986), FBI agent Jules Bonavolonta recalls an incident involving Colombo soldier Frank "The Beast" Falanga, who was arrested, brought to court, and heard, "… the grand jury, in its first count against you, has charged you with RICO." Falanga jumped up and yelled, "RICO? I don't even know any fucking RICO!"

Through the RICO statutes, authorities were able to drag leaders of Mafia families into prosecutions from which they had been previously exempt. This could be done through accomplice or expert testimony and electronic surveillance that showed the crimes were a "pattern of racketeering" activities undertaken for the benefit of the "criminal enterprise." The result is that a Mafia boss can be convicted of racketeering (running the family), even though he wasn't involved in the individual criminal acts. RICO helped strip away the insulation of the mob leaders.

Slammer Time

Some wiseguys have really been whacked by the RICO statutes. Pittsburgh mob associate John Carrabba Jr. served three years for a role in purloining FBI documents for members of La Cosa Nostra. Four years later, Carrabba was tried essentially for the same offense but as part of a RICO case: In 1991, Carrabba got five more years for contributing to the running of the Pittsburgh La Cosa Nostra family by providing the same documents.

The enhanced prison terms permitted by the RICO statutes tempted many members, even of high rank, to cooperate in return for substantially shorter prison terms. Turncoat underbosses Salvatore "Sammy Bull" Gravano of New York and Philip Leonetti of Philadelphia served about 10 years in prison for lives of crime that included 30 murders. (I discuss their cooperation in Chapter 21.) An added incentive for hoods was knowing there was a Witness Protection Program under which they could be relocated to a different part of the country and receive new identities.

A RICO Example

In January of 1988, federal prosecutors filed a multicount racketeering indictment against Philadelphia boss Nicodemo "Little Nicky" Scarfo and 16 members and associates. Through the testimony of Thomas "Tommy Del" DelGiorno and Nicholas "The Crow" Caramandi, electronic surveillance, hundreds of surveillance photographs, and the testimony of law enforcement and others, federal prosecutors demonstrated that Scarfo and the others participated in 14 murder conspiracies and countless other crimes. The government did not prove that each of the 17 defendants participated in each of the 14 killings. Each defendant was convicted of racketeering for being part of a criminal enterprise that committed murders and engaged in loan sharking, extortion, gambling, and other crimes during a 15-year period. Scarfo and his 16 co-defendants were convicted on all charges. On May 11, 1989, Scarfo was sentenced to 55 years.

The Witness Protection Program

After Joe Valachi, it became obvious that the federal government needed a specially designed full-time program to protect people who had testified against violent criminals who would try to kill them, not only for revenge but as a way of deterring others from following suit. The Organized Crime Control Act of 1970 established such a program.

The Witness Security Program was intended to take in about 30 witnesses a year. It would protect and support the witness up to and including the trial. Then the person would be given a new name, a new Social Security number, a job background, and school records for children if the witness had any. The witness would be transported to a new location and be given about $1,000 a month for housing and other essentials. The intent was to support the person for a year or so while he or she got established in the new territory.

> **Slammer Time**
>
> Before cooperating witnesses are released into the Witness Protection Program, many live in specially constructed "Wit Sec" units maintained in the federal prison system by the Justice Department's Witness Security Program.

When witnesses are relocated, marshals monitor and serve as liaisons for them but do not live with them providing round-the-clock protection. The new location and name are supposed to do that, and they have in all cases in which witnesses have abided by the rules and not contacted anyone in the old neighborhood. The witness is given a number to call in case of an emergency.

The Witness Security Program is run by the U.S. Marshals Service, an arm of the Justice Department. Persons who join the program must sign a Memorandum of Understanding, which outlines the rules and expectations on both sides. This document has been used to expel people from the program. Many who have spent their lives skirting the law return to old habits, including dealing drugs and murder. The program makes it attractive for jailed hoods to lie about events in order to gain a ticket out of prison. It is not a perfect system and requires regular evaluation.

Despite its weaknesses, the Witness Security Program has proven invaluable in the fight against La Cosa Nostra. It has provided inducements and safe havens for superstar turncoats including former Luchese family acting boss Alfonse "Little Al" D'Arco and one-time Cleveland underboss Angelo Lonardo. Both testified in key mob cases, almost always proving to be reliable and effective witnesses. Many others of lesser stature have given important testimony and have disappeared, thanks to the program. The next chapter looks at some lesser-known but still important cooperating witnesses, some of whom used the Witness Security Program.

The Least You Need to Know

- ◆ Wiretaps and bugs are key tools against the Mafia.
- ◆ RICO laws make it easier to prosecute mob leaders.
- ◆ RICO convictions usually mean heavy prison terms.
- ◆ Lengthy RICO sentences tempt mobsters to defect.
- ◆ The Witness Protection Program helps people agree to testify against La Cosa Nostra members.

Chapter

19

The Feds' Full-Court Press Against the Mafia

In This Chapter

- ◆ Joey Doves goes to the cage
- ◆ Big Ange misses his family
- ◆ Junior is a bust
- ◆ Working on Commission

By the 1980s, the Justice Department, the FBI, local police agencies, the state police, state organized crime task forces, and prosecutors had all their ducks in a line when it came to the mob. Leaders of La Cosa Nostra families began to go down one after another. In this chapter, I'll tell the stories of a few fallen bosses to illustrate what was happening across the nation and how electronic surveillance, the Witness Protection Program, and the RICO Act played in their downfalls.

As leaders were arrested to await trial or went off to prison, replacement bosses (on a temporary or permanent basis) were called on to run the different families. For each example, I will explain what happened after all the dust settled.

Indictments Sweep the Windy City

Joseph "Joey Doves" Aiuppa was born in Chicago on December 1, 1907. His formal schooling ended after third grade. He was unimposing at a little over 5'6" and weighed around 200 pounds in his middle age. Aiuppa was classified 4F and was not required to do any military service.

Aiuppa took to the streets as a young man, gradually accumulating a lengthy arrest record that included murder. His only conviction, however, was for illegally transporting mourning doves from Kansas City to Chicago. His base of operation was the Chicago suburb of Cicero. He had influence over gambling, loan sharking, labor racketeering, and assorted other rackets in the entire area.

Aiuppa was a significant-enough wiseguy to be called before both the Kefauver Committee and the McClellan hearings. He refused to testify both times, citing his Fifth Amendment privilege.

Aiuppa developed a close relationship with Anthony "Big Tuna" Accardo and maintained it throughout their lives. With Accardo's support, Aiuppa took over as Chicago Outfit boss in 1971.

As described in Chapter 12, the Kansas City FBI stumbled onto a vast skimming operation involving Teamster loans and the Las Vegas empire of Allan Glick in the 1970s. This came about as agents investigated a local murder and overheard references to Las Vegas. They sought and received a federal judge's approval to install bugs in several locations in Kansas City that led them to the Las Vegas scam.

Information from them led to further Title III approvals to bug the home of Chicago cop Anthony Chiavola, a relative of Kansas City boss Nick Civella. Aiuppa, underboss Jackie Cerone, and capo Angelo LaPietra met Civella on October 22, 1978, at Chiavola's house to discuss the Las Vegas scam.

Mafia Speak

If you're in the Chicago mob and you don't have a nickname, make sure to stay away from a horse's rear end. Anthony "Big Tuna" Accardo got one of his nicknames after hooking a huge tuna on a fishing expedition in the Caribbean. Joey Doves Aiuppa got his moniker for getting caught illegally transporting 500 mourning doves across state lines into Chicago.

Fuhgeddaboudit

Joey Doves owned up to being a bookie; he drew the line at being labeled a pimp. On July 3, 1965, then-capo Aiuppa was tape-recorded trying to convince sheriff's patrolman Donald Shaw to take a bribe, insisting he wasn't a bad guy. "All I'm interested in is the gambling. It would be different if I sold broads."

In October of 1983, Aiuppa and others were indicted on fraud, embezzlement, and other charges for using his influence on the Teamsters Union to facilitate loans to Glick so that he could purchase the various Las Vegas hotels. Their Chicago discussion of the Las Vegas situation was used against them at the trial, which began in Kansas City on September 23, 1985.

Besides electronic surveillance, federal prosecutors used testimony by Ken Eto, a one-time trusted associate of the Chicago Outfit who survived three bullets to the head during a failed rubout and became a witness. His testimony gave the jury the family structure and methods of the Chicago Outfit, including Aiuppa's role in them.

Former Cleveland underboss Angelo Lonardo said Aiuppa was the boss of the Chicago Outfit and described a meeting in the spring of 1981 in which they discussed a replacement for dying Teamsters president Frank Fitzsimmons. He also detailed a discussion with Aiuppa in 1982 to determine who would take over for prison-bound Teamsters president Roy Williams. Aiuppa was convicted on January 21, 1986.

After Aiuppa was convicted, federal prosecutors called on Jimmy "The Weasel" Fratianno to testify against him at a sentencing hearing in an effort to convince the judge that he deserved heavy time. Fratianno hated Aiuppa, believing that Aiuppa had ordered the murder of Fratianno's friend Johnny Roselli. Fratianno took great pleasure in identifying Aiuppa as the murderous boss of the Chicago Outfit.

Aiuppa was sentenced to 28 years. He was released in January of 1996 and died on February 22, 1997.

The Outfit's underboss, Jackie Cerone, was also convicted in the same Kansas City case, so veteran consigliere Anthony Accardo tapped Joe Ferriola as the new boss. The transition was peaceful, and although the Outfit lost a large monthly income from Las Vegas, it had plenty of other rackets.

Mafia Speak

Eto described former associate Phil "Milwaukee Phil" Alderisio as very hotheaded and dangerous. He said Angelo LaPietra was vicious and a sadistic killer. Makes you wonder why he hung around with these guys for 30 years!

Slammer Time

As described in Chapter 10, Teamsters president Roy Williams was convicted of conspiring to bribe a U.S. senator and was sentenced to 55 years. Scheduled to begin his prison term on April 15, 1983, Williams was allowed to remain free while appealing his conviction if he resigned from his office. He did, and later he became a government witness.

Fratianno, Lonardo, and Eto received new identities and were relocated in the Witness Protection Program, a key component of the 1970 Organized Crime Control Act.

Shakeup in the Cleveland Family

Angelo Lonardo has a storied history in the Cleveland family, avenging the 1927 death of his father, an early boss of the family who was murdered. As detailed in Chapter 7, Lonardo killed two men responsible for his father's death and escaped legal punishment for both killings.

For decades, Lonardo worked gambling and labor rackets as an associate of the family. Finally, in the late 1940s, he became a full-fledged member, earning a special place in the family when he married the sister of boss John Scalish.

> **Big Shot** _____
>
> Cleveland boss James Licavoli felt that John Nardi and Danny Greene had arranged the killing of underboss Leo "Lips" Moceri in 1976. He asked Genovese front boss Anthony Salerno to have Gambino boss Paul Castellano arrange the killing of Nardi and Greene the next time they visited Castellano in New York City. That scenario never happened, but both targets were killed by separate bombs in Cleveland.

Scalish died on May 26, 1976, and was succeeded by capo James "Jack White" Licavoli, who named his cousin, Leo Moceri, as underboss. Lonardo acted as a capo and trusted advisor. He told Licavoli about proper Mafia protocol and advised him to go to New York and introduce himself to Anthony Salerno, the Cleveland family's representative on the Commission. When Moceri was murdered a few months later, Lonardo succeeded him and traveled with Licavoli to be formally introduced to Salerno as the new Cleveland underboss.

In 1982, Licavoli went down on a federal racketeering and murder conviction stemming from a gang war that the family concluded by blowing up their two main enemies in separate incidents. Lonardo escaped arrest and was acting boss for about a year.

In April of 1983, Lonardo was convicted on racketeering and drug charges and was sentenced to life plus 103 years. The stunned Lonardo soon made overtures about defecting. He agreed to cooperate six months later. As he later told a Senate committee, "I know I will never get out of there alive, and I miss my family very, very much."

The former underboss took an odyssey across the nation, testifying at major Mafia trials. Lonardo helped bury the Chicago, Kansas City, and Milwaukee bosses by testifying about the famous Las Vegas skim of the Argent Hotels. He was a witness at the Commission trial in late 1986, giving important historical background on La Cosa Nostra and identifying Salerno and other defendants as Mafia leaders.

Lonardo is proof that lengthy RICO sentences and the safety of the Witness Protection Program can turn a veteran mobster into an important government asset.

Betrayal in the New England Family

Raymond Patriarca Jr. was out of his element as a Mafia boss. His father led the New England family with an iron hand from 1954 until his death in 1984. Because there was a vacuum in the family's leadership at the time—underboss Jerry Angiulo was in jail awaiting trial and leading capo Larry Zannino had legal and health problems— Raymond Jr. moved into the picture.

Patriarca Sr. had groomed his son to take over the top spot. Patriarca Jr. was a messenger to other families and had a personal relationship with powerful New York mobsters John Gotti and Anthony Salerno. With this important outside support and that of capo Zannino, Ray Patriarca Jr. was elected boss in 1984.

His reign was unremarkable, but the family remained relatively stable until Friday, June 16, 1989. On that day, hit teams under a renegade Boston faction led by capos Joseph "JR" Russo, Robert Carrozza, and Vincent Ferrara set out to kill two key Patriarca loyalists, underboss William Grasso and rising soldier Frank Salemme. One crew whacked Grasso in Connecticut. A second ski-masked team wearing camouflage fatigues shot and wounded Salemme in front of a pancake house outside Boston.

Prodded by Gotti, then at the height of his power, the factions arranged an uneasy truce, with renegade leader Joseph "JR" Russo made consigliere and Nicky Bianco becoming underboss. To further solidify the peace, an induction of some new members was set for October 29, 1989.

> **Mafia Speak**
>
> In a bit of gallows humor, New England underboss Jerry Angiulo and capo Larry Zannino were overheard on a wiretap joking about being put to death in a double electric chair. Zannino said he didn't want to be electrocuted without Angiulo being beside him. "They got two chairs, Jerry. We can hold hands together. I won't go any other way."

Fuhgeddaboudit

On October 29, 1989, the New England La Cosa Nostra held an induction ceremony in a private house in Medford, Massachusetts. Vincent Federico, one of the men who was "made" that day, was serving a life sentence for murder. He arranged a pass to be present for his induction!

Unfortunately for the New England family, an informer revealed the whereabouts of the ceremony, and the FBI bugged the induction ritual and captured proof that there was a Mafia family and that Patriarca Jr. was its boss.

In March of 1990, Patriarca Jr. was hit with a racketeering indictment. On December 3, 1991, Patriarca threw in the towel and pleaded guilty to racketeering and other charges. Ultimately, he received 10 years and was fined $175,000. He was released on December 11, 1998, and has maintained a low profile ever since.

When his legal problems began in 1990, Patriarca stepped down and was replaced by Nicky Bianco, but Bianco was also indicted on racketeering charges. Frank Salemme stepped in, only to be hit with RICO charges as well. The family is presently in tatters.

Patriarca Jr. wasn't a well-schooled Mafia boss, but his downfall was a testament to the key law enforcement elements examined in Chapter 18—legal electronic surveillance, the RICO statutes, and the use of informers.

Historic Convictions in New York City

The Commission case was the dream trial of every prosecutor who ever lost a case involving La Cosa Nostra. It was the time when he or she could cut through all the garbage about there not being a Mafia and nail the bosses and some key underlings to the wall.

Big Shot

Colombo soldier Ralph Scopo was tape-recorded on April 15, 1984, discussing Mafia life and how treacherous it was. Talking about Gambino soldier Roy DeMeo, who was shot to death and found in the trunk of his car, Scopo explained, "Being that he got picked up, they figure, 'Maybe this guy will rat.' That's bullshit. But not to take the chance … they went and killed him."

Investigators had gathered piles of evidence from cooperating witnesses and electronic surveillance about each of the five New York families. In 1984, the U.S. Attorney's office in Manhattan decided to use the evidence to prosecute the Mafia Commission as a criminal enterprise that oversaw the operations of La Cosa Nostra families in America. The feds said that the Commission was a "criminal enterprise" and that New York leaders engaged in a "pattern of racketeering" and committed at least two racketeering acts to keep the Commission operating as a viable entity.

On February 25, 1985, an indictment was filed charging the boss of each family and other top gangsters with violating the RICO statutes. Paul Castellano of the Gambino family, Carmine Persico of the Colombo family, Anthony Corallo of the Luchese family, Phillip Rastelli of the Bonanno family, and Anthony Salerno, the supposed boss of the Genovese family, were all arrested.

Ralph Scopo, a Colombo soldier and the family construction specialist who headed the District Council of Concrete and Cement Workers of the Laborers Union, was a key defendant.

Bonanno soldier Anthony "Bruno" Indelicato was added to the case on November 12, 1985, charged with aiding the enterprise (the Commission) by carrying out its 1979 order to kill Carmine Galante, a Bonanno capo who had tried to bully his way to the top while Rastelli, the family's boss, was either imprisoned or under indictment.

By the time the trial began on September 8, 1986, the lineup had changed dramatically. On December 16, 1985, Castellano was murdered by capo John Gotti and his allies. Rastelli had a prior racketeering case in Brooklyn and was severed from the case.

Some defendants were distracted during the trial by other important events weighing heavily on their lives. On November 18, 1986, Colombo boss Carmine Persico and underboss Gennaro "Jerry Lang" Langella were given sentences of 39 and 65 years, respectively, for RICO convictions involving the Colombo family. Anthony Salerno was facing two racketeering indictments, one for running the Genovese family enterprise and the other for his involvement in Teamsters Union activities.

> ### Slammer Time
>
> On May 4, 1988, Anthony "Fat Tony" Salerno was convicted of bid rigging in connection with Manhattan construction projects. Salerno was acquitted of fraud in the elections of Teamster presidents Roy Williams and Jackie Presser earlier in the 1980s, despite the testimony of turncoat Cleveland underboss Angelo Lonardo.

The defendants were up against a daunting amount of evidence. New York City detectives had caught a gleeful Indelicato showing up at the Ravenite Social Club just minutes after Galante was killed on July 12, 1979. The only reason for a Bonanno soldier to check in at the Gambino family's Manhattan headquarters would be to report a successful Commission-ordered job. Fred DeChristopher, a Persico relative by marriage, testified that while he was hiding Persico in his attic, the Colombo boss told him that he voted against Galante's murder but was outvoted. Indelicato's prints were found on a rear door of the car from which a hooded man with a shotgun was seen exiting and going into the restaurant where Galante was gunned down. This and other evidence proved that the Commission had sanctioned the Galante hit and that Indelicato was working on their behalf when he participated in the shooting.

Electronic evidence played a big role in sealing the fate of Ralph Scopo and the other defendants. A key government claim was that the Commission was involved in an illegal concrete club that effectively fixed the cost of major building projects in Manhattan. Scopo was taped picking up cash kickbacks from contractors and others in the industry. He detailed how bids were rigged and explained why only certain companies were allowed to be involved. He told how the four Mafia families split up the jobs and the payoffs they received from mob-linked construction companies. Some contractors testified, making the concrete club portion of the racketeering indictment a slam-dunk.

An informer played a key role in the case. On May 15, 1984, a man phoned FBI agent Joseph O'Brien and told him where a Commission meeting was going to take place that day. O'Brien and his partner, Andris Kurins, took pictures of the mob bosses leaving the private house that cleanly tied the bosses together.

Murdered wannabe Mafia boss Carmine Galante still clenches an after-dinner cigar in his teeth on the backyard patio of a Brooklyn restaurant on July 12, 1979.

(Courtesy of New York Daily News)

Hero FBI agent Joe Pistone, who penetrated the Bonanno family by playing the role of a jewel thief, gave the jurors an important overview of the structure and rules that mobsters live by as well as the function of the Commission from the witness stand. He also testified about information he gleaned about Galante's killing while working undercover against the Bonannos, as well as the Commission's involvement in the leadership affairs of the Bonanno family. Pistone was a key witness because he didn't have the negative baggage carried by mob turncoats.

The government also used Angelo Lonardo as a witness. As discussed previously in this chapter, Lonardo grew up in the Mafia. He knew Anthony Salerno and gave much of the early history of La Cosa Nostra. Lonardo also confirmed the structure, rules, and methods of the Mafia to help show that it was an illegal enterprise.

The government overwhelmed the defendants, who could do little to counter their attacks. On November 19, 1986, all were found guilty of nearly all the charges. On January 13, 1987, Judge Richard Owen unloaded on them. He gave each defendant 100 years, except Indelicato, who got 20 and was released on parole in 1998. In 2001, he was jailed for violating parole by associating with wiseguys. Salerno (July 1992), Luchese underboss Salvatore "Tom Mix" Santoro (January 2000), Scopo (March 1993), and Corallo (August 2000) all died in prison. Persico, Langella, and Luchese consigliere Christopher "Christy Tick" Furnari all remained incarcerated in 2004.

Despite this severe blow, each of the families continued to function under new leadership.

> **Mafia Speak**
>
> In the 1970s, Joseph Cantalupo became an FBI informer when he got into money problems with the Colombo family. Among his disclosures was the assertion that he had hosted a Commission meeting at his own apartment at 1460 83rd Street in Brooklyn. Cantalupo stayed outside during the two hours Joe Colombo and other bosses were inside talking.

> **Mafia Speak**
>
> Joseph Bonanno publicly acknowledged the existence of the Commission in his autobiography. Mafia boss Paul Castellano knew the revelations were a bad thing even before federal prosecutors got the idea to prosecute the Commission. "They're gonna make us be one tremendous conspiracy," he said at a kitchen meeting that was picked up on an FBI bug in 1983, according to *Mob Star* (Franklin-Watts, 1988; Alpha Books, 2002) by Gene Mustain and Jerry Capeci. Sure enough, the feds subpoenaed Bonanno to testify before a grand jury and used his testimony to obtain the Commission indictment. Fearing he would get killed if he testified at trial, Bonanno refused and was jailed throughout the trial for contempt of court.

The Gambino leaders were not present due to death—underboss Aniello Dellacroce died of natural causes and Castellano by gunshot. Castellano's assassination catapulted John Gotti to the top of the Gambino family for a wild ride of five years before he was sent away for life on another RICO case that is detailed in Chapter 23.

In the Genovese family, front boss Salerno was smoothly replaced by Vincent "Chin" Gigante, who avoided prison by feigning mental illness until July 24, 1997, when he was convicted of racketeering. He will be released in 2010.

The conviction of Luchese boss Tony "Ducks" Corallo and his underboss and consigliere brought chaos to that family. Vittorio "Vic" Amuso and Anthony "Gaspipe" Casso began a family killing frenzy that left dozens of mobsters and associates dead. Amuso was convicted of racketeering and murder and was sentenced to life on June 15, 1992. Casso bounced in and out of the Witness Security Program and then was sentenced to life on July 8, 1998.

Carmine Persico's permanent incarceration led to a civil war within his family. His son Alphonse eventually took over as acting boss. On the eve of his racketeering trial in late 2001, he pleaded guilty and was sentenced to 13 years.

The Bonanno family has had the most stable leadership. Severed from the Commission case, boss Philip Rastelli was found guilty in the Bonanno family trial and died in prison on June 26, 1991. Current boss Joseph Massino was convicted with Rastelli, was released from prison in 1992, and is the only New York Mafia boss who has not been convicted and sentenced to a lengthy prison term in the last decade, although he is facing two successive racketeering and murder trials as this revised edition of *The Complete Idiot's Guide to the Mafia* goes to press (see Chapter 28).

Other Convictions That Made the News

Many other major La Cosa Nostra figures were convicted from 1980 through the present. The following table lists bosses and/or acting bosses and the years they were found guilty. Although not an exhaustive list, it should give you an idea of the decimation of the Mafia's top ranks in the last two decades.

Name	Family	Conviction
Gennaro Langella	Colombo	1986
Victor Orena	Colombo	1993
Andrew Russo	Colombo	1999
Alphonse Persico	Colombo	2001
John Riggi	New Jersey	1991

Name	Family	Conviction
John Riggi	New Jersey	2003
Eugene Smaldone	Denver	1983
Jack Tocco	Detroit	1998
John Gotti	Gambino	1992
John A. "Junior" Gotti	Gambino	1999
Peter Gotti	Gambino	2003
Vincent Gigante	Genovese	1997
Vincent Gigante	Genovese	2003
Carl Civella	Kansas City	1984
Anthony Civella	Kansas City	1992
Dominic Brooklier	Los Angeles	1982
Peter Milano	Los Angeles	1988
Frank Balistrieri	Milwaukee	1983
Nicholas Bianco	New England	1991
Frank Salemme	New England	1999
Carlos Marcello	New Orleans	1981
Nicodemo Scarfo	Philadelphia	1989
John Stanfa	Philadelphia	1995
Ralph Natale	Philadelphia	1999
Russell Bufalino	Pittston	1981
Sam Russotti	Rochester	1984
Angelo Amico	Rochester	1989
Loren Piccaretto	Rochester	1989
Matthew Trupiano Jr.	St. Louis	1986

The Least You Need to Know

- Many Mafia leaders went to prison.
- The convictions showed that La Cosa Nostra could be damaged.
- Some families were virtually destroyed by major convictions.
- Racketeering prosecutions were used as a blueprint for future legal attacks on La Cosa Nostra.

Chapter 20

Feds Pressure Union Reforms

In This Chapter

- ◆ Auditing the Teamster funds
- ◆ Cleaning up the Teamsters
- ◆ Pushing for labor-intensive reform

On Monday, April 22, 1985, acting chairman Samuel Skinner of the President's Commission on Organized Crime announced that four major labor unions were dominated by La Cosa Nostra. He named the International Brotherhood of Teamsters (IBT), the Laborers International Union of North America (LIUNA), the Hotel Employees and Restaurant Employees International Union (HEREIU), and the International Longshoremen's Union (ILA).

In this chapter, I will examine how the government tried to eliminate mob influence over two of the unions, the IBT and the LIUNA. I will also discuss efforts to wrest control of Teamsters Local 560 from La Cosa Nostra as an example of similar efforts against other locals in the four major unions.

Dealing with the Teamster Presidency

Past experience showed that convicting and incarcerating a corrupt Teamsters president did little other than deprive the man of his personal freedom. Three of the four presidents from 1957 to 1983 went to prison. Presidents Dave Beck, James Riddle, Jimmy Hoffa, and Roy Williams all served time, but the corrupt system continued with dues-paying union workers constantly being cheated out of wages and benefits by union leaders who were in bed with the mob.

One of the first serious moves the federal government made to change the union involved the Teamsters Central States Pension Fund—a "bank" for mob-connected builders looking for financing. After great government pressure, the union agreed to turn over management of the fund to two reputable companies. Unethical practices still continued, especially with the Central States Health and Welfare Fund, but at least there was a workable system in place to try and root out the abuses.

> **Big Shot**
>
> Allen Dorfman was a key mob associate with the Central States Pension Fund. For a time after his 1982 conviction for conspiring to bribe a U.S. senator, his mob bosses worried that he might become an informer. On January 20, 1983, they stopped worrying. As Dorfman walked to his car in a parking lot, two men ran up behind him, and one poured six or seven bullets from a silenced .22-caliber semiautomatic pistol into his head.

In 1983, after years of rancorous negotiations, Teamsters officials signed an agreement with the government that provided for the Central States Pension Funds to be managed by a reputable fiduciary that would be independent of the union. The firm would hire a qualified internal auditing staff, and an independent monitor would oversee operations. In addition, the fund took back the processing of Health and Welfare Fund claims that had been controlled by Amalgamated Insurance, a firm owned by a mob associate Allen Dorfman.

Nearly two decades later, the Central States Pension Fund has assets of more than $20 billion and the Health and Welfare Fund has more than $700 million. There no longer is any serious talk of gangsters looting the fund.

In 1988, spurred by this success, the government filed a massive civil Racketeer Influenced and Corrupt Organization (RICO) suit seeking to oust the Teamsters' 18-member executive board for abdicating its responsibility to its members by selling out to the Mafia. Citing 20 murders and dozens of shootings, bombings, thefts, extortion efforts, and bribes, the government asked a federal judge to appoint a trustee to oversee new elections. The suit listed 26 high-ranked mobsters as defendants, including the leaders of New York's five families and the bosses of Chicago, Milwaukee, and Kansas City.

Ironically, the suit came a few months after the union rejoined the American Federation of Labor and Congress of Industrial Organizations—30 years after it was expelled for rampant corruption. The day the suit was filed, the executive board was in Montreal holding its quarterly meeting at the posh Ritz Carlton Hotel.

The following March, hours before the civil racketeering trial was set to begin, the Teamsters and the government reached a settlement. It called for direct rank-and-file elections of top officers and sweeping changes in the way union corruption was policed. The Justice Department dropped demands for an all-powerful, court-appointed watchdog for years, but won agreement for court-appointed officers to oversee elections and other union operations.

Teamster elections used to be easy. The mob controlled key locals and joint councils, and these entities sent delegates to the national convention to elect the president and his slate of officers. With La Cosa Nostra controlling a large block of delegates, the others would get the picture and fall in line. The facts of life, according to the Teamsters, were known to all: An incumbent president would make life miserable for a local that did not support him. Worse, he could have opponents killed.

> **Slammer Time**
>
> Local 851 of the Teamsters was based at John F. Kennedy Airport and was notorious for being controlled by the Luchese family. In 1992, secretary-treasurer Anthony Razza resisted the imposition of a trusteeship, claiming his local was free of organized crime. Two years later, Razza was sentenced to 21 months in prison after pleading guilty to tax fraud and accepting bribes.

> **Fuhgeddaboudit**
>
> In an article in *Reader's Digest*, writer Leslie Velie examined the Teamster mess circa 1975. He quoted one Teamster vice president as saying, "Without support from the boys, Fitz [Frank Fitzsimmons, president, 1971–1981] couldn't remain president for one minute." If there was any doubt about this reality, it was made abundantly clear when Jimmy Hoffa was kidnapped and murdered in July of 1975.

Under the new agreement, every card-carrying Teamster was going to be able to vote for his or her presidential pick. The agreement outlawed Teamster members from engaging in racketeering or from associating with mobsters. It set up an independent review board to root out mob-connected union officials.

For a time, the reforms seemed to be working. In 1991, veteran Teamster Ron Carey was elected president by the rank and file. His reelection in 1996, however, was marred by serious irregularities in his campaign funding, and the election results were thrown out. Carey was tossed from the union and a rerun was held in 1999. In this contest, the son of Jimmy Hoffa, also named Jimmy, won handily.

As controversial and messy as the Carey eviction was, it was a clear indication that the government was serious about union reform. Carey had been the great reformer, but he was removed even though it meant the likely return of a Hoffa—in an election by the members. This was progress. Hoffa has made seemingly serious efforts to end corruption. He has hired a number of former FBI agents as investigators to prevent the return of mob influence. The jury is still out on his efforts and will be for years to come.

Setting an Example with Teamster Local 560

The agreement, called a consent decree, played a continuous role in attempts to free various Teamster locals from the grip of the mob. I will briefly examine one of these locals to show what consistent government action accomplished.

For years, the most notorious Teamster local was 560, based in New Jersey and run by Genovese family mobster Anthony "Tony Pro" Provenzano. Numerous convictions and incarcerations of Provenzano and two brothers changed little; they played musical chairs with the various administrative positions, and Tony Pro continued to control its affairs from prison.

Ultimately, the government filed a civil racketeering suit against Local 560 in March of 1982. At trial, New Jersey Federal Judge Harold Ackerman ruled that the local was illegally controlled by the Provenzano group through fear and intimidation that included the murders of dissidents Anthony Castellito and Walter Glockner. After an appeal by the Teamsters failed, Local 560's leaders were suspended and a trustee was appointed.

Mafia Speak

On November 28, 1984, an FBI bug picked up word that the Genovese family still controlled Local 560 when front boss Anthony "Fat Tony" Salerno asked about it. "They got the control in there," said wiseguy Giuseppe "Peppe" Sabato. "Who is that now?" wondered Salerno. "Matty," said Sabato, referring to Genovese capo Matthew "Matty the Horse" Ianniello, whose Mulberry Street fish house, Umberto's Clam Bar, was the site of the storied slaying of Crazy Joe Gallo. (This is detailed in Chapter 24.)

After surviving growing pains, the trustees and the U.S. attorney's office in Newark fought off a determined bid by the Genovese family to hold on to the local through Provenzano surrogates. They prevented the candidacy of Michael Sciarra by showing that he was a mob associate controlled by the family. After his brother Daniel ran in Michael's place and was elected on December 8, 1988, the feds sued, Michael was permanently barred, and Daniel agreed to step down as president. In February of 1998, 16 years after the initial lawsuit, Local 560 was said to be free of organized crime influence and in control of its membership. It was a turnaround that many never thought possible.

Reforming the Laborers Union

The Laborers International Union of North America (LIUNA) was chartered by the American Federation of Labor in 1903. It consists of approximately 800 locals, 60 district councils, and about 800,000 members. Its locals represent general laborers, bricklayers, pavers, pipeline laborers, cement and concrete workers, and others in the construction industry.

La Cosa Nostra gradually took control of this union through fear and intimidation at the grassroots level. The families focused on key locals and district councils and used their contacts with each other to control the presidency and other national offices.

They were greatly aided by politicians who accepted political contributions from the union and looked the other way when allegations of union corruption periodically came to light. In 1994, the Justice Department alleged that four consecutive presidents, Joseph Moreschi (1926–1968), Peter Fosco (1968–1975), Angelo Fosco (1975–1993), and Arthur Armand Coia (1993–1999) "have associated with and been controlled and influenced by organized crime figures from 1926 to 1944." Coia was later found guilty of conflict of interest and federal tax fraud charges.

> **Fuhgeddaboudit**
>
> Arthur Coia, president of the Laborers Union from 1993 through 1999, had his picture taken with President Clinton and other prominent officials. He also did very well financially. He was able to afford a $1 million Ferrari. That must have impressed the boys hauling gravel and working the jackhammers in 90-degree weather.

Mafia Speak

Gaspar Lupo was president of New York's Mason Tenders District Council of the Laborers Union in 1980. In real life, however, he was controlled by James Messera, a burly 230-pound Genovese family capo. "Gaspar (Lupo) will do anything I tell him. If I tell him to jump off the roof, he'll jump off the fuckin' building," Messera told his crew one day as the FBI listened in. Messera didn't order Lupo to try any Superman stunts, and he died of natural causes.

The Beginning of the End of Mafia Rule

In 1994, the feds threatened the LIUNA with the same type of massive racketeering case they had used to bring the Teamsters into line and ultimately forced labor leaders to sign a consent decree. On February 13, 1995, the feds agreed to give the laborers a chance to reform themselves while being overseen by the federal government.

Federal prosecutors gave the LIUNA three extensions of this oversight agreement over the years, agreeing in 2000 to relax its oversight when the union appeared to be making significant progress at reform. The union adopted direct rank-and-file elections for its national officers, adopted an ethics and disciplinary code, and conducted investigations of mob-controlled locals in Buffalo, Chicago, St. Louis, Washington, D.C., and the states of New York and New Jersey. In addition, the LIUNA changed the methods for assigning work, making it more difficult for mobsters and mob-connected union officials to give it to their friends and relatives.

Capo James Messera boasted he was the real boss of the Mason Tenders District Council.

(Courtesy of GangLandNews.com)

As with the Teamsters, these reforms required the union to hire court-approved investigators to oversee that they were being carried out and that no backward steps were taken during lulls when the government's attention had shifted elsewhere.

The Case of Buffalo Local 210

The agreement between the Justice Department and the LIUNA provided that the international union would attempt to remove mob influence at the local level, particularly in Buffalo, where that city's La Cosa Nostra family had controlled Local 210 for decades.

The Justice Department's original 1995 RICO complaint alleged that the officers of Local 210 hired Daniel Domino as a business agent even though he was a Buffalo family member who had just finished a sentence for extortion. When officials discovered that federal law prevented him from holding this position, he was renamed a "clerk" but still received the same salary as a business agent. Eventually, he became president of the local. This example shows how corrupt union officials and mobsters simply ignored legislation aimed at ridding unions of mob influence.

On February 22, 1996, the LIUNA installed a trustee to oversee Local 210. For a month, some local members, spurred on by wiseguys, took over the local headquarters and prevented the trustee from conducting business there. There was scattered resistance over the next couple of years, but by late 1998, 24 members were expelled for their mob connections, and numerous internal reforms were put in place, including an equitable system for allocating jobs to union members.

> **Mafia Speak**
>
> Daniel Domino, an alleged member of the Buffalo family, was president of Local 210 of the LIUNA until he was fired in 1985. His dismissal had nothing to do with his corrupt dealings. Domino was fired because he was aligned with the Sam Pieri faction that lost power when the Commission supported Joseph Todaro as boss of the Buffalo family.

In December of 1999, however, the Justice Department was still concerned enough about the intentions of Local 210's leaders that it filed a civil racketeering lawsuit against the local. John "Jack" McDonnell, a former FBI agent, was appointed as the court liaison officer to oversee the local, even though it already had a trustee from the parent LIUNA.

Fourteen months later, so much progress had been made that the Justice Department permitted free elections, and Local 210 was returned to its members for the first time in five years. The cleanup was a tremendous blow to the Buffalo family, removing many lucrative positions and many no-show jobs from its members and associates. It was a key step in reducing the Buffalo family to a minor league operation.

During the last decade, the federal government has reached similar agreements with the ILA and the HEREIU and their locals, just as they have with the IBT and LIUNA.

"There was a time," said Jim E. Moody, former deputy assistant director of the FBI's organized crime units, "that La Cosa Nostra could have shut down the United States through the control of labor unions. The key factor in their decline has been their removal in large measure from the Big Four labor unions: Teamsters, longshoremen, laborers, and hotel and restaurant employees."

The Least You Need to Know

◆ The Mafia was entrenched in four major unions.

◆ Federal intervention was used to remove this influence.

◆ Reform required endless court intervention.

◆ La Cosa Nostra no longer controls the four major unions.

Chapter 21

Wiseguys Start Spilling Their Guts

In This Chapter

♦ Some birds start singing

♦ Some birds can sing and write

♦ The big birds start warbling

♦ Everybody seems to be singing

Informers are a vital and necessary part of the criminal investigation process. They often live in the underworld and secretly provide information to authorities. Without them, officials would solve far fewer crimes, and the public would arguably be worse off than with them. Few career criminals help the law because they have found religion. Most are jammed up and inform to avoid an arrest or to bank on goodwill with a law enforcement officer in case his or her help is ever needed in the future.

Turncoats, or cooperating witnesses, are another matter entirely. They are criminals who publicly inform on others. Some of them have been secret informers in the past, but others "go bad" when they are facing serious prison time or when they have been sentenced to a long term and hope to "buy" their way out by testifying against others.

Dealing with turncoats and informers is a tricky business that can lead to disaster in court and in personal lives. Sometimes authorities make deals with despicable people in order to convict people who are as bad or worse. Dealing with criminals, especially killers and drug dealers, will always be controversial, and it is in the public's interest for these agreements to undergo the closest scrutiny possible to safeguard abuses. In this chapter, I will look at a number of turncoats and informers to give a better understanding of this part of life in La Cosa Nostra.

Fuhgeddaboudit

Many Witness Protection Program members are criminals who have difficulty shaking old habits. Carmine LaBruno was a Buffalo associate with a long arrest record including a conviction for murder. After he testified and was relocated in the witness program, he went into hiding in Cape Coral, Florida. In 1989, he was accused of attempted murder and robbery for shooting, robbing, and leaving for dead a man with whom he had gone fishing.

The Animal Makes a Splash

Joseph "The Animal" Barboza has become the poster boy for what is wrong with the Witness Protection Program. In fact, the situation is much more complicated than that. The facts about this violent Boston criminal who helped send four men to prison for a murder they didn't commit are startling.

Mafia Speak

New England capo Larry Zannino was a ferocious mobster and had a temper to match. In 1981, the FBI overheard him reminiscing about being called to help settle a dispute on the day he was burying his eldest daughter. Zannino was so angry when the matter turned out to be trivial that he told capo Gennaro "Jerry" Angiulo, "Why don't we go in that fucking garage (the headquarters of an Irish gang) right now with fucking machine guns!"

Barboza was a violent career criminal who became an associate of the New England family in the 1960s. This connection, combined with his own ferocity, caused most "tough guys" to give Barboza a wide berth.

On October 6, 1966, Barboza was arrested on weapons possession charges after Boston police stopped him and found a rifle and a .45-caliber pistol in his car. He was locked up, and bail was set at $50,000. Two cohorts, Arthur "Tashe" Bratsos and Thomas J. DePrisco, began a series of visits to local mob hangouts, strong-arming contributions for bail money and lining their own pockets with some of the cash.

In November, the two Barboza associates went to the Nite Lite Café in Boston's North End and were shot to death by wiseguys who then drove their bodies to South Boston in Bratsos's car and parked it. The discovery of their bodies and the murder of another Barboza pal, Joseph "Chico" Amico, sent Barboza himself running to FBI agents H. Paul Rico and Dennis Condon with tall tales of murder and mob mayhem.

Barboza began testifying against major Mafia figures in 1968. He failed to convince a jury that capo Gennaro "Jerry" Angiulo was involved in a murder, but his testimony a few months later helped convict mobster Raymond Patriarca of a murder conspiracy charge. In May of 1968, Barboza, with acquiescence by the FBI, took part in a travesty of justice and sent *four* innocent men to jail for murder along with two who were actually guilty.

Barboza implicated six men—the New England underboss Henry "The Referee" Tameleo, Peter Limone, Louis Greco, Joseph Salvati, Ronald "Ronnie the Pig" Cassesso, and Wilfred Roy French—in the March 12, 1965, murder of career criminal Teddy Deegan, whose body was found in an alley in Chelsea. Barboza said that Limone brought him into the plot and that he personally checked with Tameleo to see if he approved the hit. He put Greco and Salvati in the murder with French, Cassesso, and himself. The jury believed him and convicted all six. Four defendants—including three who were innocent (Tameleo, Limone, and Greco)—were on death row until 1974, when Massachusetts abolished the death penalty.

From the day Tameleo and Salvati were arrested, stories circulated throughout the underworld and the legal community that they were framed. Vincent Teresa, another Boston mob turncoat, wrote in his book, *My Life in the Mafia* (Fawcett Books, 1974), that Salvati and Tameleo were not involved in Deegan's murder.

In addition to Salvati and Tamaleo, Limone and Greco were also wrongly convicted of the murder, and what's worse, the FBI had information from a trusted confidential informant that exonerated them, yet they never provided it to the defense or the prosecution. According to FBI reports released in December of 2000,

> **Big Shot**
>
> Barboza did not finger Martin as an accomplice because The Animal already had killed him in July of 1965, according to turncoat gangster Vincent Teresa.

the day after the murder, an informer told Agent H. Paul Rico the identities of the real killers: Vincent "Jimmy the Bear" Flemmi, Romeo Martin, Cassesso, French, and Barboza.

The prevailing wisdom today is that FBI agents Rico, Condon, and their superiors were so eager to destroy the Mafia that they helped Barboza frame guys to protect an informer who took part in the killing, Vincent "Jimmy the Bear" Flemmi, whose brother Steve was also an informer. Barboza's lies likely contributed to the uncommon zeal with which the Boston mob attempted to find and kill him. On February 11, 1976, soldier Joseph "JR" Russo gunned him down on a San Francisco street.

The evidence of a travesty of justice surfaced in the form of FBI reports at pretrial hearings in the racketeering case of New England Mafia boss Frank Salemme. In 2001, lawyers filed affidavits stating that two clients, New England wiseguys who took part in the killing, had told them that Tameleo, Limone, Greco, and Salvati had nothing to do with the murder. Lawyer Ronald Chisolm added an explosive charge: Cassesso said Agent Rico had offered him a great deal to take the witness stand and swear to Barboza's lies.

Later that month, Limone and Salvati's convictions were reversed. Salvati was released in 1997 when the Governor's Council commuted his sentence after he had served 30 years. Limone was released after serving 33 years. Tameleo and Greco died in prison in 1995. Looking back, it's outrageous that three wiseguys served decades in prison for a murder they didn't commit, but the FBI and Barboza also cost Salvati (who by all accounts was a gambler, not a gangster) 30 years of freedom. He feels he was thrown into the murder case because he owed "The Animal" $400. That's a hell of a reason to spend 30 years in prison.

> ### Slammer Time
>
> While serving life for Deegan's murder, Wilfred Roy French got religion and confessed that he was involved in the killing. In August of 1985, after serving 17 years for the Deegan murder, Henry "The Referee" Tameleo spoke to the *Boston Globe*. He acknowledged his relationship with major mob figures. "I'm not going to deny it. I knew them people very well." Unlike French, Tameleo didn't confess, most likely because he wasn't involved. "I do really and truly would like to get home," he said. Ten years later, he did—in a body bag.

Jack Zalkind, the lead prosecutor in the 1968 case, said he was "stunned" by revelations that Rico knew he had the wrong men. "I have never seen any FBI reports that were signed by Paul Rico, and I was the prosecutor. I thought Paul Rico and Denny Condon were absolutely good guys. If they were holding back on me, oh my God."

At a congressional hearing about the matter, Rico said he was convinced today that Salvati was innocent but denied framing him. Accused of showing little remorse for the miscarriage of justice to which he contributed, Rico said, "What do you want, tears?" No. But justice for Rico and other corrupt FBI agents, even belated, was certainly called for. To some degree, it was obtained, as I detail in Chapter 32.

Singing Sammy Takes the Spotlight

"I was the underboss of the Gambino organized crime family," Salvatore "Sammy Bull" Gravano said at the murder and racketeering trial of John Gotti. Gravano made Mafia history as the first underboss to testify against his boss. "John was the boss; I was the underboss. John barked and I bit." For pointing a deadly finger at Gotti and scores of other mobsters from the witness stand, Gravano was rewarded with a prison term of less than five years for a life of crime that included 19 murders.

The turncoat underboss was a superstar witness. His last testimony came at the racketeering and murder trial of Genovese boss Vincent "Chin" Gigante in 1997. He was due to testify three years later at the jury-tampering trial of a gangster who fixed Gotti's 1986–1987 federal racketeering and murder case, but a funny thing happened on the way—Gravano was arrested on drug charges, and the feds decided Gravano's credibility was gone, so they dismissed the tampering case.

Mafia Speak

Salvatore "Sammy Bull" Gravano took part in 19 gangland-style slayings and was accomplished in many facets of mob hits, as recounted in *Gotti: Rise and Fall,* by Jerry Capeci and Gene Mustain (Onyx, 1996). "Sometimes I was the shooter. Sometimes I was a backup shooter. Sometimes I set the guy up. Sometimes I just talked about it. When you go out on a piece of work, it doesn't matter what position you're in." The only time Gravano "was the shooter" was February 28, 1970, when 5'5" Sammy Bull made his bones in the back seat of a car by blowing out the brains of a friend sitting in the front.

Gravano presents both the best and the worst of the federal government's policy of getting mobsters to defect and testify against their former colleagues. He was a high-ranking mobster who testified truthfully and helped prosecute dozens of murderous wiseguys and drug dealers who might never have been nailed without him. Only a few years later, however, Gravano was caught dealing drugs with his son, his wife, his daughter, and a whole bunch of others in his new hometown of Tempe, Arizona.

As a teenager growing up in the Bensonhurst section of Brooklyn, Gravano ran with a street gang filled with young wannabe hoods who either made it to the mob or died trying. He began his Mafia career with the Colombo family, taking part in his first murder in 1970 at age 25. Two years later, Gravano was released to the Gambino family over a dispute between brother mobsters, including one who was Gravano's Colombo family sponsor.

He was placed in a crew led by capo Salvatore "Toddo" Aurello, who became his mentor in the ways of La Cosa Nostra. In 1976, the same year Paul Castellano became boss, Gravano was officially inducted into the family.

Within a few years, Gravano demonstrated that his main loyalty was to his mob family, not his real family. Gravano brother-in-law Nick Scibetta by all accounts was a wild man, constantly causing trouble. When Castellano ordered him killed, Gravano chose his life in La Cosa Nostra over the life of his brother-in-law and did nothing to save him.

Big Shot

By 1983, Gravano was a wealthy, influential mobster in the family. He often visited Castellano at home to update him on construction rackets, one of Gravano's specialties and one of Castellano's joys. Castellano also kept Gravano up-to-date on another Gravano specialty, killings, according to *Gotti: Rise and Fall* (Onyx, 1996). One day, when Castellano said he had ordered a hit on soldier Roy DeMeo, Gravano expected to be told to help out. But Castellano pulled out a newspaper clipping indicating that the deed had been done. "Is this okay with you?" Castellano tested. "If you're not mad, I'm not," said Gravano, passing the test with flying colors.

In early 1985, Gravano and John Gotti began plotting to murder Castellano. For Gravano, it was a great opportunity. Gotti was ready to make a move because Castellano had expressed anger that Gotti's brother and crewmembers were indicted for drug dealing, and Castellano had threatened to break up Gotti's crew. When underboss Aniello "Neil" Dellacroce died on December 2, 1985, Castellano sealed his fate by announcing that he was appointing key aide Thomas Bilotti as underboss. Gravano and capo Frank DeCicco decided that backing Gotti's plot was the best career move available to them.

On December 16, 1985, Gravano and Gotti were in Gotti's car across the street from Spark's Steak House in Midtown Manhattan when Castellano and Bilotti were gunned down as they stepped out of Castellano's car to enter the restaurant. Gravano's reward came within weeks as he was formally promoted to capo. By December of 1987, he was the family's consigliere, and in 1990, Gotti promoted him to underboss.

During Gravano's years with the Gambinos, he earned a reputation as an expert in the construction field. There is no question he knew the industry, but the secret behind his success was mob muscle. The Gambino family controlled key construction-industry unions and companies and used violence or the threat of it to get its way.

On December 11, 1990, the Gotti/Gravano era came to a close. The FBI arrested them, and the third member of the family's administration, consigliere Frank Locascio, along with capo Thomas Gambino. Ten days later, the Administration was in court when federal prosecutors played tape-recorded conversations in which Gotti admitted ordering three murders in a discussion with Locascio but blamed Gravano for instigating the killings. After listening, Gravano knew he was doomed. He feared Gotti might blame the murders on him. His self-preservation instincts began to kick in.

After a secret meeting with federal prosecutors, Gravano agreed to cooperate. In November of 1991, the FBI took him out of the Metropolitan Correctional Center, and he began spilling everything he knew about the family's rackets. He also discussed the five murders that he and Gotti were charged with in the indictment, including the killings of Castellano and Bilotti. On March 2, 1992, in a tense, dramatic confrontation in a packed courtroom, Gravano took the witness stand against Gotti. It was the first time an underboss had ever done so against his Mafia boss.

A classic drawing of the courtroom confrontation between Salvatore "Sammy Bull" Gravano and John Gotti by award-winning sketch artist Ruth Pollack.

(Courtesy of Ruth Pollack)

Gravano gave a full account of the planning and execution of the killings of Castellano and Bilotti. He also filled in details of the three murders that Gotti had admitted ordering on tape. When he concluded his testimony nine days later, for all intents and purposes, the case was over. On April 2, the jury made it official, convicting Gotti of racketeering, murder, and every charge in the indictment.

During the next two years, Gravano's insight and testimony (sometimes at trials, more often before grand juries) helped send more than three dozen gangsters, drug dealers, and corrupt Teamsters Union officials (as well as a juror who sold his vote to John Gotti in 1987) to prison.

On sentencing day in September of 1994, 90 law enforcement officials praised Gravano's cooperation, and prosecutor John Gleeson said he had given "extraordinary, unprecedented, and historic assistance to the government." Federal Judge I. Leo Glasser sentenced Gravano to five years in prison.

Released in March 1995, Gravano seemed to be doing quite well for himself. In April of 1997, he appeared on TV with interviewer Diane Sawyer on two successive nights, promoting a book about his life that was written by Peter Maas.

The bubble burst, however, on February 24, 2000, when he and his wife, son, daughter, and son-in-law were arrested on drug charges by Arizona authorities. Ten months later, federal prosecutors in Brooklyn charged Sammy Bull and son Gerard with buying thousands of Ecstasy tablets in Brooklyn for distribution in Arizona.

On May 25, 2001, two weeks before his federal drug trial was set to begin, Gravano and his son pleaded guilty to conspiracy charges. Sentenced to 20 years, Sammy Bull is scheduled for release in 2017, at age 74. Gerard received nine years.

Philip Leonetti Reaps a Handsome Reward

Philip M. Leonetti had the misfortune of growing up as a nephew of Nicodemo "Little Nicky" Scarfo, a violent killer who became boss of the Philadelphia family in 1981. Leonetti was raised by his mother, Nancy, and grew up in the same Atlantic City building as the psychopathic Scarfo. The future Philadelphia boss took a 12-year-old Leonetti with him to dispose of a body, figuring that a cop wouldn't suspect that a man accompanied by a little boy would be in the process of dumping the body of a murder victim.

Leonetti was the front man in Scarf Inc., a concrete placement firm that did subcontracting work on several Atlantic City casinos. When Phil "Chicken Man" Testa became boss after the murder of Angelo Bruno in 1980, he inducted nine new members to rejuvenate the family. Leonetti was one of these new recruits. The fact that Testa and Scarfo were close friends was the key reason Leonetti was made in June of 1980. He was promoted to capo in 1981 when Scarfo became boss.

In October of 1980, Leonetti, his uncle Nicky, and Lawrence "Yogi" Merlino were acquitted of the December 16, 1979, murder of Vincent Falcone, despite the eyewitness testimony of Joseph Salerno, a former Scarfo associate who testified. When Leonetti became a cooperating witness in June of 1989, he confirmed Salerno's account of the killing.

Leonetti was also involved in the corruption of Michael Matthews, a state assemblyman who became mayor of Atlantic City in 1982. Matthews pleaded guilty to an extortion conspiracy in November of 1984 but reneged on his promise to become a cooperating witness; extortion charges against Leonetti were dropped in April 1986.

> **Big Shot**
>
> Philip Leonetti was a handsome, engaging wiseguy who impressed juries with his easy smile and quiet manner. Leonetti, however, was a cold-blooded killer who fired a bullet into the back of the head of an unsuspecting friend who had dared to criticize Leonetti and his uncle, Nicky Scarfo. All told, Leonetti took part in 10 gangland-style slayings during his two decades as a Philadelphia wiseguy.

The luck of the young underboss continued in 1987 as he, Scarfo, and others were acquitted of being part of a vast narcotics conspiracy, despite the testimony of two turncoat mobsters, Thomas "Tommy Del" DelGiorno and Nicholas "Nicky the Crow" Caramandi. On December 12, 1987, Leonetti and Scarfo beat the case again.

In the 1987 acquittal, Leonetti, Scarfo, and seven other Philadelphia wiseguys were found not guilty of the September 14, 1984, killing of Salvatore Testa, a murder Leonetti admitted being part of when he began cooperating in 1989.

> **Fuhgeddaboudit**
>
> Nicky Scarfo recruited from the bottom of the barrel when he was restocking the Philadelphia family. Philip Narducci and Nicholas "Nicky Whip" Milano went into a Philadelphia store and shot down Salvatore "Sammy" Tamburrino right in front of his mother on November 3, 1983. A month later, Francis "Faffy" Iannarella repeated the scene by blowing away Robert J. Riccobene while his mother looked on. These guys made the term "Men of Honor" an obscene joke.

Leonetti's luck finally turned bad. On November 19, 1988, a federal jury found him, Scarfo, and 17 family members guilty of a vast RICO indictment that involved 10 murders, extortion, gambling, and drug dealing. Scarfo was buried with a 55-year sentence. On May 11, 1989, underboss Phil Leonetti was hammered with 45 years. A month later, he was singing to the feds.

Along the way, Leonetti testified at Mafia trials in New York, New Jersey, Pennsylvania, and Connecticut against mobsters from seven crime families. He gave federal prosecutors in New York valuable information about John Gotti's move on Paul Castellano, and he testified before the grand jury that indicted the Dapper Don in 1990. He also played a major role in a successful civil racketeering suit that federal prosecutors filed against the Hotel Employees and Restaurant Employees International Union and HEREIU's Atlantic City–based Local 54 in 1990. According to the FBI and federal prosecutors, he also provided much intelligence and insight about the Mafia beyond his testimony.

On May 29, 1992, Leonetti was handsomely rewarded. His sentence was cut to six and a half years. All told, he served five years, five months, and five days in prison.

"He was the best witness I ever saw," said George Anastasia, of the *Philadelphia Inquirer*. "He was handsome, articulate, and intelligent. He said, 'I never considered myself ruthless. We killed people, but that's just what we did.' He was there; he did the shootings; he didn't sugar-coat it. But you got the sense he had really turned his life around."

The Highest-Ranking Singer Tells Stories from Hearsay

Ralph Natale became the first La Cosa Nostra boss in history to publicly break his vow of silence when he became a cooperating witness shortly after he was arrested on drug charges in June of 1999.

Natale was a long-time associate of the Philadelphia family with a power base in Local 170 of the Bartenders Union in Camden, New Jersey. That ended when he was convicted of arson and drug trafficking in 1979. He served 15 years and missed the battles that began with the murder of Angelo Bruno in 1980.

Fuhgeddaboudit
Ralph Natale became Philadelphia boss in 1994. He felt that the previous boss, John Stanfa, was an "imposter." Natale showed how he thought a real boss should act. He began dating a young woman who was also his daughter's best friend. He set her up in an apartment and then added insult to injury by flaunting his young *commare* so that word would get around and back to his wife. To finance this "honorable" lifestyle, Natale engaged in drug dealing. Talk about an imposter!

By 1990, John Stanfa had taken over the family, but many were unhappy with his leadership and looked to Natale, even though he was locked up and only an associate.

Young rebels led by Skinny Joey Merlino engaged in shootings with Stanfa supporters, especially in 1993. In 1994, Natale was released on parole, and Merlino inducted him into the family. By this time Stanfa was in prison and out of the loop.

Before the year ended, Merlino and his loyalists orchestrated Natale's ascension to boss, a move veteran Philadelphia mob chronicler George Anastasia believes was similar to, but one better than, the upfront boss gambit employed for decades by the Genovese family. "They propped him up, told him he was the boss, let him think he was the boss, but they continued to do whatever they wanted."

A veteran drug dealer, Natale began moving methamphetamine to finance a lifestyle that included a wife, a family, and a girlfriend. He was arrested for parole violation and sent back to prison on June 11, 1998. He was indicted for drug dealing in June of 1999 and made a deal to cooperate. His prior drug convictions meant he was looking at life without parole if he went down in this case.

Natale's prosecution debut against Camden mayor Milton Milan was a seeming success; Milan was convicted of bribery and was jailed. His Merlino appearance, however, was a disaster. The jury ignored his testimony, which linked Merlino and codefendants to murders and drug dealing. It acquitted all the defendants of all the charges of violence that the feds added after Natale began to talk, convicting only on the gambling and extortion charges. Sentenced to 14 years, Merlino is scheduled for release in 2011, at age 49. "The feds fell in love with the idea of flipping a boss before they found out he was a paper boss," said Anastasia. "He came across as a pompous ass who was repeating a lot of stories he had heard, not someone who lived them."

Mafia Speak

When Ralph Natale was testifying against his underboss in Philadelphia in April of 2001, he wasn't impressed with what the turncoat boss thought were intimidation attempts by Merlino's defense lawyer, Edwin Jacobs Jr., who was merely looking over his reading glasses at him. "Listen, I had killers looking at me trying to intimidate me. You can't intimidate me," said Natale.

The Least You Need to Know

♦ Informers are a vital part of police work.

♦ Cooperating witnesses have hurt La Cosa Nostra.

♦ Many cooperating witnesses are despicable people.

♦ There are dangers with informers and cooperating witnesses.

Part 5

Battle Hymn of the Mafia

Everyone knows that the Mafia goes around shooting people. Often it happens because a bunch of drunken wiseguys get to arguing amongst themselves in a social club or in a bar with strangers. Guns get pulled out, and inevitably someone goes down with lead in various body parts.

Every now and then, however, Mafia guys engage in violence that has a little more planning behind it. In this section, I'll explain a few of the major conflicts that wracked La Cosa Nostra over the last century, and I'll try to make some sense of the carnage. I'll also take you on a trip up north to see what all the shooting was about in Canada.

Chapter 22

Mafia Rivals Fight for Supremacy

In This Chapter

- The Castellammarese War
- The stakes
- The conflict
- The winners

Out of respect for the men and women who have fought in and been victims of real wars, let's clearly state that what I call the "Castellammarese War" in this chapter wouldn't qualify as a company-size fire fight. The use of the word "war" in the Mafia context is a way to state that the disputes lasted longer than most mob conflicts and were more widespread than the usual localized shootings that occur from time to time.

The Castellammarese War is a legendary conflict that supposedly shaped La Cosa Nostra from 1931 onward. It theoretically began February 26, 1930, with the murder of Gaetano "Tommy" Reina and ended with the September 10, 1931, slaying of Salvatore Maranzano. Essentially, it was a battle over who would be the strongest Mafia leader in New York.

Ironically, the two main contenders ended up quite dead. The term "Castellammarese War" also encompasses a series of conflicts within a number of families around the nation to see who would be the boss.

In this chapter, I will look at some lead-up action to the "war," relate some of the major events of the conflict, and analyze a few myths that arose after the dust settled.

The Bad Seed

Most of the action of the Castellammarese War took place in New York City, but the alliances and intrigue included Mafiosi in Chicago, Detroit, and Buffalo. La Cosa Nostra leaders always look for partners to strengthen their position, but with the pluses come the minuses: The enemies of your new friend become your enemies, and they all begin looking for weak links in your family to get you. It's a deadly life.

> **Mafia Speak** _____
>
> Nicola Gentile was the Forrest Gump of the Mafia from about 1900 until 1937. According to his writing, Gentile was nearly everywhere that something important happened. For example, he claimed to have called a meeting of all the Mafia bosses except Joe Masseria and Salvatore Maranzano in an unsuccessful attempt to end the Castellammarese War.

New York City

Mafia life in New York City has always been a pit of intrigue, alliances, and betrayal. What follows is a brief summary of the various families who were going to take part in the "war."

The Geneveses were led by Joseph "Joe the Boss" Masseria, who was considered the most powerful of America's Mafia leaders. On the throne of the Gambino family was Al Mineo, a Masseria ally and a key strategist. Gaetano "Tommy" Reina commanded the Luchese troops. His father had been a friend of Masseria underboss Peter Morello, but Masseria was suspicious of Reina's loyalties. Over in the Bonanno camp, aging Cola Shiro was in charge, but ambitious soldier Salvatore Maranzano was looking for increased power. Finally, Joseph Profaci led what we now call the Colombo family, which appeared to be unified during this era.

Detroit

In 1930, Detroit was unstable. Sam Catalonette had managed to keep relative peace among the various factions after taking over in 1920 following violent battles for leadership. However, Catalonette died unexpectedly of pneumonia on February 14, 1930. Gaspar Milazzo, a native of Castellammarese del Golfo who was friendly with Maranzano, Buffalo boss Stefano Magaddino, and Chicago's Joseph Aiello, emerged as leader. Unfortunately for Milazzo, Detroit mobster Caesar "Chester" LaMare also coveted the top position.

Buffalo

Stefano Magaddino was also from Castellammarese del Golfo. He had moved to Buffalo after developing legal problems in New York related to a conflict from the home country. He had become boss after the natural death of the previous leader. By 1930, Magaddino was recognized as the leader of all Castellammarese Mafiosi.

Chicago

By 1930, Joseph Aiello was leader of the Sicilian family in Chicago. He resented attempts by non-Sicilian Al Capone to manipulate affairs within the Unione Siciliana, a former charitable organization that had become a clearinghouse for the production and sale of homebrew liquor and was a political force. Aiello was a good friend of Detroit's Milazzo and Buffalo's Magaddino, and they supported his efforts in Chicago.

The Stakes Are High

Turncoat mobster Joe Valachi and New York boss Joe Bonanno said the Castellammarese were the good guys, fighting the war to counter advances by the Masseria forces.

On the other hand, according to Nicola Gentile, a Mafioso who was also active during that era and who wrote about it in 1963, the Castellammarese and their allies were the aggressors. Gentile called them *fuoriusciti* or "outlaws."

At the heart of any mob dispute, whether it's between two soldiers or two families, is money and power. Ego, ambition, and petty jealousy play an important role, but the last guy standing would have not only the prestige but the income to make him and his friends super rich. This was still the era of Prohibition, and there were millions of dollars at stake.

The Plot Thickens

Here's my assessment of how this war played out, according to all the evidence that's available, including the writings of Bonanno, Valachi, and Gentile, the body count, and 30 years of experience dealing with wiseguys.

On February 26, 1930, the Joe Pinzolo faction of the Luchese family took out boss Gaetano "Tommy" Reina. Pinzolo wouldn't have done this without the support of Masseria, who liked the new state of affairs because he now had an ally running the Luchese family.

The Reina loyalists in the Luchese family were obviously not happy about the death of their mentor and protector. Outwardly they supported Pinzolo, but they were looking for allies to help them plot Pinzolo's demise.

Mafia Speak

Nicola Gentile wrote, "A lot of youths desiring to avenge their friends put themselves at the disposition of Maranzano. The group began to enlarge—and others contributed large sums."

Big Shot

Bonanno mobster Joseph Parrino was an ally of Joe Masseria. After Shiro stepped down as boss, Masseria supported Parrino as the new leader. Maranzano quickly responded to that threat by having Parrino gunned down in a restaurant in 1930. It was a bad year for the Parrinos. Brother Sam "Sasa" Parrino had been killed with Detroit's Milazzo earlier that same year.

Joe the Boss openly showed his support of Al Capone over Joseph Aiello in Chicago. This angered Aiello as well as Detroit's Milazzo, who defied Masseria's orders to support Capone. Milazzo's Detroit rival, Chester LaMare, then took advantage of this Masseria/Milazzo problem and began moving in on Milazzo's territory. He suckered Milazzo to a fake peace sitdown and blew him away on May 31, 1930.

The Detroit situation caused a leadership change in New York's Bonanno family. Salvatore Maranzano convinced the family that Masseria planned to wipe out all the Castellammarese. He brought Buffalo's Stefano Magaddino around to this way of thinking. Consequently, Bonanno leader Cola Shiro stepped down. Maranzano became family boss and leader of the resistance to Masseria.

Maranzano, ambitious and astute, used the conflict to finesse his way to the top of the Bonanno group without causing any dissension among his natural allies. One of his first moves was to order the killing of Peter "The Clutch Hand" Morello, Masseria's underboss, because the Castellammarese saw Morello as the strategic brains behind the Masseria campaign. They wanted to get Morello before "the old fox stopped following his daily routine," wrote Bonanno. This was done on August 15, 1930.

On September 5, 1930, Reina loyalists in the Luchese family lured Pinzolo to the office of Gaetano "Tommy" Lucchese where he was killed. Now the Luchese bunch, led by Tommy Gagliano, was openly allied with the Maranzano group.

Just as the Maranzano forces gathered momentum in New York, they were buried forever in Chicago. Capone's forces mowed down Joseph Aiello on October 23, 1930. This made Chicago a one-horse town, with the horse being Al Capone, a Masseria supporter. The killing also brought 70 years of peace to Chicago, as far as the leadership of the Chicago Outfit was concerned. There was no other Windy City family to complicate things.

In October of 1930, the Luchese forces, using new recruit Joe Valachi, rented an apartment in a complex in the Bronx where Masseria ally and Gambino underboss Steve Ferrigno lived. The hope was that Masseria might visit Ferrigno to plan strategy. Eventually, Valachi spotted Masseria entering the complex on Pelham Parkway, and shooters were dispatched to wait for him to leave. Over a period of days, people came and went but no Masseria. Eventually, Maranzano decided to take out Al Mineo, the Gambino boss who was also seen entering. On November 5, 1930, both Mineo and Ferrigno were gunned down by shotgun fire. Masseria was still inside and lucked out by not leaving.

Joseph "Joe Baker" Catania, another key Masseria aide, was killed on February 3, 1931, as he stood on a street in the Fordham section of the Bronx, not far from his wife, who was looking at him when the shots rang out. Shooter Bastiano "Buster" Domingo told Valachi, "You could see the dust coming off his jacket when the bullets hit."

With Masseria allies dropping like flies, Charles "Lucky" Luciano stepped up to be part of the end game. Luciano met with Salvatore Maranzano and agreed to set up his boss.

On April 15, 1931, Luciano was having a late afternoon lunch with his boss at Nuova Villa Tammaro Italian restaurant in Coney Island. At about 3 P.M., with the place empty, Luciano got up to use the men's room. When he returned, Masseria was lying dead with six bullet wounds in his body.

Big Shot

When Buster Domingo gunned down Joe Catania, he knew Catania's wife was standing nearby, watching her husband. This is a "man of honor" whom Joe Bonanno invited to serve in his wedding party.

New York Mafia boss Lucky Luciano was a big winner in the Castellammarese War and helped establish the Mafia Commission.

(Courtesy of GangLandNews.com)

With Masseria gone, Maranzano became the most powerful boss in New York, if not the nation. He held a series of meetings to clarify that point. Perhaps the most important gathering was hosted by Al Capone in late May of 1931 at the Hotel Congress in Chicago. All the La Cosa Nostra bosses were publicly introduced to each other, and a new truce was worked out.

Slammer Time

Genovese soldier Girolamo "Bobby Doyle" Santucci led a charmed life. According to Valachi, he was involved in the killings of three bosses and an underboss during the Castellammarese War. He had a piece of the hits against Maranzano, Pinzolo, Mineo, and Ferrigno and spent only a few days in the slammer as a material witness in the Maranzano hit before being released.

In June of 1931, Maranzano was honored at a banquet/fundraiser in New York City. Representatives from other families brought cash gifts. About $100,000 in tribute was raised for the new king of crime. He never got to spend much of it.

By the end of the summer of 1931, Maranzano was already in trouble. He was having difficulty with Bonanno's cousin, Stefano Magaddino of Buffalo. He was also unhappy with Lucky Luciano and some of his allies. On September 10, 1931, all the discontent surrounding Maranzano ended when he was shot to death in his Manhattan office by gangsters who were sent by Luciano and who posed as law enforcement officials.

And the Winner Is ...

Maranzano's death signaled the end of an era, and a new power emerged inside La Cosa Nostra—the Commission (which was discussed in Chapter 3).

The formation of the Commission was a very significant change, a new method of governing with ramifications for the rest of the twentieth century. Another major event that supposedly occurred—the Night of the Sicilian Vespers, the purge of so-called "Mustache Petes"—is a myth. So, too, is Joe Bonanno's claim that he had nothing to do with Maranzano's death.

The Myth of the Great Purge

The Night of the Sicilian Vespers, the great purge of old-fashioned Mafia leaders who were allies of Maranzano, never happened. Oft-repeated and written accounts place the number of slain gangsters from 20 to 90 on the same day. If true, it was an incredible massacre and an even more incredible feat of logistics and plotting.

Professor Alan Block debunked the notion in his book, *East Side, West Side* (Christopher Davis, 1979), crediting J. Richard "Dixie" Davis, lawyer for the notorious Arthur "Dutch Schultz" Flegenheimer, with setting the legend in motion in the late 1930s. Davis wrote a series of articles that included a quote from Schultz associate Abraham "Bo" Weinburg, stating that after Maranzano was killed, "… there was about 90 guineas knocked off all over the country." The purge story was repeated in *Murder, Inc.* (Woodhill Press, 1972) by Burton Turkus and Sid Feder and in *The Valachi Papers* by Peter Maas (Putnam Publishing, 1968).

Block investigated, examining newspapers in New York, Los Angeles, Philadelphia, Detroit, New Orleans, Boston, Buffalo, and Newark for the two weeks before and after Maranzano's killing.

He found three murders that were connected to the Maranzano hit. One was the killing of Sam Monaco in New Jersey. A second was the execution of Louis Russo, a close Monaco associate whose body was fished out of Newark Bay with Monaco on September 13, 1931. Valachi mentioned both in his 1963 testimony. The third was Joseph Siragusa, the Pittsburgh boss of that era. Valachi also mentioned a Jimmy Marino getting killed at the time. Authorities later identified him as James LePore. Including Maranzano, that adds up to five murdered wiseguys. As Block says, "The killing of four or five men does not make a purge."

Fuhgeddaboudit

When Joe Valachi testified about the killings surrounding the Salvatore Maranzano murder, he discussed the killings of New Jersey's Sam Monaco and Louis Russo. Not only did Valachi recall that the bodies were fished out of the drink, he also added the unnecessary and previously unreported detail that Monaco "had an iron pipe hammered up his ass."

Block speculates that the legend of the purge spread partly because Maranzano was involved in a nationwide alien-smuggling ring with contacts and associates across the country. Because Maranzano's killing curtailed the smuggling ring's operations for a time, it probably led some to believe that many ring members were killed when Maranzano was. Block suggests that the purge story also helped calm tensions after the killings. The so-called purge bolstered the belief that there would be no more violence because the supporters of Maranzano had been wiped out.

Although Block understands how criminals, and even journalists, believed the purge myth, he has little sympathy for "scholars" who have blindly repeated the myth without doing any research.

From a commonsense viewpoint, there is no way that a "purge" of 20 to 90 wiseguys took place over a few days and around the country in September of 1931. This would have made the St. Valentine's Day massacre of 1929, in which seven men were killed, look like a picnic. This type of undertaking would be beyond the capability of highly trained special forces, let alone gangsters whose successful hits are most often preceded by many aborted attempts. Some targets take months to kill for one reason or another. To think that 20 or 40 or 90 guys quietly cooperated by being exactly where they were supposed to be, all within a day or two, so that another 20, 40, or 90 teams of assassins could whack them, is just too hard to swallow.

But what of the body count that Block puts at a possible high of five? Is that all the men who were taken out during the period surrounding Maranzano's killing?

We know that the Newark underboss Sam Monaco was reported missing on September 10, 1931, the same day Maranzano was whacked. We know that his body and that of associate Louis Russo were pulled out of the river on September 13. It's logical to assume that their killings had something to do with Maranzano's due to Monaco's stature and the closeness in dates.

We only have Valachi stating that the shooting of James LePore on September 10, 1931, was associated with that of Maranzano.

Pittsburgh boss Joe Siragusa was a known associate and supporter of Maranzano, so when he was gunned down on September 13, 1931, the connection of his death to his ally's is reasonable.

What about the killing of Colorado's Peter Carlino? He disappeared on September 10, the day Maranzano died, and his body was found on September 13. Respected historian Humbert Nelli agrees that there was no purge and cites a long local feud between Carlino and Joe Roma as the most likely reason for Carlino's death.

If we move over to Los Angeles and extend our search boundaries a bit, we find Joseph "Iron Man" Ardizonne disappearing and presumed slain on October 15, 1931. He was the Los Angeles boss and was vice president of the Italian Protective League. His death would likely be related to local matters rather than events on the East Coast that occurred decades before frequent flyer bonus miles.

A nationwide search shows Maranzano dead in Manhattan, a New Jersey underboss dead in the water, a Pittsburgh boss full of holes in his basement, a Los Angeles boss missing and presumed slain, a Colorado upstart shot to death on a road near Pueblo, and two lesser lights (Russo and LePore) snuffed out. Is this a purge? It's not even a bloody Colombo war, which left 12 dead in New York from 1991 to 1993!

Webster's dictionary defines a "purge" as the elimination (in a nation, political party, and so on) of individuals held to be disloyal or undesirable. There is no mention of numbers. So perhaps there was a minor purge in 1931. Maranzano, his buddy Siragusa in Pittsburgh, and perhaps Monaco, LePore, and Russo were all taken out. We certainly don't have a "purge" as described by Peter Maas in *The Valachi Papers*. "The murder of Maranzano was part of an intricate, painstakingly mass execution—on the day Maranzano died some 40 Cosa Nostra leaders allied with him were slain across the country." This did not happen.

The Bonanno Ascension

In his book, Joe Bonanno claims he had no knowledge of the plot to kill his boss on September 10, 1930. He has got to be kidding. If he weren't part of the problem for Maranzano, he would have been part of the solution for his killers and been whacked along with him. It made no sense for Luciano to kill off Maranzano only to have him replaced by another adversary. At the Commission trial, Carmine Persico was convicted of taking part in the execution of Carmine Galante, even though he voted against the murder. Bonanno did much more to kill Maranzano than Persico did to murder Galante. If there had been a RICO case about Maranzano's murder, Bonanno would have been found guilty and served 100 years.

Mafia Speak

Nicola Gentile wrote about his supposed life in the Mafia in his Italian language book, *Vita di capomafia,* published in Rome in 1963. His work is suspect, but he has an interesting scenario for Maranzano's killing that rings true. In his account, he describes Jewish gunmen, posing as federal agents, walking into Maranzano's office with an Italian, who pointed Maranzano out to the gunmen. Gentile writes that Maranzano recognized the Italian and, still thinking the gunmen were agents, said, "Peppino, you know I am Maranzano," using the nickname of Maranzano's right-hand man, Joe Bonanno.

The Least You Need to Know

◆ The Castellammarese War involved more than nine La Cosa Nostra families.

◆ The major impact was the advent of the Commission.

◆ There was no purge of old-time leaders after the war.

◆ Too much of the war's history comes from the winners.

23

Big Troubles for the Gambino Family

In This Chapter

◆ A high-profile killing in a barbershop

◆ A well-planned ambush on Manhattan's East Side

◆ John Gotti escapes a bomb blast

◆ The end of the Dapper Don's reign

Becoming the boss of a major La Cosa Nostra family used to be a highly desired achievement. With it came prestige within a certain segment of society, financial riches, political power, and the capability to reward your friends and punish your enemies. The only problem was that others also coveted the position and were willing to kill you to get it. There was no golden parachute after a hostile takeover, although on occasion there was a big funeral with a gold-plated coffin.

Despite the dangers, many have been willing to roll the dice to achieve the top spot. In this chapter, I will examine a few gamblers who put their lives on the line to become boss of the Gambino family. The first story is an example of a perfect hit in that no one was ever charged with carrying it out. For 44 years, until I began doing research in preparation for this book, no reporter had learned that the killing was carried out by a Gambino family crew of drug dealers from the Lower East Side. The second was the most spectacular rubout in mob history, while the third is a coup attempt that failed. I conclude the chapter with a look at the way the law deposed the architect of the killing of Paul Castellano, without question the crowning achievement of the most visible, ostentatious Gambino family boss, John Gotti.

A .38-Caliber Trim

On October 25, 1957, at about 10:20 A.M., Umberto Anastasio, better known as Albert "The Mad Hatter" Anastasia, was relaxing in chair no. 4 at the Park Sheraton Hotel barbershop in Manhattan. His hair had been clipped while the shop owner, Arthur Grasso, sat and talked to him. In chair No. 5 was Vincent "Jimmy Jerome" Squillante, a close associate of Anastasia. A doctor was in the chair next to Squillante.

Big Shot

Being boss of the Gambino family virtually guarantees you riches, power, and fame, but it almost always leads to an unhappy end. From 1928 until the present, there have been eight official bosses of the family. Five of them were put out of office by violence (Salvatore "Tata" D'Aquila, Al Mineo, Vincent Mangano, Albert Anastasia, and Paul Castellano), one was forced out (Frank Scalise), and another (John Gotti) was doomed to death in prison. Only one, Carlo Gambino, had the wisdom and the luck to avoid prison and die in his own bed.

Two men walked in through the hotel lobby door. One strode up to Anastasia and opened up with a .38-caliber pistol. One shot went into the back of Anastasia's head and lodged in the left side of his brain. Two shots got him in his left hand. Another bullet went into his back at a downward angle, penetrating a lung, a kidney, and his spleen. The second shooter fired a .32-caliber pistol. One bullet went through the right side of Anastasia's hip, and there also was a grazing wound to the back of Anastasia's neck. Anastasia lurched out of the chair as shots rang out. He crashed to the floor dead.

Manicurist Jean Wineberger gave the following descriptions of the shooters:

> Shooter One: White male, 40 years old, 5'10" to 5'11", on the slim side, 175–180 lbs., blondish hair with a pompadour, fair complexion, no hat and no glasses, right handed.

> Shooter Two: white male, 45 years old, 5'7", stocky build, medium complexion, may have been Italian or Jewish.

She said the two shooters tried to run out onto the street, but the door was locked, so they exited through the door leading to the lobby, walking, not running. Squillante, who ran the family's private sanitation rackets, jumped up immediately, said "Let me out of here," and left. Police found the murder weapons nearby, a .32-caliber Smith and Wesson long-barrel revolver and a .38-caliber Colt pistol, along the route the shooters used to flee.

Anastasia's body was identified by his brother Anthony "Tough Tony" Anastasio. Three slugs were recovered at the autopsy: one in his brain, another in his left side, and a third in his underpants.

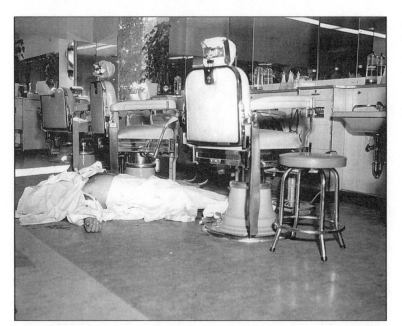

Mafia boss Albert Anastasia was shot to death in the Park Sheraton Hotel barbershop on October 26, 1957.

(Courtesy of New York Daily News)

Mafia Speak

In a rambling interview with detectives five years after Anastasia's execution, his brother Anthony "Tough Tony" Anastasio discussed the reality of Mafia life. Tough Tony, who ran the Brooklyn docks for the new boss, Carlo Gambino, accepted the killing and stressed that there were differences between the brothers in addition to the way each spelled his last name. "I ate from the same table as Albert and came from the same womb, but I know he killed many men and he deserved to die."

The shooters got away easily. No one was ever charged with any aspect of the murder plot, but there was no question that Carlo Gambino, who took over the crime family, was behind the hit. According to knowledgeable sources on both sides of the law who were interviewed for this book, the killing was carried out by a three-man hit team selected by then-capo Joseph "Joe the Blonde" Biondo, who became Gambino's underboss and remained in the post until shortly before he died in 1966. The primary shooter, sources said, was Stephen "Stevie Coogan" Grammauta, then 41, a drug dealer who was convicted of heroin trafficking in 1965. Stephen Armone, then 57, was the leader of the crew. The third member of the team, and the second shooter, was Arnold "Witty" Wittenberg, then 53, a drug dealer who was a longtime associate of the mobsters. All three men hailed from the Lower East Side of Manhattan.

Sources said that Joseph "Joe Piney" Armone, Stephen's younger brother (who was an early member of John Gotti's plot to kill Paul Castellano in 1985), would have been in on the hit but had been nabbed on a drug charge and was replaced by his brother Steve.

Stephen Armone died in 1960, Wittenberg in 1978. Grammauta was seemingly inactive for decades. He reemerged in the late 1990s as a capo of the crew. "He never showed up at the Ravenite Social Club during Gotti's reign (when Gotti demanded that all his troops show up once a week), but he's now a captain," one law enforcement official said in September of 2001.

Fuhgeddaboudit

Years after he hung up his spikes, legendary New York Yankees centerfielder Joe DiMaggio was always a sought-after celebrity when he came back to New York. In 1957, he agreed to meet Cuban businessmen who were planning to build a casino in Havana and were interested in cashing in on DiMaggio's name, as a greeter or host. Before DiMaggio met them at the Warwick Hotel, his agent took him to another room and introduced him to two big fans who just wanted to shake his hand and say hello, Albert Anastasia and Anthony "Little Augie Pisano" Carfano. Years later, when the Yankee Clipper recalled the incident for detectives, he said he was "disturbed" when his agent told him later whom he had met. "I mentioned something to the effect that you placed me in a spot."

Anastasia, who reputedly was one of the shooters in the murder of Joe Masseria in May of 1931, had served as underboss to Vincent Mangano and had taken over as boss in 1951 in much the same way that Gambino replaced him—by killing off Mangano and his brother Philip.

Until October of 2001, when I revealed on my GangLandNews.com website that the Steve Armone crew had taken out Anastasia, rival members of the first Colombo war detailed in Chapter 24 had alternately taken credit for the killing. Early on, Joey Gallo and his crew were said to have been at the scene. Many years later, Carmine Persico, by then boss of the Colombo family, bragged to a relative through marriage that although Joey Gallo had taken the credit, he had done the work.

Sidney Slater, an associate of Brooklyn's Gallo brothers, said Joey Gallo acknowledged his participation in the Anastasia murder about a week after the hit. Slater said that while they were in a bar talking about the killing, Slater wondered aloud who had done it. Gallo indicated himself, Ralph Mafrici, Joseph "Joe Jelly" Gioelli, Frank "Punchy" Illiano, and Sonny Camerone and said, "You can call the five of us the barbershop quintet."

From Slater's remarks grew the legend of Joey Gallo and his crew. In 1963, Joe Valachi added his two cents, claiming that Anthony "Charlie Bush" Zangarra, a Gambino family member in 1963, was in on the murder. Nothing came of this lead.

> **Big Shot**
>
> The City Democratic Club was formed in New York City in 1929. Among its members were gangsters Vincent Mangano, who disappeared in 1951; Philip Mangano, who was murdered in 1951; boss Albert Anastasia, who was murdered in 1957; Joseph "Joe Adonis" Doto, who was deported in 1956; and Longshoremen's Union boss Emil Camarda, who was murdered in 1941. I wonder if they had trouble recruiting new members!

Two years later, the Manhattan district attorney's office reviewed the case and included in its summary a note that a subject had "identified Ralph Mafrici and Joseph Gioelli as the perpetrators of this crime." Gioelli was already dead at this point, and Mafrici was in prison on an assault and robbery conviction. He was brought in for questioning but said nothing.

In 1973, Vincent Teresa jumped on the Gallo bandwagon in his book, *My Life in the Mafia*. He said the Gallos were part of a conspiracy run by Vito Genovese and Carlo Gambino, and the Gallos came all the way to Providence, Rhode Island, to get permission to use a New England associate as the lead shooter. Teresa's tale, like much of what he wrote, got little support from law enforcement.

In 1984, Carmine Persico put himself into the mix, although he surely didn't intend for it to become public. A longtime adversary of the Gallo brothers, Persico resented the glory they got for carrying out the famous Anastasia hit, even though he knew they didn't do it. When Persico was on the run and hiding at Fred DeChristopher's home, he told his reluctant host that he had taken care of the feared Anastasia. "That fag Joey Gallo took the credit, but I hurt Anastasia," he said, thumping his own chest for emphasis, DeChristopher told the FBI.

The Anastasia hit is a textbook example of how to carry out a high-profile killing and get away with it. For a time, the next sensational Manhattan hit seemed to be following the same path.

Big Paulie Goes Bye-Bye

Paul Castellano rode the coattails of his brother-in-law, Carlo Gambino, to the top of the Gambino family. It was a rise that probably went one step too high.

Castellano had a robbery conviction in the 1930s and spent time in prison for refusing to testify about the Apalachin meeting he attended with Gambino. By all accounts, however, he was more businessman than gangster. He was a butcher by trade and set up his sons in a successful meat and chicken distribution company that grew through the years he was a capo for Gambino. He was most definitely a crook and took advantage of his mob clout, but he left the dirty work to others.

As Gambino's health failed in 1976, Castellano served as acting boss because underboss Aniello Dellacroce, who succeeded Biondo in 1966, was serving time in prison. Gambino, who died that October, expressed a desire that Castellano succeed him. A month later, when Dellacroce was released from prison, he went along and Castellano was selected boss.

Over the next several years, Castellano stopped going to the Veterans and Friends Social Club in Bensonhurst and conducted most of the family business from his house on Staten Island. In the early 1980s, however, federal prosecutors in Manhattan and Brooklyn were each preparing racketeering cases against him.

Things really began to go seriously wrong in 1984. On March 30, Castellano was arrested on a multicount racketeering indictment that put him at the top of a violent car-theft ring run by crazed soldier Roy DeMeo. He was released on $2 million bail but was right back in the soup on May 15, when he attended a Commission meeting that was under surveillance by the FBI. Castellano and others were photographed leaving the scene.

As he awaited trial for being the boss of the DeMeo crew, Castellano was arrested on a racketeering indictment in the Commission case. (This was detailed in Chapter 19.) The next day, Castellano was released on another $2 million bail. He soon learned that his home had been bugged in 1983, and this put him on a path that crossed John Gotti's again and again. In the course of preparing for trial, Castellano became more and more angry at Gotti and his crew.

The FBI had recorded Gotti's brother Gene and sidekick Angelo Ruggiero talking about Castellano during an investigation into their heroin-distribution ring. Castellano was upset about the drug dealing, was angry that they had talked about him, and was furious that the feds had used their idle talk about him to bug his house. He indicated that he was going to play this card and break up the Gotti crew, robbing Gotti of his power base.

As 1985 progressed, Castellano's problems escalated. Underboss Aniello Dellacroce was dying from cancer. Dellacroce had been keeping a rein on the ambitious Gotti, but as Dellacroce faded, his control over Gotti waned, a fact that Castellano failed to notice as he went to trial in the DeMeo racketeering case.

Mafia Speak

Paul Castellano didn't mind being tagged as a murderer, but his nose got out of joint when he thought a detective implied that he was less than a gentleman, according to *Murder Machine* (Dutton, 1992) by Gene Mustain and Jerry Capeci. When Detective Kenneth McCabe placed Castellano under arrest for heading a band of wiseguys who killed 25 people, the Mafia boss didn't utter a word of protest. But when McCabe mentioned matter-of-factly that his late brother-in-law Carlo Gambino had been a "real gentleman," Castellano looked hurt and then blew up, "What? I'm not a gentleman?"

During this period, Gotti got all his ducks in a line for a possible move to the top. He was a degenerate gambler, but he was no fool. Before he would roll the dice in a high-stakes game in which his life and those of his buddies were on the line, he was going to prepare. By late September of 1985, Robert "DeeBee" DiBernardo, an influential soldier who had the ear of Castellano; capo Frank DeCicco; Salvatore "Sammy Bull" Gravano; Gotti's close friend Angelo Ruggiero; and capo Joseph "Joe Piney" Armone all agreed that Paul would have to go. Gotti's use of DiBernardo and his inclusion of DeCicco and Gravano and then Joe Piney were brilliant moves that would assure them support from the rest of the family, if and when they pulled the trigger on the plot and the wild plan actually came to fruition.

DeCicco and Gravano decided to back Gotti's play, especially after a veteran of wild and crazy assassination plots, Armone, told them that consigliere Joe N. Gallo wouldn't be involved but would support them if they succeeded. The coup attempt was going to go ahead. All that remained was to decide when.

This plot was the biggest undertaking known to La Cosa Nostra. Looking back at how it evolved two decades ago, Gotti's incredible gamble, feat of nerve control, and brilliant planning are evident. At every step, he was in danger of being betrayed and killed, but each important step he took was the right one, from using DeeBee to bringing in DeCicco and Gravano and then Armone.

Other major leaders had gone down in a hail of gunfire, but the instigators were always backed by other major players. In the Anastasia killing, Gambino was supported by the Genovese boss, the Luchese boss, and most likely the Colombo boss. When Lucky Luciano took out Joe Masseria, he knew the move was backed by the other four New York families. This type of support was typical of most, if not all, the Mafia coups in New York.

Fuhgeddaboudit

When Paul Castellano was gunned down on December 16, 1985, he was on trial with capo Anthony "Nino" Gaggi and three members of Roy DeMeo's crew of wiseguys for running a multimillion-dollar-a-year auto theft ring that stole gas guzzlers in Brooklyn and shipped them to Kuwait for resale. When the trial resumed, Gaggi and hit man Henry Borelli were convicted. Anthony Senter and Joseph Testa were acquitted. At a second trial, Senter and Testa were convicted of racketeering and 11 murders and sentenced to life without parole, according to *Murder Machine*.

Gotti was making the move alone. He felt he had the support of Joseph Massino of the Bonanno family, but Massino wasn't even the family boss yet. Ruggiero had gotten unofficial backing from Gennaro Langella, acting boss of the Colombo family, who said, "What are you waiting for?" when Ruggiero mentioned the idea. If things went wrong, Gotti knew, Langella would have denied such remarks. For all intents and purposes, Gotti was alone as he planned to take out the friend of Vincent "Chin" Gigante, head of the powerful Genovese clan.

Gotti settled on attacking Castellano as he arrived at a Midtown Manhattan restaurant at the height of the evening rush hour during the Christmas shopping season. It was a bold move. If successful, they would look brilliant. If it failed, they would look like idiots. So many things could go wrong, but there was no hope of luring Castellano to someone's basement for a fake meeting and putting two behind his ear like a typical Mafia hit.

The night before the hit, 11 men gathered in the basement office of Gravano's Brooklyn construction firm—Gotti, DeCicco, Gravano, Ruggiero, Joe Watts, John Carneglia, Iggy Alonga, Eddie Lino, Anthony "Tony Roach" Rampino, Salvatore "Fat Sally" Scala, and Vincent Artuso. Gotti and DeCicco outlined the plan to shoot two targets the next day as they entered a downtown restaurant. In several respects, things broke well for Gotti and his gang of 10. Both Castellano and key aide Thomas Bilotti, whom Castellano had just announced would be his new underboss—Dellacroce had died two weeks earlier—were always together. They had planned to meet DeCicco and three other capos at the restaurant that evening. Four shooters—Carneglia, Lino, Scala, and Artuso—were designated, while the others would serve as drivers or backup shooters. DeCicco would be in the restaurant with unsuspecting capos Thomas Gambino, Daniel Marino, and James Failla.

The next day, the men gathered at a small park and went over their roles in the ambush. Gotti stressed that once they began, they had to make sure both Castellano and Bilotti were dead, no matter what. He and Gravano would be the primary backup shooters, parked nearby. The four shooters donned nearly identical long coats and black fur hats to help make individual identification difficult. The crew proceeded to its positions around Sparks Steak House and waited for Castellano.

Rampino was on East 46th Street, across the street from Sparks, just in case. Down the street toward Second Avenue was another backup shooter, along with the drivers of the two getaway cars. On the corner of East 46th Street and Third Avenue, Gotti sat behind the wheel with Gravano riding shotgun. He was to climb out and gun down the targets if they tried to escape in his direction, or he was to shoot anyone who tried to interfere with the primary gunmen. There was a lot of firepower.

Bilotti pulled the Lincoln right up in front of Sparks. As Castellano began exiting the car, two gunmen walked up and fired at least six bullets into his big frame, including a final shot to the head. As Bilotti stepped out, he was approached by the other shooters. One fired several shots, toppling the new underboss to the street. The gun of the fourth designated shooter jammed. One of the Castellano shooters came around the front of the car, squatted down next to Bilotti, and fired a shot into his head. Then all four shooters and Rampino headed down the street toward Second Avenue, piled into the two getaway cars, and drove off.

Meanwhile, Gotti and Gravano watched the shooting take place, moved into traffic, slowly drove by the scene, and then headed back to Gravano's Brooklyn office to compare notes.

Inside the restaurant, Frank DeCicco was sitting with Failla and Marino, who were stunned when they found out who was shot. DeCicco immediately told them they would not have been hurt, which was his way of saying he was in on the plot. As they hurriedly left, they ran into the just-arriving Gambino, son of Carlo and nephew of Castellano. DeCicco also told Gambino he was in no danger and to go home. DeCicco drove to Brooklyn to report what had happened from his vantage point.

> **Mafia Speak**
>
> Vincent Artuso was the designated shooter whose gun jammed. All four shooters were using automatic pistols, which, although capable of pumping out a lot of bullets in a short period of time, are also notorious for jamming. "… Eddie Lino had reported back that Vinnie Artuso's gun jammed and he didn't shoot," Gravano told the FBI when he cooperated six years later. It was critical for Artuso to report this immediately so that no one would think he had backed out.

It was an incredibly successful hit. Looking back, it was unquestionably the high-water mark of Gotti's regime. The execution was well-planned and not plagued by any number of unlucky breaks that could have screwed things up in this hustling, bustling area of Manhattan, normally well covered by police. Within a few weeks, Gotti was elected boss by a cowed group of capos. He would go on to fleeting fame and death behind bars in June 2002 (see Chapter 27).

A Case of Mistaken Identity

Not everyone was happy with Gotti's rise to the top of the Gambino family, especially with his method of achieving this lofty perch. Most angry was Genovese family boss Vincent "Chin" Gigante. Chin was a friend and contemporary of Castellano, but he also felt safer with someone he could control on the Gambino throne. To justify plotting against Gotti, Gigante invoked the Mafia Commission rule against unsanctioned executions of family leaders.

Gigante contacted Anthony "Gaspipe" Casso, a rising power in the Luchese family, who agreed to a plot to bomb Gotti and his underboss Frank DeCicco with the help of a Genovese associate who was a one-time U.S. Army munitions expert. After weeks of surveillance and dry runs, Casso and Vittorio "Vic" Amuso, brother Robert Amuso, a capo, and bomb expert Herbert Pate were set to move into action on Sunday, April 13, 1986, outside the Veterans and Friends Social Club in Bensonhurst, Brooklyn. Gotti regularly met DeCicco there on Sundays before driving to his Manhattan headquarters at the Ravenite Social Club.

As Casso and the Amusos watched from a parked car, Pate ambled by with a bag of groceries, dropped something near DeCicco's car, and "while picking it up, placed a bag containing explosives under [the] car," Casso told the FBI in 1994 when he began cooperating with authorities.

The Luchese and Genovese families avenged the unsanctioned killing of Paul Castellano with a remote-controlled car bomb that killed Gambino underboss Frank DeCicco on April 13, 1986.

(Courtesy of New York Daily News)

They waited about an hour—with Pate in a car across the street and the others in another car equipped with a police scanner—for DeCicco and Gotti to leave the club and get in the car.

"Pate pulled up alongside DeCicco's car with the window rolled down, detonated the bomb. When the explosion went off, Pate's car was hit with glass and debris," said Casso. They rendezvoused minutes later at a nearby mall. "Herbie was bleeding from his ear, and the (car) had damage to the driver's side door," said Casso.

Unfortunately for the plotters, Gotti had changed his usual routine, and Pate mistook a Luchese soldier for him. DiCicco was killed and the associate injured. A passing police officer took the associate to a nearby hospital, where he recovered from his injuries.

Casso, whose cooperation deal ultimately fizzled, said Gambino capos James "Jimmy Brown" Failla and Daniel Marino were in on the plot and had provided intelligence about Gotti and DeCicco's normal routine. No one was ever charged with the crime. Of the plotters, Gigante is in prison until 2010, Failla died behind bars, Casso and Vic Amuso will never see freedom again, and Marino was released from prison in 2001.

Casso told the FBI that he and Gigante decided to use a bomb to divert suspicion away from them because mobsters are not supposed to use explosive devices. This part of the plan worked, according to a conversation between Gotti and Gravano that was recounted in by Jerry Capeci and Gene Mustain (Onyx, 1996).

"The bomb was fuckin' something," said Gotti. "The car was bombed like they put gasoline on it. You gotta see the car. You wouldn't believe the car."

"I saw it, John. I pulled Frankie out."

"I heard, Sammy. I heard it was too late," said Gotti.

"Who the fuck did it?"

"I don't know ... Who the fuck knows?" said Gotti.

"Chin?"

"Nah, he wouldn't use fuckin' bombs, he'd want you to know. It's some renegade element," said Gotti.

Gotti Falls Prey to the Feds

The boss of the Gambino family will always be a prime target of the FBI, but John Gotti was an especially attractive prey. His brazen coup in downtown Manhattan propelled him into the limelight. Within days, Gotti appeared for a pretrial hearing for his then-pending racketeering and murder trial, dressed to the nines in a double-breasted Armani suit. The Dapper Don loved the attention. His stunning 1987 acquittal in the federal RICO case and his subsequent victories in two state court cases made him the Teflon Don. His confident, cocky manner magnified his stature and irked law enforcement no end.

The feds launched an all-out offensive to get him. From informers the FBI learned that Gotti used an apartment over the Ravenite Social Club to hold top-secret meetings with Gravano and consigliere Frank Locascio. They bugged the apartment on November 20, 1989, and doomed Gotti even before his February 9, 1990, acquittal of assault charges in Manhattan Supreme Court.

Gotti provided federal prosecutors with overwhelming evidence that he was involved in three murders—his own admissions to them in a talk with Locascio on December 12, 1989. The conversation, in which Gotti blamed Gravano for the murders and questioned his loyalty, also spurred the underboss to cooperate. As I detailed in Chapter 21, after hearing the tapes on December 21, 1990, Gravano began pondering his options. He soon decided to roll over on his boss.

On November 10, 1991, Gravano was escorted out of his prison cell at the Metropolitan Correctional Center and was whisked to a secret location to be debriefed by the FBI. Gotti must have heard the prison door slamming shut permanently that night.

At trial, the prosecution hammered Gotti with videotapes taken outside the Ravenite and with his own words on the audiotapes. On March 2, 1992, Gravano took the stand and told all about the plot to kill Paul Castellano, the murders of three soldiers, and assorted other violence. The jury returned a guilty verdict on April 2, 1992. "The Teflon is gone. The don is covered with Velcro, and every charge stuck," said New York FBI boss Jim Fox.

Gotti was sentenced to life on June 23, 1992. Hours later, Gotti was awakened, taken to a local airport, flown to a maximum security prison in Marion, Illinois, and placed in solitary confinement that is designed to break the will of incorrigible criminals and make them conform.

Sustained by great pride and stubbornness, Gotti refused to knuckle under and remained at Marion instead of beginning a gradual procession to less onerous prison levels. According to the feds, he continued to try to run the Gambino family from behind bars. In late 2001, after two battles with cancer, Gotti was incarcerated in a federal prison hospital in Springfield, Missouri. He died on June 10, 2002.

The Least You Need to Know

- Many New York bosses have been promoted by gunfire.
- The Anastasia hit was a perfect coup.
- John Gotti demonstrated incredible self-confidence in the assassination of Paul Castellano.
- Luck plays a big part in coups.

24

Mob Wars Cripple the Colombos

In This Chapter

- ◆ Joe Profaci feels the pressure
- ◆ The Gallo brothers join in
- ◆ Joe Magliocco replaces Profaci
- ◆ Carmine Persico takes the reins

The family became known as the Colombo family in 1970, but in this chapter, I will use the term "Colombo family" to refer to it even during the years when it was headed by Joseph Profaci.

From the late 1920s until 1960, the Colombo family was a relatively stable clan, especially when compared to others, such as the Gambino family. However, once the peaceful mold was broken, the Colombo group has periodically engaged in bursts of violence as various factions battled for control of the powerful New York family.

In this chapter, I will recount attempts by the Gallo brothers to wrest control of the family from a fading Joseph Profaci and his chosen successor,

Joseph Magliocco, in the early 1960s. I will also examine the wild shooting war that broke out in the early 1990s as the Carmine "Junior" Persico faction fought to retain power even though Persico was in prison for life.

Joe Who?

Joseph Profaci, who had a minor criminal record in Italy, rose quickly to the top of a New York La Cosa Nostra family after emigrating from Sicily in 1921. Within seven years of arriving, he attended a gathering of major Sicilian Mafia figures in Cleveland that was raided by cops. An ally of Joe Bonanno before, during, and after the Castellammarese War of 1930–1931, Profaci was based in Brooklyn, but his rackets were far flung. Through close ties with Bonanno and other Mafia leaders, he was a powerful, influential crime boss for decades.

> ### Fuhgeddaboudit
>
> Joseph Profaci emigrated from Villabate, Sicily, and arrived in the United States on September 4, 1921, a few weeks before his twenty-fourth birthday, along with many other Italian immigrants aboard the ship *Providence*. Seven years earlier, 15-year-old Giuseppe "Joseph" Magliocco arrived in New York on the ship *Taormino* with his father, Giovanni, and four siblings: Ninfa, 19, Ambrogio, 13, Antonio, 4, and Giovanni Jr., 3. Eventually, Ninfa "Nina" Magliocco would marry Joe Profaci, and Nina's brother Joseph would become Profaci's brother-in-law and his longtime underboss.

By 1960, Profaci and Magliocco had been in power for 30 years without any assaults on Profaci's power, neither from within his family nor from outside. He maintained alliances with Bonanno, Stefano Magaddino of Buffalo, and the Detroit family (through the marriage of two daughters to sons of powerful Detroit mobsters) and was a close friend of Vincent Mangano, boss of what we now call the Gambino family. Profaci's throne seemed very secure, but the 1960s brought assaults from within that seemed to trigger chaos for the next four decades.

In 1961, Carlo Gambino, Tommy Lucchese, and the Genovese family were raising a serious challenge to the established order that Bonanno, Profaci, and Magaddino had maintained for decades. As always, the way to power in New York was to secure allies on the thrones of other families and use them to increase one's own influence. Gambino was a master at this and was the prime mover in an alliance among the Gambino, Luchese, and Genovese families.

Instrumental to the Gambino plan was the Gallo crew from the Red Hook section of Brooklyn. The core of the group consisted of brothers Lawrence, Joseph, and Albert Gallo. Along with crew members Frank "Punchy" Illiano, John "Mooney" Cutrone, and Joseph "Joe Jelly" Gioelli, they hammered out a living by running jukebox rackets, loan sharking, and gambling, along with many other illegal ways to make a buck or two. Rich they were not, but they wanted to be.

The Gallo brothers were very willing revolutionaries because of the November 4, 1959, murder of Frank "Frankie Shots" Abbatemarco, a crewmember killed on orders from Profaci. From the Gallo perspective, Abbatemarco was a loyal Profaci numbers banker who was killed for falling behind in his tribute to Profaci, not usually a capital offense. Profaci felt Abbatemarco was a disloyal member who was encouraging the Gallo brothers to revolt and needed to be whacked.

The Gallos Roll the Dice

In February 1961, the Gallos made a bold move. They snatched several Profaci leaders off the streets and held them for ransom. The hostages included Profaci's underboss Magliocco, Profaci's brother Frank, and future boss Joseph Colombo. They were held in separate locations as Profaci tried to negotiate a peaceful settlement through the efforts of consigliere Charles "The Sidge" Locicero, who shuffled back and forth between the warring camps.

Within a few weeks, the hostages were released, and a peaceful settlement was accomplished. The Colombos were one big happy family again, or so it seemed for a few months.

Mafia Speak

Joe Colombo earned the respect of his kidnappers during the early stages of his abduction, according to knowledgeable sources. "Early on," said one, "they were acting like assholes, and Colombo said, 'Hey, you treat us like men! We're brothers here. You do what you gotta do but don't abuse us. If you're gonna shoot us, you shoot us, but don't abuse us.'"

Getting Serious

On Sunday, August 20, 1961, Larry Gallo arrived at the Sahara Lounge in Brooklyn to meet mobster John Scimone, a Profaci wiseguy who had been kidnapped six months earlier. They met outside the bar and walked in to talk and share a drink at about 5 P.M., an hour before the bar could open legally because of Sunday "blue laws" then in effect. Owner Charles Clemenza was behind the bar. Suddenly, one of two hoods hiding in the shadows looped a rope around Gallo's neck and tightened it enough to render him near unconsciousness. They pressed the semiconscious Gallo to call his brothers and get them to the bar. He refused. The hit men were about to finish him off when Police Sergeant Edward Meagher, who had noticed a door ajar, walked in to investigate what he thought was a violation of the Sunday blue laws.

The fluke saved Gallo's life. Scimone and the others ran out yelling threats at Clemenza, the bartender. Outside the building, one of them fired a shot into the face of a police officer who had waited outside. The three fled in a white Cadillac.

Big Shot

About six weeks after the attempt on the life of Larry Gallo, one of his young associates made a very bad decision to verbally abuse a Profaci capo on October 4, 1961, when he saw him on a street corner in South Brooklyn, according to *Revolt in the Mafia* by Raymond Martin. Joey Magnasco jumped out of a Gallo car yelling and screaming and grabbed the capo around the collar. As passersby ducked for cover, the capo's brother pulled out a pistol and killed Magnasco.

Within minutes, dozens of squad cars responded, and police found a dazed Larry Gallo and a bartender who claimed to have seen nothing. Four blocks away, police recovered the Cadillac with a shaken John Scimone lying on the sidewalk, claiming to be an innocent victim and saying two hoods had taken him hostage.

Mafia Speak

Joseph Gallo was a shrewd, fearless street fighter who was very, very dangerous. He was often called Crazy Joe Gallo by his peers and the media, but he became something of a folk hero in the early 1960s. He was controversial, quick with one-liners, and often quoted in newspaper stories. When called before the McClellan Rackets Committee in the late 1950s, he walked into the office of chief counsel Robert Kennedy and said, "Nice carpet ya got here, kid. Be good for a crap game."

Larry Gallo said he didn't know his assailant. The prevailing wisdom is that Carmine "Junior" Persico and Salvatore "Sally D" D'Ambrosio were the key players. The white Caddy belonged to Alphonse Cirillo, another Profaci soldier. Gallo refused to cooperate, and no one was charged in the attack.

Unknown before the attempt on Larry Gallo, a few days earlier, one of the crew's most feared soldiers, Joseph "Joe Jelly" Gioelli, disappeared and was killed by the Profaci side. The makers of *The Godfather* movie combined Gioelli's reputation and the attempt on Larry Gallo to create the horrible murder scene involving the Godfather's hit man Luca Brasi.

Two days later, police responded to public pressure and raided the Gallo headquarters in South Brooklyn to give the impression that they were doing all they could to stop the mob violence. Sporadic shooting continued with little consequence except to the families of the dead and wounded. Early in 1962, Carlo Gambino and Tommy Lucchese proposed that the Commission force Profaci to step down after a long and distinguished career for the ultimate good of his family and theirs, too. Joe Bonanno vigorously opposed the suggestion. Bonanno saw Profaci as an important ally who would help sustain Bonanno in power. No decision was made, but the lines were drawn.

Profaci's death due to cancer on June 6, 1962, eliminated one serious topic on the Commission's agenda. However, the dump-Profaci motion was quickly replaced by a dump-Magliocco move when Magliocco called for a quick election and was selected as boss. Gambino and Lucchese were not happy and moved to oust him.

Joe Magliocco's Turn

The rival Colombo factions stalked each other into 1963. Carmine Persico survived a car bombing without serious injury. His longtime enforcer, Hugh McIntosh, was ambushed and shot but suffered only minor injuries. On May 19, 1963, things got very serious. Persico was pulling away from the curb when a Gallo truck slowed in front of him, the back door opened, and three rifle shots hit Persico in the face, shoulder, and hand. Again, the tough gangster survived and came back for more.

By the fall of 1963, the Gallo revolt was over. Joey Gallo was in prison, sentenced on November 15, 1961, to 7 to 14 years for extortion. Crewmembers Ali Waffa and Louis Mariani had been killed in separate incidents, and on December 9, 1963, a grand jury returned an indictment charging 17 Gallo crewmembers with loan sharking, bookmaking, and other crimes.

Throughout this period, Persico was in and out of jail (mostly out) as he battled state and federal indictments through trials and retrials. In 1968, he was convicted of federal hijacking charges in a controversial trial at which Joe Valachi was a prosecution witness. It was the only time Valachi testified at a trial. After years of delays, Persico was jailed in 1971 and served eight years in prison.

In the meantime, Joseph Magliocco and Joseph Bonanno gambled and lost big time. They plotted to eliminate their antagonists on the Commission, Lucchese and Gambino, and were exposed by Joseph Colombo. Magliocco admitted his transgressions and was deposed. The Magliocco/Bonanno plot also helped lead to the overthrow of the Bonanno dynasty in 1964. (This is detailed in Chapter 25.)

Joe Magliocco died on December 28, 1963, and it was all over. Capo Joe Colombo was supported by Gambino and Lucchese and was selected by the Profaci troops as family boss. Larry Gallo died of cancer in 1968. Joey Gallo languished in prison until 1971 and was killed a year later.

Carmine Persico's Turn

After the 1971 shooting and incapacitation of Joe Colombo (which is detailed in Chapter 17), the Persico clan took over leadership of the family. Carmine Persico was in and out of prison, but various acting bosses carried on for him. Persico went down heavily, however, in two major racketeering cases in 1986: the historic Commission case and one against the Colombo family. Sentenced to 139 years, he knew he was done and looked to his son to carry on his legacy.

Alphonse Persico, a college-educated capo, had been convicted with his dad in the Colombo family case and was due out of prison in 1993. In the meantime, the elder Persico named capo Victor "Little Vic" Orena as acting boss. As often happens, the temporary leader began to like the view from the throne. Orena made a pact with John Gotti, cited a bunch of alleged transgressions of Mafia rules by Persico, and asked the Commission to make him official boss.

As tensions increased, loyalists of Carmine Persico, led by consigliere Carmine Sessa, made the first move. On June 20, 1991, Sessa, capo John Pate, and soldiers Henry "Hank the Bank" Smurra and Robert Zambardi drove to Orena's Long Island home armed to the teeth, looking to end the dispute before it began. Orena spotted them, however, escaped, and appealed to the other families. They urged calm, and for a few months, there was no violence. Orena pressed the Commission to depose Persico, while Persico loyalists, led by Sessa, sought to convince the Commission (representatives of the Gambino, Luchese, and Genovese families) that Orena had overstepped his authority as acting boss and was fomenting a revolt.

The situation exploded in violence on November 18, 1991, when two cars of soldiers and associates ambushed Persico capo Greg Scarpa Sr. as he drove his daughter and granddaughter down the Bensonhurst, Brooklyn, block where he lived. No one in Scarpa's car was shot. Several bystanders were hurt by careening cars and ricocheting bullets, but there were no fatalities. The first of 12 to die during the bloody war would come days later.

On November 23, 1991, a crew under Orena loyalist William "Wild Bill" Cutolo ambushed Henry "Hank the Bank" Smurra and pumped three bullets into his head as he sat in his 1988 Lincoln outside a donut shop in Sheepshead Bay, Brooklyn. Cutolo's crew led the way for the Orena faction, killing three of the four Persico faction members who were murdered during the war.

The Persico supporter who got away in the opening salvo of the war came back to haunt the Orenas, however. Scarpa Sr., then 63, wounded Orena capo Joel "Joe Waverly" Cacace in a wild shootout on a busy commercial street in Brooklyn. He killed three Orena loyalists, including one as he was hanging Christmas lights outside his home.

Greg Scarpa Sr.'s resumé is the stuff of mob legend. Standing with Colombo and Persico in the 1960s, he helped beat back the Gallo revolt, was promoted to capo, and was a big moneymaker, earning millions for his mob family, a family he raised with his wife, and one he raised with his *comare*. He picketed the FBI with Joe Colombo in 1970 and killed more than a dozen gangsters over the years, according to court records. "I love the smell of gunpowder," Scarpa told his crew after one shooting.

"If he'd lived 400 years ago, he would have been a pirate," said Scarpa's former lawyer Joseph Benfante.

All the while, however, starting in the late 1950s, Scarpa led a double life as a top echelon informer for the FBI. He secretly explained the Mafia Commission, the induction ceremony, and the Mafia's rules and regulations years before Valachi did it publicly. He informed on Profaci, Colombo, Persico, and scores of other gangsters.

As Tom Robbins and I reported in the *New York Daily News* on June 21, 1994, the FBI sent him on a special mission to the Deep South to help break open a stalled investigation into the 1964 slayings of three civil rights workers by Ku Klux Klansmen. On a J. Edgar Hoover–approved trip to Philadelphia, Mississippi, from July 27 to 30, Scarpa used gangster tactics to learn where the Klan had buried the bodies of Michael Schwerner, Andrew Goodman, and James Chaney when they were killed on June 21.

After FBI agents fingered a Klansman they described as a weak link, Scarpa kidnapped him and brought him to a shanty hidden among tall loblolly pines, as FBI agents waited outside. He tied the man to a chair and demanded to know where the bodies were buried. The first story, which Scarpa relayed to the agents, was phony. So was the second. Scarpa asked one of the agents for his gun, walked inside, put the barrel into the Klansman's mouth and said, "Tell me the fucking truth or I'll blow your fucking brains out." The terrified Klansman gave him the location and the names of the culprits.

During the Colombo war, Scarpa terrified the Orenas, whose members made several search-and-destroy missions without success. Scarpa's work ethic also caused Sessa to goad other Persicos to step up the pace and kill a few guys. "Scarpa's the only one getting anything done," he screamed at one Persico strategy session, Sessa said after he began cooperating. After Sessa's pep talk, a Persico crew killed Orena soldier John Minerva and an associate in front of Minerva's Long Island home.

While Scarpa was killing rival gangsters, he was telling his FBI control agent Lindley DeVecchio what was going on, sort of. On January 7, 1992, Scarpa told DeVecchio the war was still on and the Persico faction was planning to retaliate. Later that day, Scarpa executed capo Nicholas "Nicky Black" Grancio while he sat in his car. "This one's for Carmine," he shouted as he blew Grancio's brains out. The next day, Scarpa told DeVecchio that the Persico faction had whacked Grancio. A week later, he implicated a capo who had no role in the shooting.

Scarpa never worried about dying in a gunfight. He was even more fearless and reckless during the 1991–1993 war, according to friends and enemies alike, because he knew he was dying of AIDS. Scarpa contracted the deadly virus from tainted blood he got from a crewmember in a transfusion he received while undergoing an emergency hiatus hernia operation in 1986. Scarpa's bullheadedness did him in. He forbade doctors from using previously screened blood, insisting that only blood from crewmembers he called to the hospital be used during any transfusion.

Big Shot

On December 8, 1991, Orena faction members killed an 18-year-old worker at a Brooklyn bagel store as they hunted for two Persico loyalists suspected of shooting the son of Orena faction mobster Louis "Bobo" Malpeso. Malpeso sent an inept father and son team, Anthony and Christopher Liberatore, to a bagel shop that the suspects owned with instructions to whack them. As Anthony waited in a car, son Christopher walked in, spoke briefly to the youth, Matteo Speranza, panicked, and shot him to death. The Liberatores pleaded guilty and testified against Malpeso. The jury could not reach a verdict on a murder charge but convicted Malpeso of the attempted murders of a Persico associate and a bystander who were shot and wounded in another Orena assault gone awry.

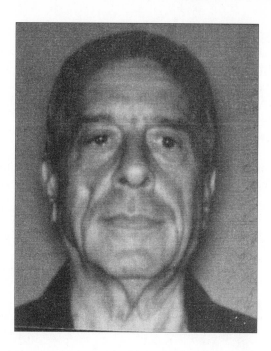

AIDS-ravaged Greg Scarpa Sr. killed three rival gangsters in the bloody 1991–1993 Colombo mob war.

(Courtesy of GangLandNews.com)

On August 26, 1992, Scarpa received a $300,000 settlement from a malpractice suit he filed against Victory Memorial Hospital for negligence in allowing him to contract the AIDS virus from tainted blood supplied by crewmember Paul Mele. When Scarpa appeared in court for the case, police arrested him on a gun rap and for conspiring to murder William "Wild Bill" Cutolo in the fall of 1991. Scarpa pleaded guilty and died in a federal prison hospital ward in June of 1994. By then, his informant work was an open secret, and only his relatives attended the funeral.

Meanwhile, on April 1, 1992, Victor Orena and a key capo, Pasquale "Patty" Amato, were indicted on wartime racketeering charges and for a family murder that took place in November 13, 1989. They were convicted and sentenced to life in prison without parole.

With Scarpa out of the picture after August of 1992, the Persico faction resorted to a teenaged wannabe for its *coup de grace*, the last fatality in the war—capo Joseph Scopo, one-time Orena faction underboss. On October 20, 1993, John Pappa, then 18, killed Scopo in front of his Queens home. The son of slain Genovese mobster Gerard Pappa, young Pappa idolized his father and wanted to become a made guy. He has a macabre tattoo on his back, an Italian inscription saying *morte prima di disonore*—"death before dishonor"—as a headline over two all-seeing eyes that peer out from the middle of his back. Eric Curcio, 25, and John Sparacino, 23, accompanied Pappa on the hit, but when he heard they were taking credit for shooting Scopo, Pappa killed them both.

Convicted of four murders (including Scopo, Curcio, and Sparacico), Pappa got four life terms plus 45 years. If he lives long enough, he could set a record for most time in federal prison. If this is the future of La Cosa Nostra, it's all over for the Mafia.

During these two years, there were scores of murder attempts by both factions. When the shooting stopped, two bystanders, four Persico loyalists, and six Orena supporters were dead; 15 others were wounded by gunshots. In the many court cases that stemmed from the war, Orena and 15 faction members were convicted of various charges, and 13 were acquitted. On the Persico side, 41 were convicted and only one, Alphonse Persico, acquitted. He eventually took control over a much-weakened family.

This eerie tattoo adorns back of wannabe Colombo mobster John Pappa.

(Courtesy of GangLandNews.com)

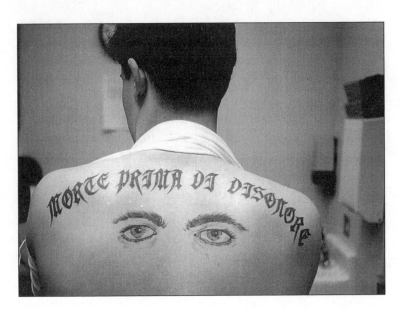

Mafia Speak

From his deathbed, FBI informer Greg Scarpa tried to make amends with Alphonse Persico as Persico neared trial for racketeering and murder for taking part in the Colombo war. In an affidavit, Scarpa said Persico was "a nobody" who was "never earmarked to take on any position in the family at all." Rival hoods "shot at me while I was in a car with my daughter and 2-year-old grandchild," he said. "I was so upset over this that my only intention was to retaliate … I had no instructions to retaliate from anyone, especially Allie Persico … I did not need anybody's permission to act … Allie Persico had nothing to do with any of these events."

The double-crossing and the killings continued, however. In the aftermath of the war, Persico appointed Cutolo, who was also acquitted of all war-related charges, as underboss in a seeming overture for peace. The move was, in reality, a diabolical plot to lure Wild Bill to his death, rather than a promotion. In May of 1999, Cutolo was called to a meeting by Persico and disappeared. His body has not been found, but there is no doubt that he is dead. In Chapter 31, I detail the efforts of William Cutolo Jr. to bring his father's killers to justice. Persico, who pleaded guilty to racketeering charges in a plea bargain that calls for him to spend 13 years in prison, is a suspect in his death.

The Colombos have been battling each other for 40 years. There is no reason to think that will change anytime soon.

The Least You Need to Know

◆ There has been constant turmoil in the Colombo family since 1960.

◆ More than 20 people have died in leadership battles.

◆ Innocent people have been killed in these conflicts.

◆ The leadership of the Colombo family is obviously worth fighting over to some people.

The Joe Bananas Split

In This Chapter

- ◆ A profile of the Bonanno boys
- ◆ How the Bonannos perceive themselves
- ◆ Capeci's opinion of the Bonannos

Joseph Bonanno was a legendary La Cosa Nostra boss. In 1931 at age 26, he took over one of New York's five families when the Mafia Commission was formed at the end of the Castellammarese War. He was the youngest boss approved by the Commission and the only one of the original 24 bosses to be deposed by it. His son, Salvatore "Bill" Bonanno, was a member of his father's mob family and was a major reason why the Commission dethroned the elder Bonanno in 1964 and essentially banished them from Mafia life.

Joe and Bill Bonanno are La Cosa Nostra outcasts who refuse to give it up. For years, they have been telling stories, not to avoid prison terms like so many mob turncoats of the last two decades, but for what seems to be an insatiable need to tell all to anyone who will listen. They broadcast how great they are and have been and how terribly they have been treated by the Mafia and the law. Father (twice) and son (three times) have been convicted of several relatively minor crimes and have served prison terms ranging from one to three years. All things considered, they have done pretty well for themselves. In May 2002, Joe died at age 97 in Tucson. At press time, Bill, 72, was talking about writing yet another book, with, of all people, Joe Pistone, the former FBI agent who infiltrated the Bonanno family in the late 1970s.

In this chapter, I look at their careers and examine their writings to see if, as they assert in their books, they are men of honor who are bound by honor or are severely flawed, whining self-promoters who have gotten away with murder and more for decades.

Introducing the Bonanno Boys

Three generations of Bonanno family men have chosen to live a way of life that outsiders refer to as the Mafia. It is impossible for an outsider to fully comprehend the circumstances that led them in that direction. More than any other family, however, the Bonannos have given their side of the story, in violation of the code of silence they agreed to follow when they were inducted into the secret society they refer to as La Cosa Nostra.

Grandpa Bonanno

Salvatore Bonanno—Joseph Bonanno's father—was a crook, a liar, and perhaps a murderer, according to his son. In 1899, while studying to be a priest, Grandpa Bonanno stole a gold candelabrum, got caught, and was expelled. His explanation was that he did it so his mommy wouldn't make him go back to the seminary. As an adult, Grandpa was accused of murder. To get off, he used his mother to help him fabricate a story that destroyed the reputation of the wife of his main accuser. His mother convinced the woman to go to a midwife for a gynecological exam and obtained intimate physical details of the wife's anatomy—she had a mole near her vagina. Grandpa used this information from the witness stand to support his false claims that he was having an affair with the woman. In his autobiography, *Man of Honor* (1983), Joe Bonanno called his archrival Carlo Gambino a "squirrel of a man." Grandpa Bonanno sounded like a worm.

> **Mafia Speak**
>
> Joe and Bill Bonanno each called rival Carlo Gambino a "squirrel of a man." We don't know what Gambino called Bonanno, but FBI agent and author Bill Roemer described him as "a constant whiner. He complained, he cried, he got sick—anything to gain sympathy. He did not live up to the 'tradition' he speaks about so much in his book."

Daddy Bonanno

Joseph Bonanno arrived in the United States in December of 1924 on a fishing boat that brought him from Havana, Cuba, to Tampa, Florida, the final leg of his journey from Castellammare del Golfo, Sicily. After being detained for a few days by immigration officials in Jacksonville, Florida, Bonanno made it to New York, where he quickly moved into the booming bootleg liquor business. Using powerful Mafia connections—Bonanno implied that his father was a man of honor in Sicily—he beat back an effort by a New York gangster to move in on his operation. At a sitdown to decide who was in the right, Bonanno had three powerful mobsters sitting on his side of the table, including cousin Stefano Magaddino (the Mafia boss of Buffalo) and Salvatore Maranzano (the boss whom Bonanno would ultimately replace). The deck was stacked for him, but reading the account in his book, you might get the impression he had beaten off a man-eating shark.

Fuhgeddaboudit

Joe Bonanno wrote that "one of the proudest moments of my life was the day I became a naturalized U.S. citizen in 1945." According to Rosalie Bonanno, a daughter-in-law of this "great American citizen," one of the contributions made by Bonanno and other Mafia bosses to America was to buy farms so that "they could list the men who worked for them as farm workers and in that way make them ineligible for the draft."

A regular theme of Joe Bonanno's book is that he has been unfairly persecuted by authorities because of false charges that have ruined his reputation. Ironically, Bonanno does what he accuses others of doing in his book, smearing all Irish-American police officers of his day with a simple six word sentence:

"All the Irish cops took payments."

When Joe Bonanno took over for the murdered Salvatore Maranzano in 1931, his economic situation brightened considerably. He became heavily involved in the garment center, owning pieces of the B&D Coat Company and the Morgan Coat Company. Bonanno wrote that his success in this field depended on contacts within the Ladies Garment Workers Union and the merchant's association. He doesn't mention that labor-racketeering schemes with corrupt or frightened union officials gave his companies an unfair advantage over strictly legitimate concerns.

The cheese business would always have an attraction to Bonanno. A Brooklyn family reached out to him to purchase a Wisconsin cheese factory that had been wracked with violence as Chicago hoods battled for control of the enterprise. Bonanno became a partner, and his stature as a Mafia boss prevented the Chicago gangsters from muscling in on the operation.

Bonanno wrote that he also owned part of the Anello and Bonanno Funeral Home and the Brunswick Laundry Service of Brooklyn. In addition, Bonanno bought the 280-acre Sunshine Dairy Farm in upstate New York, near Middleton, which was managed by his uncle John Bonventre. Arizona was home to other Bonanno businesses, including the Alliance Realty and Insurance Company of Tucson and a cotton ranch outside that city.

Although Bonanno wisely invested much of his vast illegal earnings in so-called legitimate businesses and spent much of his time masquerading as a legitimate businessman, his men were also looking for the usual gangster means to make a buck. Bonanno and a number of family members were actively involved in the numbers business.

Carmine Galante was in Montreal muscling into gambling, nightclubs, and other rackets as the Bonanno family asserted control over that Canadian city. Galante also had New York interests, including the Rosina Costume Company and Latamar Shipping. Capo Natale Evola controlled Belmont Garment Delivery service, which required union connections to succeed. Some members, including Vito DeFilippo, ran gambling joints in Haiti. His family, with Bonanno and Galante leading the way, made tons of money in the heroin-smuggling business. All in all, Bonanno controlled a powerful family with legitimate and illegitimate interests around the nation and in Canada and Haiti.

In their books, Joe and Bill constantly praise the elder Bonanno's intelligence and wisdom, but sometimes the actions they describe indicate the exact opposite. In 1963, when the Commission was trying to oust Joe Magliocco from the throne of what we now call the Colombo family, Bonanno permitted his son to live at the Magliocco estate, even though Magliocco was plotting against the powerful bosses. Bill's presence not only suggested that the Bonannos were involved in Magliocco's schemes, it also placed Bill, his wife, and his kids in a dangerous situation.

Bonanno made another stupid move involving his son. In 1964, the failing health of consigliere John Tartamella would not allow him to remain in that position. Bonanno pushed the election of Bill as consigliere. Not only did Bill lack the necessary experience, the action also angered the mobster most deserving of the high post, veteran capo Gaspar DiGregorio, as well as many others. With the backing of Buffalo boss Stefano Magaddino, DiGregorio broke away from the Bonannos, splitting the family.

The Bonannos have consistently denied any involvement in drug dealing by themselves or their family, but the evidence indicates that they knew about it, profited from it, and encouraged their members to continue their drug-trafficking operations. The drug dealing of Bonanno underboss Carmine Galante was discussed in Chapter 11, but there are other examples. In February of 1959, Vincenzo "Vic" Cotroni, leader of Bonanno's Montreal rackets, was arrested in Miami on conspiracy to violate the narcotics laws. In October of 1959, Cotroni's brother Giuseppe pleaded guilty to heroin conspiracy charges lodged after a joint undercover operation by Canadian and American authorities. Despite the guilty plea by Giuseppe and Vic's arrest on drug charges, Bonanno kept Vic in place as his man in Montreal.

Mafia Speak

Some sections of Joe Bonanno's autobiography are difficult to read without closing the book and saying, "You have got to be kidding!" For example, at one point, he writes, "In my family, some activities were clearly considered out-of-bounds. I did not tolerate any dealings in … narcotics." Later on, Bonanno writes, "My tradition outlaws narcotics. It had always been understood that 'men of honor' don't deal in narcotics." Bonanno and his family made millions of dollars in the heroin business.

In the early 1960s, three family bosses accused Bonanno of plotting to kill them in an attempt to maintain or expand his power. New York bosses Carlo Gambino and Tommy Lucchese, as well as Buffalo boss Stefano Magaddino, ordered Bonanno to appear before the Commission to respond to murder conspiracy charges. Bonanno refused and tensions rose dramatically in 1964.

The Commission deposed Bonanno and recognized longtime Bonanno capo Gaspar DiGregorio as family boss. Over the next four years, an undeclared war of nerves and periodic shootings broke out. Eventually, Bonanno gave up his family and conceded defeat by retiring to Arizona. His vain attempts in his book to say that he had unified the family and then voluntarily retired simply do not stand up to the evidence. Bonanno was outfought and outthought by his rivals as his retreat clearly shows.

Slammer Time

Bonanno capo Natale Evola is another family member who was convicted of a narcotics conspiracy during Joe Bonanno's reign. Evola was sentenced in 1960 to five years and a $10,000 fine. Evola would go on to become boss of the family from 1970 until his death from natural causes on August 28, 1973.

Billy Boy Bonanno

Bill Bonanno was 22 years old when he was inducted into his father's crime family. He recalls the day well. "I remember that it was a chilly gray day in Brooklyn. It was in the spring of 1954. I took my 'oath of office' in a large warehouse in Brooklyn. The heads of the other four New York families—Joe Profaci, Tommy Lucchese, Frank Costello, and Albert Anastasi—were there, along with several other bosses from Buffalo, Milwaukee, Chicago, and Philadelphia."

In those four sentences, Bonanno puts the lie to his entire 282-page book, *Bound by Honor* (St. Martin's Press, 1999). There is as much chance that eight visiting Mafia bosses attended his induction ceremony as there is that I attended. In fact, there is less chance that they all attended. At least I was in Brooklyn in 1954.

As Bill Bonanno knows, only family members can attend an induction ceremony. Not La Cosa Nostra members, but members of that family. Every FBI informer, every Mafia turncoat, every organized crime expert who has ever testified about it in federal court has made that clear, from Joe Valachi on down. This information was confirmed at two inductions that were tape-recorded by authorities. There have been several occasions when mobsters were excluded from induction ceremonies of their sons or brothers because they were being "made" by other families. But Bill Bonanno wants us to believe that the Bonanno family let the boss of Milwaukee attend an induction. Bonanno's assertions are laughable.

Fuhgeddaboudit

With all those Mafia bosses supposedly at Bill Bonanno's induction, there probably wasn't enough room for Bonanno soldier Joseph "Bayonne Joe" Zicarelli. At least he never mentioned being there when he was picked up on an illegal FBI bug 10 years later, talking about Bill: "This guy is sick and I think he is a little crazy … or else he's immature to a point where from being born with a silver spoon in his mouth, and don't know what hardship is." Rosalie Bonanno never used the words "silver spoon" in her book, but she did write that "at 14 he had his own car."

Where's Big Daddy Bonanno?

In the fall of 1964, a decade after Bill Bonanno was inducted into his father's crime family, father and son were living together at Bill's East Meadow home. On October 20, the night before Joe was scheduled to appear before a grand jury, he dined with his New York lawyer William Maloney and two others. After dinner, three of the group, including Bonanno, took a taxi to Maloney's Park Avenue apartment.

About midnight, as Bonanno exited from a cab, two men grabbed him by the arms and moved him toward a waiting car. Maloney told police he pursued them but backed away when one of the kidnappers fired a shot at his feet. They shoved the Mafia boss into the back seat and sped away.

It was a stunning development and made news all over North America. For many, it looked as if Bonanno was history; but for those in the know, the event made no sense. Few knew what actually happened, and the federal government began pulling mobsters in front of grand juries to try to get to the bottom of the affair.

Nearly two months later, Maloney announced that Bonanno was alive and would be appearing before the grand jury on Monday, November 21, 1964. The media went wild, but on Monday there was no banana. In fact, Bonanno didn't publicly appear again until May 17, 1966.

Mafia Speak

On Thursday, October 22, the boys over at Simone "Sam the Plumber" DeCavalcante's plumbing business were speculating along with the New Jersey boss about the Bonanno kidnapping. At one point, DeCavalcante said that none of the bosses knew what was going on. Underboss Frank Majuri then offered what the feds and everyone but the Bonannos have concluded: "Then he must have done it himself."

The Bonanno Tales

Joe and Bill Bonanno wrote about this incident in their books, and Bill gave information to author Gay Talese for his book *Honor Thy Father* (World Publishing, 1971). Joe says the two men grabbed him and threw him into a car, and they took off into the night, finally stopping at a remote New York State farmhouse. There, over the next six weeks, Bonanno claimed, he engaged in debate with his cousin and rival Stefano Magaddino, the man who was behind the kidnapping.

A month and a half later, Bonanno was driven for two days and nights into Texas and was dropped off in El Paso. From there, he phoned a trusted man from Tucson, Arizona, who called his wife in New York, assured her that he was fine, and then picked him up and drove him back to Tucson. On Thursday, December 17, 1964, Bonanno's friend called Bill Bonanno at a Long Island phone booth that the two had previously agreed to use if an emergency ever arose.

The next day, Bill Bonanno phoned his father's lawyer, Bill Maloney, with the resulting press conference and the no-show of Daddy Bonanno on Monday, December 21. After this, Bill Bonanno claims that he lived in fear until May of 1965, not knowing whether his father was dead or alive. At that time, while Bill was jailed briefly for refusing to testify before a grand jury about his father's disappearance, his uncle Frank Labruzzo visited him, and by code, let him know that the senior Bonanno was alive.

Legendary Mafia boss Joe Bonanno claims to be a man of honor who has been wronged by the Mafia as well as the law.

(Courtesy of GangLandNews.com)

Joe Bonanno claims that he hid in Tucson for some time and then secretly moved back to New York, where he used disguises to move around. Bill was kept in the dark about his dad's whereabouts so that he wouldn't have legal problems by refusing to testify or lying about his father's whereabouts. (The thought that a made guy would worry about lying to a grand jury is an insult to anyone who has passed the age of reason.) The essential Bonanno points are that Joe was kidnapped, then went into hiding, and Bill didn't know he was alive until May of 1965. Let's see how that story stands up.

Capeci's Analysis

The Bonanno story of the kidnapping was a hoax from start to finish. The so-called man of honor wanted to avoid a grand jury appearance. He didn't want to testify, and a refusal would have meant a jail term of indeterminate length, something Bonanno really wanted to avoid.

In the early 1950s, Bonanno managed to avoid testifying before the Kefauver Committee. In the late 1950s, he evaded the grand juries inquiring into the circumstances of the 1957 Apalachin meeting. In the early 1960s, he ducked the McClellan hearings.

In fact, Bonanno went to prison in Canada in the summer of 1964 in a vain attempt to avoid being sent back to the United States and subpoenaed to appear before a grand jury.

In support of this theory, I offer a summary of an FBI tape recording made on Wednesday, December 23, 1964, of a conversation in the office of Simone "Sam the Plumber" DeCavalcante, the New Jersey boss. DeCavalcante was talking to Joe Notaro, Bonanno's most loyal capo. He told Notaro that the Commission would probably ask Notaro about "this kidnap move." To this, Notaro replied, "This was regarding an indictment that was supposed to be coming up." Notaro didn't want to talk further about the event, but his words clearly show that Bonanno faked a kidnapping to avoid testifying to the grand jury.

Another factor that cries hoax is Bonanno going out without bodyguards despite the state of insurrection within his family.

> **Mafia Speak**
>
> Before her 1956 marriage, Rosalie Profaci spoke to hubby-to-be Bill Bonanno about religion. His remarks show how people like Joe and Bill Bonanno justify their way of life. Rosalie quotes Bill as saying, "A person who sees things the way you do might think I have sinned, and I might think I have simply done what I had to do." In his autobiography, her father-in-law justified his criminal ways much the same way: "The way of life I and my friends had chosen was but a means to attain social advancement and respectability. We didn't consider ourselves criminals."

There are many other discrepancies in the Bonanno stories about the kidnapping, but the boys at Sam the Plumber's office, who didn't know the FBI was tape-recording their conversations and had no reason to make up stories, put the lie to Bill's claim that he was living in fear, not knowing whether his father was alive or dead until he received a phone call from a mysterious stranger on Thursday, December 17, 1964.

On December 23, 1964, the FBI bug in DeCavalcante's New Jersey office picked up Bonanno mobsters Joe Notaro, Vito DeFilippo, and Joe Zicarelli visiting DeCavalcante to discuss the Bonanno affair. Notaro and DeFilippo were staunch Bonanno loyalists; Zicarelli, at this point, was sitting on the fence.

Notaro said he had met with Bonanno, who had agreed to step down effective whatever date was convenient for Notaro, who still had to negotiate some details with the Commission about the last few Bonanno members still allied with Bonanno. At this point, DeFilippo said that the meeting took place two weeks earlier and that

Bonanno, underboss John Morales, consigliere Bill Bonanno, and six or seven capos who were still loyal to the Bonannos were all there.

So Daddy and Billy Boy Bonanno sat down together at a meeting more than a week before the supposedly dramatic December 17, 1964, phone call informing Bill Bonanno that his dad was safe.

There is no doubt about this. Joe Bonanno tried to avoid problems with the law and the Commission by faking his own kidnapping. He and his son tried to protect Bill from government efforts to have Bill tell where his father was. The idea that Bill didn't have a clue and thus would not be lying if he said that before a grand jury is preposterous. Everyone but the Bonannos seems to recognize how ludicrous the story was and is.

It was a hoax that backfired. The publicity forced the government to apply constant pressure to find the elusive Mafia boss. In turn, the pressure tied the Bonannos in knots. Bill even served time for contempt. With Daddy Bonanno absent, other mob bosses were even more paranoid than usual and were even more anxious to have Bonanno removed from power. They tried to entice his men to defect. The net result was that Joe and Bill Bonanno had to retreat west to stay alive. Tactically and strategically, the kidnapping was a disaster as well as a hoax.

We are fortunate that Bill Bonanno and his late father possessed huge egos and tried desperately to rewrite history throughout the years. Their contributions have done little to increase our knowledge of La Cosa Nostra but have done much to convince us, and others, that they are anything but men of honor. After reading their books, watching their movies, and listening to some of their interviews, we have a much better understanding of why mob powers like Carlo Gambino, Tommy Lucchese, and Stefano Magaddino didn't trust them. We also know why Sal Profaci, son of the late boss Joe Profaci, and his cousin, also named Sal Profaci, a brother-in-law of Bill Bonanno, refused to support the Bonannos when Joe Profaci died in 1962. The Bonanno boys were bad news.

The Least You Need to Know

- Joe and Bill Bonanno have tried to rewrite history.

- Their efforts to rewrite history continually fail.

- The Joe Bonanno kidnapping was a hoax.

Chapter 26

The Canadian Mob Hits

In This Chapter

◆ Canada's king of the bootleggers

◆ The case against Albert Agueci

◆ The story of Paolo Violi

Canada has long had numerous organized crime organizations operating within its borders. Some, like Montreal's West End Gang, are entirely homegrown; others, like La Cosa Nostra, are offshoots of foreign enterprises from countries such as Nigeria, Russia, Jamaica, China, and Italy.

No one group dominates organized crime in Canada. Some groups are more structured than others, but even these have an ebb and flow to their membership, activities, and the rackets in which they engage. Before the mid-1960s, when Canadian laws were heavily weighted in favor of European immigrants, there was no problem with Jamaican gangs or Nigerian scam artists. Now, however, there are criminals of every ethnic background in Canada.

That being said, the focus of this book is La Cosa Nostra, the unique American version of the Sicilian Mafia. In this chapter, I discuss some major murders that took place in Canada that were related to La Cosa Nostra. The New York–based Bonanno family had a crew in Montreal,

Quebec, and the Buffalo, New York, family had influence all through the Niagara peninsula, including Hamilton and Toronto, Ontario. The murders I discuss have connections to these two organizations.

Rocky Goes for a Walk

Rocco Perri was one of Canada's prime crime figures during the 1920s and 1930s. Perri emigrated from Plati in the Italian province of Calabria, arriving in North America in 1903. He landed in the United States but by 1912 was living in the Toronto/Hamilton area of Ontario. Within a few years, Perri was actively involved in bootlegging, taking advantage of various prohibitions against alcohol in Ontario and Canada.

In 1920, when Prohibition went into effect in the United States, Perri and his organization were well versed in the illegal movement and sale of liquor and beer, and they became major players in moving booze into the United States. They were aided greatly by Canadian laws that made it legal to transport and sell liquor to customers outside Canada, no matter what the liquor laws of the receiving country were, until June 1930. It was a golden opportunity, and Perri quickly took advantage.

For about 10 years, Perri was one of Canada's major bootleggers, Canada's Al Capone, in more ways than one: A number of Calabrian competitors had been killed earlier during the Prohibition era, and the prevailing wisdom is that Perri played a role in their demise. Until James Dubro and Robin Rowland wrote *King of the Mob* (Penguin Books, 1987), however, few Canadians of the last 50 years had even heard of Perri. Much of the information that follows comes from their writing and research.

According to Dubro and Rowland, two Perri common-law wives took part in his bootlegging operations. Bessie Starkman left her husband for Perri back in 1913 when they were both penniless. She rose to become the business brains behind their extensive bootlegging operations and had a reputation of being very tight with a buck.

> **Big Shot**
>
> The August 13, 1930, murder of Bessie Starkman appears to break the Mafia rule about killing women. That restriction was meant to apply to women who were not directly involved in Mafia affairs, however. This clearly was not the case with Bessie.

On August 13, 1930, Perri and Starkman arrived home and parked in a detached double garage behind their large home in Hamilton, Ontario. After getting out of the car, Starkman headed for the door leading toward the back of the home. Three shotgun blasts rang out, and two hit her, killing her instantly. Perri was unharmed. He told police that by time he got to the murder scene, Bessie's killer was gone.

Within days, Antonio Papalia, a member of Perri's organization, was arrested. He was linked to two stolen New York State license plates that were found a few blocks from the murder scene. But after a lengthy investigation, no additional evidence was discovered, charges were dropped, and Papalia was released.

Papalia wasn't the only suspect, however. Most of the credible theories about Starkman's death revolved around her personality. The one involving Papalia was based on her failure to support members of the gang who had met misfortune, legal or otherwise, while working for the Perris. Another connected her death to her difficulties with a Rochester, New York, gang that had supplied her with dope which she failed to pay for. Perri was also a suspect for reasons including infidelity. Some of the theories intertwined, but no one was ever charged with her murder.

Mafia Speak

Antonio Papalia was a member of the Rocco Perri bootleg gang during Prohibition. When Rocco's common-law wife Bessie Starkman was gunned down on August 13, 1930, Papalia was a suspect. According to *King of the Mob*, Papalia denied involvement in a newspaper interview. "Rocco is my friend … even if I knew who did it, I would tell him first … not the police."

If Perri did her in, his actions didn't help his business. Over the next 13 years, his fortunes gradually declined. The end of American Prohibition in 1933 and Ontario's decision to control liquor sales cut into his income dramatically. He also had lots of enemies, perhaps the same ones who took out Bessie. On Sunday, March 20, 1938, a bomb destroyed the front porch of his Hamilton home. Eight months later, the gangster's DeSoto was blown up with Perri and associates Frank DiPietro and Fred Carlo inside. Incredibly, Perri wasn't injured but the other two were seriously hurt. Like the murder of his wife, no one was ever charged in these attacks.

Fuhgeddaboudit

Despite a La Cosa Nostra rule against the use of explosive devices, bombs have been a part of Mafia life for nearly a century. In an apparent botched attempt against Buffalo boss Stefano Magaddino, an assailant threw a bomb into the home of his next-door neighbor on May 19, 1936, killing the occupant, Magaddino's sister, Mrs. Nicholas Longo. In 1963, the Gallo gang planted a bomb in the car belonging to rival Carmine Persico. In 1981, Philadelphia boss Phil Testa was murdered by a bomb. As detailed in Chapter 23, Gambino underboss Frank DeCicco was killed by a bomb—it was also meant for his boss John Gotti—that was placed under DeCicco's car and detonated by remote control in 1986.

World War II brought more difficulties for Perri. For Canadians, the war began in 1939, and the government carried out a plan, now accepted as illegal and immoral, to inter Japanese and Italian residents of Canada because Japan and Italy were allies of Nazi Germany. According to Dubro and Rowland, the federal government used this roundup as a backdoor attack on suspected criminals of Italian descent. Perri was included in this group. He was picked up on June 10, 1940, and was interred until October 10, 1943. By then, Italy was out of the war and no longer viewed as an enemy.

During his absence, new alliances were formed in the Italian organized crime community. Buffalo family boss Stefano Magaddino had extended his influence in Ontario, and some of Perri's former men, including Antonio Papalia, had signed on.

In the spring of 1944, Perri was trying to re-establish some of his rackets in Hamilton, without much success. He obviously rankled someone with ties to Magaddino. On the morning of Sunday, April 23, 1944, he left his cousin's home in Hamilton and went for a walk. He was never seen again. Since then, the Buffalo family has exerted considerable influence in Ontario—via members, associates, and allies—right through the century.

Rocco Perri, Canada's Al Capone, survived bomb blasts at his home and in his car, but he never returned from a quiet Sunday walk in April of 1944.

(Courtesy of GangLandNews.com)

The Story of Poor Albert

Albert Agueci and his brother Vito, members of the Buffalo La Cosa Nostra family, lived in Toronto, Ontario. They emigrated from the Sicilian town of Salemi, where they were closely connected to the Mafia family there. They arrived in Canada in 1950. Both were arrested for a huge "French Connection" heroin conspiracy that employed French criminals as middlemen between the Sicilian Mafia and the North American La Cosa Nostra, which wholesaled the drugs. Often, the illegal product would be moved to Canada first and then smuggled across the border to American customers. This is where the Aguecis fit in.

Albert was in the bakery business in Toronto with Benedetto Zizzo, whose brother was the Mafia boss of their hometown. By the end of the 1950s, Albert was very well connected and was a made member of the Magaddino family, whose territory included the Toronto neighborhood where Agueci lived.

It was during this period that Albert and Vito Agueci became intertwined with Joseph "Joe Cago" Valachi in the heroin business. The Aguecis would receive the product from Europe and smuggle it across the United States border to Valachi and other members of the Genovese family in New York City.

At the time, Valachi and mobster Vince Mauro worked in a crew under capo Anthony "Tony Bender" Strollo. Both Strollo and Magaddino, the boss of the Aguecis, would have received a piece of their respective gangsters' profits. However, at around that time, the Apalachin era, there was a "ban" against drug dealing in La Cosa Nostra, so it is likely that Magaddino pretended not to know the source of the tribute he was receiving from the Aguecis.

In the spring of 1959, Joe Valachi was indicted on heroin conspiracy charges but learned of his impending arrest and fled to Connecticut. On November 19, 1959, after a tip from an informer, Valachi was arrested. He was fortunate to receive bail while his lawyers tried to make a deal with the government. He was set to go to trial in February of 1960 if he didn't make a deal. As February approached, he fled to Canada with the help of Albert Agueci.

Valachi was in Toronto for a day or two when Strollo ordered him back to New York. Valachi claims he was told not to worry, that a light sentence had been negotiated. On June 3, 1960, he was shocked when he received 15 years. Fourteen days later he was locked up in an Atlanta prison.

A year later, Valachi was charged in another heroin-trafficking conspiracy and returned to New York. While awaiting trial, he was housed in the Federal House of Detention on West Street in New York City with Albert Agueci. The Aguecis were indicted in the same case as Valachi, and Albert was angry that the Buffalo family hadn't raised bail money for him and his brother.

Valachi claims that Albert Agueci was vocal in his criticism of Magaddino's lack of action, particularly for not arranging bail. According to Valachi, Albert threatened to implicate Magaddino in the drug conspiracy if he didn't arrange the release of his brother. In September of 1961, Albert got out when his wife sold their new Toronto home and raised the bail money. Brother Vito remained behind bars.

> ### Slammer Time
>
> Joe Valachi told author Peter Maas (*The Valachi Papers*, 1968) that while awaiting trial for narcotics conspiracy in the Federal House of Detention in New York in September 1961, he met Albert Agueci, a Toronto-based member of the Buffalo family. Valachi said he knew that Agueci couldn't stand being in prison and would do anything to get out. "I could see right away that Agueci wasn't going to last long."

When Albert Agueci returned to Canada, he immediately arranged to confront Magaddino. Just what happened next is unclear, but Albert ended up dead. On October 8, 1961, Agueci left Toronto on his way to a court appearance in New York. An illegal FBI bug in a Buffalo mob haunt picked up some partial information about a man being taken to a farm to be cut up. On November 23, 1961, his mutilated body was found in a field near Rochester, New York.

No one was charged in the murder, but law enforcement officials believe that Agueci's death stemmed from his wild threats toward Magaddino. No Mafia boss will tolerate a threat by an underling to inform against him. After Vito heard what happened to Albert, he was no longer interested in making bail. In March of 1962, Vito was sentenced to 15 years for drug dealing.

The Rise and Fall of Paolo Violi

In the early 1950s, Montreal, Quebec, was a wide-open city with gambling, prostitution, and hundreds of clubs featuring live entertainment. Corrupt politicians controlled a police force that was weakened by political appointments and members on the take. It was also a key stop for heroin on its way into New York City. Overseeing this wild scene was Carmine "Lilo" Galante, a powerful Bonanno family capo and a favorite of boss Joe Bonanno.

Not everyone favored this wild-west atmosphere, and a strong reform party won the election in 1954 under the leadership of lawyer Jean Drapeau, who was elected mayor. After taking office, Drapeau applied pressure to Galante and some of his key American aides. A year later, Galante was expelled, and the Bonanno leadership in Montreal fell to Salvatore Giglio until he, too, was shown the border in 1957.

Fuhgeddaboudit

Montreal wasn't the exclusive domain of the Bonanno family. Many other gangs have existed side by side with them. A small sampling—from the 1970s era—includes the Montreal Chapter of Satan's Choice, the Popeye Motorcycle gang that evolved into the Montreal Chapter of the Hells Angels; the Dubois brothers who carved out drug territory in the downtown and old section of Montreal; and the West End Gang who engaged in drug dealing in their section of Montreal.

Luigi Greco and Vincenzo Cotroni became the Bonanno family's key players in Montreal. Greco was a Sicilian; his friend Cotroni was Calabrian. Between them, they put together a strong crew of made members of the Bonanno family, along with a much larger gang of associates who were involved in gambling, hijacking, counterfeiting, stock-market scams, prostitution, robberies, and many other rackets. A large chunk of the profits from these scams would be sent south on a regular basis as tribute to the Bonanno leadership.

By the 1970s, times were once again changing. The rise of French nationalism had the political situation in turmoil. On the crime front, the balance of power shifted quickly on December 7, 1972, when Luigi Greco was killed in an explosion, and the Sicilian faction of the Montreal crew died with him. Ironically, his death resulted from the unusual work ethic Greco had when it came to a pizzeria he owned. He was personally scrubbing down the kitchen with gasoline to remove caked-on grease when the fumes were ignited by a pilot light.

Meanwhile, Vincenzo Cotroni was aging, ailing, and jailed, and the leadership of the Montreal mob fell to Paolo Violi, a Calabrian Canadian who married into a powerful Calabrian family from Ontario that was in the orbit of Buffalo's Magaddino family.

In November of 1973, Violi traveled to New York to cast his vote for Philip Rastelli as the new Bonanno boss to replace Natale Evola, who had died earlier that year. It was a sure sign of his rise to the top.

Cotroni was in and out of prison, fighting a one-year sentence for refusing to testify at the Quebec Police Commission Inquiry into Organized Crime. According to Royal

Canadian Mounted Police wiretaps, Violi seized the opportunity and got permission from boss Phil Rastelli to take charge of the family's Montreal crew.

Cotroni, and later Violi, had lots of trouble with the Sicilian wing of the crew after the death of Greco. Things got so bad that Violi sought permission from Rastelli to kill the emerging leader of the faction, Nick Rizzuto. Rastelli refused the request, but Rizzuto and some of his key men moved to Venezuela for a period of time, and they built a lucrative heroin network there.

Slammer Time

When Montreal hood Paolo Violi was arrested for refusing to testify before the Quebec Organized Crime Commission in 1977, he was incarcerated. He didn't waste all his time behind bars. Every day, he wrote elaborate love letters to his wife. "Violi wrote to her five times a day, every day," according to an article by Ann Charney in *Weekend Magazine*. "Even more amazing, the letters are not hastily tossed off notes. Each sheet has its margins decorated with drawings of birds, animals, hearts, flowers. The writing is sometimes in verse and, like the drawings, is beautifully executed."

Around this time, on January 24, 1974, Carmine Galante was released from federal prison after a long stretch for heroin trafficking. Galante had one thing on his mind—a return to power. To do that, he would need to win the support of the capos and make money. Those desires brought about changes in Montreal.

Slammer Time

Frank Cotroni was a younger brother of Vic Cotroni, the long-time Bonanno capo in Montreal. Frank was a media darling and was credited with power that didn't really exist. He was a glorified drug dealer who kept getting caught at his trade. He was convicted and jailed three times for narcotics conspiracies. In addition, he was given an eight-year sentence in 1987 for a murder conspiracy.

Galante was New York born but of Sicilian heritage. He aligned himself with Montreal's Sicilian wing, took advantage of legal problems that had befallen Rastelli, and made a power play for the top spot of the Bonanno family.

This was bad news for Violi, who was handicapped by two consecutive one-year sentences for failing to testify at the Crime Inquiry and for an extortion charge. On February 8, 1977, while Violi was in prison, his brother Frank was shot to death by two gunmen who surprised him at an import/export firm that he ran. This was a sure warning to Violi that he was a target, and everyone on the street was aware of his precarious position. In late 1977, Violi was released from prison to face an open rebellion by the Sicilians.

On December 20, 1977, cops became suspicious about a group of men they thought were stalking someone, but they failed to identify the intended victim. They tailed the suspects to an alleyway behind the Jean Talon Bar, which was next to Violi's head-quarters. But police failed to link them to Violi.

A month later, on Sunday, January 22, 1978, Violi was playing cards in the Jean Talon Bar when a masked gunman fired both barrels from a sawed-off shotgun into Violi's head, killing him instantly.

Police quickly arrested four men as material witnesses, including a brother-in-law of Nick Rizzuto. Eventually, three associates of the Sicilian faction pleaded guilty to conspiracy to murder. Any lingering thoughts of revenge disappeared on October 17, 1980, when Rocco Violi, the last of the Violi brothers, was killed.

The Sicilians were now clearly back on top in Montreal. Vic Cotroni had little choice but to accept the death of his protégé and be content that he hadn't been whacked. He faded into the background and died of cancer in September of 1984. The Rizzuto crew was in control.

Giuseppe "Joe" LoPresti was a very important player in Rizzuto's crew. They came from the same Sicilian hometown, and LoPresti lived in a luxurious home in Montreal on a secluded cul-de-sac with Rizzuto, his son Vito—a key crew member whose Bonanno family exploits are detailed in Chapter 28—and Nick's son-in-law as his only neighbors. LoPresti was well plugged-in to Montreal's Mafia powers and was a major player in the heroin trade.

In 1982, LoPresti was overheard on an FBI bug making major heroin deals with Gambino family soldiers Angelo Ruggiero and Gene Gotti. Bonanno soldier Gerlando Sciascia, of Montreal, and Eddie Lino and John Carneglia, two of the shooters John Gotti used to take out Paul Castellano in 1985, were also picked up on the bug. All were indicted on heroin-trafficking charges.

Big Shot

John "Johnny Pops" Papalia, son of Buffalo family soldier Antonio Papalia, was one of Canada's most famous gangsters in the last quarter of the twentieth century, acting as an Ontario representative for the Buffalo family. On May 31, 1997, a street punk killed Papalia with a shot to the head in a parking lot, later claiming he did so on the orders of Calabrian hoods Pat and Angelo Musitano. In a plea bargain, the Musitanos pleaded guilty to murder conspiracy in the killing of a Papalia lieutenant, and murder charges in Papalia's murder were dropped. The shooter, Ken Murdock, was sentenced to life with a likelihood of parole in 13 years. The Musitanos received 10 years.

After two mistrials, Gene Gotti and Carneglia were convicted in 1989 and were sentenced to 50 years. LoPresti, Lino, and Sciascia went to trial separately and were acquitted in 1990. Gambino turncoat Sammy "Bull" Gravano revealed the following year that he had paid $10,000 to a juror to fix the case.

Good luck didn't last too long for LoPresti. On April 29, 1992, he left his exclusive Montreal home and was found later that day wrapped in plastic beside a train track with a bullet in his head. No one has been charged with his killing. Seven years later, Sciascia, who had been kicked out of Canada, was shot to death in Manhattan—his body was dumped on a Bronx street—allegedly on orders from Bonanno boss Joseph Massino (see Chapter 28 for more on this).

Bonanno soldier Joe LoPresti was killed in 1992, two years after he was acquitted of shipping heroin from Montreal to Gambino family soldiers in New York.

(Courtesy of GangLandNews.com)

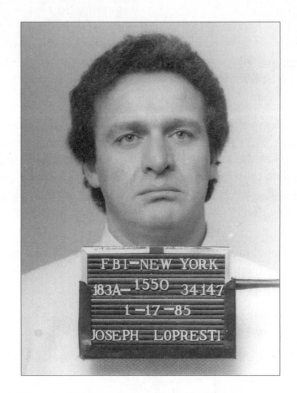

The Least You Need to Know

- Canadian wiseguys made hay—and cash—during the Prohibition Era in the United States.

- Canada has its own serious Mafia hoods.

- Toronto had some Buffalo Mafia members.

- Montreal has a branch of the Bonanno family.

Part 6

The New Millennium

The New Millennium found the law enforcement community battling some old, veteran gangsters in the never-ending cat-and-mouse game that the longtime adversaries have been waging for decades. In this section, I will detail racketeering and other charges against new leaders of New York's five families, as well as the death in federal prison of the most well-known mobster of his generation, John Gotti, the one-time swashbuckling Dapper Don.

You'll also meet several up-and-coming Generation X gangsters who grew up with Madonna, bungee jumping, and *The Simpsons,* and will learn about some new age schemes and scams they've used to reap tremendous rewards and an all-out assault from The Law. I'll also update decades of scandalous activity by some FBI agents in Boston and examine the latest revelations about the disappearance and murder of former Teamsters Union president Jimmy Hoffa.

Chapter 27

The End of an Era

In This Chapter

♦ The Dapper Don dies in prison

♦ More Gottis go to jail

♦ Chin Gigante gives up his insanity act

♦ "Little Al" D'Arco gets his due

On June 10, 2002, John Gotti died of throat cancer in a federal prison hospital. He had been diagnosed with the cancer four years earlier as he served a life sentence for his racketeering and murder conviction at the federal penitentiary in Marion, Illinois.

In this chapter, I examine the death of the once swashbuckling Dapper Don and the crime family he left behind. I also discuss an important but somewhat less dramatic milestone of Gotti's longtime rival and nemesis, Vincent "Chin" Gigante, the boss of the city's most powerful Mafia family: his public admission that he had feigned insanity for years in an effort to avoid prosecution. And I detail the very impressive credentials of one-time Luchese acting boss Alphonse "Little Al" D'Arco, the most important mob defector to testify in both the twentieth and twenty-first centuries.

John Gotti Dies in Prison

The last decade of John Gotti's life was far from what he would have wanted, but when Gotti finally succumbed to throat cancer, he got a showy, spectacular sendoff he surely believed he deserved.

A remembrance card for mourners at John Gotti's wake.

(Courtesy of GangLandNews.com)

JOHN GOTTI

A huge motorcade of about 75 limousines, including 19 flower cars and a police escort, guided the late Dapper Don to his final resting place in St. John's Cemetery in Middle Village, Queens, next to his father and his son Frank, who died in a tragic accident in 1980 at age 12.

Along the way, the 10-block-long procession snaked through Gotti's Howard Beach neighborhood past his modest home as throngs of residents waved their good-byes to their larger-than-life neighbor. It was the same scene in Ozone Park, as the motorcade passed his Queens headquarters, the Bergin Hunt and Fish Club, where Gotti had spoken so glowingly about himself, predicting a superlative legacy for himself as boss of the Gambino family only a few days after his predecessor had been laid to rest at a much more serene sendoff.

Mafia Speak

Listen carefully to me. You'll never see another guy like me if you live to be 5000.

—John Gotti, January 29, 1998

"We're going to put this thing together where they could never break it, never destroy it, even if we die," he had said 16 years earlier, his words—as they often were during his tumultuous reign—recorded for posterity.

> ### Fuhgeddaboudit
>
> Laminated cards that were distributed to mourners at John Gotti's wake had a smiling photo of the Dapper Don on one side and the following words on the other:
>
> Do not stand at my grave and weep;
> I am not there, I do not sleep.
> I am a thousand winds that blow;
> I am the diamond glints on snow.
> I am the sunlight on ripened grain;
> I am the gentle autumn's rain.
> When you awaken in the morning's hush,
> I am the swift uplifting rush
> Of quiet bird in circled flight.
> I am the soft star that shines at night.
> Do not stand at my grave and cry.
> I am not there; I did not die.

From the time his brother Richard, his son Peter, and six other pallbearers carried his bronze coffin into a gray hearse outside the Papavero Funeral Home in Maspeth, Queens, at 10:30 A.M. on Saturday June 15, 2002, until two hours later when Gotti's widow, other family members, and close friends placed red roses around his coffin and left gravediggers to do their work, scores of reporters and photographers—including four media helicopters—accompanied the late Dapper Don to his final resting place.

The former New York City sanitation worker followed his brother John into the Gambino crime family and into federal prison.

(Courtesy of GangLandNews.com)

His son John A. "Junior" and brothers Gene and Peter were scattered in separate federal prisons and unable to take part, with Peter having been jailed only a week earlier following a racketeering indictment. But wife Victoria and daughters Angel and Victoria paid homage to him, and after the funeral, the family gathered at the home of Gotti's favorite child and most outspoken family member, daughter Victoria, for a traditional family meal.

Dissed by His Peers

Despite all the pomp and circumstance, and like much of Gotti's reign atop the Gambino crime family, the wake and funeral were much more form over substance when it came to respect from Gotti's peers.

Except for members of his crime family, a dearth of wiseguys showed up to pay their final respects. Not even a handful of mobsters from New York's other four crime families showed up, according to law enforcement officials who monitored the comings and goings. Most notable by his absence was Gotti's Howard Beach, Queens, neighbor and longtime close mob associate Joseph Massino, boss of the Bonanno crime family.

Massino was a frequent visitor to Gotti's Bergin Hunt and Fish Club headquarters when both were earning their mob stripes during the 1970s and 1980s. Massino quietly backed Gotti's move to take over the Gambino family in 1985 by assassinating Paul Castellano. And in return, a few years later, Gotti had supported the lifting of sanctions by the Mafia's Commission against the Bonanno family as Massino was poised to assume control. And unlike the bosses of the city's other crime families, Massino wasn't under indictment, or on parole, and so he could have attended if that were his choice.

> **Slammer Time**
>
> For the last 12 and a half years of his life, from December 10, 1990, when he was arrested on racketeering charges and detained without bail, until he died on June 10, 2002, John Gotti was incarcerated in one federal facility or another. He officially began his last prison sentence on June 23, 1992.

Massino, like the overwhelming majority of wiseguys from the New York Metropolitan area purposely stayed away, sending a message, according to law enforcement officials and underworld sources, of disdain and disapproval.

Even Bruce Cutler, Gotti's longtime lawyer, was hard pressed to explain Massino's absence, acknowledging that "Joe is definitely a friend of John's" and that he was surprised that he hadn't paid his final respects. Still, said Cutler: "It was a very large turnout because he has so many admirers and so many friends. He's a much beloved man. This is a testament to his popularity."

Feds Nab Three More Gottis

A week before John Gotti died, his brothers Peter and Richard, and Richard's son, Richard G. Gotti, were indicted on federal labor racketeering charges stemming from the Gambino family's longstanding control over the Brooklyn and Staten Island docks. The huge 68-count indictment, which also charged 14 additional family members and associates, identified Peter as the family boss, his brother as a captain, and the younger Richard Gotti as a soldier in the crime family.

In one fell swoop, the three Gottis achieved the unenviable distinction of being the largest number of Gotti family members to be charged as defendants in a single federal racketeering indictment. The following year, all were convicted of sharing in hundreds of thousands of dollars in extortion payoffs that were funneled up the chain to them from a number of underlings, including capo Anthony (Sonny) Ciccone, the wiseguy who had been the crime family's man on the Brooklyn and Staten Island docks since John Gotti took over the crime family in 1986.

In 2004, Peter, who had turned down a plea bargain before trial that called for four years in prison, was sentenced to nine years and four months after his conviction at trial. His brother and nephew, who were free on bail until after they were sentenced, received less severe prison terms. Before the year ended, the number of imprisoned Gottis would jump to five.

As this updated edition went to press, Peter was waiting trial in Manhattan on additional racketeering charges that could doom him to a similar fate as his late brother. Peter was charged with engaging in construction industry extortion scams from 1991 through 2003 and taking part in a conspiracy with several Gambino family underlings to kill turncoat underboss Salvatore "Sammy Bull" Gravano in 1999 and 2000. Those charges are detailed in Chapter 29.

On the Waterfront (Brooklyn and Staten Island)

On January 17, 1986, a few days after John Gotti had become boss of the crime family, the late Dapper Don explained to an aide that capo Anthony "Sonny" Ciccone was raking in $2,000 a month in labor payoffs and earning even more each week from "small scores" as the family's man on the waterfront. Ciccone had replaced legendary Gambino mobster Anthony Scotto on the docks in the early 1980s after Scotto was convicted of taking $250,000 in payoffs while he served as an International Longshoremen's Association (ILA) vice president and imprisoned for 39 months.

The first Christmas tribute Gotti had gotten from Ciccone came to about $26,000, Gotti said with pride, quoting Ciccone as relating exactly the way Ciccone had explained it to him. "Every week," Ciccone had said, "there's a score, $300, or $500 from the dock, so I bring it inside. Then I bring it in (to you at Christmas)."

Two decades later, Ciccone was still in place, funneling the boss's share of his waterfront extortion payoffs up the line, but to Peter Gotti, instead. Another difference, according to tape-recorded conversations obtained during a lengthy Waterfront Commission investigation, was that the size of the payments had increased more than five-fold.

In one discussion, ILA vice president Frank "Red" Scollo, who also served as president of ILA Local 1814 in Brooklyn, the largest in the country, was overheard telling a Ciccone crew member that he would soon collect and pass on to Ciccone a $20,000 payoff from the president of the Howland Hook Marine Terminal, a huge waterfront warehouse on Staten Island.

Mafia Speak

During a 20-month undercover investigation, investigators installed court-authorized bugs in one barbershop, one car, two social clubs, and four restaurants. They also tapped four cell phones, one home phone, and one fax line.

The barbershop bug, placed in a Staten Island unisex hair salon called Guys & Dolls, picked up Ciccone badmouthing his predecessor racketeer Anthony Scotto for being a cheapskate.

On April 12, 2001, Ciccone blasted Scotto, a former ILA union boss who was convicted of labor racketeering in 1979, for trying to up his union pension by $280 per month, and related that he had told soldier Jerome Brancato to set Scotto straight.

"I said, 'Go, Jerry, go tell him (Scotto) that I said stop with this fuckin' thing, you're getting everybody in trouble. You're calling Red (Scollo); you're fuckin' terrorizing Red. Johnny Bowers (an ILA official) is scared shit. Just forget about it. What the fuck is with you? $280! You ain't got enough money?'"

Ironically, Ciccone was blowing his stack about something he had tried years earlier: "I was entitled (too)," he said. "When I went there (to the ILA), they told me that, that my appearance there terrorized every fuckin' body."

Another time, after Scollo told Ciccone that a rival union leader was "changing the rules on the piers," Ciccone enlisted his hulking 220-pound right-hand man Primo Cassarino to contact 350-pound enforcer Richard "The Lump" Bondi and pay the union leader a visit.

"Get Richie," said Ciccone. "Stop by, ring his bell, and just tell him, 'You know what? You'd better stop it ... otherwise you know what's gonna happen here!' and that's all." Later that night, Waterfront Commission investigators watched as Primo and The Lump did what they were told. So did the rival union official.

Another conversation between Scollo and Ciccone, a former ILA official who was ousted from his post in 1991 because of his organized crime ties, clearly demonstrated that despite his official ouster, Ciccone was a modern-day real-life version of the mob dock boss character played by Lee J. Cobb in the 50-year-old movie classic, *On the Waterfront*.

When Scollo asked if he could fire a wayward ILA union delegate, Ciccone bellowed, "Kick him out. Fuck him. Let him come to me."

Life Imitates the Movies

Eight months into the labor-racketeering probe, the ears of Waterfront Commission investigators perked up when they heard Sonny Ciccone and enforcer Primo Cassarino discussing an upcoming movie that would star actor Steven Seagal, the action movie star who had been a partner in the movie business, with a longtime Ciccone associate who lived in Staten Island.

For more than a decade, Seagal and Julius Nasso had been partners in a company that grossed hundreds of millions of dollars producing Seagal films. They had been close friends. They often dressed alike, in black, and Seagal had bought a house on Staten Island next door to Nasso's home. Their friendship and partnership had dissolved, however, and they were in the midst of a bitter dispute at the time.

"This guy Steve's got money, too ... and the movie may cost ten million dollars," Ciccone said.

Over the next few months, Ciccone, Cassarino, Nasso, and his brother Vincent, embarked on a campaign to extort $700,000 from Seagal. They traveled to Toronto where Seagal was filming the movie, *Exit Wounds;* to Hollywood, where he was promoting it; and to a landmark restaurant in Brooklyn, where Ciccone, Cassarino, and the Nasso brothers did their best to convince Seagal to fork over $150,000 a picture to them, or else.

In January 2001, Ciccone—with Cassarino and the Nassos in attendance—met Seagal in a private dining room of Gage and Tollner, the landmark Brooklyn eatery, and threatened him.

"Look at me when I talk to you," Ciccone sneered at him during the shakedown effort, Seagal recounted later from the witness stand. "We're proud people .... Work with Jules and we'll split the pie."

During the meeting, Seagal, who was carrying a licensed handgun, tried to buy time by agreeing to re-unite with Nasso, even though he had no intention of doing so. At the end of the session, Nasso told Seagal he had made the right decision. "These were people who were not going to let it go," he told Seagal. "If you would have said the wrong thing, they would have killed you."

Fuhgeddaboudit

As the wiseguys dined with Seagal, his assistant Neil Prashad sat at the restaurant's bar with 350-pound mob associate Richard Bondi, who forbade Prashad from joining Seagal.

Under questioning by assistant U.S. attorney Katya Jestin at trial, Prashad testified that every time he looked at his huge companion, "I thought there was something bulging out of his right side. It could have been a weapon or it could have been a cell phone." He never asked Bondi which it was, but at the time, Prashad recounted, he was too frightened to even go to the bathroom.

A few days later, on February 2, Cassarino, Ciccone, and Vincent Nasso were overheard joking and laughing about how terrified Seagal was at the restaurant sitdown. "I didn't acknowledge the fuck," Ciccone bragged, noting that Seagal had been "petrified" during the session.

"I wish we had a gun on us, that would have been funny," said Cassarino.

"It was like right out of the movies," said Vincent Nasso.

On the Waterfront (New York and Florida)

As the Gambinos entered the New Millennium with their Brooklyn and Staten Island waterfront rackets intact, the Genovese family did likewise with the piers in Manhattan, New Jersey, and Miami. Federal prosecutions had snared some mobsters and corrupt union officials for labor racketeering over the years, but the family kept on trucking.

The Genovese family controlled those ports through its domination of ILA Local 1804-1 and its sway with the Metropolitan Marine Maintenance Contractors Association, a trade group that had been created in the early 1970s to organize container repair companies that formed when containers were introduced into the shipping industry to cut down on labor costs.

Metro, as the trade association is known, handles all collective bargaining with the key ILA locals, including Local 1814 in Brooklyn, and Local 1804-1 in North Bergen, New Jersey. Its officers are also trustees of ILA pension and benefit funds worth hundreds of millions of dollars.

Until he was indicted in 2002, Metro's chief negotiator with the unions was vice president Pasquale "Patty" Falcetti, a Genovese crime family soldier with persuasive negotiating talents, according to discussions he had about two pending labor union negotiations that were recorded by the FBI in 2000 and 2001.

"I hate these fucking Albanians," he exclaimed about one. "I hate them. If you have a beef with them, you have to kill them right away. There's no talking to them."

Slammer Time

Rather than take a chance at trial, all the Genovese family members and associates charged with racketeering on the New York, New Jersey, and Miami waterfronts in 2002 reached plea bargains that included an agreement to sever all ties with the shipping industry, including the ILA.

Andrew Gigante received the lowest sentence—two years—but paid over $2 million in fines and restitution.

Soldier Pasquale "Patty" Falcetti, a former Metro vice president, and family associate Thomas Cafaro, a Metro employee, received the stiffest sentences—seven years.

One-time acting boss Liborio "Barney" Bellomo, who had been jailed in 1996, took four more years. Ernest Muscarella, who succeeded Bellomo as acting boss, got five. Capo Charles Tuzzo and soldier Michael Ragusa, a Metro employee, received 30 months.

About another problem, one between two mob-connected tow-truck companies, Falcetti had this solution: "Take a few guys and go beat the shit out of the kid. That's what I would do."

The chief Genovese family operative during the last three decades, according to federal prosecutors in Brooklyn, was a son of family boss Vincent "Chin" Gigante who has worked on the New Jersey docks for 28 years, Andrew Gigante. He is not an inducted member of the crime family, and until February 2002, had never been charged with a crime.

When indicted on labor racketeering charges in 2002—essentially as his imprisoned father's key representative on the docks—Andrew was a supervisor for A. G. Ship Maintenance Corporation. He also owned substantial interests in two waterfront companies and $4.2 million in property.

Chin Gigante Gives Up the Ghost

On April 7, 2003, Andrew Gigante and six other Genovese family racketeers pleaded guilty in Brooklyn Federal Court to labor racketeering on the waterfront, but they were only supporting players in the proceeding. Though important, their admissions took second billing that day.

Vincent "Chin" Gigante, the longtime boss of the crime family, was the main act. Despite being the leader of the group, he didn't admit taking part in the family's waterfront rackets, but with obstructing justice through a long discredited "crazy act" that had him walking through the streets of Greenwich Village in his pajamas for years.

As the proceeding began, it looked for a fleeting moment like Gigante was going to put on his old mumbling, bumbling, Daffy Don routine, the one that had fooled shrinks and frustrated law enforcement for more than three decades.

Old Habits Die Slow

His hair and prison duds were disheveled, and as courtroom deputy Louise Schaillat began the pro forma reading of the "promise to tell the truth" oath that all defendants take, Gigante started to raise his left hand.

But after a few seconds, Chin raised his right hand and followed the new script that had been crafted for the day. He pleaded guilty to obstructing justice for seven years by deceiving doctors from the time of his indictment in 1990 until his conviction at trial in 1997.

And although his guilty plea was accomplished primarily through the use of short responses to questions from Judge I. Leo Glasser, Gigante answered them all coherently. After concluding his plea—and being sentenced immediately (three years) in an unusual concession that allowed him to return that day to the federal prison where he was serving the sentence he received in 1997—he left no doubt about his lucidity when Glasser allowed Gigante to say his good-byes to Andrew in the well of the courtroom.

Father and son hugged and after a long embrace, the scene played a lot like a 10-minute silent movie. His words could not be picked up by reporters, but we could all see the relaxed, elder Gigante cracking jokes, smiling often, and looking alert. The smiling, animated Gigante shook hands with defense lawyers as his son introduced them to him.

He blew kisses to his other children—sons Vincent and Salvatore, daughters Carmela and Lucia—and his brother, Father Louis Gigante, who were seated in the spectator section. For many years, the priest had walked arm-in-arm with pajama-clad Vincent as the straight man for his crazy-man act.

By pleading guilty, Gigante spared his family members from being dragged into the case as witnesses or as participants in tape-recorded conversations they had with Gigante while he was in prison. Federal prosecutors had said they would play many during the trial in which he sounded lucid to prove that he had been feigning insanity for decades.

In one conversation, on April 30, 2001, four days after dozens of Genovese family mobsters were indicted, Gigante called his wife and asked if he had been indicted. When she said he hadn't but there were allegations he was "running" a "certain family," he said the only running he did was "around the park" at the prison. Then, Gigante told her to "Call everyone," and hung up.

According to prison medical records that were filed in the case, Gigante walks three miles a day, his heart, blood pressure, and other vital signs are excellent, and when a prison guard once asked him if any younger prisoners had been taunting him, he said, "Nobody fucks with me."

He's due out of prison in 2010, at age 82.

Little Al D'Arco Gets His Reward

Superstar turncoat Alphonse "Little Al" D'Arco received his just rewards from the federal government in an unannounced, early morning proceeding on October 10, 2002.

Little Al D'arco standing in a doorway in Little Italy during his heyday as a Luchese family wiseguy.

(Courtesy GangLandNews.com)

D'Arco, a former Luchese family acting boss who had pleaded guilty to a slew of crimes including 10 murders, was sentenced to no time in prison in return for his testimony as a prosecution witness at a dozen mob trials.

In deference to his age—70 at the time—and various ailments he suffers, D'Arco didn't have to come to court. He was sentenced via a remote television hookup much like those used by Larry King or Barbara Walters to interview a pop idol or icon.

Federal Judge Charles Brieant was able to hear and see D'Arco on a television monitor that was placed in the well of Brieant's courtroom in White Plains, New York, for the 8:30 A.M. session.

Brieant told me he approved the unusual setup because D'Arco "has serious medical problems, his life is at risk when he travels, and there was no reason for him to have to come to White Plains."

D'Arco, who made a brief statement, could see and hear the judge, his lawyer, prosecutors, and the chief criminal investigator for the Manhattan U.S. Attorney's office, Kenneth McCabe, on a monitor set up near his undisclosed permanent home.

D'Arco thanked his lawyer, his family, and the many law enforcement officials who kept him "on the straight and narrow" after he walked into FBI offices and began cooperating against the mob in September 1991 when he became convinced the Luchese family was set to kill him.

"They helped me tremendously to achieve this and to turn my life around. I'll never let their confidence down at any time," he said.

Mafia Speak

Little Al D'Arco's syntax wasn't always great, but he got the point across when he gave a federal court jury a primer on loan sharking in January 2004.

On what wiseguys would tell loan-shark customers when giving them loans: "'You got to pay every week. Do you know what you're doing when you take this money? If you don't know what you're doing, don't take this money, you know.' And you tell them they've got to pay every week. Don't ask them. That's it. And don't duck."

On why they invariably found a way to pay up: "That's the threat of violence. That's always there. When they know that you're a member of the mob, you convey that threat, you know."

Brieant, who presided over a 1995 racketeering trial at which D'Arco testified, gave the Luchese defector "time served"—which was no time at all because he has been free on bail since pleading guilty to racketeering in 1992. He also assessed him a $50 filing fee. The entire proceeding, whose outcome was a foregone conclusion, took less than 10 minutes.

A high-school dropout—the Brooklyn-born gangster quit school at age 15 and began running with older relatives and friends who were mob connected—D'Arco possessed an uncanny ability to recall dates, incidents, and anecdotes going back decades.

He met Luchese boss Vittorio Amuso in 1959 at a "bust out operation" at Washington and Flushing Avenues in Brooklyn, and he went "on record" with the family in March 1966. He was first proposed for membership in 1974, and he finally became a made man on August 23, 1982.

A drug dealer and loyal soldier, D'Arco moved up to capo in 1988 and became acting boss on January 9, 1991, the day he began to suspect he was marked for death.

During his decade working for the government, he was a key witness against Amuso, Gigante, acting Colombo boss Victor (Little Vic) Orena, and other top gangsters who were convicted of racketeering, including Bonanno consigliere Anthony Spero and Genovese consigliere James Ida.

He told the feds about efforts by the Luchese and Genovese families to kill John Gotti as payback for killing Paul Castellano and provided a wealth of intelligence information about all five families.

He testified in Brooklyn, Manhattan, White Plains, and Camden, and four years ago was set to testify in Detroit at the racketeering trial of Motor City wiseguys about, among other things, Henry Ford's mob connections during the 1930s, until a federal judge canned that idea.

"If Al said it happened, it happened," said one former federal prosecutor. "And he never stretched the truth," he said, recalling that during preparation for one trial, D'Arco corrected him about an important fact. "I'm sure he done it," said Little Al, "but I never seen him do it, so I ain't gonna say I did."

The Least You Need to Know

- John Gotti died serving a life sentence.
- Gotti's mob peers shunned his wake.
- Chin Gigante admitted faking mental illness.
- Little Al D'Arco was an excellent prosecution witness.

Chapter 28

The Last Don

In This Chapter

- Bonanno consigliere Anthony Spero gets life in prison
- The Feds go after Joe Massino
- Several Bonanno's turn on Joe
- Massino's seven murders

Since 1986, when Bonanno boss Philip "Rusty" Rastelli was convicted of racketeering, the feds have convicted 15 bosses or acting bosses of New York's other four families.

The Luchese family leads the parade with five: Antonio "Tony Ducks" Corallo, Vittorio "Vic" Amuso, Joseph "Little Joe" Defede, Louis "Louie Bagels" Daidone, and Steve Crea. The Colombos had four: Carmine "Junior" Persico and his son Alphonse, Victor "Little Vic" Orena, and Andrew Russo. The Gambino family had three: John Gotti, son John A. "Junior" Gotti, and Peter Gotti. (A fourth, Paul Castellano, suffered a worse fate while he was on his way to a racketeering conviction.) And the Genoveses had three, Vincent "Chin" Gigante, Anthony "Fat Tony" Salerno, and Liborio "Barney" Bellomo.

In this chapter, I take a look at Bonanno boss Joseph Massino, who has run the crime family since 1992. At press time, the feds were seeking to make him the second Bonanno leader they have brought down since 1986. He, on the other hand, was hoping to follow in John Gotti's footsteps, and become the second Mafia boss in history to beat a racketeering case, as the Dapper Don did in 1987.

Joe Massino Takes a Big Fall

On January 9, 2003, 10 years after getting out of prison and enjoying a hugely successful run atop the resurging Bonanno family, Joseph Massino was arrested on a racketeering indictment that charged him with a storied 22-year-old murder. He was sent back to prison a day before his sixtieth birthday, and held without bail to await trial.

The feds moved then, sources said, as a preemptive strike to prevent him from heading for the hills like he did in 1982 when he suspected he was going to be indicted. That time, he returned following the trial of his codefendants, more than two years later, and was acquitted at trial.

"He had a 10-year run," one law enforcement source said. "We wanted him off the streets now."

After a decade atop the Bonanno crime family, Joseph Massino went to trial for racketeering and seven murders that were committed years before he became boss.

(Courtesy GangLandNews.com)

During the next 16 months, things would only get worse for Massino and the entire family. On May 24, 2004, by the time he went to trial, the racketeering charges were expanded to include six additional murders between 1981 and 1987, and a litany of other lesser charges. In a separate indictment, more than two dozen Massino loyalists had also been hit with racketeering charges, with most also facing at least one murder charge. Massino was also accused of arson, loan sharking, and running a variety of illegal gambling businesses—a seasonal baccarat game, a sports betting operation, and the distribution of joker poker machines in restaurants and bars in the Metropolitan area.

And the Bonannos—once the most impenetrable of the fabled five families—were reeling from defections of at least eight made men who had spilled their guts to the feds and were prepared to testify against their boss and the still loyal members of the crime family, who had begun referring to themselves as members of the "Massino family" about the time that it all started falling apart.

The Anatomy of Massino's Prosecution

After years of plodding along against the cagy, surveillance conscious Massino, the FBI moved its investigation of the Bonanno boss into high gear on April 15, 2002. On that day, the family's longtime consigliere, Anthony Spero, was sentenced to die in prison for ordering three gangland style slayings a decade earlier.

Spero, who had served as acting boss briefly in 1992—following Philip Rastelli's death and before Massino was released from prison—stood as tall as he could as he got the bad news.

Dressed in drab prison blues, 73-year-old Spero smiled broadly and waved at relatives and friends, including many who showed up to support him in his three-year-long losing battle.

Anthony Spero was sentenced to life in prison for three murders committed by the Bath Avenue Crew of young hoodlums that he controlled.

(Courtesy GangLandNews.com)

Spero's conviction—stemming from the murderous activities of a crew of young toughs based on Bath Avenue in Bath Beach, Brooklyn—was like a dark cloud hanging ominously over Massino as his trial began.

Spero was found guilty solely on the testimony of a few low-level associates—without the help of any tape-recorded conversations or direct testimony from any made men who heard or saw Spero order the murders of any of the three victims.

Against Massino, assistant U.S. attorneys Mitra Hormozi, Robert Henoch, and Greg Andres had much much more. They had six Bonanno made men who were prepared to testify about the seven murders he was charged with as the trial began.

Mafia Speak

When FBI agents Kimberly McCaffrey and Jeffrey Sallet arrived at Joe Massino's house to arrest him at 6 A.M. on January 9, 2003, they were a little taken aback when he answered the door fully dressed and said he had been expecting them.

"He stated he thought we were coming yesterday," McCaffrey testified. "He thought he was going to be arrested the day before."

As the agents drove him to FBI headquarters for processing, he again caught them by surprise. "You must be Kimberly and you must be Jeffrey," he said with a smile.

Massino wasn't done tweaking his antagonists. After arriving at the FBI office in Downtown Manhattan, he told McCaffrey that he had heard the FBI recruited her "right out of high school," obviously enjoying himself.

"You know a lot about me," she said.

"You do your homework and I do mine," he replied.

In addition, the prosecution had myriad banking and other financial records that linked Massino to several companies involved in shady dealings that dovetailed nicely with the testimony of the cooperating witnesses. The lion's share of the material had been unearthed by two FBI agents with accounting backgrounds, Kimberly McCaffrey and Jeffrey Sallet. The records tied Massino to a bakery, a parking lot, and a restaurant where Massino often held court with family members.

The Bonanno Family Defectors

In late 2002, capo Frank Coppa Sr., who began a three-year stretch for securities fraud earlier that year at a federal prison in Fort Dix, New Jersey, was the first to roll over. Coppa, then 61, had been hit with three extortion counts around the same time he was incarcerated, and, in the words of one source, "was not looking to add any more time to his stay."

His defection made him the first Bonanno mobster to agree to publicly break the Mafia vow of silence that has been breached dozens of times by wiseguys from New York's other four families since 1962, when Genovese soldier Joe Valachi paved the way.

Richard "Shellackhead" Cantarella, then 59, and his son Paul, then 31, were quick to follow Coppa's lead. Both were defendants in the same case. Among other crimes, Paul was charged with a kidnapping/home invasion robbery. The elder Cantarella took part in the 1992 murder of a *New York Post* delivery superintendent in an effort to thwart a state probe into widespread racketeering and fraud at the *Post* stemming from the family's control of the Newspaper and Mail Deliverers Union. In that case, Shellackhead had been caught on tape boasting that Massino had supported his induction into the crime family while he was serving six years for labor racketeering that ended in November 1992.

"The guy who did it was Joe, the guy you met. He was in jail and he sent (out) the word," Shellackhead had said.

Within two months of his 2003 arrest, Massino got the absolutely worst possible news. His underboss, Salvatore "Good Looking Sal" Vitale, who had been indicted with Massino and charged with the same 1992 murder as Cantarella, also defected. Vitale, who is Massino's brother-in-law, is discussed in Chapter 29.

Sonny Black's Body?

The murder of Dominick "Sonny Black" Napolitano was the centerpiece of the government's case, the first of seven murders Massino was charged with. A capo, Napolitano paid the ultimate price for allowing FBI agent Joe Pistone to infiltrate the Bonanno family during his five years of undercover work that ended in July 1981.

On August 17, 1981, in the basement of Ronald "Monkey Man" Filocomo's Staten Island home, he and Bonanno soldier Frank "Curly" Lino blew Dominick "Sonny Black" Napolitano's brains out, according to the testimony of several Bonanno turncoats at the trial. Filocomo, a longtime member of Lino's crew, had been proposed for membership in the crime family but was rejected because he had once worked as a corrections officer.

> **Big Shot**
>
> In his book, Pistone described how Sonny Black, on learning that the man he knew as Donnie Brasco was really an agent, went up to the pigeon coops on the roof of his Brooklyn home, where he often retreated for private thought. A few weeks later, when the coops were taken down, Pistone said he knew Sonny Black "was history."

For two decades, authorities have maintained that they recovered Sonny Black's badly decomposed body on August 12, 1982, when remains of a man were fished out of a creek in a swampy area of Staten Island. The location is where cooperating witnesses say Napolitano's body was dumped.

But Massino's lawyer, David Breitbart, raised serious questions about the remains, telling trial judge Nicholas Garaufis during pretrial arguments that he would prove that the remains cannot possibly be Napolitano's remains.

The expected testimony that Lino and Filocomo each fired two bullets from .38 caliber handguns into Napolitano's face is not backed up by the physical evidence, the lawyer said. The victim, said Breitbart, was killed by a single shot to the back of the head that created a half-inch circular hole, which is much more likely to have been created by a .45 caliber bullet than a .38 caliber slug, according to his reading of the autopsy report.

"What they now have," said Breitbart, "are individuals who are purported to have put more holes in Mr. Napolitano than the corpse they have from 1982. Not only are they going to be unable to prove that Mr. Massino had anything to do with it, they are creating a charade transaction by purporting to have a corpse that is not the corpse of Sonny Black Napolitano."

Breitbart also claimed that the clothing that was recovered was not Sonny Black's and that the foot size of the recovered body was three sizes larger than Napolitano's feet. "He wore seven-and-a-half–size shoes, not size eleven, the shoe size of the body that the FBI would have you believe is Sonny Black," said Breitbart.

Although Massino is charged with six other murders and it is not necessary to have recovered Napolitano's body to convict Massino of his murder, Breitbart hoped to cast doubt on the entire case by convincing jurors that the remains are not Sonny Black's.

Donnie Brasco II

On February 18, 1982, six months after Napolitano was killed, Bonanno soldier Anthony Mirra, 60, was shot to death at a Manhattan parking garage. Like Sonny Black, Mirra was ostensibly whacked for enabling Pistone to penetrate the family while he played the role of jewel thief "Donnie Brasco," which is the title of Pistone's book as well as the hit movie about his undercover work starring Johnny Depp and Al Pacino.

The execution took place several months before Bonanno soldier Benjamin "Lefty Guns" Ruggiero and four cohorts went to trial on racketeering and murder conspiracy charges stemming from Pistone's undercover work. At the 1982 trial, Pistone conceded he told Ruggiero "why don't we just kill him" during a discussion about Mirra, but insisted that he said it to "maintain" his credibility in his Brasco role and "knew [Ruggiero] wouldn't kill [Mirra] on my encouragement."

At the time of the conversation, which Pistone taped and turned over to his superiors, Mirra and "Brasco" had been engaged in a feud over what defense lawyers charged were narcotics sales by the undercover detective that were never reported to the FBI. Pistone insisted the dope deals were concocted by an undercover police officer as part of their cover.

Breitbart, who represented the only defendant to be acquitted of all charges in the 1982 trial, said he and Massino are "ready for trial and convinced the result will be the same as the first time I cross-examined Pistone."

In the 2004 trial, however, Breitbart would not be questioning Pistone about the Mirra hit. In early 2003, around the same time that Bonnano underboss Vitale decided to cooperate, Bonanno soldier Joseph "Joey Mook" D'Amico, who killed Mirra, also defected and was primed to testify that Massino was behind the killing.

The Three Capos

On May 5, 1981, Bonanno capos Alphonse "Sonny Red" Indelicato, Philip "Philly Lucky" Giaccone, and Dominick "Big Trin" Trinchera were shot to death in a bloody coup that was carried out at a Brooklyn social club.

For decades, details about the killings remained a closely guarded secret shared, amazingly, by dozens of Bonanno family members and a select group of Gambino mobsters, who somehow managed to keep the specifics from becoming common knowledge. Indeed, for weeks, until Indelicato's body was found in a shallow grave in a Queens lot, there was no physical evidence confirming that the three capos had been eliminated.

The murders were carried out after Massino, acting for then-imprisoned Bonanno boss Philip Rastelli, received an official sanction from the Commission, the Mafia's ruling body detailed in Chapter 3.

The Commission, which had approved the execution of cigar-chomping Carmine "Lilo" Galante only two years earlier, initially vetoed the hits with a "no bloodshed" edict. But with Gambino boss Paul Castellano taking the lead, the Commission reversed itself after learning that the rebel capos were planning an all-out assault against Rastelli's supporters.

"It was a kill-or-be-killed situation for the two factions," said one law enforcement official. "And when you think about it, it's really no surprise that the Commission (made up of Mafia bosses) came down on the side of the sitting boss. It just took us a while to find out."

Fuhgeddaboudit

Following the news that an FBI agent working undercover had been proposed to be "made" in the early 1980s, the Bonannos paid very close attention to rules against inducting former law enforcement officers.

A few months after the killings, when the mob learned that "Donnie Brasco" had been an FBI agent, the Bonannos would lose their seat on the ruling body, but in May 1981, the family was in good standing with the panel.

The new insight about the murders came from Vitale, who wielded a machine gun during the slayings. He told the feds that Massino got Commission approval through Castellano, for whom Massino had done a big favor in 1975 (for more on that favor, see Chapter 29).

And several Gambino mobsters, including then-underboss Aniello "Neil" Dellacroce, helped plan the slayings and helped dispose of the bodies, according to accounts provided by Vitale and other Bonanno defectors.

Sources say that Curly Lino, who was aligned with the slain capos and escaped the carnage, was prepared to testify that he was confronted after the slayings by Dellacroce and Gotti's brother Gene and asked if he had notified police. When Lino responded negatively, Dellacroce was pleased, and told Lino he hadn't been slated for death, and then, turning to Ruggiero and DeCicco, told them it was now "safe to clean up the club" and to proceed there.

In Vitale's account, the triple execution ran into a few snafus. One was the accidental wounding of Santo Giordano, a member of the Sicilian faction that was allied with Massino. Giordano was hit by mistake in the wild shootout that began when the three capos entered the club for what they believed were peace negotiations.

The other was Vitale's own screw-up. He was handed a submachine and told to position himself in a closet. He was unfamiliar with the weapon, however, and as a result, he precipitated chaos and a near-crisis when he "accidentally discharged the weapon before the three capos arrived."

Despite the prosecution's seemingly overwhelming case, Massino, who was acquitted of conspiring to kill the three capos in 1987, is confident he'll be vindicated again, says lawyer David Breitbart. "Mr. Massino was acquitted of the captains' murders once, so fundamental fairness dictates he should not have to stand trial for those charges again. But because the courts have ruled otherwise, Joe will be found innocent again." The other murders, Breitbart added, "are more of the same lies by Vitale and other cutthroat killers looking to save their asses by pointing fingers at the man the government has singled out."

The Canadian Connection

When Massino learned about Indelicato, Trinchera, and Giaccone's plan to overthrow Rastelli, he moved quickly. He gained the support of the family's Sicilian faction and decided to import several gunmen from the group's base in Montreal. The family's connections there are discussed in Chapters 4 and 11. Massino reasoned that their faces would be unknown in New York and they could leave soon after the murders, according to court papers that assistant U.S. attorney Nicolas Bourtin filed in Montreal.

A key player in the slayings was capo Gerlando "George from Canada" Sciascia, whose heroin smuggling schemes during the 1980s with Gene Gotti are discussed in Chapter 26. Sciascia was involved in the planning and played an important role on May 5, 1981, according to Vitale and other sources.

The plan called for Sciascia to accompany Massino to what the three capos were told was to be peaceful discussions to iron out their differences and once again become a unified family. Four hit men wearing ski masks would be waiting in a partially closed closet. Sciascia would signal the shooting to start by running his fingers through his hair. The closet door was ajar just enough for the killers in waiting to see Sciascia give the signal.

In the closet, Vitale was armed, he said, with a "tommy gun." Three other hit men, including two Sicilian faction members from Montreal, Vito Rizzuto and Emanuele Ragusa, had a shotgun and two handguns. Sciascia also had a piece. At the time, Rizzuto's father, Nicholas, was a Bonanno capo and the leader of the Montreal crew.

> **Big Shot**
>
> George from Canada Sciascia was a key player in the three capos murder, but 18 years later he had fallen out of favor and Joe Massino decided that "George has got to go," turncoat Bonanno underboss Sal Vitale testified, adding that after Sciascia was killed, Massino ordered Vitale to attend Sciascia's wake to deflect suspicion away from the hierarchy of the Bonanno family.

When the capos arrived, Sciascia gave the signal. "This is a stickup," shouted Rizzuto, who jumped out and launched the carnage by shooting Trinchera first, according to Vitale. Trinchera, who weighed about 300 pounds, "kept coming at them," Massino reportedly said later. Also, Vitale told the feds, he saw Sciascia shoot Indelicato in the head and Massino later told him that he punched Giaccone to stop him from escaping.

The shooters fled, leaving Vitale behind to escort the other capos out to a waiting car. Vitale then went back for double duty with a cleanup crew headed by Dominick "Sonny Black" Napolitano.

"The bodies of Indelicato, Giaccone, and Trinchera were wrapped in painter's drop cloths and placed in a van that was driven to Howard Beach," wrote Bourtin.

Another old Massino buddy, Duane "Goldie" Leisenheimer, told the feds that he drove the car that spirited the capos away, and that in addition to his chauffeur's role, he later put up Massino, Rizzuto, and Ragusa at his apartment.

In January 2004, Rizzuto, then 59 and described by Canadian authorities as the godfather of the Mafia in Canada, was indicted by a Brooklyn federal grand jury on racketeering and murder charges for his alleged role in the three capos' murders. Arrested by the Royal Canadian Mounted Police, Rizzuto has contested extradition. At this writing, he is incarcerated in Montreal as his case winds its way through the court system in Canada.

As this book went to press, Massino was still on trial, which was expected to conclude in late July or early August 2004. No matter the outcome, things are likely to get worse for the beleaguered Bonanno boss. Massino is charged with the execution of Bonanno capo Gerlando "George from Canada" Sciascia, who was killed in March 1999, allegedly on orders from Massino.

Since Sciascia's killing occurred after U.S. federal laws were changed to permit capital punishment, there is little doubt that Attorney General John Ashcroft would order prosecutors to seek the death penalty for Massino in that case. In fact, many legal experts, and this author, believe that Ashcroft would order prosecutors to bring Massino to trial and seek the death penalty even if he were convicted of the seven murders and destined to die in prison.

The Least You Need to Know

- Joe Massino was Bonanno boss for a decade when he was hit with racketeering and murder charges in 2003.

- Bonanno consigliere Anthony Spero will die in prison.

- With a large supporting case, Massino allegedly orchestrated the killing of three rebel Bonanno capos on May 5, 1981.

- Vito Rizzuto, the godfather of the Mafia in Canada, played an important role in the slayings of the three capos.

Chapter 29

The New Turncoats

In This Chapter

- Good Looking Sal
- Mikey Scars
- Fat Sal Mangiavillano
- Cookie D'Urso
- George Barone

As I stated in Chapter 21, cooperating witnesses are essential tools of the trade for the law enforcement community when it comes to making successful cases against mobsters. Some of the turncoats are "made men" who have defected from their respective crime families to lessen their own time in prison. Others are mob associates who have turned on their cohorts for the same reason.

In this chapter, I will tell you about five important turncoats who have wreaked havoc with wiseguys in the new millennium by agreeing to become cooperating witnesses. They are a diverse group. One, a Gambino capo who was once part of John Gotti's inner circle, has yet to make his courtroom debut. The others, two mobsters and two associates, have already testified and are likely to have encore appearances. They include a Bonanno underboss—the second to testify against his Mafia boss—and an aging

Genovese soldier who belonged to the Jets, a Hell's Kitchen gang of mostly Irish hoodlums that was made famous in the 1957 musical about gang violence, *West Side Story.*

Good Looking Sal

In February of 2003, Bonanno boss Joseph Massino got some bad news, arguably the worst he could possibly receive—his longtime underboss had become a turncoat and was telling the feds about more than a quarter century of murders and other mob mayhem they had committed together.

The defection by Salvatore "Good Looking Sal" Vitale was a staggering blow to Massino, probably hurting him much more than a similar decision by Salvatore "Sammy Bull" Gravano a decade earlier had hurt his boss, John Gotti.

Good Looking Sal Vitale turned his back on the Bonanno crime family in an effort to save himself from a life sentence.

(Courtesy GangLandNews.com)

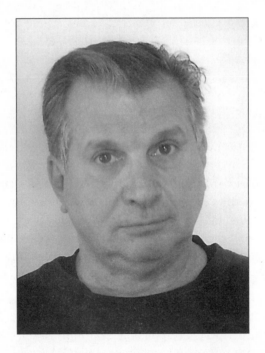

"It was like an ice pick in the eye," said one gleeful law enforcement official.

Not only had Vitale been Massino's underboss for more than a decade, he was also his brother-in-law, and uncle to Massino's three children. And when they were kids growing up in Middle Village, Queens, in the summer of 1954, and young Sal was six and Joey was 11, Big Joey taught Little Sal how to swim at a local swimming pool.

But when the feds quietly moved Vitale into a special unit for cooperating witnesses, he didn't tell them about the swimming lessons Massino gave him 50 years ago. Instead, he told them about nine murders they were involved in together, including the first one in 1975, when Massino did a big favor for Paul Castellano.

Vitale described how Massino got together with another young gangster on his way to becoming a Mafia boss, John Gotti, to kill a boyfriend of Castellano's daughter for insulting Castellano. Vitale had nothing to do with the killing, he said, but was called to the scene of the crime to help remove the body when a van that had been stolen for that purpose wouldn't start.

> **Mafia Speak**
>
> Joe Massino and John Gotti were buddies and partners in crime in their younger days, but Massino often criticized Gotti's swashbuckling style and his murder of Gambino boss Paul Castellano to take over the family, said Salvatore Vitale.
>
> "He used to say" about Gotti, Vitale testified: "He broke every rule in the book, John destroyed this life. John set us back a hundred years."

The boyfriend's fatal mistake was saying that the powerful gangster, a butcher by trade, looked a lot like Frank Perdue, a resourceful businessman/self-promoter who named his chickens after himself. Perdue, who starred in his own TV commercials, seemed to resemble a chicken as he squawked: "It takes a tough man to make a tender chicken." Vitale also implicated Massino in the storied 1979 murder of Carmine "Lilo" Galante, saying Massino delivered a message from then-incarcerated boss Philip Rastelli to his loyal troops that the cigar-chomping pretender to his throne had to go. Two years later, on May 5, 1981, he said, Massino organized the murders of three family capos who were fomenting another rebellion against the imprisoned Rastelli (see Chapter 28).

Vitale also tabbed Massino for the murders of two Bonanno wiseguys held responsible for permitting FBI agent Joe Pistone to infiltrate the crime family from 1976 to 1981—capo Dominick "Sonny Black" Napolitano in 1981 and soldier Tony Mirra the following year (see Chapter 28). Vitale, who testified against Massino at his murder and racketeering trial that began in Brooklyn Federal Court on May 24, 2004, will likely have at least a few encore appearances before he ends his career as a prosecution witness.

"He fills a big void at the top of the charts," said one law enforcement official, citing a paucity of high-level turncoats since Gambino underboss Sammy Bull Gravano and Luchese acting boss Alphonse "Little Al" D'Arco turned on the mob in 1991.

Mikey Scars

In November of 2002, an up and coming Gambino capo with close ties to jailed boss Peter Gotti rocked the crime family by deciding to cooperate with the feds.

Michael "Mikey Scars" DiLeonardo, a Staten Island gangster who had been a close pal of John A. "Junior" Gotti—and an alleged partner of the Junior Don in strip joints in New York, Atlanta, and Boca Raton—turned as he awaited trial for murders.

His defection was a devastating blow for the already reeling crime family. "He's been part of the inner circle for 10 years and can hurt a lot of people," said one law enforcement official.

A regular at John Gotti's Little Italy headquarters during the Dapper Don's reign, DiLeonardo had learned the gangster trade from Gotti's murderous underboss Salvatore "Sammy Bull" Gravano. Under Gravano's tutelage, he became a key player in the family's construction industry rackets as a member of Teamsters Local 282. And like his mentor, DiLeonardo reached out to the feds while detained without bail and awaiting trial for murder and other racketeering charges that could put him away for life.

Mikey Scars—his nickname conjures up knife fights but stems from dog bites on his face and taunts by classmates when he was eight—hadn't testified by the time this book went to press. But information from DiLeonardo has led to an important indictment against Peter Gotti, as well as investigations that were expected to result in charges against top Gambino family members Junior Gotti and capo Nicholas "Little Nick" Corozzo.

DiLeonardo has told the feds that Junior and Little Nick ordered the 1992 shooting of Guardian Angels founder and radio host Curtis Sliwa. The outspoken Sliwa was shot, DiLeonardo told the feds, "to teach him a lesson" for his repeated portrayals of the late Dapper Don as a lowlife gangster who deserved to be jailed for life for his April 1992 racketeering and murder conviction.

"The guys should go straight to hell without an asbestos suit," said Sliwa, who was critically wounded by two gangsters on June 19, 1992—four days before Gotti was sentenced to life. His assailants picked him up in a stolen taxicab outside his East Village apartment as he left for his early morning talk show and shot him in the back and both legs.

Sliwa underwent two operations, and spent three weeks in Bellevue Hospital. On his release, Sliwa resumed his show and accused associates of Junior Gotti with being responsible for the attack. "I've been right about this all along," Sliwa said. "This is the way the Gottis have been doing business ever since the beginning. Thank goodness that it's starting to change. I won't be happy though until they're all either in jail or pushing up daisies."

The wheelman in the plot, according to Mikey Scars, was soldier Joseph D'Angelo, another one-time Gravano protégé. The shooter was Michael "Mikey Y" Yannotti, a member of Corozzo's crew. Yannotti and D'Angelo both become made men following the shooting.

Mikey Scars DiLeonardo claims that Junior Gotti ordered the shooting of Guardian Angels founder Curtis Sliwa.

(Courtesy GangLandNews.com)

The feds have additional plans for DiLeonardo. In November 2004, he was slated to testify against Peter Gotti and soldiers Thomas "Huck" Carbonaro and Edward Garafola at their trial in Manhattan Federal Court. All are charged with conspiring to kill Gravano in late 1999 and early 2000 in a belated effort to seek retribution for his defection.

Following interviews in 1999 in which Gravano, then living relatively openly in the Phoenix area, essentially dared the family to exact revenge, the family deemed it was necessary to kill him, if only to save face with other New York families.

Fat Sal Mangiavillano

When the leaders of the Gambino family decided to whack Gravano in 1999, they plucked an Italian-born techno whiz off the mean streets of Bensonhurst, Brooklyn, for the job.

Salvatore "Fat Sal" Mangiavillano brought only an eighth-grade education to the task, but the self-taught wizard was so adept at surveillance that he rigged a remote video camera in the grill of a rented panel truck to spy on Gravano at his Phoenix pool construction company. Using a laptop computer from a safe distance away, the techie monitored the comings and goings of the transplanted gangster.

By helping to track down the superstar witness who had helped bring down John Gotti, Mangiavillano hoped to "make his bones" and become a made man.

The rotund hit man who "learned how to be mechanical" by chopping up stolen cars also planned to make a remote-controlled bomb to whack Gravano, he testified at the murder conspiracy trial of Huck Carbonaro in October 2003.

Mafia Speak

While Mangiavillano was working to kill Gravano, Carbonaro spilled the beans about the Sliwa shooting to Fat Sal, according to a report by FBI agents Cindy Peil and Theodore Otto.

"Sliwa was shot because he was badmouthing John Gotti," Huck told Fat Sal, adding that Sliwa wasn't the only one who got under the Gambinos' skin.

"During the same conversation," the agents wrote, "Carbonaro told (Mangiavillano) that he felt columnist Jerry Capeci should have been shot instead for 'all the shit he writes.'"

Thankfully, that never happened. I assume—and hope—that Huck was speaking hyperbolically, much the same way that John Gotti used to about me, albeit with a bit more vitriol than the Dapper Don ever used in any of his invectives.

Fat Sal, who trimmed down from 400 pounds to a svelte 300 for his debut as a prosecution witness, had gotten approval from Gambino boss Peter Gotti to violate mob rules against using bombs "because Sammy broke the rules first."

The plot fizzled when Gravano was arrested on drug charges in February 2000. Two years later, though, Fat Sal put his travels to Arizona to good use by breaking the same rules as Gravano did to get out from under some heavy time he was facing for a string of bank robberies.

From the witness stand, Mangiavillano pointed a damning finger and helped convict Carbonaro of murder conspiracy charges.

In November 2004, Fat Sal will team up with Mikey Scars and face off against Carbonaro again, along with codefendants Peter Gotti and Edward Garafola at their racketeering and murder conspiracy trial in Manhattan Federal Court.

Cookie D'Urso

The murder of Tino Lombardi and attempted murder of Cookie D'Urso on November 20, 1994, played out like an episode of the long-running hit TV drama *Law & Order*, one that took nine years to bring the killers to justice.

And along the way to guilty verdicts on January 28, 2003, D'Urso, who survived a shot in the back of the head in 1994, brought down 50 Genovese mobsters and associates on a variety of racketeering and other charges.

D'Urso, a brash young mob wannabe who tried but failed twice to seek revenge the normal mob way, decided to obtain his vengeance with the help of the feds after he was arrested on murder charges nearly four years later.

He wore a wire for nearly three years, helping the feds bring racketeering and murder charges against top Genovese gangsters, including family boss Vincent Chin Gigante and others (see Chapter 27).

He tape-recorded conversations with capos Salvatore "Sammy Meatballs" Aparo and Joseph Zito and more than a dozen other mobsters, including Aparo's son Vincent and Gigante's man on the docks, Pasquale "Patty" Falcetti. But he never could get close to the five men with whom he and his cousin Tino had been playing cards when he and Tino were riddled with bullets and he somehow survived.

That November 1994 night, they were at the San Giuseppe Social Club in Williamsburg, Brooklyn, when he was shot in the head and lost consciousness, waking up to find Lombardi dead and the others gone.

Before going into surgery, not knowing if he'd survive, D'Urso named the five men who were there at the time, telling cops he knew three of the men had guns but he never saw who shot him. Seven years later, despite a hugely successful undercover operation, the feds still had no other evidence than the five names they had a few days after the killing.

So, the Brooklyn U.S. Attorney's office did what *Law & Order's* A.D.A. Jack McCoy would. It got indictments against all of them, charging the three men D'Urso had seen with guns with murder and attempted murder charges. The others were charged with engaging in a conspiracy to cover up the killing. And the feds hoped for the best.

Fuhgeddaboudit

Years ago, when they first spotted each other at a Staten Island amusement park, DeCavalcante capo Anthony Rotondo and Bonanno capo Richard "Shellackhead" Cantarella played a cat-and-mouse game trying to feel each other out.

Rotondo, who followed his father into "the life," and Cantarella, who pulled his son into the mob, each *knew* the other was a wiseguy, but Mafia protocol made it difficult for them to nail it down without violating the rules.

Finally, Rotondo, a college graduate who chucked his degree, struck up a conversation and asked Cantarella if he knew Anthony "T. G." Graziano, a Bonanno capo from Staten Island that Rotondo had been looking to meet.

Sure enough, Cantarella knew him and said he did, but didn't say he knew him as a member of the Bonanno family.

"Do you know Danny Annunziata?" asked Cantarella, who had been angling to meet the DeCavalcante soldier.

FBI agent Nora Conley explained the problem: "They both realized the other was a member of organized crime, but needed to have another made guy do the (formal) introduction."

Where there's a will, there's always a way. They arranged for Graziano to introduce them to each other. Then Rotondo introduced Cantarella to Annunziata.

In 2002, Rotondo and Cantarella became turncoats. Now, if they meet in a secure federal prison unit for cooperating witnesses, there are different "Witsec" rules they have to follow, for "witness security" purposes. No names, only initials are permitted. Can you just hear Rotondo say, "Hey, R.C. How's it going?" And Cantarella reply, "Couldn't be better A. R. I'm so glad to be here."

If truth be told, assistant U.S. attorneys Paul Weinstein, Dan Dorsky, and Paul Schoeman had no real idea how they would prove it.

It didn't take long for them to figure it out.

Anthony Bruno, one of the men D'Urso had seen standing behind him with a gun, was first in the door to make a deal. Anthony "Rookie" Cerasulo, who had been poised at the social club door as a lookout and getaway driver, was next.

On the eve of the trial, John Imbrieco, who shot and killed Lombardi after Bruno shot D'Urso in the head, pleaded guilty and took 20 years.

Carmelo "Carmine Pizza" Polito, who makes pizza, robs banks, and owed the cousins $60,000 in 1994, and Mario Fortunato, an owner of a landmark Brooklyn bakery and occasional bank robber, rolled the dice and went to trial.

The jury convicted both men. On May 30, 2003, Judge I. Leo Glasser sentenced Polito, 43, and Fortunato, 55, to life without parole, sentences mandated by federal law.

As Glasser pronounced the sentence, Lombardi's sister Assunta Rozza, said: "I hope they both live long, healthy lives in prison." Her mother, Pasqualina, completed the sentence: "And burn in hell."

Meanwhile, D'Urso and wife Vanessa, who built a healthy $4.5 million real estate portfolio as he worked undercover, now have new identities under the Witness Protection Program, and are having no problems making ends meet.

Sometimes, crime does pay.

George Barone

Of all the mobsters snared in D'Urso's celebrated three-year FBI undercover operation, the most important might have been an aging, ailing, battle-weary Hell's Kitchen gangster.

George Barone was a powerful waterfront racketeer in the days when the mob ruled supreme on the city's docks. In his prime, in the 1950s, Barone was a character right out of *On the Waterfront*, a "Johnny Friendly" type who used guns, knives, and his fists to enforce the rules of his then-boss and close pal, Mafia chieftain Vito Genovese.

Barone, 79 when he was nabbed in 2001 for extortion, walked hunched over and suffered from lung disease, heart disease, diabetes, and cancer. He was so hard of hearing that he needed a teleprompter to read questions from lawyers when he took the witness stand in his debut as a government witness.

But his memory was pretty darn good when Barone, only the third Genovese soldier to defect since Joe Valachi paved the way in 1962, testified at the waterfront racketeering trial of Gambino boss Peter Gotti. (He was poised to testify against his mob boss Chin Gigante and seven others before Chin and Company copped guilty pleas.)

Most defectors have little insight about the mob's glory days and a limited historical perspective about the Mafia. Barone, however, has firsthand knowledge about a half century of crime.

A World War II veteran who took part in five Allied invasions, including the assault on Iwo Jima, Barone spent a couple years at Pace College before acquiring an accelerated education about the waterfront while scrubbing down ships at Manhattan piers in the late 1940s.

He joined the International Longshoremen's Association around 1949 as a working foreman for a ship-cleaning company controlled by Albert Anastasia, boss of what is now known as the Gambino family, according to FBI reports.

After fending off efforts by Anastasia capo Carmine "The Doctor" Lombardozzi to use nonunion workers, Barone got in bed with Genovese—a fierce Anastasia rival—and began taking payoffs to allow Genovese to use nonunion labor.

By the mid-1950s, Barone was an ILA official and "very close" to Genovese, so close that Don Vitone confided that he had learned about a diabolical plot in which his underboss, Frank Costello, and Anastasia planned to kill Genovese, and told the feds how Genovese responded.

"Genovese directed Chin Gigante to kill Costello, (and) Genovese was also responsible for Anastasia's murder" in October 1957, Barone said, according to a report by FBI agents Michael Campi and Joy Adam.

Barone was a personal hit man for acting boss Anthony "Fat Tony" Salerno in the 1960s and 1970s. He spent most of the 1980s in prison, but he got back into "the life" in the 1990s, flourishing as the family's man on the Miami docks until his arrest.

Fuhgeddaboudit

In his day, George Barone was involved in so many murders, he can't remember them all.

"I didn't keep a scorecard, but it was probably ten or twelve," said Barone, who dispatched most of his victims in the 1950s, when he belonged to a Hell's Kitchen gang of mostly Irish hoodlums whose name, the Jets, was made famous in the 1957 musical about gang violence, *West Side Story*.

"I am a mongrel. I'm partly Italian, Irish, and Hungarian," Barone testified when asked about his own heritage.

His lucrative labor racketeering partnership with Genovese ended in 1958 after the leader of the Jets, the Hell's Kitchen gang Barne belonged to, was killed. Barone aligned himself with Salerno, who later sponsored his induction into the family.

Barone became a favored hit man for his mob masters. In the mid-1960s, he traveled to Covington, Kentucky, and killed a Salerno nemesis who was causing problems for a gambling operation Fat Tony controlled there. In 1967, he again did Salerno's bidding, killing John Biello, a New York wiseguy who had moved to Miami and earned Salerno's wrath.

Before going to prison in 1983, Barone was ordered to meet Chin Gigante and several wiseguys and ILA officials to smooth the way for Andrew Gigante to take over some of Barone's responsibilities on the docks.

As they waited for Gigante to arrive, Barone saw a man who "looked like the 'man from LaMancha,'" the fabled Don Quixote character, and for a brief moment, "thought this person was there to kill them," according to an FBI report.

"As the person came closer, he realized it was Chin dressed in a robe with the hood up over his head. Gigante embraced (Barone), told the others how much he loved (him) and how they were together years ago with Vito Genovese."

Turning his back on the mob after 50 years was a difficult decision, Barone said, but made easier when he was cheated by the Gigantes and suspected that they had marked him for death.

"I wanted to get even. I wanted to survive. I didn't want to get killed by them," he said.

The Least You Need to Know

- Sal Vitale was the second Mafia underboss to testify against his boss.
- Gambino capo Michael "Mikey Scars" DiLeonardo is an important government witness.
- Salvatore "Fat Sal" Mangiavillano wanted to become a made man but became a cooperating witness instead.
- Cookie D'Urso helped put scores of gangsters away.
- George Barone was the oldest wiseguy to become a cooperating witness.

Chapter 30

Generation X Gangsterism

In This Chapter

- ◆ Richard Martino's phone sex scheme
- ◆ Andrew Campos plays telephone company
- ◆ The "Night Drop Crew" makes some big withdrawals
- ◆ John Micali represents the new American gangster
- ◆ Christopher Colombo dabbles in the movies

In March 2004, the New York FBI determined that members of the Gambino family had perpetrated the largest consumer fraud in U.S. history, one that fleeced consumers of an eye-popping $750 million from 1996 through 2002. Worse yet, said New York FBI boss Pasquale D'Amuro, "The estimated income figure is fast approaching a billion dollars."

In this chapter, I examine two extremely lucrative white-collar style fraud schemes that generated those massive amounts, as well as other money-making schemes by so-called Generation X gangsters, those born in the 1960s and 1970s who grew up with cable TV, Atari, bungee jumping, Tom Cruise, *The Simpsons*, personal computers, and Madonna.

Richie from the Bronx: King of Phone Sex

Most lawbreakers and law enforcers agree that John Gotti was a lousy crime boss. With his strut and swagger, he taunted the feds and assured his eventual downfall. He also surrounded himself with wiseguys who were in way over their heads. Older brother Peter, the former garbage man tapped to serve as acting family boss, is a good example.

But on January 4, 1990, the Dapper Don picked a winner when he approved the induction of an underling of then-underboss Frank "Frankie Loc" Locascio—Bronx hoodlum Richard Martino, known to his mob cronies as Richie from the Bronx.

"I want guys that done more than killing," said Gotti, praising Martino in a conversation that was picked up by an FBI bug.

"I like the Richies," he said. "They're young, twenty something, thirty something …. They're beautiful guys …. Ten years from now, these young guys we straightened out. They're gonna be really proud of them."

Since his induction, Martino, a virtually unknown soldier until he was indicted on massive racketeering and money laundering charges in 2003, put more money into the family's coffers than any other wiseguy, according to court records and organized crime experts with the FBI. Martino, then 32, hit the ground running, earning millions for himself and the mob in the early to mid-1990s as a pioneer in the lucrative phone sex trade, according to federal law enforcement officials and a 1995 investigation by *New York Daily News* reporter Tom Robbins.

By age 35, Martino was the mob's emerging king of phone sex. Using satellite hook-ups, high-speed computers, and scores of telephone lines, his companies offered a wide range of phone sex choices in several languages for charges ranging from $3.95 to $30 a minute. He had offices on Manhattan's East Side. He hired "artists" in the Dominican Republic to talk dirty for minimum wages. He used a phone-switching station in Kansas to obtain the telephone lines. And he became a multi-millionaire.

By 1995, Richie from the Bronx had moved north, and was living in a plush split-level home in Tuckahoe, New York, a tiny Westchester County community a few miles from his old haunts in the Bronx. His lifestyle, however, was light years away from the days when he worked as a runner, drove a getaway car during a robbery, and smashed a bottle over two patrons' heads during a barroom brawl. He drove a white 1994 Roll Royce and a top-of-the line black Mercedes Benz, and was building a five-bedroom, $4 million summer hideaway in "The Estates," an especially exclusive section of ritzy Southampton, Long Island.

He had some minor legal hassles, civil lawsuits from disgruntled customers and regulatory agencies, but escaped criminal charges until the feds hammered him in 2003. Martino was charged with heading an Internet-based porn scheme that bilked consumers in the United States, Asia, and Europe of $230 million from 1996 to 2000 by tricking gullible surfers to submit credit or debit card information as a come-on for "free tours" of adult entertainment sites.

Instead, the sites, featuring raunchy content from *Playgirl*, *Climax*, *High Society*, and *Young Girls* magazines, contained a cyber-age gimmick that temporarily disabled the "back" button and all other exit modes from the site. As viewers paged through the site, their charges mounted. The average cost of the "free tours" was about $60.

Martino and his codefendants—they include Salvatore "Tore" Locascio, son of the jailed-for-life former family underboss—were charged with stealing $230 million, but privately, authorities say the total plunder from the Internet fraud scheme was more than $300 million.

For years, Tore Locascio, who took over his father Frank's crew when he was convicted with Gotti in 1992, was on the payroll of one or another Martino telecommunications company. Martino had more than a dozen that were based in a converted carriage house that served as his office on Manhattan's East Side. One year, Locascio earned a cool $1 million, and in 1999 and 2000, after Tore and Junior Gotti were indicted on racketeering charges, Martino funneled $8 million to Tore to help fray the cost of his legal fees, fines, and restitution.

Telephone Cramming

Not too many attendees at John Gotti's wake recognized the stocky dark-haired mourner in a white suit and tie who showed up to pay his respects to the late Dapper Don.

But the crime family's hierarchy knew that Andrew "Andrew Campo" Campos was an important friend of theirs, and a key player in a huge moneymaking scheme that poured millions of dollars into the crime family's coffers.

Two years later, however, on February 10, 2004, the feds let everyone in on the secret. They obtained a racketeering and money-laundering indictment that accused Campos of operating eight shell companies around the country that generated anywhere from $50,000 to $600,000 a day from 1997 to 2001 in an innovative and ingenious "telephone cramming scheme" that grossed more than $200 million, with a cool $100 million in profits.

"The telephone cramming and 'free' Internet pornography schemes were innovative and highly profitable," said FBI boss D'Amuro. "They demonstrate how the mob continually seeks new ways to generate cash, unconstrained by concerns for legality or propriety."

FBI agents arrested Campos at his $1-million home in the suburbs without incident. Campos, authorities said, had recently been inducted into the crime family. Viewed as a "moneymaker," Campos was quickly moved up to acting capo by acting boss Arnold "Zeke" Squitieri, the sources added.

Although the Campos surname suggests a Greek ancestry, his father's lineage is Italian, according to a law enforcement official, who also reported that the crime family conducted an extensive investigation into his heritage before he became a made man.

The telephone "cramming" scam, according to court records, was similar to the Internet fraud scheme that Locascio, Martino, and another member of Frank Locascio's Bronx crew, Zef Mustafa, used to bilk thousands of unwitting world-wide-web consumers of upward of $230 million. Indeed, they were also participants in the "cramming" scheme.

In the Campos scheme, callers were solicited through ads in magazines, newspapers, and on TV to dial toll-free "800 numbers" to obtain free samples of sex, psychics, or horoscopes. Instead of the promised free chat lines, dating services, phone sex, and other services, the callers' phone numbers were logged and they were billed an average of $40 a month for voice mail service they never requested or received.

The charges were placed on consumers' phone bills by a mob-controlled company that entered into billing and collection agreements with telephone companies that allowed the wiseguy firm to insert a bill page into the phone company bills. Telephone companies all over the United States have similar agreements that enable legitimate companies—so-called "billing aggregators"—to insert bills for a variety of goods and services into bills they send out each month to their customers.

The scheme was the family's most profitable enterprise and generated more cash than even the family leaders realized, according to FBI investigators and analysts who determined that consumers lost some $520 million in the cramming scheme.

To pull off the swindle, the mob used a number of shell companies around the country, including a Kansas City billing company, USP&C Inc., and a small 8000-subscriber telephone company 25 miles away in Peculiar, Missouri. On the surface, the company, Cass County Telephone, was headed by an otherwise upright local citizen. According to the feds, it belonged lock, stock, and telephone lines to the Gambino crime family.

The gangsters' strategy—to take over and operate a small rural telephone company behind the scenes—was ingenious. The Telecommunications Act of 1996 mandated that federally regulated fees be tacked onto every local phone bill and allocated to companies serving districts where maintenance and other costs are high. Federal records show that Cass County reaps some $6.4 million a year in these subsidies.

The wiseguys provided the capital needed to buy so-called access lines from larger phone companies, according to the feds. After that was accomplished, the wiseguys were off and running—to the bank.

Martino, LoCascio, Campos, and Mustafa have all pleaded not guilty to the charges, and are set for trial in October 2004. Federal prosecutors Eric Komitee and Jeffrey Goldberg are also seeking $430 million in forfeitures from the defendants. Their attorneys say that their clients might have been guilty of sloppy business practices, and perhaps civilly liable for violating complicated regulations governing Internet and telephone communications, but that their operations were proper and above board.

Bank Burglaries

Willie "The Actor" Sutton was only stating the obvious when he uttered his famous response to a New York newsman who wanted to know why he robbed banks— "Because that's where the money is"—but his words remain pertinent more than 50 years later when it comes to the *raison d'etre* of a loosely knit gang of Colombo and Gambino family associates.

But while Willie Sutton was essentially a local New York phenomenon, members of the "Night Drop Crew" logged many thousands of frequent flyer miles during their modern-day efforts to go "where the money is." Using the tools of carpenters, laborers, and demolition workers, the "Night Drop Crew" flew across the country robbing banks and burglarizing night deposit boxes.

On September 17, 2003, however, the feds ended, at least temporarily, the activities of the brazen cross-country bank heist artists who plied their trade from 1993 through August of 2003.

Using crowbars and similar tools, the crew would pry night deposit boxes from the bank wall and remove the deposit bags containing cash, often using gaffing hooks to fish them out. Other times they rented heavy duty SUVs, attached chains to the bumper, and ripped the night deposit box from the bank wall.

Slammer Time

The timing of the massive racketeering indictment of nine suspects was especially troubling for "Night Drop Crew" member John Micali and his fiancé, Lori Daidone, daughter of Louis "Louie Bagels" Daidone, the acting Luchese boss discussed in Chapter 31.

Micali's arrest, and detention without bail, forced them to postpone their gala wedding celebration, planned for October 10. Thinking optimistically, they rescheduled it for December 21, paying for all the arrangements, including wedding favors, the rehearsal dinner, and gifts for the bridal party.

"I have dreamed of this day since I was a little girl," said Lori, in a letter to Brooklyn Federal Judge Sterling Johnson, begging him, without success, to grant Micali a 10-day furlough and make her lifelong dreams come true.

Among other places, they hit banks in Ft. Lauderdale, Miami, Coconut Creek, Pinecrest, and Hollywood, Florida; in Green Bay, Milwaukee, and Grand Chute, Wisconsin; in Jefferson County, Tennessee; in Minnetonka, Minnesota; in Springfield Massachusetts; and in Las Vegas, Nevada. After hitting a few Las Vegas banks on May 30, 2000, crew members laundered the stolen cash in casinos.

According to court papers filed by Brooklyn federal prosecutor Joey Lipton, the crew didn't discriminate against banks closer to its base in New York, however, hitting many banks in Brooklyn, Queens, and Long Island, as well as in cities in New Jersey and Pennsylvania.

Principal organizers of the crew, said Lipton, were two 30-year-old mob associates from Brooklyn with several prior arrests and very close ties to Gambino soldier Thomas "Huck" Carbonaro, John Micali, and Thomas Dono, a nephew of Carbonaro.

Both also operated a lucrative cocaine business and served as enforcers for a gambling operation Dono ran for his Uncle Huck at a Brooklyn social club. One night, wrote Lipton, after a tapped-out gambler couldn't pay, Dono and Micali "beat the individual with a hammer causing him to bleed all over the couches that were in the back room of Dono's club."

In January 2000, according to court papers, Micali agreed to take part in what he learned later was the Gambino family plot to kill Sammy Bull Gravano. At the time, however, Carbonaro merely gave Micali an electronic pager along with instructions to fly to whatever city he called from. Micali, expressing blind loyalty befitting a wannabe wiseguy, agreed to do as instructed but was never called. If the call had come, Micali surely would have been up to the task, according to his resumé. Micali, who took part in at least 14 successful bank burglaries and 9 failed bank jobs, pleaded guilty in early

2004 and faced about five years at sentencing. At press time, Dono, who would face about the same prison time even though he was implicated in fewer heists, was still considering whether or not to go to trial.

John Micali led a band of young mob associates dubbed the "Night Drop Crew" who robbed and burglarized a slew of banks across the country.

(Courtesy GangLandNews.com)

The New American Gangster

Like many people from all walks of life, Micali has good reason to regret a tattoo he got many years ago that probably seemed like such a swell idea at the time.

The artwork fills his upper back. It is a powerful portrait of a suave, nattily-dressed man pointing a gun at the head of a beaten, handcuffed victim kneeling on a cobblestone street under a lamppost.

The victim's hands are behind his back. His head is bowed. He is prepared to die. The Sicilian words that frame the kneeling man are: *"Ammazza a tutti i Sbirri Cu Na Pistuta NA Testa."* According to the FBI, the English translation is: "Kill all the police with a shot in the head."

"The depiction reveals a new era of American gangsters, ones who obviously subscribe to the old world ways of killing police and prosecutors that plagued Italy for decades," said one law enforcement official, describing Micali and eight others indicted as members of the "Night Drop Crew."

"They used guns, baseball bats, hammers, anything and everything they could to get what they wanted," he said.

The artwork on John Micali's back sends a powerful message. So does the translation of the Italian words that accompany it. "Kill all the police with a shot in the head."

(Courtesy GangLandNews.com)

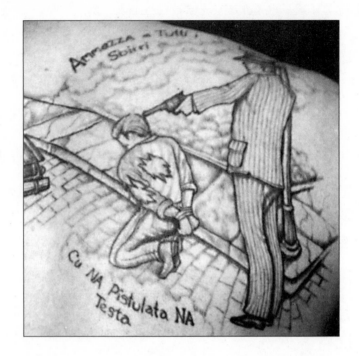

"It's certainly not your normal Mafia mentality," said N. G. Berrill, a forensic psychologist at John Jay College of Criminal Justice. "He needs to demonstrate his bravado or machismo in a very graphic way. For him, it's not sufficient that he develop his reputation based on deed; he needs to splash a billboard on his back."

Berrill, who does profiling work for the Justice Department, said the tattoo "reminds me a lot more of a biker slogan, or a neo-Nazi, neo-fascist kind of mentality. What it says is that 'I am at war with the police.'"

Don John Testosteroni

In an early scene of an unreleased 1989 full-length movie spoof, *Godfather III: The Unauthorized Sequel*, maniacal mob boss Don Testosteroni is seen walking through a cemetery in Palermo, Sicily. He stops at the headstone of his Uncle Virgil, and in a long, often hilarious rant, he tells his dead uncle that that he is on his way to America to avenge his death. And when he does, he will return to Palermo, exhume his remains, and plant them at St. Patrick's Cathedral.

"Revenge will be my word. And death will be my message ... And don't worry, I'll have a safe flight," he proclaims, as the scene fades.

This spoof of the Godfather films, a college thesis project at the School of Visual Arts, won a Special Recognition Prize for best full-length feature in 1989.

Starring as "Don John," in a story that he wrote and in a film for which he served as executive producer, was budding actor/screenwriter Christopher Colombo, the youngest son of the late Mafia boss Joe Colombo, whose life and death from gunshot wounds suffered in 1971 is featured in Chapter 17.

Four years later, however, when his older brother Anthony was released from federal prison, his younger brother eschewed any entertainment industry aspirations he might have had to follow the same path as his father and three older brothers, according to a racketeering indictment filed in Manhattan Federal Court in April 2004.

In a blast from the underworld past, Christopher, 42, and Anthony, 59, were hit with charges that included gambling, loan sharking, and shakedowns of several construction firms and a hot publicly traded Internet advertising company, DoubleClick.

Such lucrative scams would have made their late father—a Coast Guard dropout who took over the Profaci family in 1964 and died in 1978 from the gun shot wounds inflicted seven years earlier—proud. According to the indictment, their crew earned up to $10 million that included no-show jobs for relatives and crew members from 1999 to 2002.

But surely the elder Colombo, who wore $1,000 suits and $500 shoes decades before John Gotti burst on the scene as the Dapper Don, would have blanched at the sight of Christopher in court, unkempt and unshaven and wearing a T-shirt and jogging pants.

Anthony, a soldier in the crime family, was held without bail. Christopher, described as an associate, was ultimately released on a $1 million bond. They were awaiting trial at press time.

Shelved but Not Shut Out

Amazingly, the Colombo brothers were able to engage in mob-sanctioned activities for a decade while they were officially ostracized by their crime family, and supposedly, the entire mob. In court, prosecutors Preet Bharara, Benjamin Lawsky, and Meryl Lutsky declared that the Colombo Brothers Crew had been on the outs with boss Carmine Persico and had been "placed on a shelf" and prohibited from engaging in "family affairs."

The Commission created a "shelf" designation years ago to give mob bosses some lee-way when a made man violated one or more rules and, out of fear or favor, the family desired a punishment other than execution. A mobster on the shelf is essentially sus-pended from all family business activities, but like many mob rules, many wiseguys ignore the ruling.

Sources say that even though the Colombo family had told the city's four other fami-lies about the suspension, members of the Bonanno and DeCavalcante family each engaged in "sitdowns" with the crew to resolve disputes over turf.

"Twenty years ago it was pretty rare, but today, it's gotten to be a pretty common thing, especially since the Commission called for a moratorium on most mob killings in the mid-90s," said one knowledgeable Gang Land source, pointing to similar sanc-tions in recent years by the Gambino, Luchese, and Bonanno families.

The family beef with Christopher and Anthony Colombo goes back to the bloody 1991 to 1993 internal family feud detailed in Chapter 24. The Colombo brothers—including unindicted brothers Joe Jr. and Vincent—backed the losing faction. Worse, when the war ended, they refused to profess their allegiances to the winning side, headed by Persico's son Alphonse, or to share their spoils with him.

During Carmine Persico's reign, Anthony, Vincent, and Joe Jr. headed a violent armed robbery gang whose members often posed as police officers to gain entrance to the homes of wealthy victims on Long Island, who they then often beat and terrorized. They pleaded guilty in 1986.

Anthony, who served the longest stretch, was released in August 1993, and, according to the latest racketeering indictment, got back into action with erstwhile actor Christopher and many crew members who worked for the Colombo Brothers in the 1980s.

The Least You Need to Know

- ◆ John Gotti was right about the moneymaking talents of Richard Martino.

- ◆ Martino and other Generation X gangsters made hundreds of millions of dollars in high-tech frauds.

- ◆ Some Generation X gangsters used tools of blue collar workers to make their fortunes.

- ◆ Some young gangsters act more like biker or neo-Nazis than old-style wiseguys.

- ◆ After a fling in the entertainment world, Christopher Colombo reverted to the underworld.

Chapter 31

Louie Bagels, Allie, and John Riggi

In This Chapter

- Louie Bagels gets life
- Frankie Pearl takes 15 years
- Allie Persico and John Rigggi are in until 2012
- Joe Waverly could get life

Often, as the saying goes, the more things change, the more they remain the same. In some Mafia families, however, the more things stay the same, the more they change.

Since becoming boss of the Luchese crime family, Vittorio "Vic" Amuso has spent more time in federal prison than not. Likewise for Carmine "Junior" Persico, boss of the Colombo family, and John Riggi, boss of the Newark, New Jersey–based DeCavalcante family.

Although the names of the people at the top of the three families haven't changed for quite some time, the activities of the crime families and their respective battles with the law have been anything but static in the new millennium. In this chapter, I take a look at some of these goings-on in the three families.

Louie Bagels and the Rip Van Winkle Murders

Born and raised in Bensonhurst, Brooklyn, Louis Daidone was an all purpose quarterback for New Utrecht High School who was good enough to be offered a football scholarship to Indiana State University in 1963. He didn't take to the Hoosier state—he told friends the feeling was mutual, that they didn't much like Italian-Americans there—and soon returned to Bensonhurst, made his bones with the Luchese family, and moved up to acting boss for Amuso around 2000.

Louie "Bagels" Daidone was found guilty of the Rip Van Winkle murders that carried a sentence of life in prison.

(Courtesy GangLandNews.com)

In 2004, Daidone went to trial in Manhattan Federal Court on racketeering charges that included two murders that took place so long ago (1989 and 1990) that his lawyer had dubbed them the Rip Van Winkle murders, saying they were based on old and sleepy information that would be discredited when the case finally went to trial.

At trial, however, the feds used the testimony of an old-timer, one-time acting boss Alphonse "Little Al" D'Arco, and that of a much younger family defector to recount the murders, including one in which Daidone used talents he had picked up during his football days.

D'Arco, who was "made" on the same day as Daidone in 1982, said that Daidone had killed soldier Bruno Facciola in 1990, and, under his instructions, had placed a canary in his victim's mouth as a warning to others not to talk to the feds. Turncoat soldier Frank Gioia Jr. related that Facciola had tried to run out of a garage where he had been cornered, but Daidone "tackled Facciola and dragged him back into the building" where he was shot and killed by another gangster on the hit team.

Mafia Speak

By the time Louie "Bagels" Daidone went to trial in 2004, it was for murders that could mean the rest of his life in prison. But when first busted in December 2002, Daidone was hit with less serious extortion charges that led to some sarcastic banter with arresting FBI agents.

When one noted he had a "nice wine collection," Daidone replied: "Yeah. I got it with all my extortion money."

As they drove to their office for processing, Daidone complained about one of two nicknames that the FBI had been using for him, one that referred to the name of a Boulevard in Queens that housed a bagel store he owned.

"I don't know anybody who calls me Crossbay Louie," said Louie Bagels, who had no complaints about the nickname that referred to the foodstuffs he sold on Crossbay Boulevard.

The jury convicted Daidone quickly, but not without examining the government's case closely. Very closely.

Before reaching their verdict, the only thing the jurors asked for was a magnifying glass, apparently trying to spot the canary that D'Arco said Daidone had placed in the murder victim's mouth, explaining that Daidone had told him he killed a bird and preserved it in a freezer until he was ready to move on Facciola.

During closing arguments, prosecutors Karl Metzner and Diane Gujarati had told jurors that if they looked closely at the picture of the slain gangster that was introduced into evidence, they "could see something in there."

Less than two hours after getting the magnifying glass, the jurors found what they were looking for and pronounced Daidone guilty on all counts. He faces a mandatory life sentence.

The Freeport Caper and Loud Music

A week before Daidone was arrested in the Manhattan case, 22 Luchese mobsters and associates were indicted on racketeering charges filed in Brooklyn stemming from the family's takeover of a Freeport, Long Island, nightclub that poured $7,000 to $10,000 a night into the organization's coffers.

The Brooklyn case was based on extensive wiretaps that picked up many Luchese wiseguys close to Daidone, including family consigliere Joseph "Joe C" Caridi, in criminal conversations involving loan sharking, extortion, and drug dealing. The focal point of the case, however, was the lucrative shakedown of the owners of a very popular waterfront restaurant bar that lasted for nearly a year.

Mafia Speak

Louis Daidone had a reputation of being tough on his loan-sharking customers, according to former acting boss Joseph "Little Joe" Defede. "He was a little hard-boiled, from what I understand. He was, like, hard to deal with, in other words. I learned this here from associates of Daidone, that he was hard to deal with, as far as loan sharking. That he was tough. When he wanted his money, that it had to be on time."

Once, Defede recalled, Daidone was very upset with a debtor because he was 10 or 15 minutes late with his payment. He was angry, said Defede, that the victim "was holding his money too long, that he was supposed to be there at the same time he should be there."

Ironically, the owners had solicited the Lucheses to oust Lewis Kasman, a self-described adopted son of John Gotti, an investor in the club who had allegedly begun diverting assets to himself. Daidone had been picked up in several discussions with his men, but the feds decided to develop further evidence linking the extorted loot to Daidone before seeking to indict him.

But the case against the others was so strong that they all pleaded guilty, and federal prosecutors in Brooklyn opted to use tape-recorded evidence that implicated Daidone in loan sharking and a beating that he had ordered to bring him to justice. Daidone was charged with ordering wiseguys to slap around a Brooklyn landlord.

Daidone had been overheard giving one of his men directions to the home of the Brooklyn landlord who was threatened, and later beaten, because one of tenants played music too loud. In light of the life sentence Daidone would receive for his murder conviction in Manhattan, a conviction for the beating and the loan-sharking charges would have no real impact, but they were still pending as this book went to press.

Frankie Pearl and the Garbage Haulers

A year before Daidone killed Facciola, another Luchese hit team traveled to East Northport, Long Island, and murdered two brothers-in-law in the tiny offices they used to operate a private garbage-hauling business. The men were killed on August 10, 1989, at about 6 A.M., a few minutes after they got to work. One, Donald Barstow, 35, died instantly. The other, Robert Kubecka, 40, somehow managed to get close enough to grapple with one of the gunmen, who was injured during the struggle, leaving behind a trail of blood as he and his cohort escaped.

Two months later, in October 1989, unbeknownst to the law enforcement community, the wounded gunman, Frank "Frankie Pearl" Federico, was rewarded for his work and inducted into the crime family during a special initiation rite conducted by family boss Vic Amuso, who was a fugitive at the time but returned to Brooklyn to perform the ceremony.

The genesis of the murders was obvious—the men had testified against capo Salvatore Avellino, the Luchese gangster who controlled the family's monopoly in the private sanitation industry on Long Island. But because authorities had no individual suspects, the case lay dormant until March of 1993.

That's when former underboss Anthony "Gaspipe" Casso began cooperating and named all the participants in the plot, telling the feds that Federico was the gunman who had been wounded in the assault. Subpoenaed for blood and hair samples, Federico fled. During the next few years, the other players in the hit, and Avellino himself, were able to wangle sweet plea deals in the murder because Casso self-destructed as a prosecution witness and the feds had no physical evidence tying any of them to the killings.

The Feds did have Frankie Pearl's blood, but they didn't have him. On January 27, 2003, at 6:50 in the evening, they got him, too. Looking very dapper in a gray suit and black cashmere coat, Frankie Pearl arrived at a Bronx coffee shop looking to replenish his dwindling supply of cash. He was down to his last $3,000.

Instead of being met by an old friend with cash, he was greeted by cops and agents with cuffs, who arrested him for the 1989 execution murders. A year later, on March 22, 2004, after exhausting all efforts to suppress the blood evidence from his case, Federico, at age 76, pleaded guilty to the murders of Kubecka and Barstow for an agreed-upon sentence of 15 years in prison.

If he lives long enough, with normal time off, he'll be released in 2016, at age 88. That's bad, but Frankie Pearl made out a lot better than Luchese boss Vic Amuso. Federico had 10 years of freedom after the killings, and although it's a long shot, he has some hope of getting out of prison. Amuso, who was arrested and jailed in 1991, has no hope of ever getting out of prison.

Allie Bites the Bullet, Again

Through bloodshed and bloodlines, Alphonse "Allie" Persico took over the day-to-day operations of the Colombo crime family in the mid-1990s, fulfilling the dream of his father, Carmine, the jailed-for-life official boss of the crime family.

For both of them, the dream has become a nightmare.

The younger Persico's ascension was put in motion in August 1994, following his acquittal on racketeering and murder charges and release from federal prison. With the backing of his father, Alphonse was a shoe-in to take over the crime family. Mobsters loyal to his father had crushed an insurrection by a rebel group in a bloody two-year long war (1991–1993) with 12 fatalities and many more injuries. His rise to acting boss was hastened in 1996 by the jailing of his cousin Andrew Russo, a caretaker acting boss Carmine selected to tutor Alphonse and prepare him for his birthright.

Since October 1999, however, when Alphonse was arrested by FBI agents, who found $25,000 in cash and $1 million in loan-sharking records during a search of his Brooklyn apartment, he has been in one federal prison or another. And he's not due to be released until 2012. What's worse for him, the feds are pulling all the stops in an effort to keep him there until he dies, as they have with his father.

Fuhgeddaboudit

It was Friday, September 4, 1988, the start of a glorious Labor Day weekend, and Alphonse Persico was tooling around the Florida keys in his 50-foot-speed boat, *Lookin' Good*, when a Coast Guard cutter, *Courageous*, signaled him to cut his engines for a routine search of his vessel.

The boarding party found two loaded weapons—a Browning .380 semi-automatic pistol and a Mossback 12-gauge shotgun—hidden away, but Persico caught a big break. Everything else was in order and a quick check failed to turn up a prior conviction that would have automatically barred him from possessing a gun. The crew merely unloaded the guns, and sent Persico on his merry way.

You'd think that a bright, prison-hardened, college-educated gangster like Persico would have breathed a sigh of relief, and then, as soon as the *Courageous* was out of sight, dumped both guns overboard.

Think again. At about 1:00 A.M. on September 5, the Coast Guard discovered his 1986 federal racketeering conviction, and a team of Coasties and Key West police returned to the marina where the *Lookin' Good* was docked. They found Persico and both guns still onboard.

The search that led to Persico's loan-sharking arrest occurred while FBI agents were looking for a cell phone they believed would link Persico to the May 1999 disappearance and suspected murder of underboss William "Wild Bill" Cutolo.

Held without bail, Persico pleaded guilty to possessing loaded guns on his boat in Key West the previous year, and began serving a 15-month sentence. The loan-sharking charges were dropped, but on the day his sentence for weapons possession ended, January 26, 2001, the feds used the seized loan-sharking records to charge him with engaging in a loan-sharking conspiracy from 1993 to October 1999.

Two weeks later, the feds let Persico know that the case would be more than a minor annoyance when they disclosed that Cutolo's son, William Jr., had been responsible for the search of Persico's Brooklyn apartment and had been working with the feds to obtain evidence against his father's killers in an investigation he dubbed, "Operation Payback."

In addition to Persico, the racketeering indictment included underboss John "Jackie" DeRoss, who succeeded the slain Cutolo as the family's number two mobster and was also a suspect in Cutolo's murder, and several other members of DeRoss's crew.

On the eve of trial in December 2001, Persico threw in the towel, and pleaded guilty to racketeering, loan-sharking, and money-laundering charges for an agreed-upon sentence of 13 years.

In the process, he admitted he was a high-ranking member of the Mafia because the indictment accused him of being "the acting boss of the Colombo family," earning some razzing from other inmates at the Metropolitan Detention Center (MDC) when he returned there from Brooklyn Federal Court.

"They said you admitted you were the boss," said one wiseguy.

"No, just some legal mumbo jumbo," said Persico, who took some prelaw courses at St. Johns University before dropping out to follow his father and uncles Alphonse and Theodore into the Colombo crime family—and federal prison. Uncle Alphonse died there in 1989 at age 59. Uncle Teddy is due out in 2013, at age 75. Carmine, 70 when this book went to press, is scheduled for release in 2043.

Alphonse, who was badmouthed by DeRoss for admitting membership in the Colombo family, later tried to withdraw his plea and proceed to trial when federal prosecutors decided not to use Cutolo Jr. as a witness, for a variety of reasons, including mental instability. His efforts failed.

Meanwhile, DeRoss, a veteran gangster who rejected a plea deal calling for much less time than Persico agreed to because it entailed admitting membership in the crime family, proceeded to trial in early 2002.

In February, when, after four days of deliberations, the jury announced it had reached a verdict, DeRoss loosened his tie and stood to hear the verdict. He was acquitted of racketeering, money laundering, extortion, conspiracy—all charges stemming from Cutolo Jr.'s undercover work—but found guilty of a lone unrelated extortion charge.

He left his tie on the defense table, gave his coat to a nephew to take home, and was led off to join Persico in the MDC with his head held high. Sentenced to seven years, DeRoss is scheduled for release in 2008, at age 70.

Joe Waverly and the Judge

On January 22, 2003, nearly 16 years after the heinous and baffling execution of a 78-year-old retired civil lawyer working as an Administrative Law Judge, Colombo consigliere Joel "Joe Waverly" Cacace was nailed for the crime.

Cacace, who was serving as the family's acting boss, was charged with the March 20, 1987, murder of George Aronwald, the father of a one-time mob prosecutor, who was shot to death in a bizarre mistaken-identity gangland-style rubout.

More than 15 years after a retired 78-year-old lawyer was executed for no apparent reason, the feds charged Joe Waverly Cacace with his murder.

(Courtesy GangLandNews.com)

Aronwald was killed as he stood at the counter of Young's Chinese Laundry in Long Island City picking up his shirts in the middle of the day. The killer followed him in and emptied his gun at him. Hit twice in the head and three times in the chest and body, he died instantly.

For years, police had no clues or possible suspects. Right after the murder, detectives scoured Aronwald's civil practice, his workplace as a PVB hearing officer, and his son William's career as a prosecutor in search of a motive. They even looked into whether Aronwald was mistaken for the late Gambino consigliere Joseph N. Gallo, who was of similar age and stature and lived nearby.

The key witness against Cacace is Luchese associate Frank Smith, the only surviving member of a three-man hit team that intended to kill Aronwald's son William, a former federal prosecutor who had been marked for death by the jailed-for-life Colombo boss, Carmine "Junior" Persico.

Smith and two incredibly inept cohorts who were killed a few months later, Vincent Carini and his brother Enrico (Eddie), mistook their slight, frail 78-year-old victim for his burly 46-year-old son, according to court documents filed in connection with the racketeering and murder indictment against Cacace.

The first real break in the case came 10 years after the murder, on July 9, 1997. That's when turncoat Luchese soldier Frank Gioia Jr. learned that Smith's sister Kim—the mother of Gioia's only son—had tape-recorded telephone conversations she had with him and sold them for $10,000 to wiseguys Gioia was cooperating against.

Mafia Speak

From the witness stand, Frank Gioia Jr. explained why, after holding back for two years, he began to tell the feds in 1997 about crimes in which members of his girlfriend Kim's family had been involved: "I learned that she secretly recorded me on tape for the mob. The same day when I learned of the tapes—(that) she taped me for Bones, (Frank Papagni)—that's when I decided to come clean about her family. That's the first time I ever spoke to them about her Uncle Tony, her brother Frank Smith, her father, her cousin Michael, and her cousin Vincent. I felt that she had crossed the line. If you want to go out with somebody else, you don't want to wait for me, that's one thing. If you want to hold my son from me—maybe later on you'll see the reasons why I'm doing these things and maybe you'll settle down and maybe I will get a chance to see my kid. But once you want to go against me and you want to go with the people that tried to kill my father and abuse my family, you want to sign in with the mob, then … I can't trust you any more."

"Once Gioia heard this," said FBI agent Stephen Byrne, "he told me in substance to get my pen out and get ready to write. Gioia then provided us with a list of crimes committed by (her) relatives, including several unsolved murders."

Gioia, whose cooperation has helped convict more than 80 mobsters and drug dealers, and one cop killer, had spared his then-fiancé's family when he defected in 1995. He gave Smith up for Aronwald's murder and the slayings six months later of two mob associates around the corner from Smith's Bath Beach, Brooklyn, home.

Cacace is also charged with ordering the slaying of the two mob associates in Bath Beach, and the 1987 murder of a corrupt police officer, Carlo Antonino.

Smith told Gioia about the hits during jailhouse visits Gioia made to Smith in the early 1990s. At the time, Smith was incarcerated for drug dealing for which he was wrongly convicted.

Ironically, Smith's wrongful drug conviction, which kept him locked up and out of harm's way for 16 years, and a little dumb luck, helped save his life.

Three months after Smith and the Carini brothers killed Aronwald, they were allegedly targeted for death by Cacace to silence them forever. The Carinis were both killed on June 11, 1987, on a night that Smith was supposed to have been with them. He arrived home late, so they left for their execution without him.

Following their murders, according to law enforcement accounts, Smith sought help from members of the Luchese family he knew. They prevailed at two high-level sit-downs with the Colombos, who agreed to spare Smith. Nevertheless, Smith always feared that Cacace would ignore the agreement and have him killed. "I always figured they would kill me," Smith told Gioia. "They killed Eddie and Vinny. I never figured Joe Waverly would let me live since I'm the only one left who could tie him to the killing."

Joe Waverly Cacace is scheduled for trial in late 2004. Gioia and mob associate Salvatore "Fat Sal" Mangiavillano, one of the New Defectors featured in Chapter 30, are also expected to testify against Cacace.

John Riggi Gives Up

John Riggi held out until the bitter end, but the longtime DeCavalcante boss eventually gave up the ghost.

In late summer of 2003, Riggi, the aging and ailing New Jersey mob boss, was about to become the oldest Mafia boss to go to trial for racketeering. Instead, on the eve of trial on September 4, 2003, he became the oldest don to cop a plea to racketeering charges, agreeing to a sentence of 10 years.

Riggi pleaded guilty via a remote television hookup between Manhattan Federal Court and the federal prison hospital in Butner, North Carolina, one of several facilities where he had been confined since he went to prison for a variety of federal crimes on October 25, 1990.

Normally, getting 10 years for a racketeering case that includes three mob hits and three failed murder plots would be a steal. But for a 78-year-old wiseguy suffering from high blood pressure, prostate cancer, and heart disease, the move was at odds with the most optimistic actuarial tables.

Fuhgeddaboudit

On Sunday mornings for three decades—the 1960s, 1970s, and 1980s—virtually the entire DeCavalcante family would spend a few hours at John Riggi's Elizabeth, New Jersey, coffee shop on John Street. The coffee shop was where Riggi and mob associates who paid homage to him conducted their crime business.

Across the street from the coffee shop was the Ribera Social Club that Riggi also ran, ostensibly to raise money for poor kids in Italy.

Each year, the Ribera club raised money for the St. Joseph's Orphanage in the old country. And while family members appropriated some cash for themselves once in a while, "usually it went to the orphanage," according to turncoat capo Anthony Rotondo.

His guilty plea was the culmination of a four-year federal assault by the feds against the Garden State gangsters who fancy themselves the models for *The Sopranos*. The sentence will keep him incarcerated until December 2012, at age 87.

Riggi, who moved into the family's inner circle and began his climb to the top under legendary Mafia boss Simone "Sam the Plumber" DeCavalcante, pleaded guilty to doing a favor for a powerful New York Mafia boss, something DeCavalcante had tutored him to do four decades ago.

Back then, Carlo Gambino had asked DeCavalcante to kill Joseph "Joey Surprise" Feola, an associate in the garbage business who suddenly fell out of favor with his bosses. So Joey Surprise was lured to a garage, where he was strangled, wrapped in a burlap bag, and buried.

In late 1989, Gambino's successor, John Gotti, asked Riggi for a similar courtesy—the execution of Fred Weiss, a jammed-up private sanitation magnate—and Riggi could not bring himself to say no.

"This is a favor for John Gotti. It will put us on the map," he told capo Vincent "Vinny Ocean" Palermo on September 6, 1989, setting in motion Weiss's killing five days later.

Riggi took over as acting boss in the early 1980s when DeCavalcante retired to Florida and enjoyed the fruits of his years of plunder in the Sunshine State. He eventually left the official post to his longtime understudy.

Years later, in 1997, Sam the Plumber died of natural causes at age 84, but his patronage and tutelage has meant lots of trouble, with the mob, as well as the law, for his former star pupil and loyal follower.

Mafia Speak

During a private talk with his boss on October 2, 1964, a day John Riggi would later be promoted to capo, he praised Simone "Sam the Plumber" DeCavalcante as a fair and more honest boss than predecessor Nick Delmore, according to a bug the FBI had at the Kenilworth Plumbing and Heating Co. in Newark, Sam the Plumber's headquarters.

"The veil has been lifted and no one is afraid to speak the truth," Riggi told DeCavalcante, who heartily agreed.

Riggi's problem with the Mafia stemmed from a decision DeCavalcante made decades earlier. He eliminated the traditional use of a gun, knife, and a burning holy card during induction ceremonies, having decided they were an unnecessary waste of time.

Up until late 1998 or early 1989, Riggi followed suit. About that time, however, a New Jersey soldier spilled the beans to a New York wiseguy. Word spread throughout New York's Five Families, and the Mafia Commission ordered the family to re-induct its entire membership.

Large group re-inductions were held. At one, according to Palermo, underboss John D'Amato "placed a gun and a knife on the table and said that these were their tools, just like a carpenter has a hammer and screwdriver. When called upon, these tools must be used."

The Least You Need to Know

- Louie "Bagels" Daidone and Vic Amuso are each serving life sentences for multiple mob murders.

- Frankie Pearl Federico is serving 15 years for two mob murders.

- Allie Persico is due out of prison in 2012.

- Joe Waverly is facing life behind bars.

- John Riggi will get out of prison in 2012, if he lives that long.

The FBI: Scandals Abound in Beantown

In This Chapter

- ◆ Paul Rico makes the ultimate escape
- ◆ FBI agent John Connelly doesn't get off so lightly
- ◆ Home sweet home for Cadillac Frank
- ◆ Steve "The Rifleman" gets hit with life
- ◆ Whitey Bulger remains a fugitive

In 1968, it has been established beyond all doubt, mob informant Joseph "The Animal" Barboza helped frame four innocent men—including gangster Louis Greco—for the 1985 murder of small-time criminal Teddy Deegan.

A few days after the conviction, according to testimony 35 years later by former New England Mafia Boss Francis "Cadillac Frank" Salemme, FBI agent Dennis Condon came to his garage, "elated about getting these guys convicted, and he made the statement, 'I wonder how Louie Greco likes it on death row, and he wasn't even there.'"

Former agent Condon has denied making that statement, has denied any wrongdoing in the case, and denied knowing that at the time of Barboza's testimony, the FBI had confidential information that showed Barboza to be lying.

In this chapter, I examine developments concerning some of the major players in the scandal and the progress of the continuing investigation by federal and local authorities.

Paul Rico Beats the Rap

On January 17, 2004, H. Paul Rico, an aging and ailing accused killer awaiting trial for a 23-year-old execution murder—and a suspect in a 1965 mob rubout—passed away from natural causes in the medical unit of a state prison in Tulsa, Oklahoma.

Rico was 78 when he died. He had spent four months in prison for the murder of businessman Roger Wheeler, a pillar of the Tulsa community who was shot in the head at a country club in Tulsa on a beautiful spring day in 1981 as kids frolicked nearby at a swimming pool. In the end, as many a wiseguy has said about gangsters who enjoy the fruits of their crime unimpeded for the lion's share of their lives, Rico beat the rap. He proved the old adage that crime often pays.

But Paul Rico was not a made man. He was worse than most, though. Technically, he could be described as a mob associate—he engaged in criminal activity with organized crime figures for decades—but that label doesn't do justice to the depraved criminal activity that he engaged in for most of his adult life.

Rico, who retired from the FBI in 1975, was a corrupt agent who spent most of his career as a G-man working organized crime in Boston. According to testimony by two former gangsters—one a longtime informer, the other a Mafia boss—Rico helped them kill a rival gangster in 1965 and framed several other hoodlums for a murder they didn't commit. His partner at the time was Dennis Condon.

Rico's death saddened many law enforcement professionals, not due to any sympathy for him, but because it will likely forestall a full public accounting of all the dirty deeds he committed while carrying a badge. But enough is known about them, and other FBI agents who investigated organized crime in New England, as a result of prosecutions in Boston and Tulsa and through a voluminous report by a special House Committee on Government Reform about the FBI's use of confidential informants.

Ironically, one of Rico's informants, Steve "The Rifleman" Flemmi, ultimately did him in. Rico had worked as a security specialist for Wheeler and was under investigation by his boss for skimming funds from World Jai Alai, a Miami company Wheeler owned. According to Flemmi, Rico commissioned three old Boston cronies to whack his boss to end the inquiry.

Tulsa Detective Sergeant Mike Huff, who had investigated Wheeler's murder for 22 years, was angry that by dying (three years earlier Rico arrogantly told a congressional investigator: "I'm an old man. I'll be dead before you can do something."), Rico had deprived Tulsans of their need for closure. But the dogged detective had some hope the case wouldn't die with Rico. Another of Rico's informants, James "Whitey" Bulger, also took part in the killing, and is still alive, albeit a fugitive (see the section titled "Whitey Bulger Stays on the Run" later in this chapter for more on Bulger).

"He needs to be caught and stand trial," said Huff. "The public has the right to some answers."

John Connolly

John Connolly was another corrupt FBI agent who worked the Mafia in Boston. Like Rico, he also received bonuses and commendations for great accomplishments in rooting out organized crime. He wasn't quite as lucky as Rico, however. He was caught, convicted, and sentenced to 10 years.

Connolly was convicted in May 2002 of racketeering and obstruction of justice for warning then–New England Mafia boss Francis "Cadillac Frank" Salemme and two other gangsters in late 1994 that the feds were about to arrest them on racketeering charges. The other gangsters, Whitey Bulger and Steve "The Rifleman" Flemmi, were longtime informers for Connolly. Salemme escaped but was arrested seven months later in Florida. Flemmi was arrested on January 5, 1995. At press time, Bulger remained a fugitive on the FBI's Most Wanted list with a $1-million reward posted for information leading to his apprehension. Connolly, at age 63, still had seven more years to serve before his projected release date, June 28, 2011.

Based on new information the feds have received from Flemmi, however, the convicted agent might face additional charges that could keep him incarcerated forever. During the 1970s and 1980s in Boston, Flemmi and Bulger ran a criminal organization that controlled gambling, drug trafficking, and loan sharking that rivaled the Mafia, in part, because Connolly looked the other way at their rackets while using information they supplied to focus on their mob rivals.

In court documents, Flemmi claimed that in 1976, Connolly warned Bulger that nightclub owner Richard Castucci was an FBI informant against his gang, and in 1982 Connolly told Bulger that a mob-connected financier, John Callahan, was being investigated as an intermediary in the murder of Roger Wheeler and would likely cooperate against Bulger and Flemmi.

The U.S. Attorney's office in Boston was investigating Connolly for suspected involvement in at least two murders that Bulger and Flemmi committed, allegedly with important help from the rogue G-man. The feds were examining various options to prosecute Connolly for those crimes, even though a jury acquitted him in 2003 of leaking confidential information to Bulger that prompted Bulger and Flemmi to kill Castucci and Callahan. At the same time, the feds were reportedly looking to get him to cooperate in their efforts to locate Bulger and assist in additional investigations of corruption by other FBI agents and police officers.

Cadillac Frank

Former New England Mafia boss Francis "Cadillac Frank" Salemme is one of a kind. After doing what many other wiseguys, including one other boss, have done—break his vow of omerta—Salemme moved back to his hometown and got himself a legitimate job.

In early April 2004, WCVB-TV reporter David Boeri spotted Salemme having lunch in one of his favorite eateries, the Busy Bee restaurant on Beacon Street, the same diner that state police had bugged years earlier to help nail him on federal racketeering.

A year earlier, sporting a new Irish name under the federal Witness Protection Program, he relocated to an apartment complex in the southwest. But he couldn't resist the lure of his hometown. Besides, he joked to Boeri, the medical care wasn't what it was cracked up to be: "I expected I was going to Walter Reed and they sent me to Walgreen's instead."

Salemme's decision to testify against corrupt FBI agent Connolly wasn't a joke for the retired G-man. The only charge for which the jury convicted Connolly was based on Salemme's testimony about a chance meeting he had in late 1994 with Connolly, who had arrested him in New York in 1972 when he was a fugitive in an attempted murder.

Salemme testified that Connolly had said, "I hope there's no hard feelings, I was just doing my job."

Salemme assured Connolly there were none, and as they departed, Salemme testified, Connolly said that he was working nearby, adding, "You have an open invitation to come to my office."

A day or two later, Salemme took him up on his offer. He stopped in at Connolly's office, looking for information about a federal probe of him, Flemmi, and Bulger that Salemme had learned about.

Surprisingly, Salemme testified, Connolly was very cordial and forthcoming with him and said he was still plugged into goings-on at the FBI and would get a message to him through Flemmi when the indictment was about to come down.

From the witness stand, Salemme said he had nothing against Connolly, but merely decided to break his Mafia vow of *omerta* and testify against him because he was granted immunity, and threatened with another 18 months in jail for contempt if he refused.

At that stage of his life, he was 68, with more than three years to serve, he said, "I wasn't going to do 18 hours for anybody, never mind 18 months." By testifying, Salemme got 28 months off his 11-year, 4-month term that had been scheduled to end in 2005.

Fuhgeddaboudit

In testimony before the House Committee on Government Reform, Cadillac Frank Salemme tried to explain how he and Steve Flemmi decided how to pull off their criminal endeavors, including murder.

"I planned them. Stevie wasn't a planner. He would go if you took him by the hand, but he wasn't a planner at all. He had his own agenda, and he wasn't deviating from that. He had somebody to do the grunt work, and that was me. So I planned them and (we) executed them, him and I."

Although he testified against Connolly and admitted taking part in eight murders in the 1960s, Salemme has refused to turn on his old mob cohorts. For example, Salemme hasn't given up assailants who shot and wounded him in a rubout attempt in June 1989.

Sitting in a window booth at the Busy Bee two years after his testimony, Salemme displayed little anxiety about being exposed.

"No, I don't feel unsafe at all," he said, insisting that he was going to resist any urges to return to "the life" and will remain far away from his old stomping grounds in the North End, avoiding restaurants and cafes where he might run into old cohorts.

"Shame on me if I get back in the game, or even attempt to. That life is so inundated with top-echelon informants you couldn't survive half a day in it," he said.

Steve "The Rifleman" Takes Life

On January 27, 2004, as the sons, daughters and other relatives of his many victims watched, Stephen "The Rifleman" Flemmi was sentenced to die in prison for the murders of eight men and two women he admitted killing from 1974 to 1985.

Steve "The Rifleman" Flemmi on the prowl in the streets of Boston in this police photo.

Flemmi, his voice hushed, apologized for behaving like a vicious animal during his life of crime, but the grieving relatives of his victims were not assuaged by the apology or the life sentence that the 69-year-old Flemmi received as part of a plea bargain worked out between his lawyers and lead prosecutor, assistant U.S. attorney Fred Wyshak.

"Because of you, I have never for a minute known what it's like to grow up with a father," said 29-year-old Timothy Connors, whose father Edward was killed by Flemmi in June 1975. "You were able to enjoy your life, go on vacation, have girl-friends …. Your troubles are over today, and mine will go on until the day I die."

Flemmi's plea deal calls for him to spend the rest of his life in prison. It eliminates the possibility of capital punishment for his participation in the murder of Roger Wheeler in Oklahoma and another slaying in Florida. In addition to those slayings, Flemmi pleaded guilty to eight other murders, including his girlfriend, whom he strangled when he learned she was going to leave him; the daughter of another girlfriend in a fit of anger; and a host of other crimes, all while working as a paid informant for the FBI, first for Rico, later for Connolly.

In his signed plea agreement, Flemmi admitted being a leader of a "violent criminal organization" known as the Winter Hill Gang. The gangs consisted of "well over a hundred" members who shared Boston area rackets like gambling, loan sharking, and drug dealing with the Mafia but also engaged in numerous other crimes including extortion and murder from 1972 to 2000.

Flemmi and his longtime partner-in-crime, James Whitey Bulger, would often bury their victims' bodies to lessen the chance of prosecution. Occasionally, Flemmi admitted, he pulled out his victims' teeth to make their remains more difficult to identify.

Mafia Speak

"There's two things with Flemmi paramount to everything, his money and his women," Cadillac Frank Salemme told the House Committee on Government Reform. "He was a womanizer, and you know what happened with this case, what took place with this stepdaughter and the other little girl, Debbie Davis. But that was his MO all along. That's what it was to him, his money and his women, not necessarily in that order."

Flemmi and Bulger got away with murder for years, but their criminal organization began to crumble in January 1995, when they were hit with federal racketeering charges. In 2000, after their long sordid history of bribing cops and FBI agents with cash and information was exposed, the feds upped the ante, charging Flemmi with 10 murders and Bulger with 19.

In court, Wyshak, who had begun the investigation in the mid-1990s noted that it had been a "grave mistake" for the FBI to use Flemmi and Bulger as informants, labeling that decision as "a scar on this city" that fostered mistrust among law enforcement agencies. He added a poignant observation: "These wounds will not heal overnight."

Whitey Bulger Stays on the Run

After spending a few years at Alcatraz decades ago for bank robbery, James "Whitey" Bulger has always managed to come out on top in his continuing cat-and-mouse game with the law. In May 2004, the FBI announced that its latest gambit to snare the cunning and vicious killer from Southie had failed.

A month earlier, the FBI had released three never-before-seen pictures of Bulger in an effort to get the one tip it needs to apprehend him after nearly a decade on the run. Taken before he fled, the photos—one of which showed Bulger cuddling a black poodle that had belonged to the woman he is believed to be with, Catherine Greig—were broadcast on Fox TV's *America's Most Wanted.*

Following the broadcast—the twelfth time that the popular crime show had featured Bulger—viewers called in 18 tips about Bulger sightings in South America, Canada, and Florida.

"All 18 washed out," said Kenneth Kaiser, head of the Boston FBI, which has a task force of 12 to 14 investigators and analysts working full time on the case.

In its latest wanted flyers about Bulger and Greig—another new photo showed Bulger holding a baby goat—the FBI noted that Greig "has an affinity for animals" and that the couple often enjoys "walking on beaches and in parks" together.

Whitey Bulger in a 1994 photo released by the FBI.

In 2002 and again the following year, there were sightings of Bulger in London that authorities believe are credible, causing the task force to devote much of its investigative resources in the United Kingdom, Ireland, and throughout Europe.

"This involves the credibility and the reputation of the FBI," said Kaiser. "I want to get this situation resolved so we can move forward."

The Least You Need to Know

- Several corrupt FBI agents have damaged the agency's credibility in Boston.
- Former Mafia boss Cadillac Frank Salemme says he's now legit.
- The Winter Hill Gang was a vicious organized crime group that flourished for years in Boston.
- Steve "The Rifleman" Flemmi will die in prison.
- Whitey Bulger is a huge black eye for the FBI.

33

Jimmy Hoffa: The Murder Mystery Solved?

In This Chapter

- ◆ Jimmy Hoffa gets whacked
- ◆ The FBI identifies suspects in Hoffa's murder
- ◆ Frank the Irishman writes a very revealing book
- ◆ This author's analysis of the Hoffa murder

On July 30, 1975, at about 1:35 in the afternoon, James Riddle Hoffa, the former president of the International Brotherhood of Teamsters, left the offices of an airport car service in Pontiac, Michigan, in a bit of a rush. He was there, he told employees, to ask the owner of the company, a friend, to attend a meeting with him.

But Louis Linteau, a former Teamsters Union official, was out. So Hoffa, who was punctual to a fault, departed. As he left, he told an employee who stopped him to ask about a problem with his Teamsters Union pension that he didn't have time to discuss it. "I've got this meeting and I've got to meet on time."

About an hour and fifteen minutes later, about 2:50 P.M., Hoffa was seen leaving the parking lot of the Machus Red Fox Restaurant in Bloomfield, another suburb of Detroit, in a maroon Mercury with three other men. He hasn't been seen since.

In this chapter, I look at the disappearance of Jimmy Hoffa, perhaps the most successful mob rubout of a prominent personality in the history of the American Mafia, one that has been the subject of late-night talk shows, gossip columns, and jokes. I discuss the circumstances of his disappearance, and the many suspects who emerged in the FBI's investigation. I also examine and analyze the gripping, and seemingly authentic, account of Hoffa's slaying in *I Heard You Paint Houses*, a book by Charles Brandt (Steerforth, 2004).

The Hoffex Memo

Six months after Jimmy Hoffa disappeared, FBI Director Clarence Kelley convened a meeting of FBI agents and federal prosecutors from around the country investigating the case, which everyone knew by then was a murder.

In a list of 12 suspects that the FBI prepared for the two-day conference, one suspect was described in more detail than any others: Francis Joseph "Frank" Sheeran, then 43.

> ### Fuhgeddaboudit
>
> Early on, the FBI tabbed Frank "The Irishman" Sheeran as a key suspect in Jimmy Hoffa's disappearance, including this description of him in an internal memo: President Local 326, Wilmington Delaware; resides in Philadelphia and is known associate of Russell Bufalino, LCN Chief, (North) Eastern Pennsylvania. His vehicle seen at meeting of LCN figures in Wilkes Barre, Pennsylvania, August 29, 1975, and also in Detroit, December 4, 1975, during FGJ (federal grand jury) appearance of New Jersey Teamsters. Known to be in Detroit area at the time of JRH disappearance and considered to be close friend of JRH.

Bufalino, then boss of the Pittstown, Pennsylvania, family, wasn't listed as a suspect, and except for a mention of him in a lengthy paragraph about Sheeran, neither Bufalino nor Sheeran were mentioned again in a 55-page memo that was distributed at the conclave.

Two other listed suspects, Charles "Chuckie" O'Brien, then 41, a so-called "adopted son" of Hoffa and a Teamsters Union official, and Salvatore "Sally Bugs" Briguglio, a trusted associate of Genovese capo and powerful Teamsters Union power Anthony "Tony Pro" Provenzano, were said by two witnesses to have been in a car with Hoffa that left the restaurant parking lot at about 2:45 P.M. The report had O'Brien driving and Sally Bugs directly behind him in the back seat of a maroon Mercury that was owned by a son of Detroit capo Anthony "Tony Jack" Giacalone, a longtime associate of Hoffa.

Hoffa had been in the back seat, according to evidence obtained from three German Shepherd scent dogs that detected a "strong indication of JRH scents in the rear seat" of the car, the memo stated.

That day, Hoffa had taped to the lamp shade in his office—where he usually posted important messages—a note that he had a 2:30 appointment with Tony Jack at the "Fox Rest." Hoffa, however, had told Linteau, and his wife Josephine, that he had a 2 P.M. appointment at the restaurant. And at about 2:15, he called home, angry that he had been stood up, wondering if anyone had called.

The Two Tonys

The "Hoffex" memo also lists two important "Tonys" as suspects in the mysterious disappearance of James Riddle Hoffa—Anthony "Tony Jack" Giaccalone and Anthony "Tony Pro" Provenzano. Hoffa thought he was going to meet both men that fateful day, the memo states.

Giaccalone, then 57, was a longtime friend and business associate. His former girlfriend was Chuckie O'Brien's mother and a good friend of Josephine Hoffa. Giaccalone was the mob's "contact man" with the Teamsters through the 1950s and 1960s. By 1971, however, when Hoffa was pardoned by President Richard Nixon and released from prison, they had drifted apart, essentially because Hoffa was then an outsider, and of no real use to Tony Jack, or the mob, for that matter.

Provenzano, then 58, had served time with Hoffa in Lewisberg Federal Penitentiary in the late 1960s and was an officer of Teamsters Local 560 in Union City, New Jersey. They hated each other and Hoffa resisted all efforts by Giaccalone to settle his differences with Provenzano. On May 15, 1975, Tony Jack met Hoffa at his son's law offices and pressed Hoffa to meet with Tony Pro, who would meet him anytime, anyplace.

"There's got to be a meeting," Giaccalone said, according to the memo. Hoffa refused to meet him anywhere, saying Tony Pro was "a bum."

In mid-July 1975, Tony Pro called Hoffa at home, and Hoffa had dismissed him, telling his wife that he wasn't planning to help Tony Pro in any way, said the memo, concluding that "JRH resisted" Giaccalone's mediation efforts "for a lengthy period" but that for reasons that were unclear, Hoffa had eventually relented and agreed to meet with him.

But, according to the "Hoffex" memo, neither of the Tonys was anywhere near the Machus Red Fox Restaurant on July 30, 1975. Each had airtight alibis. Tony Pro was in Union City, at Local 560's offices, according to secretaries and other office workers who testified before a federal grand jury. Tony Jack was having a massage and a haircut at the Southfield Athletic Club in Detroit and had been seen by more people during the three critical hours before and after Hoffa's disappearance than usually spotted him in a week. Indeed, so many people saw him, the memo concluded: "Giaccalone definitely appeared to be establishing an alibi, inasmuch as he made himself very visible, which is not his normal style."

Two other suspects, brothers Thomas, then 38, and Steven Andretta, 42, also "trusted" allies of Provenzano, were said to have been playing cards with Tony Pro at Local 560's offices but unlike Provenzano, their alibis were less than airtight, the Hoffex memo concluded. The accounts of their whereabouts at the time of the Hoffa murder were discounted for a number of reasons, none of which warranted an indictment for perjury.

Of all the suspects listed above, only Chuckie O'Brien and Thomas Andretta were alive in June of 2004, when this book went to press.

Frank "The Irishman"

In the opinion of Frank "The Irishman" Sheeran, the "two greatest" men that he met during his life were Jimmy Hoffa and Russell Bufalino. When Sheeran died in an assisted living facility in December of 2003, he wore a gold watch encircled with diamonds that Hoffa had given him nine months before he disappeared. On his finger, he wore a gold ring topped by a three-dollar gold piece surrounded by diamonds that Bufalino had given him the same night.

Mafia Speak

Frank Sheeran's first brush with the law took place on February 4, 1947. He was beating up "two big stiffs" on a street corner in Philadelphia and cops told them to "get off the corner," according to his account in *I Heard You Paint Houses*.

"I told the cop I wasn't going anywhere until I was finished with them. Next thing you know I'm fighting three cops. They booked me disorderly conduct and resisting arrest."

At six-foot-four, Sheeran, president of Teamsters Local 326 in Delaware, towered over both men. They differed in style and demeanor. Bufalino was low-key and soft-spoken. Hoffa loved publicity and was loud. But each possessed qualities that Sheeran admired: intelligence and both mental and physical toughness. They obviously thought highly of Sheeran. That night, at Frank Sheeran Appreciation night at the Latin Casino in Philadelphia, a gala event attended by 3,000 paying guests, they each gave him a gift he treasured and wore until the day he died.

The night before, Sheeran recalled in *I Heard You Paint Houses*, a book by lawyer Charles Brandt about Sheeran and his relationships with Hoffa and Bufalino, how the three men had a sitdown at which Bufalino warned Hoffa to give up his stated goal to run for Teamsters Union president and thus avoid offending the mob, which had replaced Hoffa when he was convicted of jury tampering and incarcerated in 1967. But Hoffa refused to get the message, Sheeran recalled, and at the end of the session, as Sheeran was about to drive Hoffa back to his hotel, Bufalino pulled Sheeran aside and said: "Talk to your friend. Tell him what it is."

The seemingly innocuous words were "as good as a death threat," said Sheeran, relating that when he told Hoffa that their friend Bufalino, who had introduced the two men in the 1950s, had implored Sheeran to lay it out for him, Hoffa still refused to get the message.

"They wouldn't dare," growled Hoffa, his eyes glaring at Sheeran's. That night, for all intents and purposes, Hoffa assured his own death at the hands of his best friend. Hoffa failed to recall the significance of the first words he had said to Sheeran the night they first spoke: "I heard you paint houses." The paint, Sheeran explained, "is the blood that supposedly gets on the wall or the floor when you shoot somebody."

To Paint the House

Early Wednesday afternoon, July 30, 1975, Frank Sheeran pulled his big black Lincoln into a small airstrip at Port Clinton, Ohio, on the southern tip of Lake Erie, and walked toward a small plane that was waiting for him. He left Russell Bufalino in the passenger's seat. When he returned, they would drive back to a restaurant where they had left their wives and Bufalino's sister-in-law and continue on to Detroit, some three hours away, where they were heading to attend a wedding of lawyer William Bufalino's daughter.

Two days earlier, Hoffa had called Sheeran and told him that he would be meeting "the little guy," code for Tony Pro, at 2:30 P.M. that day. Sheeran quickly agreed to meet him at 2 P.M., along with "his little brother," code for a gun, and serve as his backup for the sitdown that had been finally arranged by Tony Jack Giaccalone. The following day, however, Sheeran learned from Bufalino that Hoffa wasn't going to meet with Tony Pro and Tony Jack, but with him.

When the plane landed in a Pontiac airfield, Sheeran got into a plain, gray, dusty Ford that had been left there and drove a few miles to a "house with brown shingles, a high backyard fence, and a detached garage in the back." He met Sally Bugs Briguglio there, and they waited for Chuckie O'Brien to pick them up and drive them to the parking lot of the Machus Red Fox Restaurant to pick up Hoffa and bring him to the house for what Hoffa and Chuckie believed was an important "meeting." He didn't say a word to Thomas and Steven Andretta, who were in a back room, waiting for cleanup duty.

Sally Bugs got in the back seat, behind Chuckie. Sheeran sat in the front passenger seat. They got to the restaurant at about 2:45, saw Hoffa's green Pontiac, and Sally Bugs directed Chuckie to a spot where Hoffa would have to pass in order to get to his car. They wanted to be sure he got into their car, not take his own, believing he would have his own "little brother" in the glove compartment. The scenario was well planned, but getting Hoffa into the car would be the hardest part of the job.

A minute later, they spotted Hoffa walking from the area of a hardware store, looking around impatiently, for Sheeran, or the two Tonys, who were all late. When Chuckie pulled up to him, Hoffa railed at him, and then at Sally Bugs in the back seat, whom he didn't know.

"Who the fuck is he?" said Hoffa.

"I'm with Tony Pro," said Briguglio.

"What the fuck is going on here? Your fucking boss was supposed to be here at 2:30."

"People are staring at us, Jimmy," said Briguglio, pointing toward Sheeran, whose face Hoffa hadn't seen yet, and said, "Look who's here."

As Hoffa lowered his head to look inside the car, Sheeran lowered his, and waved to him, a signal for Sally Bugs to put everything into the proper perspective for Hoffa, and explain the change in plans.

"His friend wanted to be at the thing," said Sally Bugs, a reference to Bufalino, a private person who would be uncomfortable meeting in a public place. "They're at the house waiting," he added. Seeing Sheeran, and knowing that Bufalino would be at the meeting, was "the final bait" to lure Hoffa into the car. With Sheeran there as his backup, and with Bufalino waiting at the house, Hoffa let his guard down and sat in the empty seat behind Sheeran.

"I thought you were supposed to call me last night," he barked at Sheeran. "I waited in front of the restaurant at 2:00 for you. You were going to be sitting in my car with me when they showed. I was going to make them get in for the sitdown."

"I just got in," said Sheeran. "We had a delay in plans. McGee had to rearrange things so that we could do this meeting right—not sitting in a car," Sheeran continued, using a nickname for Bufalino that he and Hoffa used.

For the next few minutes, until they arrived at the house with brown shingles, Hoffa peppered Sheeran with comments and questions.

"I called Jo. You could have left a message," he said.

"You know how McGee is about the telephone when it involves his plans," said Sheeran.

"SOMEbody could have told me 2:30. At the very least. With all due respect to McGee …."

When the car stopped at the brick steps near the front door of the house, Hoffa bolted toward the house with Sheeran right behind him. Sally Bugs, who wasn't important enough to attend a meeting this important, got into the front seat as Chuckie drove away.

"Jimmy Hoffa always walked out front, way ahead of people he was walking with," recalled Sheeran. "He took short steps but he was fast. I caught up to him and got right behind him the way you get right behind a prisoner you're taking back behind the line, and when he opened the front door, I was right behind him up the front stoop and into the small vestibule, shutting the door behind us.

"When Jimmy saw that the house was empty, that nobody came out of any of the rooms to greet him, he knew right away what it was. If Jimmy had taken his piece with him he would have gone for it. Jimmy was a fighter. He turned fast, still thinking we were together on the thing, that I was his backup. Jimmy bumped into me hard. If he saw the piece in my hand he had to think I had it out to protect him. He took a quick step to go around me and get to the door. He reached for the knob and Jimmy Hoffa got shot twice at a decent range—not too close or the paint splatters back at you—in the back of the head behind his right ear. My friend didn't suffer."

After waiting a few seconds to make sure that none of the cleanup men were there to send him to the same place as Hoffa, Sheeran dropped the gun on the floor, drove back to the airfield, and was soon back in Port Clinton, Ohio, waking up Bufalino by starting his car.

They picked up the women and arrived in Detroit about 7 P.M. The only conversation they had about the Hoffa matter after his return flight, Sheeran recalled, was when Bufalino woke up, winked at him, and said: "I hope you had a pleasant flight, my Irish friend."

"I hope you had a good sleep," replied Sheeran.

Capeci's Analysis

On Wednesday, July 30, 1975, I was living and working in Brooklyn, New York, covering the state and federal courts there for the *New York Post*. I have no first- or secondhand knowledge of what happened to Jimmy Hoffa that day.

As a newspaper reporter for more than three decades, I have spoken to a handful of law enforcement officials who have been involved in the investigation of Hoffa's murder. By no stretch of the imagination am I a "Hoffa expert." But from all I have read and heard about the case, both officially and unofficially, the account that Frank Sheeran provided of Hoffa's demise, to use an expression I have heard repeated countless times at murder and racketeering trials, "has the ring of truth."

So, too, does his description of the execution three years later of Sally Bugs Briguglio, a suspect in the plot to kill Hoffa from day one. So much so that if Sheeran hadn't died in late 2003, he surely would have received a visit or two from the law when the book was published. There is no statute of limitations on murder in Michigan, New York, or anywhere else in the United States.

There is no doubt in my mind that Sheeran discussed that with co-author Brandt, a former prosecutor and defense lawyer, when he agreed to tell his story in this unique book. Unique because while many mob killers have written tell-all books before, none have done so—to my knowledge—without having previously gotten immunity from prosecution through a cooperation deal with federal or local authorities.

In addition to clearing up the most celebrated Mafia murder mystery of the century, Sheeran described the inner workings of the International Brotherhood of Teamsters and the small but influential Bufalino crime family, and the often deadly internal machinations of both organizations. Sheeran provided those special little details about Hoffa and Bufalino that bring them back to life—toward the end, Hoffa often referred to himself in the third person; the angrier Bufalino got, the softer he spoke. He told about scores of low-level hoodlums, Mafia leaders, and Teamsters Union officials he met during his life of crime. Guys like Jack Ruby—yes, *that* Jack Ruby, the guy who killed Lee Harvey Oswald on national television—Sam "Momo" Giancana, the Chicago Outfit boss who was gunned down a month before Hoffa; Tony "Pro" Provenzano; and Frank Fitzsimmons, the Teamsters president who took Hoffa's job when he went to prison in 1967, and for whose job Hoffa lost his life.

For me, the most intriguing chapter in *I Heard You Paint Houses* was Chapter 24. In it, Sheeran asserts that he was the reason that I spent a few hours at Umberto's Clam House on Mulberry Street in lower Manhattan during the early morning hours of April 7, 1972.

That day, I was re-routed from my usual 6 A.M.-to-1 P.M. shift covering police head-quarters to that Little Italy landmark to report about the execution of renegade Colombo family gangster Joseph "Crazy Joe" Gallo. He was blown away in the wee hours of the morning as he celebrated his forty-third birthday with his wife, her daughter, an entourage of Gallo-phites, and his bodyguard, Peter "Pete the Greek" Diapoulos.

> **Big Shot**
>
> For a hit like the one on Crazy Joe Gallo, Frank Sheeran preferred to have two guns handy, one in his waistband and a backup in an ankle holster, and neither equipped with a silencer, he explained in *I Heard You Paint Houses*.
>
> "You'd use something like a .32 and .38 revolver because you wanted more stop-ping power than you could get with a .22. You wanted to do some noisy stray shoot-ing all over the place to send the witnesses scurrying for cover. But not the kind of noise that a .45 makes, which you could hear in a patrol car blocks away."

No one has ever been charged with Gallo's murder. Until now the prevailing wisdom—from two cooperating witnesses, including Diapoulos—has laid responsibility for the hit on a Genovese soldier who, when last heard from, had relocated somewhere in California. If he's still alive, he'd be about the same age as Sheeran, who wrote that after first shooting Diapoulos, he took out Gallo as he ran out of the restaurant.

In his detailed account, Sheeran said he later "heard that some Italian guy took credit for the whack they put on Gallo. That's okay by me." I got to the murder scene too late to make an opinion based on fact. But if I were forced to make a choice, I'd say Frank Sheeran did the work.

The Least You Need to Know

- Jimmy Hoffa was killed by the mob in 1975.
- It's a safe bet his body will never be found.
- Frank "The Irishman" Sheeran said he killed Hoffa.
- Sheeran's account has the ring of truth.

A Chronology of Major Events

Many events in the history of the American Mafia have been influential in making it what it is today. What follows is a list of some of these occurrences to aid the reader in placing the many individual stories in this book into a wider, more complete, context.

1890–1914   Mass immigration of millions of honest Italians occurs, along with a handful of criminals familiar with the ways of the Sicilian Mafia, the Calabrian Mafia, and the Cammora.

1890–1920   Rudimentary Mafia organizations begin to form based on the patterns of the Sicilian Mafia, the Calabrian Mafia, and the Cammora. Ethnic exclusivity of the organizations fades as Italian-Americans are incorporated into them. Most criminal activities are limited to local or regional areas.

1900–1920   Widespread use of an extortion technique called the Black Hand creates the myth that all who practice Black Hand activities are part of the Mafia. Most Mafia violence involves internal problems within the gangs or struggles for control of local rackets with other gangs.

1920   Prohibition begins, signaling the beginning of an escalation of violence as various groups compete to control the lucrative illegal liquor trade. Political corruption becomes more widespread.

1930   The Castellammarese War and other Mafia conflicts create turmoil in the world of Italian-American criminals.

1931 The killings of two major Mafia leaders, Joseph Masseria and Salvatore Maranzano, lead to the formation of the Commission, a board of directors type of body that oversees La Cosa Nostra.

1931–1950 A period of relative stability takes place in La Cosa Nostra. Individual leaders like Charles "Lucky" Luciano, Al Capone, and others are removed from power by law enforcement rather than by bloodshed from internal problems or inter-family disputes.

1950 The Kefauver hearings bring attention to the menace of the Mafia's gambling syndicates with their connections to corrupt local politicians.

1957 The discovery of 58 Italian-Americans—many with extensive criminal records—meeting together in Apalachin, New York, raises fears of a powerful, secret, national movement called the Mafia. These fears spawn many inquiries and headlines.

1957–1960 The Senate Rackets Committee exposes some of the connections between major Mafia figures and powerful union leaders.

1957–1964 The FBI begins a massive intelligence-gathering operation focusing on La Cosa Nostra. One of its techniques involves widespread illegal buggings of major Mafia criminals.

1961–1964 Attorney General Robert Kennedy makes La Cosa Nostra a prime target of the resources of the Justice Department.

1963 Joseph Valachi, a Mafia soldier, testifies publicly before a U.S. Senate committee and outlines the structure and leaders of La Cosa Nostra.

1963–1970 The FBI secretly feeds a media interest in the Mafia by leaking information about top gangsters to select reporters.

1967–1976 Carlo Gambino of New York and Anthony Accardo of Chicago emerge as the two most powerful Mafia leaders in America.

1967–1970 After recommendations by a presidential commission, Congress passes the Omnibus Crime Control Act (1968) and the Organized Crime Control Act (1970), both of which would prove instrumental in crippling the Mafia in the 1980s.

1970–1971 New York Mafia boss Joseph Colombo launches an ill-conceived Italian-American Civil Rights League. Colombo damages legitimate concerns of honest Italian-Americans with his massive con game. He is shot and incapacitated in 1971, ending his Mafia career as well as his charade as a civil rights leader.

1976–1982 FBI agent Joe Pistone infiltrates the Bonanno family as federal law enforcement officials begin to grasp the power of the Racketeer Influenced and Corrupt Organizations (RICO) Act and learn how to use it against entire crime families.

1980–2000   The FBI spearheads a massive assault on La Cosa Nostra. An extensive intelligence-gathering operation, in cooperation with state and local police agencies, combined with the widespread use of the RICO statute to result in the crippling of all the Mafia families and the virtual elimination of many of the smaller organizations. The federal government exerts continuous pressure against four major, Mafia-controlled, international unions to force reform that significantly decreases the financial and political power of La Cosa Nostra.

1985–1987   Gambino capo John Gotti orchestrates the spectacular assassination of his Mafia boss as federal prosecutors bring major racketeering cases against New York's five families.

2000   Major Mafia powers such as John Gotti, Vincent Gigante, Carmine Persico, Victor Amuso, John Riggi, Jack Tocco, Nicky Scarfo, Andrew Russo, Victor Orena, and many others have been convicted of racketeering and murder and are behind bars. Many others have died, either in or out of prison, including Anthony Salerno, Anthony Accardo, Anthony Corallo, Santos Trafficante, Carlos Marcello, Russell Bufalino, Nick Civella, Frank Balistieri, and Eugene Smaldone.

2001   Serious La Cosa Nostra families continue to operate in New York and Chicago, adapting to changing times and law enforcement tactics. Less powerful but still viable groups remain in other cities.

2002–2004   John Gotti dies of throat cancer. The feds convict brothers Peter and Richard Gotti and a nephew of racketeering charges as the federal onslaught against his family and others continues, especially in the New York/New Jersey area. Genovese boss Vincent Gigante, DeCavalcante boss John Riggi, and the acting bosses of the Colombo and Luchese family, Alphonse Persico and Louis Daidone, are also convicted and receive long stretches in prison. And four decades after Joe Valachi became the first mobster to publicly break his oath of allegiance to the Mafia, the FBI coerced and cajoled eight "made members" of the Bonanno to cooperate in an effort to send "Last Don" Joseph Massino back to federal prison forever.

A Word About Mafia Nicknames

Nicknames are not unique to La Cosa Nostra. Many husbands and wives have endearing terms for each other. Anyone who follows team sports is familiar with nicknames. Many legendary figures have had familiar labels, including George Herman "Babe" Ruth, Dwight "Ike" Eisenhower, Richard "Tricky Dick" Nixon, and Maurice "The Rocket" Richard.

Contrary to most reports, mobsters don't take on nicknames to try to confuse the cops, although that is an added bonus. What often occurs is that a wiseguy becomes noted for something that results in a moniker being attached to him. For example, Colombo associate Joseph Luparelli preferred fish to meat and hence became Joe "Fish" Luparelli. The machine gun was the weapon of choice for Capone-era hood Jack McGurn; hence he became "Machine Gun" Jack McGurn. Carmine Galante, the 1970s-era Bonanno boss, sported two nicknames. Most common was "Lilo," which was a short form of his baptismal name, Camilo. And because he usually had a cigar stuck in his mouth, he was often called "The Cigar." Mob turncoat Jimmy Fratianno said his nickname "The Weasel" came during his youth when cops had a hard time physically grabbing the elusive little brat who would be running about.

Nicknames often refer to the physical size of the hood. Few Mafia guys fit a physical workout into their busy day of scheming, robbing, eating, drinking, and cheating on their wives. Not surprisingly, a number of the guys have had weight problems; hence you had Dominick "Fat Dom" Borghese, Vincent "Fat Vinnie" Teresa, Dominic "Fats" Corrado, Joseph "Joe Jelly" Gioelli, and Anthony "Fat Tony" Salerno.

Nicknames sometimes differentiate between two relatives with the same given name. "Big Paul" Castellano's cousin was "Little Paul" Castellano.

Mob guys love unflattering nicknames, ones that zero in on physical traits besides size. Cleveland underboss Leo "Lips" Moceri had prominent lips; Bonanno underboss Nicholas "Nicky Eye Glasses" Marangello wore thick corrective lenses. Tommy "Three Finger Brown" Lucchese, boss of his own family, had lost two digits in an accident and was given this nickname by a cop who used a label already attached to a famous ballplayer with the same physical problem.

Chicago boss John "No Nose" DiFronzo apparently got his nickname after losing part of his nose in a shootout. From his picture, it seems obvious why Nick "Big Nose Nick" Tolentino got his label.

Sometimes the name has to do with the man's personality. Joseph "Crazy Joe" Gallo took on his moniker after displaying erratic behavior. Previously he was "Joey the Blond" because of his hair color. Colombo boss Carmine Persico is "Junior" to his buddies. However, some wiseguys, behind his back, call him "The Snake" because of a reputation for being sneaky and deadly, especially after word got out that he tried to strangle Larry Gallo in 1962. Genovese boss Frank "The Prime Minister" Costello was known for his ability to mix with all levels of society and favored negotiations over the use of violence. Henry Tameleo of the New England family was known as a peacemaker and became "The Referee."

In the 1960s, the Colombos had two associates called Larry "Big Lollipop" Carna and Joseph "Little Lollipop" Carna. Looking at them, the nicknames made no sense because Big Lollipop was noticeably smaller than Little Lollipop. The nicknames stemmed from their ages, not their size.

Others get labeled because of their occupation. Buffalo boss Stefano Magaddino ran a funeral parlor and hence was called Stefano "The Undertaker" Magaddino. Ciro "The Artichoke King" Terranova controlled the market in that commodity, hence his nickname. At one time, New England hood Frank "The Cheeseman" Cucchiara was in the cheese-making business.

Some wiseguys are large in size compared to their buddies. Large does not necessarily mean he looks like a football player. Generally, it means someone who is over 5'8" and big in build. In this group we have Detroit capo Big Mike Polizzi, Cleveland underboss Big Ange Lonardo, Luchese drug-dealing capo Big John Ormento, murdered Cleveland boss Big Joe Lonardo, Colombo capo Big Sal Micciotta, and Gambino boss Big Paul Castellano.

Now and then, you come across a hood with a nickname that refers to a physical location. It might have been the place where he was born or where he hung out. Chicago boss Phil "Milwaukee Phil" Alderisio had a Milwaukee background. Gambino soldier Steve Armone lived on East 14th Street. He was "East 14th Street Steve." Bayonne Joe Zicarelli didn't come from Newark. John "Bath Beach" Oddo of the Colombo family and Joseph "Staten Island Joe" Riccobono, one-time consigliere of the Gambinos, obviously had a connection to those New York City locations.

Salvatore "Tom Mix" Santoro of the Luchese family bore a resemblance to old-time cowboy film star Tom Mix. Genovese capo Joseph "Joe Adonis" Doto earned his label for his good looks, like the mythical Greek Adonis. Gambino capo Jack "Good Looking Jack" Giordano also had a few admirers of his profile.

Albert Anastasia was the Gambino boss during the mid-1950s. An early reputation for being quick to kill to enforce his will as head of the mythical Murder Incorporated earned him the name "Lord High Executioner." Still others used the label "The Mad Hatter," which suggested that he was crazy like the character from *Alice in Wonderland*. (By the way, the term "mad hatter" comes from the practice of using mercury in the making of top hats. Constant contact with this substance damaged the brains of the workers, hence the name "mad hatter.")

A few Mafiosi had nicknames that were a reference to sex. Albert "Kid Blast" Gallo's name came not from his use of a gun but from the teasing of his fellow hoods. Every time Gallo would return from a date, the guys would ask him if he "blasted" her. One can only guess if sex had anything to do with the nickname of Detroit hood Anthony "Tony Long" Cimini!

The late FBI agent and author Bill Roemer claims he gave Chicago hood Anthony "Tony the Ant" Spilotro his nickname before Spilotro ended up buried in a farm field by his friends. Roemer and Spilotro didn't like each other, and Roemer began referring to Spilotro as "Pissant." The media cleaned that up a little and settled on "Ant."

Here are a few other favorites—you can guess how they got the label:

Theodore "Teddy the Bum" DeMartino

Angelo "Four Cents" Salerno

Antonio "Tony Bananas" Caponigro

Joseph "Socks" Lanza

Joseph "Pip the Blind" Gagliano

Joseph "Shoes" Caruso

Ralph "Bottles" Capone

Joseph "Misery" Moceri

Peter "Petey Pumps" Ferrara

One last thing about nicknames. If you hear the boss and his friends using a three-letter nickname for you that rhymes with cat, you're about to go bye-bye.

Appendix C

Further Readings

Abadinsky, Howard. *Organized Crime.* Chicago: Nelson-Hall Inc., 1996.

Anastasia, George. *Blood and Honor: Inside the Scarfo Mob—The Mafia's Most Violent Family.* New York: Zebra Books, 1993.

———. *The Goodfella Tapes.* New York: Avon Books, 1998.

———. *Mobfather: The Story of a Wife and Son Caught in the Web of the Mafia.* New York: Pinnacle Books, 1993.

———. *The Last Gangster.* New York: ReganBooks, 2004.

Block, Allan. *East Side–West Side: Organizing Crime in New York, 1930–1950.* Swansea, U.K.: Christopher Davis, 1979.

Blumenthal, Ralph. *Last Days of the Sicilians.* New York: Times Books, 1988.

Bonanno, Joseph. *A Man of Honor: The Autobiography of Joseph Bonanno.* New York: Simon & Schuster, 1983.

Brandt, Charles. *I Heard You Paint Houses: Frank "The Irishman" Sheeran and the Inside Story of the Mafia, the Teamsters and the Last Ride of Jimmy Hoffa.* Hanover, NH: Steerforth Press, 2004.

Brill, Steven. *The Teamsters.* New York: Simon & Schuster, 1978.

Campbell, Rodney. *The Luciano Project.* New York: McGraw-Hill, 1977.

Capeci, Jerry. *Jerry Capeci's Gang Land: Fifteen Years of Covering the Mafia*. New York: Alpha Books, 2003.

———. *Wiseguys Say the Darndest Things*. New York: Alpha Books, 2004.

Capeci, Jerry and Gene Mustain. *Gotti: Rise and Fall*. New York: Onyx, 1996.

Cressey, Donald. *Theft of the Nation*. New York: Harper Row, 1969.

Demaris, Ovid. *The Last Mafioso: The Treacherous World of Jimmy Fratianno*. New York: Time Books, 1981.

Dubro, James and Robin F. Rowland. *King of the Mob*. Markan, Ontario: Penguin Books, 1987.

Fox, Stephen. *Blood and Power: Organized Crime in the Twentieth Century*. New York: William Morrow, 1989.

Kobler, John. *Capone*. New York: G. P. Putnam's Sons, 1971.

Lehr, Dick, and Gerard O'Neil. *Black Mass*. New York: Public Affairs, 2000.

Maas, Peter. *The Valachi Papers*. New York: G. P. Putnam's Sons, 1968.

Mustain, Gene, and Jerry Capeci. *Mob Star*. New York: Alpha Books, 2002.

———. *Murder Machine*. New York: Dutton, 1992. New York: Onyx, 1993.

Pileggi, Nicholas. *Wiseguy: Life in a Mafia Family*. New York: Simon & Schuster, 1985.

———. *Casino*. New York: Simon & Schuster, 1995.

Pistone, Joseph, and Richard Woodley. *Donnie Brasco: My Undercover Life in the Mafia*. New York: Signet, 1988.

Roemer, William. *Man Against the Mob*. New York: Ballantine Books, 1989.

Schwartzman, Paul, and Rob Polner. *New York Notorious*. New York: Crown Publishers, 1992

Smith, Dwight. *The Mafia Mystique*. New York: Basic Books, 1975.

Sondern, Frederic Jr. *Brotherhood of Evil: The Mafia*. New York: Farrar, Straus, and Girioux, Inc., 1959.

Zeigler, Henry A. *Sam the Plumber*. New York: New American Library, 1970.

Index

M